DISCARD

THE PEACEKEEPING ECONOMY

LLOYD J. DUMAS

The Peacekeeping Economy

USING ECONOMIC RELATIONSHIPS TO BUILD

A MORE PEACEFUL, PROSPEROUS, AND

SECURE WORLD

Yale UNIVERSITY PRESS

NEW HAVEN AND LONDON

Published with assistance from the foundation established in memory of Philip Hamilton McMillan of the Class of 1894, Yale College.

Yale University Press books may be purchased in quantity for educational, business, or promotional use. For information, please e-mail sales.press@yale.edu (U.S. office) or sales@yaleup.co.uk (U.K. office).

Set in Scala type by Westchester Book Group.
Printed in the United States of America.

Library of Congress Cataloging-in-Publication Data
Dumas, Lloyd J.
The peacekeeping economy : using economic relationships to build a more peaceful, prosperous, and secure world / Lloyd J. Dumas.
p.   cm.
Includes bibliographical references and index.
ISBN 978-0-300-16634-7 (hbk. : alk. paper)
1. International economic relations.   2. Peace—Economic aspects.
3. International relations.   4. International security—Economic aspects.   5. Disarmament—Economic aspects.   I. Title.
HF1359.D848 2011
341.5'84—dc23
2011017733

A catalogue record for this book is available from the British Library.

This paper meets the requirements of ANSI/NISO Z39.48-1992 (Permanence of Paper).

10 9 8 7 6 5 4 3 2 1

To the dove, the olive branch, the rainbow
and all the other signs of peace,
in the hope of helping to fulfill
the promise they represent

CONTENTS

Preface   ix

Acknowledgments   xiii

PART ONE: A NEW PARADIGM FOR ACHIEVING NATIONAL
AND INTERNATIONAL SECURITY

1 The Hopeful Science   3

2 Laying the Foundations   16

3 The Core Principles of Economic Peacekeeping   37

4 Making It Happen: Building a Peacekeeping Economy in
the "Real World"   98

5 Making It Stronger: Organizations and Institutions   152

6 Does Globalization Contribute to Economic Peacekeeping?   208

PART TWO: THE ECONOMICS OF DEMILITARIZED SECURITY

7 The Economic Promise of Demilitarized Security   251

8 Removing Barriers to Demilitarized Security: Managing
the Transition   277

9 Extending Demilitarized Security: Economic Peacekeeping
and Nonviolent Action   298

10 Demilitarized Security, Development, and Terrorism   320

PART THREE: THE PEACEKEEPING ECONOMY

11 Bringing It All Together: Toward a More Prosperous and
Secure World   347

Notes   367

Index   405

PREFACE

For all of my professional life, I have been deeply concerned about the extent to which the United States has embraced military force as the guarantor of the nation's security and that of the wider world. It is easy enough to understand why the country turned in this direction. After the existential threats posed by the Second World War and the ultimate spectacular victory of the U.S. and its allies, it seemed obvious that those who would do us and our way of life grievous harm could not be stopped by mere diplomacy and negotiation. They had to be faced down with overwhelming force. And so the U.S., a country that had essentially disbanded its military after every other war in its history to return to the ordinary business of life, built and maintained, through years of war and years of peace, the world's most powerful military.

As an economist, I understood that prosperity, whether of a company or of a nation and its people, depended crucially on how it used its productive resources—the skill and effort of its workforce, the productive power of its machinery and equipment—especially in the long run. While I did not and do not deny that the threat or use of military force is sometimes helpful, even unavoidable, I became concerned that, as rich and capable a people as we are, the enormity of our military burden would eventually drag the country down. In the presence of the diversion of so much of the country's critical economic resources (especially technological talent) in support of our military power, it seemed we were in danger of losing the widely shared prosperity basic to the American dream. So, in the mid-1980s, I wrote *The Overbur-dened Economy*, the first book in what was to become an unintended trilogy on the multiple connections between security, the economy, and the primacy accorded to military force.

The second book in the trilogy, *Lethal Arrogance*, came thirteen years later and took a very different turn. Having nothing to do with economics, it relied heavily on my training as an engineer as well as a social scientist. I argued that our implicit assumption that we could always control whatever technologies we produced, no matter how complex, no matter how power-ful, was a lethal piece of arrogance. Our innate fallibility as human beings made it impossible for us to design, build, operate, and maintain extremely dangerous technologies with any real assurance that nothing would go cat-astrophically wrong, by accident or by intention. Focusing heavily on tech-nologies capable of causing the most devastating harm, most especially nuclear and other weapons of mass destruction, the book was an attempt to explain, on the simple grounds of who we are, why even our own arsenals of weapons of mass destruction threaten us, rather than making us more secure. (A revised and updated version of this book was published in 2010 under the title *The Technology Trap*.)

This book, *The Peacekeeping Economy*, completes the inadvertent trilogy. For if we are to reject high levels of military spending on the grounds that they seriously injure the economy in the long run, and accept that accumu-lating massive military force can endanger rather than protect us, then what are we to do to achieve the security we value so highly? The core argument here is that it is possible to structure international (and intranational) eco-nomic relationships in ways that create strong positive incentives to build and keep the peace. A peacekeeping economy does not rely on any funda-mental change in human nature, ethics, or deep social understanding. It is instead an approach primarily focused on harnessing the power of self-interest to provide both prosperity and security. It does not require altruism or empa-thy, although it is compatible with any empathetic or altruistic impulses there may be. I certainly do not claim that it is a complete security strategy by itself, obviating the need for diplomacy or even military force. But it should strengthen the hand of the diplomats and make the need or impulse to call on military force much more rare.

I have tried to lay out here not only the principles underlying a peace-keeping economy, but also practical strategies for putting it in place. While I cannot provide a blueprint, I have provided approaches to implementation that can be undertaken by the public at large, as well as by government and the private sector. If the efforts of any one of these actors fall short, there are always alternative approaches the others can take to continue to move the project of building a peacekeeping economy forward.

It is difficult to change long-held and deeply embedded habits, such as the belief that military force is the essential and ultimate source of security. But that habit of thought has cost the world a great deal in terms of both blood and treasure. There are enormous benefits to be had and dangers to be avoided by considering that there may be a better way to achieve security. I offer the peacekeeping economy as one serious and practical attempt at finding that way.

ACKNOWLEDGMENTS

In a telephone conversation more than twenty years ago, my friend and colleague, international lawyer Burns Weston, raised an important challenge: What can economists contribute to the search for security without reliance on nuclear weapons? The thinking he inspired with that simple question lies at the core of this book, and for that inspiration, I am deeply grateful.

The book brings together a number of threads of my work, spun over quite a few years. As always in such an enterprise as this, there are many people to thank for their stimulation and encouragement. Seymour Melman, my teacher, my colleague, and my friend, was always an impassioned voice for peace and constant source of provocative ideas. With his usual insight, wit, and style, Kenneth Boulding created the "chalk theory" of war and peace, providing just the right perspective from which to see the potential of a peacekeeping economy most clearly. John Ullmann, Greg Bischak, Joel Yudken, and Miriam Pemberton were important partners in the development of strategies for economic conversion. Gene Sharp completely changed my thinking on the viability of nonviolent action as a pragmatic element of security strategy.

The list of old and new friends who have motivated and encouraged this work is long. Among others it includes Lynne Dumas, Roger Kallenberg, Alice Barton, Martha Hurley, Dana Dunn, Yolanda Eisenstein, Warren Davis, Joelle Rizk, Leila Bendra, and Jennifer Hubert. Thanks to Kaikaus Ahmad for his support and valuable research assistance. In this and every other project I have undertaken, I have been buoyed by the unswerving confidence and encouragement of my parents, Marcel and Edith Dumas. And I will always be grateful for the day this work led me to a chance meeting in a Houston classroom that began a long personal journey of discovery, infused with the inspiration, adventure, and optimism that underlies this work, in the company of my intellectual partner and soul mate, Teresa Nelson Dumas.

PART ONE

A NEW PARADIGM FOR ACHIEVING

NATIONAL AND INTERNATIONAL SECURITY

The Hopeful Science

The international system that relies on the national use of
military force as the ultimate guarantor of security, and the
threat of its use as the basis for order, is not the only possible
one. To seek a different system with a more secure and a more
humane basis for order is no longer the pursuit of an illusion,
but a necessary effort toward a necessary goal.

—Carl Kaysen, Professor of Political Economy, MIT

WE LIVE IN A TROUBLED AND INSECURE WORLD. As the economic, political,
and cultural processes of globalization draw us closer together, enabled by
technological revolutions in transportation and telecommunication, it becomes increasingly obvious that the problems of any one part of the globe
are now problems for us all. The collapse of the Thai currency in 1997 not
only caused major economic shock waves in nearby Malaysia, Korea, the
Philippines, and Indonesia but also threatened the economies of nations
as far away as Russia, Nigeria, and Brazil.[1] The discontent of a handful of
Saudis, encouraged and supported by the scion of a wealthy Saudi-based
family holed up in Afghanistan, destroyed a world-famous New York City
landmark on September 11, 2001, and with it the lives of thousands of innocent people, in the single worst international terrorist attack to date.[2]
The SARS virus, contracted in China in 2003, became, with alarming
speed, a serious threat to the health of people living in Europe and North
America. When an avian influenza virus that could infect and kill humans
made its way from Asia to Europe in 2005—despite desperate attempts at
containment—fears of a lethal flu pandemic propagated around the world.
By late 2008, problems that began to surface in one piece of the U.S.
mortgage market (sub-prime mortgages) only a year and a half earlier had
propagated around the world, brought down a number of major financial
institutions, and threatened the world's economy with the worst global

retrenchment since the Great Depression. In such an interconnected world, security has become everyone's business.

Seventeen centuries ago, the Roman military analyst Vegetius wrote, "If you want peace, prepare for war." For many years, national and international security analysis and policy have been dominated by those who believe that Vegetius was right, that force and the threat of force are the most effective means of keeping the wolves (or should I say, the hawks) at bay. The long stretch of history over the millennia since the time of Vegetius has been filled with attempts to deter aggression through military strength, to preserve peace by improving the technology and building up the capacity to use powerful military force. It has also been filled with many hundreds of wars, taking a sickening toll in human life and wasted treasure. In the twentieth century alone—a century in many ways remarkable for its scientific, economic, and political progress—there were over 230 wars, more than half of which were fought after the end of World War II.[3] The cost of these wars in human lives was somewhere between seventy and one hundred million dead, despite the fact that we somehow managed to avoid a nuclear holocaust, the war we all feared most. The cost in wasted economic resources, in economic opportunities foregone, may be incalculable. All this, and still we do not have peace. All this, and still we are not secure.[4]

Not only have our vast arsenals of powerful weapons and other military preparations failed to prevent war, they have proven to be nearly useless against the threat to peace and physical security that most troubles and constrains the daily lives of those of us who live in the relatively politically stable and economically prosperous parts of the world—the ongoing threat of terrorism. The world's most powerful military, backed up by thousands of nuclear weapons, failed to deter or defeat those who attacked the United States by flying hijacked American airliners into the twin towers of New York's World Trade Center and the headquarters of the U.S. military command itself. Virtually all of the successes we have had in capturing terrorists and in thwarting terrorist attacks have been the result of a combination of accurate intelligence, international cooperation, and quality police work, not the threat or use of military force. It seems that Vegetius was wrong: preparation for war brings neither peace nor security. Seventeen centuries of following the same failed advice should be enough. It is time for a paradigm shift, time for us to change our ways of thinking.

Economic Thinking and Security Strategy

Rather than thinking of national and international security strategy so much in terms of weaponry and coercive physical force, maybe it is time to think more in terms of creating the conditions that make keeping the peace a natural outcome of the pursuit of regional, national, local, and individual self-interest. In this, the way economics looks at the world has much to offer. For we economists do not live in a world dominated by violence and power. Our paradigms have much more to do with choice and incentive than with force and coercion.

The fact is, security is not and never has been primarily a matter of weapons and violence. Security is primarily a matter of relationships. The proposition that security depends primarily on relationships, not on weaponry, is easy enough to illustrate. During most of the Cold War, the Soviet Union was not the only nation with sufficient nuclear weaponry and delivery systems to launch a devastating nuclear attack against the United States. Britain and France also had that capability. Yet for all the time, money, and energy that we devoted to thinking about how to counter the Soviet nuclear threat, I doubt that we spent ten dollars or ten minutes worrying about a British or French strike. Why not? We had our disagreements with Britain and France, but underneath it all, the French and British were our friends, our allies. And in the late 1980s, when our relationship with first the Soviet Union and later Russia began to warm, we all felt (and were) more secure. All that nuclear weaponry was still there, still ready to go. But the relationship had change profoundly for the better, and that made all the difference.[5]

Economists are especially well positioned to understand and explore this question of security because, at its most fundamental, economics is not really about money, nor is it about statistical analysis, or mathematical or game theoretic models; it is about relationships. Economists are not simply technicians manipulating models and data; we are students of human behavior. Most of economics may focus on behavior in relationships that lie within the systems people have created to satisfy their material wants and needs, but some of the most basic insights we have gained into human behavior have power well beyond that realm.

In the market economists' paradigm, behavior is most effectively influenced not by the threat or use of force, but by incentives of one kind or another. There is no reason to believe that this insight into human behavior does not also have some currency in the pursuit of security, even in the most narrow, traditional sense of preventing the outbreak of war.

There are many motivations that lead to war, civil as well as international. Some of these are economic—seizing economic assets controlled by others or maintaining control of economic assets others are trying to seize from us. Other motivations have little or nothing to do with economics. It is surely a mistake to believe that potential combatants can always be bought off with economic incentives. But it is an even bigger mistake to believe that economic relationships do not play a critical role in creating the conditions that can either lead to explosions of violence or prevent them.

Isn't it at least impractical, if not entirely utopian, to propose that we should seriously consider stepping away from such heavy reliance on the threat or use of military force as our primary guarantor of security in a contentious world of nations and peoples that still have so much to learn about getting along with each other? Isn't it hopelessly politically naïve to argue for such a reorientation of security strategy in a nation in which record military budgets routinely sail through Congress with broad bipartisan support? Well, that depends. It is unrealistic to expect that we would abandon overnight a deeply ingrained belief that military strength is virtually equivalent to national security. But it is not unrealistic to believe that, if we become convinced that the ways of thinking that lie behind our foreign policy and domestic political behavior are based on false premises, we are capable of changing our minds—and our behavior. We have done it before.

There was a time when we were a deeply isolationist country, convinced that our natural wealth and broad oceans protected us against the consequences of political and military conflicts in other parts of the world. By the end of World War II, it had become crystal clear to us that the fundamental premise on which that thinking was based was no longer true, and our way of thinking and behaving changed. There was also a time when a deeply ingrained belief that women were not intellectually capable of exercising independent political judgment barred them from voting and other forms of political participation in this country, both as a matter of custom and as a matter of law. But (after a long struggle) when we ultimately came to understand that the fundamental premise on which this way of thinking was based was false, both custom and law changed. Nothing seems as inevitable as the status quo, but nothing is as inevitable as change. In the final analysis, though it may take us a while, we are capable of recognizing reality and changing our approach to the world accordingly.

The proposal for a new, less military-centered way of thinking about security would also be naïve and politically unrealistic if it were premised on a basic change in human nature.[6] Of course it is true that if all people became kinder, gentler, and more caring toward each other, if they learned to put the needs of all of their fellow human beings above their own selfish interests, the world would be a more peaceful and secure place. But though I do not rule out the possibility, or at least the hope, that that might happen some day, I'm afraid it will be a very long time before even a distant glimpse of such a world appears on the horizon. In this world, the world in which we will live out our lives, Adam Smith seems to have had it right. Whether enlightened or unenlightened, broadly or narrowly defined, self-interest is a powerful driver of human behavior.

The ascendance of (more or less) free market economies over the last 230 years makes it clear that a system structured to harness self-interest for the general good is eminently practical and can be highly effective. The key to harnessing self-interest successfully is precisely to rely on choice and incentive, rather than on force and coercion. Since it has worked so well for so long in the hard-nosed world of business and economic relations, it is the essence of pragmatism to at least seriously consider that it might also work well in the hard-nosed world of national and international relations. In the final analysis, it must be effectiveness rather than familiarity or conditioned reflex that drives the approach we take to something as critical to our well-being as security strategy, precisely because we live in a world of nations and people that have so much to learn about getting along with each other.

There are times when simply penetrating misperceptions to reveal the true cost/benefit structure facing those making self-interested choices is enough to change their understanding of which choices actually support their interests, and thus to affect which choices they make. But even when that is not enough, economists believe that the most effective and efficient way to influence behavior for the general good is not by threatening or using force but by creating incentive structures that align the interests of those we are trying to influence with those of the wider society.

For example, if a factory is discharging waste into a river and polluting the water supply of a community downstream, the economists' solution is to put a per unit pollution tax on the firm (or to offer a per unit payment to the firm to reduce its waste discharge), not to threaten to blow up the factory or to imprison or kill the management. Such a pollution tax (or cleanup subsidy) creates the conditions that make it in the interest of the firm to voluntarily choose to do what the downstream community wants it to do. In addition, since pollution abatement involves costs as well as benefits, it may not make sense to expend all the resources required to return the river to pristine condition. A tax or subsidy set at the proper level can be expected to induce not only a cleanup, but also the most socially desirable amount of cleanup (the amount of pollution reduction that gives society the greatest net benefits).

Economics also provides perspectives that can help us see past the purely short-term impacts of our actions to their longer-run implications. It is wholly consistent with economic thinking to recognize that doing what is expedient in the short run may not be optimal, or even viable, in the long run. Perhaps thinking more along those lines might help us avoid the traps into which the short term "power game" view of international security has caused us repeatedly to fall, such as imposing the backbreaking reparations to punish and cripple Germany after World War I that played such an important role in triggering the rise of the Nazi regime, and with it the horrors of the Holocaust and World War II; or supporting the "freedom fighters" resisting the Soviet incursion into Afghanistan in the late 1970s, and so inadvertently helping to give rise to the brutal Taliban regime and train a whole generation of terrorists (including those who attacked the New York World Trade Center in 1993).

Economists are taught to look not only at the most obvious direct effects of actions, but also at the reactions and adjustments those actions are likely to trigger over time. When any given path people are accustomed to taking becomes relatively more difficult to follow, we know that they will seek and, given enough time, find new ways to achieve their goals. We are accustomed to recognizing that their immediate response and their ultimate response may be very different. And we know the difference can be very important in determining whether the actions we take, the policies we implement, the strategies we follow in trying to influence their behavior, will have the results we are seeking.

The formal mathematical models and empirical tools that economists use can be helpful in analyzing specific elements of the problem of national and international security.[7] But I want to emphasize that the real power of economics in confronting the real world of security lies not in the applications of these technical approaches, but in the fundamental concepts and ways of thinking that underlie them. It is the way economists look at the world—their understanding of the importance of choice, the use of incentive structures to harness self-interest in the service of an overriding goal, the creation and activation of opportunities for mutual gain—that has the most to offer in the search for practical paths to a more secure and prosperous world.

For example, one of the most important contributions of the field of economics to clear thinking may be the concept of "opportunity cost." This simple yet powerful idea is that making intelligent choices requires us to think in terms of not only the direct costs and benefits of what we choose to do, but also the foregone benefits (and costs) of those things we could have done instead but chose not to do. Every choice we make has consequences in terms of choices we failed to make. The choice of one course of action can and often enough does destroy the option of choosing alternative courses of action that were viable before that decision was made. It is thus critical to keep in mind what options are being lost, as well as what might be gained by the choice we have decided to make.

For example, when the Bush administration decided to launch a preemptive military invasion of Iraq in 2003 to forcibly disarm Iraq of weapons of mass destruction, it destroyed the option of allowing United Nations weapons inspectors the time and resources they wanted and needed to verify by peaceful means their earlier (correct) conclusion that there no longer were any significant stores of such weapons or active programs to develop them in Iraq. It may take some time before we can assess the full range of other useful security options that may have been foreclosed as a result of the hostility the United States generated by taking such action, against the advice of most of our allies and the wishes of nearly every other country in the world.

The failure of Vegetius's advice and the usefulness of economic ways of thinking in finding a more successful approach to peace and security are even more obvious if we consider that real peace—what Johan Galtung called "positive peace"—is more than just the absence of war. After all, it is not bullets and bombs alone that kill and maim people. There is also such a thing as "structural violence"—violence that is built into the structure of political, social, and economic systems. People whose poverty causes them to die of malnutrition in a world with more than enough food, or who are blinded, crippled, or killed by preventable diseases; or who become the targets of vicious crimes committed by desperate, marginalized people who have lost their sense of humanity—these are not the victims of war. They are the victims of structural violence. Yet they are just as damaged, just as dead as those we count as war casualties. Any reasonably comprehensive concept of security should incorporate protection against this kind of victimization as well as the threat of menacing armed forces. Positive peace is more than just the absence of war; it is the presence of decency.

Implicit in economics is the idea that raising the material well-being of one group of people does not require reducing the material well-being of another. Economic growth and development are not, as game theorists would put it, zero-sum games. In a zero-sum game (like poker), the gains of the winners must exactly equal the losses of the losers. Nothing is added to the pot being divided among the players; it is a game of redistribution only. Productive economic activity is a "positive-sum" game, a game in which the "pot" grows as new wealth is created. Any positive-sum game has the potential of being a game in which everyone wins, provided the rules of the game are structured to distribute some of the gains to every one of the players. Economic development requires the rules to be structured this way. In low-to-middle-income countries, economic development is a necessary (though not sufficient) condition for creating positive peace.

What Does Security Really Mean?

In common usage, "national security" refers to the protection of the nation-state, and "international security" to the prevention of violent conflict among nation-states. But when you think about it, it is not the security of the nation-state as such that is fundamental; it is the security of the individual. Nations are, after all, artificial constructs that have been created by real human beings in pursuit of objectives that seemed more attainable collectively than individually.[8] Security is certainly among the most important of those objectives. In short, *people do not exist to protect nations; nations exist to protect people.* Nations are abstractions; people are not.[9]

Groups are a critical intermediary between the individual and the huge collection of individuals that make up the nation-state. It is through group action that individuals often have the most effective impact on the policies and institutions of the state and of the economy. At the same time, group identities and norms have considerable impact on the lives of individuals. They are critical to some of the most compelling aspects of the immediate social context within which individuals live. Therefore, the nature of group identities and the distribution of power among them, both within societies and across them, have important implications for the security and prosperity of nations, and for the security, prosperity, and wider quality of life of their people.

Still, personal security is the most basic concept. National security is relevant only to the extent that maintaining the integrity of the state is an effective way of maintaining the security and well-being of the people who live within its jurisdiction. That being so, it seems a little odd that we spend so much time talking about protecting the nation, and so little time talking about whether the policies we follow to protect the nation actually increase the security of individuals who live within it. We assume that they do, but we should not blithely make such an assumption.

Since concern for national security derives from the more basic concern for personal security, it makes sense to begin at this less abstract level.

Personal Security

Much of life flows in a fairly continuous way, from moment to moment, from day to day. For most of us, things generally follow a fairly predictable pattern within a more or less stable range of variation. Changes in the underlying pattern normally occur only slowly over time. But life is occasionally subject to sudden, sharp changes. Such dramatic shifts, both good and bad, shatter the normal routine, and may alter the flow of our lives for extended periods of time. Some of these sharp changes come as a bolt out of the blue; others may be the result of a long and gradual process that builds to a sudden good or bad change in the status quo. Marriage, divorce, the birth of a child, graduation from school, severe injury or illness, the collapse of a business, a large financial windfall, the loss of a job, imprisonment, release from prison, sudden fame, the death of a loved one—all are common examples of life discontinuities with a potentially long reach.

Personal security begins with protection against the more damaging and unpleasant of these abrupt changes. Life is inherently uncertain, and nothing can completely remove the possibility that any given individual will experience such changes. Yet there is no question that we are personally more secure the lower the probability of encountering bad changes, and less secure the higher this probability.

Some of these personal earthquakes are natural in their origins. Others are artifacts of the particular social and political structures we have created. For example, severe illness or injury could exist even in a "state of nature" (though its probability is certainly influenced by social and political factors), while imprisonment or bankruptcy could not. If the society and the political system are able to reduce the probability or severity of those negative shifts that would occur anyway, and provide buffers or protections against those that are social or political in origin, they increase real personal security.

But personal security goes beyond this. It includes the ability to carry on a normal flow of life activities without constant stress or worry about being able to maintain them. A person who is constantly struggling to cover expenses, living in a precarious balance between income and outflow, can scarcely be said to be secure.[10] Finally, personal security also means the ability to exercise basic human rights without fear, in ways that are sensitive to the human rights of others.

In practical terms, then, personal security requires at least a decent material standard of living, along with reasonable assurance it will continue (or improve). It means being able to freely exercise basic human rights. And, of course, personal security includes protection against illness, injury, and death, especially from "unnatural" causes, whether those causes are criminal activity, repression by the domestic government, or attack by foreigners.

National Security

If a nation's political and social organization successfully provides security to the individuals it encompasses, there will be a clear and compelling linkage between national and personal security. The protection of the artificial entity we call the nation then will be connected to the protection of the real people who give it life.

It is common to think of national security as being linked to personal security only in the sense that a nation protects its people against subjugation, illness, injury, and death arising from external attack. But it is clear that an individual who is protected against external attack yet in imminent danger of being arbitrarily arrested, assaulted, or murdered while walking the streets of the city in which he/she lives is certainly not secure. Even if its citizens are well protected against outside invasion and conquest, a society is failing to provide personal security in the fullest sense when it creates conditions that foster economic deterioration, crimes against persons, or internal repression.

It is therefore particularly important to consider the internal socioeconomic and political consequences of the policies, strategies, and tactics that are chosen in the quest for national security. Even if such choices reduce the probability of external attack, they may still be counterproductive if they create internal conditions that substantially reduce personal security. For example, suppose in response to a perceived threat a nation undertakes a massive military buildup that puts a heavy burden on its economy.

The public may be forced to make substantial economic sacrifices in the short run. Worse still, if the economy continues to bear this heavy burden for an extended period of time, the nation's general economic performance may well go into a prolonged slide (see Chapter 7).

If that happens, the economic problems created by the military buildup will tend to increase the probability of job loss and bankruptcy, and will generally make it harder for a significant part of the population to make ends meet. The economic dimension of personal security will clearly have been reduced. If times get exceedingly hard, it is quite likely that crimes against property will increase, as some people steal what they can no longer afford to buy. Crimes against people may also increase as worsening economic conditions raise the level of frustration and anger, leading to violence both inside and outside the family.[11] We can be sure that the military buildup actually increased overall security only if the resulting gain in personal security from reducing the danger of external attack is greater than the negative impacts on personal security that result from its internal socioeconomic effects. Even so, the question still remains as to whether other feasible approaches to addressing the external threat might have had larger net security benefits.

Clearly, *any program promoted for the purpose of increasing any dimension of security should be carefully analyzed in terms of all the dimensions of security.* It is impractical and counterproductive to consider its effects on only one aspect of security. That is likely to lead to foolishness comparable to spending so much money on buying security systems to protect your belongings that you can no longer afford to own anything worth stealing.

The potential contribution of economics to solving the problems of international security has been greatly underappreciated and undervalued, even by most economists. Since the grim musings of the Reverend Thomas Robert Malthus two hundred years ago, economics has had a reputation as "the dismal science." But I do not see it that way. While I make no claim that economic perspectives alone will reveal all the answers, I see in the economic approach a source of hope, one key element in the paradigm shift that can lead us to much more effective and much less violent and costly ways of keeping ourselves physically secure and materially healthy.

As we look back at history's most brutal, murderous, and insecure century, we do not have to be dreamers or utopians to look forward to the future with hope. In the pages that follow, I will argue that there is great value to taking a more economic approach to the problems of national and international security, and that the economic perspective can shed light on these problems and serve as a guide to finding workable, realistic paths—grounded in historical and present day realities—toward a safer and more prosperous world.

It is, of course, impossible for any one book to deal comprehensively with the many different dimensions of national and international security narrowly construed, let alone the much broader issue of positive peace. But I do believe it is possible to show how important a role properly structured economic relationships can play in defining practical, real world policies that are effective in meeting the global challenge of security—and in so doing hopefully (in both senses of the word) to stimulate more productive thinking about how to most effectively harness the power of economic behavior to that purpose. Therein lies the key. For the collective application of human intelligence is capable of reaching far beyond what even the most creative individual human mind can achieve.

We already have in our grasp the seeds of ways of thinking and acting that can help this increasingly globalized, interconnected, and contentious world find its way to a lasting, if less than perfect, peace. We must now develop the wisdom and will to nurture them and let them grow.

2

Laying the Foundations

War and the Economy

FOR THOUSANDS OF YEARS, there was only a marginal relationship between war and the economy. As human settlements grew larger, rulers had to raise sufficient funds to pay for the tools of war and the armies to wield them. But most of the population had little stake in the conduct or outcome of war. Their lives, particularly their economic lives, went on as before. All that began to change a little more than two hundred years ago.

The last decade of the eighteenth century saw the birth of the first mass army raised by conscription from the general population, as the French attempted to defend their revolution against attack by the professional armies of nearly all the monarchies of Europe. Within a few years, that massive army of poorly trained French conscripts turned into a fearsome fighting force, spending many lives in the conquest of much of Europe under the command of Napoleon Bonaparte. War was no longer the business of relatively small professional armies. It increasingly involved large numbers of people, drawn from the ordinary population.[1] Part of what had been the labor force of the economy had become the backbone of the military.

The twentieth century saw even more remarkable changes in both the nature of war and the relationship between war and the economy. A century after the defeat of Napoleon, the Great Powers were once again locked in deadly combat, this time in history's first industrialized war. World War I followed the enormous increase in mass production capability that was the result of more than 150 years of industrial revolution. It was the worst war in human history to that point, a brutal, depersonalized affair that took the lives of more than eight million soldiers and wounded perhaps twenty million more.[2] This butchery was in no small measure the result of a startling shift in the tools of war, from the sword and single shot musket or rifle to the machine gun, capable of filling the air with a blizzard of bullets. Mechanization was the hallmark of industrialization, with its capacity for rapidly repeating the same precise task. It had come to the battlefield with appalling results.

The machines of war—and the ammunition they so rapidly expended— were spewed out in huge quantity by the machines of industry. More than ever before, the productive capacity of the economy had become an integral part of war-making. Since the civilian labor force was now crucial to the war effort, anything that would wound or destroy them, disrupt their lives, or terrorize or demoralize them into ineffectiveness could be justified by the terrible logic of war. As a result, the civilian population, as well as the places where they worked and lived, all became targets for direct attack.

The intentional bombing of civilians in cities began in World War I, but the air raids of that war were primitive, with few casualties and little effect on the war effort. In 1915, for example, the first major air raid on London produced its greatest casualties at the Dolphin Pub on Red Lion Street, where a total of seventeen patrons were killed or injured in the attack.[3] At the time, attacks on the civilian population were generally considered acts of barbarism and widely condemned as illegitimate to the "civilized" conduct of war. Yet by the end of World War II, only thirty years later, air raids that left entire cities in ruin had become a normal and accepted part of military combat.[4]

The devastation caused by the atomic bombing of Hiroshima and Nagasaki in the last days of that war shocked and frightened the world. It seemed as though something entirely new and unexpected had happened. Yet in important ways, it was neither new nor unexpected. It was instead the result of the working out of the inexorable logic of total war that had had its beginnings in the reaction of the European monarchies to the French Revolution.

Since 1945, the world has lived constantly with the fear of nuclear weapons. Armed with arsenals that ultimately bristled with many thousands of nuclear weapons aimed at each other and ready to launch in a matter of minutes, the United States and the Soviet Union (and their allies) confronted each other in a long Cold War. If, by accident or intention, we had triggered an all-out nuclear war during those decades of confrontation, it is a certainty that many millions would have died and a real possibility that we would have become the first species responsible for its own extinction.

Although it would be foolish to assume that the possibility of general nuclear war no longer exists,[5] the peaceful end of the Cold War has certainly made it less likely, at least for the time being. Still, the proliferation of nuclear weapons—to mutually confrontational states such as Pakistan and India, to so-called rogue states such as North Korea, and to subnational terrorist groups or networks such as Al Qaeda—remains high on the list of national and international security concerns. The nuclear age that dawned secretly in the deserts of New Mexico and burst into history in the skies over Hiroshima and Nagasaki is still very much with us.

It would not take a general nuclear war to ruin the world's economy. Even a limited nuclear exchange could easily destroy the confidence of investors and tear to pieces the highly interdependent global system of production, trade, and finance. For that matter, full-scale conventional war, fought with modern weapons far more destructive than those of World War II, could well produce a global depression. The economy has become much more fragile than the society, and there is little question that, as it has in the past, economic disaster can set the stage for severe social and political disruption.

For more than two centuries, economic progress has made war larger and more destructive. At the same time, the growing destructiveness and expense of war have become an ever-greater burden on and potential threat to an increasingly sophisticated and interdependent economic system. Even the preparation for war has become more of a burden, draining the economic vitality of heavily armed nations by diverting key resources needed to keep their economies productive and efficient (see Chapter 7).[6] War, the threat of war, and the preparation for war have the potential to undermine the global economic system. The question at hand is whether the global economic system can be structured and organized in such a way that it has the potential to undermine war.

Do Economic Relationships Precipitate or Prevent War?

There has long been a debate about the connection between economic relationships and violent conflict. On the one hand, many have argued that virtually all wars are fought for economic reasons. There is always some ultimate motivation relating to the control of natural resources, access to markets, or simply the desire to take valuable goods and services from others (including their labor). Furthermore, ongoing economic relationships create conflicts that can and often do grow to the point of explosion, erupting in wars within or among states. No matter who wins, the economic relationships that emerge from these conflicts often sow the seeds of future wars, as those who find themselves disadvantaged at the end of the last war sooner or later seek once again to gain the upper hand.

It has also been argued that economic relationships tend to reduce the likelihood of war. A web of economic relationships binds the participants together. While their growing interdependence does not prevent conflicts, it does create strong incentives to settle whatever conflicts arise as amicably as possible. And because ongoing economic relationships imply continuing personal contact and interaction, they also tend to break down national and ethnic stereotypes that lower the threshold of violent conflict by picturing the people of some other nations or ethnic groups as strange, untrustworthy, or perhaps even less than fully human. As it has been succinctly put, "When goods cross borders, soldiers don't."[7] From this perspective, the strengthening and expansion of economic relationships on a global scale may be the single strongest force for world peace.

A Brief Look at the Foundations of the Theoretical Debate

In the formal literature of international relations and political economy, the role of economic relationships has been an important area of disagreement about the causes of war between the so-called realist-neorealists and the liberal-neoliberals.[8] In general, realists believe that the nation-state is the principal actor in an international arena characterized by anarchy. In such a world, dominance is good, and power is therefore primary. Because of the inherently conflictual nature of state behavior in an anarchic world, realists believe that trade will weaken the position (and thus the security) of those states that gain relatively less, even if it produces absolute benefits for all trading partners. In contrast, liberals focus more on the individual than on the state, and see greater possibilities for and likelihood of ongoing stable cooperation among the people and governments of different nations. Although they recognize that the gains from international trade are often unequally distributed, they believe that the existence of absolute gains will still be a binding force in the international system, as long as those gains are substantial. Liberals also believe that international institutions solve some of the "collective action" problems that exist in an international system that has no overarching political authority. Robert Keohane points out that liberals so often stress institution building not because they are naïve about "harmony among people," but because they agree with realists that a world without rules or institutions would be "a jungle in which governments seek to weaken one another economically and militarily, leading to continual strife and frequent warfare."[9]

Old school realists such as Hans Morgenthau argue that, given the anarchic nature of the international realm, the accumulation of power for its own sake is a rational goal for the nation.[10] Neorealists such as Kenneth Waltz see power less as an end in itself and more as a useful means to achieving national objectives, the most crucial of which is security.[11] Realists believe that the more power a state has the more secure it is, but neorealists argue that a state can have too much power for its own good, as well as too little. There is a "security dilemma," long ago identified by John Herz,[12] resulting from the fact that actions taken by one state to enhance its security, such as building up its military forces, diminish the security of other states.[13] This leads the other states to react in ways that tend to undo any security advantage that has been temporarily achieved. Waltz agrees. "In an anarchic domain, the source of one's own comfort is the source of another's worry,"[14] and he believes that "excessive strength may prompt other states to increase their arms and pool their efforts against the dominant state."[15] Waltz sees the tendency toward balancing power as natural and predictable.[16] Yet he acknowledges that the idea that there is such a thing as too much national power has been a hard lesson for political leaders to learn: "In international politics, success leads to failure. The excessive accumulation of power by one state or coalition of states elicits the opposition of others. The leaders of expansionist states have nevertheless been able to persuade themselves that skillful diplomacy and clever strategy might be able to transcend the normal processes of balance of power politics."[17]

Realists and neorealists agree that the distribution of power is the central issue in keeping the peace, though they disagree about whether a unipolar (hegemonic), bipolar, or multipolar distribution works best. They either see economic relationships as irrelevant to the question of war and peace or believe that they are more likely to provoke war than inhibit it. In the latter belief, realists draw philosophical support from the works of Jean-Jacques Rousseau. While Rousseau recognized that trade brought wealth, he believed it also brought growing inequality, which was dangerous. Furthermore, he argued, "interdependence breeds not accommodation and harmony, but suspicion and incompatibility."[18] Waltz takes this a step further: "The fiercest civil wars and the bloodiest international ones have been fought within areas populated by highly similar people whose affairs have become quite closely knit together."[19]

For realists, economic interdependence creates weakness, vulnerability, and insecurity because it conveys leverage to other nations that allows them to constrain a dependent nation's behavior by threatening to reduce or cut off trade flows. Robert Gilpin points out that realists find economic interdependence especially threatening when it takes the form of dependence on others for key strategic goods—goods (such as military equipment) needed for security purposes, or resources (such as oil) critical to the functioning of the military sector and/or the wider economy.[20] The security-reducing effects of unbalanced strategic dependence make the outbreak of military conflict more likely.

Joanne Gowa combines the realist premise that the anarchy of the international system requires states to look to their own security with the recognition that trade provides real economic gains, to create a more nuanced realist perspective on the impact of international economic relationships on security.[21] Since the distribution of power is critical to keeping the peace, and wealth is one important dimension of power, wealth-enhancing trade affects the distribution of power, and consequently the prospects for peace. In particular, because trade permits nations to focus on producing the goods they produce most efficiently ("specialization according to comparative advantage"), it can free up other resources that those nations can then use to build their military capabilities. While all trade enhances a nation's own wealth and therefore its military capability, trading with foes also strengthens the foes' military capabilities, thus canceling part or all of the security advantage gained through trade. Gowa draws the obvious conclusion that nations should trade primarily with their military allies. This allows them to achieve the economic benefits of trade and boost their own military power, while at the same time strengthening their allies, therefore making themselves even more secure. From the realist perspective, the only problem with this idea is that alliances may be subject to sudden and arbitrary shifts, as soon as self-seeking nations see advantages to realigning themselves.

For different reasons Paul Papayoanu also argues that a nation should trade with its allies rather than with its potential adversaries. He believes trading with democratic military allies has positive security effects because it gives those allies a stronger stake in each other's well-being. This makes it easier for a nation's leader to mobilize its allies to balance the power of any opposing nation or alliance that becomes a potential threat. Trading with potential adversaries, however, creates a situation in which vested domestic economic interests that want to avoid confrontation with those adversaries may grow strong enough to constrain the nation's leader in trying to balance the threat those adversaries pose if at some point they actually do become aggressive.[22]

In contrast, realists like Hans Morgenthau believe that the outbreak of war has no systematic connection with economic interdependence, because they believe wars result primarily from political and strategic military factors. Barry Buzan, for example, argues that there has been no general decline in wars among *nonmajor* powers since World War II despite growing trade, and that the lack of war among the *major* powers during the Cold War was the result of military deterrence and the bipolar (two superpower) distribution of power, not trade considerations.[23] Kal Holsti contends that economic interdependence does not really affect the outbreak of war because security interests trump economic interests during times of serious conflict.[24]

Both realists and liberals agree that cooperation is more desirable than conflict. Peter Gourevitch points out, "That cooperation produces benefits superior to conflict has not been challenged by different system theorists; the collective gains from coordination outweigh the solo benefits of conflict. The divergence has always been over whether cooperation will occur."[25] Although liberals also recognize that there is no overarching form of government that dominates the international arena, they see it as less unstable and the actors within it more prone to self-interested cooperation than do realists. Liberals believe that the realist notion of the state as a unitary entity with a well-defined national interest does not give sufficient weight to the interests and actions of diverse individuals. Robert Keohane argues that the interaction of individual and organizational actors within nations, engaging in behaviors that cut across nations, constitutes a form of "transnational" relations that undercuts the centrality of the state. International business and economic relationships may be among the most important transnational behaviors.

Liberals are also not as pessimistic as realists that the combination of anarchy and unequal distribution of the gains from trade is a recipe for ongoing interstate conflict. Keohane lays heavy emphasis on building institutions, which he defines as formal or informal organizations to which nations voluntarily belong because of the benefits of cooperation.[26] He contends that international institutions are capable of facilitating cooperation that would otherwise be difficult to accomplish or sustain in their absence, given the lack of international government.[27] Of course, many international organizations and arrangements have already been created—including the United Nations, the World Trade Organization, and the European Union, along with international agreements on airlines, the mails, and the environment.

Keohane and Martin argue that institutions help overcome particular obstacles to cooperation in specific ways: "Realists interpret the relative gains logic as showing that states will not cooperate with one another if each suspects that its potential partners are gaining more from cooperation than it is. However, just as institutions mitigate fears of cheating . . . so can they alleviate fears of unequal gains from cooperation. Liberal theory argues that institutions provide valuable information, and information about the distribution of gains may be especially valuable."[28] That is, of course, providing the gains of cooperation actually are evenly divided over time, which they may or may not be.

Keohane claimed that, under the right conditions, states can and do find effective ways to cooperate, even in the absence of international government. Perhaps the best illustration of how independent units, uncoordinated by any central authority, find ways of cooperating to their mutual advantage is the market system itself. Markets amount to a network of ongoing, voluntary cooperative interactions that take place among economic units. The glue that holds the market system together is an incentive structure that plays on self-interest. There is no sovereign to compel cooperation, but there is a system of norms of behavior, which can be usefully reinforced by agreed institutions, such as contract law and systems of adjudication of contract disputes. The meaningful enforcement of some of these reinforcing institutions (such as contract law) on subnational actors (such as firms) can be accomplished by national institutions, even in the absence of international government or institutions. For example, if a U.S. firm violates a contract with a French firm, the French firm can sue for breach of contract in U.S. courts, and enforce the contract or punish the violator without access to an international authority.[29] States operating under the right set of incentives can also find creative ways of cooperating and enforcing agreements without establishing anything remotely resembling world government.[30] "Bad behavior" (such as failure to pay back loans) can be punished by loss of cooperation (unwillingness to provide loans in the future) and thus loss of the benefits of further cooperation. This works best when there is no player in the market system so dominant that it can get away with breaking the rules. All this is also true in the case of an international political system.

Joseph Nye argues that more sophisticated forms of liberal theory are needed because the simplest forms were discredited by the outbreak of World Wars I and II: "The proposition that the gains from commercial transactions would overcome the problems inherent in the security dilemma and make war too expensive were belied in 1914. Hopes that a system of international law and organization could provide collective security, which would replace the need for self-help inherent in the security dilemma, were disappointed by 1939."[31] Together, he and Robert Keohane developed the idea of "complex interdependence": states interact with each other in a variety of areas (migration, environment, culture), not just in terms of economics or military national security concerns. Each of these areas of interaction has a number of dimensions.[32] Gourevitch explains, "The definition of country interests, the influences on countries from actors within them, and the way countries interact flows [sic] through a network of relationships only some of which pass through the formal institutions of the nation-state. Some of these networks are embodied in formal institutions . . . but most are not, being comprised of very influential patterns of norms or relationships."[33] Keohane and Nye also believe that military force has become less useful and authority within the state more fragmented.

In a useful summary, Susan McMillan identifies four categories of liberal theory—political, economic, sociological, and sophisticated—all of which have important implications for the issues of war and peace.[34] A main tenet of *political* liberalism (as, for example, espoused by Immanuel Kant) is that republics in which individuals have fundamental civil rights are less likely to go to war than are autocratic forms of government. A modern variant, the so-called democratic peace argument (as, for example, espoused by Bruce Russett), holds that because of shared norms of peaceful dispute resolution and the unquestionable political legitimacy of governments freely chosen by their own people, liberal democracies do not go to war with each other, though they may well go to war with authoritarian nations.[35] Early *economic* liberals (e.g., Baron de Montesquieu) argued that "the natural effect of commerce is to lead to peace," but were not all that specific as to how that connection operated.[36] In the twentieth century, economic liberalism focused on the idea that international trade would inhibit war because widening trade made war a more costly and less effective means of pursuing the self-interest of states.

Richard Rosecrance made perhaps the best and most comprehensive version of this economic liberal argument in his 1986 book, *The Rise of the Trading State:*

While trading states try to improve their condition and their own domestic allocation of resources, they do so within a context of accepted interdependence. They recognize that the attempt to provide every service and fulfill every function of statehood on an independent and autonomous basis is extremely inefficient, and they prefer a situation which provides for specialization and a division of labor among nations. One nation's attempt to improve its own access to products and resources, therefore does not conflict with another state's attempt to do the same. The incentive to wage war is absent in such a system for war disrupts trade and the interdependence on which trade is based. Trading states realize that they can do better through internal economic development sustained by a world wide market for their goods and services than by trying to conquer and assimilate large tracts of land.[37]

In his thought provoking 1990 review essay, "Is War Obsolete?," Carl Kaysen argued that, by the twentieth century, changes in the nature of both war and the economy had transformed the economic cost-benefit calculus of war:

Industrial wars involved the whole nation, not the typically small fraction of population and output drawn into earlier wars. . . . Destruction of a significant part of the stock of tangible capital in the battlefield countries was one element . . . in the economic costs of the great wars. . . .

On the other side of the ledger, the extent to which the conquest of new territory added to the economic strength of the conqueror is questionable. The question is whether the economy of a different society . . . can be effectively incorporated by conquest against the will of its inhabitants. The continuing political hostility of the conquered, and its effects on the level of energy and efficiency with which their economy operates, may lead to poorer results than those the conqueror could have achieved by . . . investing the equivalent in production for home consumption or trade with the rest of the world.[38]

The American-led 2003 invasion of Iraq and its subsequent occupation certainly provides strong evidence for Kaysen's proposition that a hostile conquered population can interfere with "the level of energy and efficiency with which their economy operates," and therefore the success of efforts at postwar reconstruction led by an occupying power.

Sociological liberalism emphasizes the importance of connections among people that form in the course of commercial relationships. The communication and cooperation those ongoing links imply will increase people's knowledge and appreciation of each other and their customs and culture. Frequent close contacts among people could, of course, lead to more rather than fewer conflicts among them if their interests or behaviors are not compatible. Even so, Karl Deutsch argues that "conflicts can still be reduced by increasing the salience and weight of parallel or interlocking interests among the countries concerned," making collaboration so rewarding that it is potentially capable of overcoming tendencies toward conflict.[39] What McMillan calls *sophisticated liberalism* is a generally hopeful combination of political and economic liberalism that nevertheless recognizes the potential for conflict. Peace is encouraged by international institutions that facilitate free trade as well as by fostering broader forms of international cooperation.

Edward Mansfield combines the realist fixation on the distribution of power with the liberal focus on the importance of trade, arguing that both concentration of power and extent of trade are theoretically relevant to the outbreak of war.[40] He then goes on to claim that neither of the key relationships—that between concentration of power and trade, or that between concentration of power and war—is as simple, direct, and consistent as most realist and liberal theorists imply. Mansfield instead argues that "both the highest and lowest levels of concentration give rise to the highest levels of global trade, while intermediate levels of concentration give rise to the lowest levels of such trade,"[41] and that "both the highest and lowest levels of concentration give rise to the lowest incidence of major power warfare, while intermediate levels of concentration give rise to the highest incidence of such warfare."[42] In the end, Mansfield's argument supports the liberal point of view. If the least amount of trade and the highest incidence of major power war both occur at intermediate level of concentration of power, then trade and war should be inversely related, as liberal theorists claim.

Dale Copeland put forth the interesting idea that it wasn't just historical or current levels of trade that were relevant to conflict, but also expectations of future trade:

High interdependence can be peace-inducing as liberals maintain, as long as states expect . . . trade levels to be high in the future: positive expectations for future trade will lead dependent states to assign a high expected value to a continuation of peaceful trade, making war the less appealing option. If, however, a highly dependent state expects future trade to be low due to the policy decisions of the other side, then realists are likely to be correct: the state will attach a low or even negative expected value to continued peace without trade, making war an attractive alternative.[43]

If this argument is correct, it substantially complicates the problem of distinguishing whether observed behavior is consistent with the liberal or realist hypotheses. For example, if conflict erupts when current levels of trade are low, we might conclude that the liberals are right. But if no conflict erupts when levels of trade are low, we cannot tell whether the realists are right (since low interdependence is associated with low conflict) or the liberals are right, and the reason there is no conflict is that future trade levels are expected to be high.[44] Consequently, to the extent that expectations of future trade are key to the likelihood of present conflict, it is critical to have an accurate way of determining future expectations to properly discriminate empirically between the liberal and realist hypotheses.

A Brief Background Look at Some Empirical Evidence

After reviewing a diverse group of twenty empirical studies bearing on the realist/liberal debate, Susan McMillan reported that only four were consistent with the realist contention that greater international interdependence either had no effect on military conflict or actually made it more likely, while ten supported the liberal hypothesis that increased economic interdependence was associated with less military conflict. The other six studies produced either mixed results or results that were conditional.[45]

The realist argument was supported by one of the earliest statistical analyses of this issue, done by Bruce Russett in 1967.[46] He found that states that were part of the same group of trading partners between 1946 and 1965 were at least twice as likely to have participated in military conflicts as states that were not. Because the trading groups in his study included many that were involved in colonial relationships, he recognized that his results might illustrate the effects of *unequal* trade, rather than trade as such. Russett further noted that since trade tended to be highly correlated with geographic proximity, and geographic proximity tends to be correlated with military conflict, the observed relationship between trade and conflict might even have been spurious.

Anne Uchitel's case study of Nazi Germany, Imperial Japan, and Great Britain in the period between the two world wars provided additional support for realists, although she argued that a specific type of economic dependence—on imports of militarily and economically strategic materials—seemed to be more important than interdependence in general.[47] Particularly in the case of Germany and Japan, dependence on external sources for strategic supplies created "incentives for states to adopt expansionist policies and offensive military strategies."[48] Dependence on world export markets, however, did not seem to be important, probably because that kind of dependence does not directly threaten supplies of critical materials. Uchitel also found that there was inequality in the distribution of costs and benefits of interdependence, and concluded that this inequality was dangerous. In a related result, Katherine Barbieri found that the more balanced the gains from trade, the less likely that pairs of trading nations would engage in conflict with each other, a finding consistent with the realist argument that asymmetries in trade provoke conflict.[49]

Among the earliest empirical studies supporting the liberal hypothesis was a simple (bivariate regression) analysis on data on country pairs from 1958 to 1967, published by Edward E. Azar in the *Journal of Conflict Resolution* in 1980.[50] In the same issue of that journal, Solomon Polachek presented formal and statistical models he had developed, based on the assumption that trade produces net benefits. As a consequence, Polachek reasoned, introducing disruptive conflict into a previously peaceful trading relationship would be expected to cause losses of those benefits. As he put it, "The implicit price of being hostile is the diminution of welfare associated with potential trade losses."[51] Over the years, in a series of statistical studies of country pairs with various coauthors based on those models, Polachek found a consistent, inverse relationship between trade and conflict, supporting the liberal hypothesis. For example, in 1982, Gasiorowski and Polachek found an inverse association between trade and conflict in an analysis of trade between the Soviet- and the U.S.-led blocs during the period of détente from 1967 to 1970.[52] Tests confirmed that the direction of causality ran from trade to conflict and not the other way around.[53] They also found some evidence that the type of good traded made a difference.

Four years later, Mark Gasiorowski published his own analysis of the relationship between economic interdependence and international conflict, correcting for what he argued were deficiencies in Polachek's earlier work.[54] Looking at the period 1960–1977, his regressions once again showed an inverse relationship between trade and conflict, confirming the liberal hypothesis. But he also found that the fewer countries from which a given country imported goods, the higher the level of conflict, and the fewer goods a country exported, the higher the level of conflict. Since fewer suppliers of imports and a narrower range of types of exports imply greater vulnerability to disruptions of trade, Gasiorowski's results also provide some support for the realist point of view.

In 1992, Polachek once again analyzed the conflict/trade relationship for pairs of countries, this time for the period 1948–1978. Using a variety of (regression-based) statistical analyses, he found once again that pairs of countries that traded the most had the least conflict, even after controlling for the characteristics of the countries involved. The consistent pattern revealed by Polachek's analyses provides strong support for the liberal hypothesis. A later study of country pairs, by John Oneal et al., that controlled for other issues related to conflict still found that a higher level of trade was associated with fewer "militarized international disputes."[55] This reinforced Polachek's conclusions and strengthened support for the liberal claim that trade does help to promote peace.

When Edward Mansfield put a number of ideas arising from his theoretical analysis of the connection between international trade and war to the statistical test, the results were once again overwhelmingly in support of the liberal point of view. Looking at the average number of wars for each five-year period from 1855 to 1964, Mansfield found that there was a strong and robust inverse relationship between the level of international trade and the frequency of wars. This conclusion held whether he looked at wars between major powers, wars that did not involve any major powers, or all international wars.[56] He also found that, despite his belief that concentration of power was critically important to the relationship between trade and war, "there is little evidence that the effect of the level of international trade on war is due to the influence of the distribution of power on both commerce and war."[57]

The period preceding World War I has often been used as evidence for the realist point of view. It is argued that the European powers were heavily engaged in trade in the period leading up to World War I, yet that did not stop them from going to war.[58] But liberals do not necessarily accept this interpretation. Rosecrance, for example, has argued, "This claim is largely specious. Though foreign investment was then a larger proportion of GDP than it is today, it was overwhelmingly liquid portfolio investment which could be quickly disposed of in a crisis. To the extent that direct investment in physical facilities was involved, it was largely confined to a metropolitan power's empire. European Great Powers did not have a significant stake in the economies of brother nations."[59] Less than two decades later, the protectionism of the 1930s reduced international interdependence, and World War II subsequently erupted, giving apparent support to the liberal argument. On the other hand, realists point out that the two states whose aggression initiated the war—Germany and Japan—were also the most highly dependent on external sources of supply for critical raw materials, supporting their point of view.

Dale Copeland gives his own historical analysis of both those periods, leading to his interesting conclusion that "trade expectations," not actual observed levels of trade, hold the key to understanding why high levels of Japanese and German trade dependence failed to prevent World Wars I and II. For example:

> Germany in the 1930s . . . would always remain highly dependent on outsiders for the food and raw materials vital to its economic health, unless it expanded. Moreover, since the surrounding great powers were better able to fashion self-sustaining imperial realms, should they ever move in this direction by closing their borders to trade . . . long-term German economic viability and therefore security would be threatened.[60]
>
> After the U.S., British and Dutch severed all oil trade to Japan in August 1941, Japanese leaders agreed that unless oil imports were restored, economic decline would imperil long term security. Hence, following the failure of desperate diplomatic initiatives in November 1941, the plan for all-out war was accepted by the emperor. In short Japan's extreme dependence, coupled with very negative expectations for future trade, pushed the country into a war.[61]

Civil Wars

Up to this point, we have focused primarily on the connection between economic relationships and international war. Because international wars

are initiated and directed by governments, which have the formal authority to mobilize an entire nation's human and economic resources, they are
fought with larger, better-equipped forces and far more destructive weaponry. They also pose the greatest risk of escalation, both horizontal (drawing more nations into the conflict) and vertical (increasing the power of
forces deployed and the destructiveness of weapons and tactics used). But
wars between nations are not the only violent conflicts that can undermine economic progress and cause enormous trauma, pain, and suffering. Particularly in the twentieth and early twenty-first century, wars within
nations have crippled life-supporting economic activity, taken countless
lives, and created human rivers of refugees.

Although it has become commonplace to think of civil wars, at least in
modern times, as being caused by deep-seated social grievances, ideological
rivalries, and ethnic hatreds, the fact is that economic agendas can and do
play an important role. Paul Collier writes, "I have investigated statistically
the global pattern of large-scale civil conflict since 1965, expecting to find a
close relationship between measures of . . . [intergroup] hatreds and grievances and the incidence of conflict. Instead, I found that economic agendas
appear to be central to understanding why civil wars start. Conflicts are far
more likely to be caused by economic opportunities than by grievance. . . .
Civil wars create economic opportunities for a minority of actors even as
they destroy them for the majority."[62]

The popularity of the idea that grievances are the main cause of civil
wars is reinforced by most of what we hear day-to-day from those engaged
in ongoing violent civil conflicts. The rebels are always rebels with a cause;
there is always a terrible wrong to be righted, an injustice to be undone.
The government is always trying to protect the public against disruption,
instability, and lawlessness, to support the mainstream of society against
the rebel extremists who would contaminate, pervert, or destroy it. This
is neither accidental nor the result of misinterpretation. To put it simply,
grievance agendas are better public relations than economic agendas. It is
usually easier (and cheaper) for rebels to recruit soldiers, broaden support,
and raise funds by emphasizing grievances, because of the nearly universal emotional appeal of participating in the struggle for what is right and
true and just. For similar reasons, it is easier for governments to rally pub-

lic (and international) support by trying to delegitimize rebel grievances and raise the specter of the grievous wrongs the rebels would commit if they were successful. Even if the leadership on one or both sides were more concerned with who will have control over and thus be able to exploit diamond mines or oil fields, their public discourse about the war will still be cast in terms of grievance.

None of this is by way of saying that grievances are always concocted or even exaggerated in the service of a good sales pitch. The grievances may be very real, and the pain they cause may run very deep. But whether the grievances are real or fabricated, they are likely to be used to cover any economic agenda that might really be driving the conflict. Even when an economic agenda is paramount, on the surface it will not seem to be.

More perversely, the outbreak of war "legitimizes" activities that are punishable crimes in times of peace, creating incentives to keep the conflict going. War relieves those who pursue profits of a variety of constraints that exist in peacetime: They can threaten or carry out violence against rival traders legitimately; they can forcibly take what valuable goods or resources others have without compensation; they can play a "protection game," extorting money and other valuable commodities under the threat of violence. In other words, knowing they can use the fact of war as an excuse for committing what amount to criminal offenses, they may see the breakdown of law and order as an economic opportunity.[63] As William Reno pointed out for a sample of twentieth century civil wars, "Experiences in Sierra Leone, Liberia, Sudan, Somalia, El Salvador, Chechnya and Cambodia show that the economic interests of belligerents may be a powerful barrier to the termination of conflict. They may use war to control land and commerce, exploit labor, milk charitable agencies, and ensure the continuity of assets and privileges to a group."[64]

Indra de Soysa investigated the empirical relationship between natural resource wealth and civil conflict (involving at least twenty-five battle deaths) for the period 1989–1998.[65] After taking into account a number of other relevant economic and social factors, de Soysa found that the greater the abundance of *nonrenewable* subsoil resources (known mineral deposits), the higher the probability of civil war. Interestingly, he did not find any significant relationship between the abundance of *renewable* resources and civil war. This might be because the exploitation of intense concentrations of nonrenewable mineral resources, especially those that are easily extractable, does not involve the extent of territorial control or require the kind of ongoing, large-scale cooperative effort that is involved in taking economic advantage of control of cropland, pasture, or even forest.

For a global sample of countries, Paul Collier tried to predict whether or not a country would have a civil war during each five-year period from 1960 to 1995 on the basis of factors related more to economic agendas or to grievances.[66] Collier found, "The results overwhelmingly point to the importance of economic agendas as opposed to grievance. . . . [A] country that is heavily dependent on primary commodity exports, with a quarter of its national income coming from them, has a risk of conflict four times greater than one without primary commodity exports. . . . Thus, some countries are much more prone to conflict than others simply because they offer more inviting economic prospects for rebellion."[67] Collier goes on, "The only result that supports the grievance approach to conflict is that a prior period of rapid economic decline increases the risk of conflict."[68] It appears that even when they are the cause of grievances rather than direct motivation, economic factors play an important role in civil war.

The formal theoretical and empirical literature related to the matters at hand is extensive and ongoing. Our brief look at this literature seeks only to establish the main theoretical and empirical underpinnings of the idea of economic peacekeeping.

The Peacekeeping Economy: Synthesizing and Extending the Theory

I do not see the realist and liberal philosophies as disconnected and irreconcilably hostile. Realists do not dispute the liberal claim that international trade is economically beneficial, but rather are quite rightly concerned about the implications of unequal trade gains and of excessive dependence on external sources of supply for goods that are critical to the nation's economy and security. Liberals, particularly sophisticated liberals, do not dispute the realist claim that inequalities can easily arise from trade; nor do liberals claim that economic interdependence necessarily overrides all other forms of interaction, wiping out all other sources of conflict and hostility. Liberals do believe that international economic relationships create incentives to avoid war, and can set in motion sociological, psychological, and perhaps political processes that reinforce those incentives. Realists, particularly neorealists, are certainly less sanguine about the binding power of economic interdependence and more likely to see international economic relations as a sideshow, but they do not deny that economic factors are relevant to national and international security. And both agree that cooperation, if it can be brought about, is a superior strategy to conflict.

The anarchic nature of the international realm highlighted by realists is recognized by liberals as well, but liberals do not find it as inherently troubling as realists do. While realists see the world of nations as prone to continuing conflict in the absence of a dominant power (hegemon) or a carefully constructed balance of power to block that tendency through explicit or implicit threat or use of force, liberals see the potential gains of interdependence in an anarchic world as implying strong incentives to build effective international institutions and other cooperative arrangements.

Though realist and liberal philosophies are not entirely incompatible, they illuminate different key aspects of the connection between economic relationships and war. From liberals comes the importance of interdependent economic relationships in creating positive incentives to avoid conflict; the possibility that the personal interactions involved in ongoing economic relationships can help to strengthen those incentives; and the importance of seeing international relations as relations between individuals and organizations reaching across national boundaries, as well as relationships between nation-states. From realists comes the importance of paying attention to how equally the gains of trade are distributed; the strategic risk involved in depending too heavily on foreign sources of supply of goods vital to the nation; the importance of power; and the value of a certain healthy skepticism about the assumption that nations will always act in an economically self-interested way.

Taking note of the fact that, on balance, the findings of empirical studies are far more supportive of liberal than they are of realist hypotheses, the challenge is nevertheless to extract the most useful elements of both theoretical perspectives, to combine and extend them in an attempt to weave what we know about the relationship between war and the economy into a paradigm for preventing war. It is to that challenge that we now turn.

3

The Core Principles of
Economic Peacekeeping

If you want to change the old reality, don't fight against it.
Build a new reality that makes the old one obsolete.

—Buckminster Fuller

SINCE THE END OF WORLD WAR II there has been great progress in establishing treaties and institutions aimed at creating a working body of international law and acceptable practice. Still, the international legal and political environment remains essentially anarchic. It is not possible to rely confidently on an overarching, authoritative, and enforceable system of international law or governance to bind the behavior of nations, and only slightly more possible to rely indirectly on such a system to bind the behavior of global businesses or individuals.[1]

As a result, nation-states are still more or less independent actors, able to accept or reject constraints as they see fit. Therefore the central question in constructing a peacekeeping international economy is, How can economic forces best be used to get sovereign nations to voluntarily cooperate with each other in resolving conflicts without resorting to organized violence? The answer to this question lies in creating a combination of positive incentives and negative sanctions that naturally guides nation-states to more peaceful patterns of behavior.[2]

The impact of incentives on voluntary behavior is one of the core themes in market economics. Economists assume that human behavior is purposive, not random or capricious, and that there are always underlying goals driving us to do what we do. To the extent that this is true, it becomes possible to change behavior by creating conditions that change the way in which the goals we seek can best be achieved. For example, a tax credit for business investment will stimulate investment because it lowers the cost of buying equipment and therefore makes investment a more attractive route to the firm's underlying goal, higher profits.

It is also generally assumed that both positive and negative incentives ("carrots" and "sticks") influence behavior, so either can be used. This follows from the assumption that behavior is driven by the logical pursuit of underlying goals. By this reasoning, imposing high enough fines on firms that continue to exceed established limits on pollution will have essentially the same effect as giving large enough tax credits to firms that do not. In either case, profits will be significantly lower if the firm continues polluting at current levels, so either approach will be just as likely to get them to reduce pollution. That is not to say that *exactly equal* positive and negative incentives can be expected to have exactly the same effect.[3] I will return to this matter later in this chapter.

Economic sanctions are the main form of negative economic incentive used to affect international political conduct. They fit easily into the realist model of influencing behavior through coercive power, though in this case the force threatened or used is economic, rather than military. Even so, economic sanctions do not have a particularly good reputation among realists, who argue that they are relatively ineffective, especially compared with the threat or use of military force. But the historical record of economic sanctions does not appear to support such a negative assessment.[4] Applied in the right way and under the right conditions, they can be an effective tool for influencing national and international behavior (see Chapter 5). And even though sanctions can cause a great deal of damage, they do not inflict the carnage that results from military action. If they can be made to work, they are almost always preferable to armed conflict. Nevertheless, economic sanctions are still a part of the paradigm of threat; they are still an attempt to influence behavior through punishment. While they can be an important tool for ending undesirable behavior, threats are not likely to work as well as positive incentives in reinforcing desirable behavior. Positive economic incentives not only are more likely to be effective, they also have much lower human and economic cost.

In his intriguing book *Stable Peace* Kenneth Boulding sets out what he calls the "chalk theory" of war and peace.[5] A piece of chalk breaks when the strain applied to it is greater than its strength, its ability to resist that strain. Similarly, a war breaks out when the strain applied to the international system exceeds the ability of that system to withstand strain. Establishing stable peace therefore requires reducing strain, increasing strength, or both.

The chalk theory is a useful mental frame of reference, because it helps us avoid the trap of dogmatism and the folly of seeking a single cause or a single cure for the scourge of war. It helps us to think about war in probabilistic terms. Anything that increases strain or weakens resistance to that strain adds to the probability of war; anything that reduces strain or increases the ability of the system to withstand strain helps keep the peace. There is no constant, dependable, clear-cut threshold of hostility beyond which war occurs.

In the midst of this complexity and uncertainty, maximizing the peacekeeping potential of the international economic system is part of the answer to establishing stable peace. For the international economy to make its greatest contribution to keeping the peace, there must be a potent combination of economically based strain-mitigating and strength-enhancing strategies. That sounds more complicated than it actually is, at least in concept. It comes down to four basic principles that define the character of a peacekeeping economy.

Principle I: Establish Balanced, Mutually Beneficial Relationships

The liberal claim that higher levels of international economic activity help to keep the peace, and the realist claim that they create conflict and war, seem utterly contradictory. But they are both right—higher levels of international economic activity can make war either more or less likely. Which of the two they actually do depends crucially on the nature of the activity, not just on the amount. Unbalanced, exploitative relationships tend to increase the number and severity of conflicts, while balanced, mutually beneficial relationships tend to reduce them.

The economic theory underlying the liberal view that free trade is intrinsically beneficial (the theory of comparative advantage) contains nothing that either guarantees or prohibits a balanced flow of benefit. Furthermore, although most of the literature exploring the connection between international economic activity and conflict is focused on trade, trade is not the only form of international economic activity relevant to preventing or provoking violent conflict. Foreign direct investment (FDI), capital flows in the form of loans and transfer payments, and flows of labor in the form of physical (or virtual) immigration can also play an important role.[6] The concepts of balance and mutual benefit are important to these kinds of economic relationships as well.

A relationship is "balanced and mutually beneficial" if its benefits flow to every participant and there is a rough equivalence between everyone's contribution to the relationship and the benefit they derive.[7] It does not mean that all parties to the relationship benefit equally regardless of their contribution. A balance of benefit implies that those who participate are compensated for their participation in a way that truly reflects the value of their contribution rather than differences in their bargaining power.[8] Unbalanced, exploitative relationships are thus those in which the flow of benefit is overwhelmingly in one direction, and does not correspond to relative contribution.

The enormous trade imbalance between the United States and China, for example, does not necessarily mean that the two nations have an unbalanced exploitative economic relationship. The U.S. may be buying a much larger dollar value of goods from China than China is buying from the U.S., but if the U.S. is paying China a price that reflects the true value of the goods it is purchasing, and China is paying the U.S. a price that reflects the true value of the goods it is purchasing, their trading relationship is balanced, mutually beneficial, and thus unlikely to provoke war. And what price reflects the true value of the goods purchased? It is the price that would be paid with open competition and no distortions arising from differences in economic or political power between the trading partners.[9]

However, a balance of trade in the more conventional sense (the volume of exports relative to imports) also matters to issues of war and peace. As the realists have pointed out, if two nations are not equally dependent on each other, the less dependent nation will have a degree of leverage over its more dependent trading partner. That may make the more dependent partner insecure, leading that partner to bring other, more coercive forms of power (such as military power) to bear to overcome its perceived disadvantage. Realists believe that the likelihood of that kind of reaction is greater the more critical the goods being traded are to the well-being of the more dependent country, and the weaker the supplying country is militarily. If a nation whose economy is very dependent on oil imports, for example, buys most of its oil from a militarily weaker nation that buys little or no important goods from it, the oil importing nation may feel tempted, even compelled, to threaten the weaker nation militarily or even to try to seize control of critical oil fields by military force. Trade that is balanced in the sense of volume and significance, as well as in the sense of benefit relative to contribution, is therefore more likely to prevent war than trade that is balanced in only one of those senses. Much the same can also be said of forms of international economic relationships other than trade, such as investment.

In addition to the problems created by unequal dependence, realists also see unequal benefits arising from unbalanced trade as creating or increasing power differences among states, potentially disrupting the balance of power that keeps the peace. Yet there is a more basic reason why economic relationships that are unbalanced (especially in terms of benefit relative to contribution) create conflict: they are inherently unfair. Psychological studies have concluded that "the idea of justice or fairness may be more centrally related to attitudes toward violence than are feelings of deprivation. It is the perceived injustice underlying the deprivation that gives rise to anger or frustration,"[10] both of which are common precursors of violent behavior.

There is also some interesting evidence from the field of experimental economics that people understand the importance of treating others fairly in economic transactions, if only out of self-interest. The Ultimatum Game is a one-time, two person game in which one person, the Proposer, makes an offer to divide a sum of money (say, $100) provided by the Experimenter with another person, the Responder, in a specified proportion—say 60–40 percent, or 90–10 percent. If the Responder accepts the offer, they divide the money the way the Proposer suggested; if not, neither gets anything. After running the experiment a large number of times in various countries under various conditions, experimenters have noted that rather than trying to get a very lopsided deal, the majority of Proposers offered the Responders 40 to 50 percent of the sum of money, and about half of the

Responders rejected any offer below 30 percent. We do not know whether most Proposers made a relatively balanced offer out of a sense of fairness or out of pure self-interest, but it is clear that half the Responders preferred to walk away empty-handed rather than take an offer they considered patently unfair.[11]

If any party to an unbalanced relationship is suffering a net loss, that party will certainly feel ill-used and hostile. But even if everyone is gaining something, the fact that the vast majority of benefit flows elsewhere is bound to create or aggravate resentment among those who receive less value than they contribute, giving them reason to want to disrupt the status quo. They will lose little and may actually gain both "psychic income" and economic benefits by destroying the relationship. There is certainly little or no incentive for them to resolve whatever conflicts might occur, economic or otherwise. And if they see disruption as key to rebalancing or replacing the relationship with more beneficial economic arrangements, there will be an incentive to raise the intensity of those conflicts, even to the point of war. That is part of what drove the American Revolution.

Balanced relationships tend to have the opposite effect. Since everyone gains benefit at least equal to their contribution, out of pure self-interest no one will want to see it disrupted. Furthermore, when gains are more equitably divided, the economic growth and development of all of the parties are stimulated. Resources are more effectively used, producers become more productive, the size of the market grows. As a result, they have more to offer each other as time goes by, both as sources of products and as sources of profits. The advantage of balanced relationships grows over time.

The mercantilists of times gone by (and the dependency theorists of more recent times) saw the economic world as something of a zero-sum game, a game of redistribution (such as poker), the gains of one party coming at the expense of another. Unbalanced, exploitative economic relationships have something like this static, redistributional character. But balanced, mutually beneficial relationships do not simply divide a fixed pie of benefit; they help the pie to grow. Balanced relationships distribute the gains of the larger pie in a way that is more likely to create a "virtuous circle," a positive feedback loop that keeps the pie growing.

When relationships are balanced, current gains and the prospect of still greater gains in the future create strong self-interested incentives to settle more peacefully the conflicts that inevitably arise in any relationship, as liberals and neoliberals argue.[12] As those conflicts are successfully resolved time after time, the idea of allowing them to fester to the point of desperate confrontation comes to seem more and more absurd. The thought of brandishing the threat of war against valued economic partners slowly recedes, and war itself ultimately comes to be seen as unnecessary, undesirable, and inherently counterproductive.

The idea that conflict is heightened by exploitation and relieved by balance has power across a wide range of human relationships, from the interpersonal to the international. Even though it is often convenient to talk about "China" trading with "the U.S.," at their core, international economic relationships are not really relationships among the unitary (indivisible) nations of realist theory or even the depersonalized, mechanistically profit maximizing firms of microeconomic theory. They are relationships among people—people who may be playing different personally or organizationally defined roles, but people nonetheless. In international trade as well as in friendships and marriages, domination typically produces resentment and hostility, while balance builds trust and cooperation.

It is easy to see why people who are being exploited would be better off if the relationship were to become more balanced. It is harder to see that even those doing the exploiting would also gain from greater balance, especially over the long term. The discontent of the exploited motivates them to resist control—and to try to force a greater degree of balance, end the relationship, or even reverse the direction of domination. If the exploiter comes under stress from external sources, there will be a strong incentive for those being exploited to take advantage of the exploiter's weakened position, adding to that stress. Knowing this makes exploiters insecure, leading them into a high pressure state of constant vigilance, and requiring that they put an inordinate amount of effort and expense into maintaining control. This is much more of a drain than is generally realized.

When relationships are balanced, there is no need to expend extra effort to keep them going. Because they are fair and mutually beneficial, balanced relationships do not provoke antagonism. On the contrary, as each party begins to perceive how much it is gaining, both start to see the well-being of the other party as in their own best interest. The mutual flow of benefits binds the parties together. Because the relationship benefits all participants more or less equally, they will all be more likely to look for ways of maintaining or strengthening it, out of self-interest. When conflicts occur, they will try to settle them amicably rather than take actions that might make them worse. If their relationship partners come under stress from external sources, they will have an incentive to relieve, rather than increase, the pressure. In this situation, everyone in the relationship will feel more secure; no one will need to expend extra effort and expense just to keep it going. In economists' terms, *a balanced relationship is a more efficient relationship: the benefits are achieved at a much lower cost.*

Adam Smith saw this clearly more than 230 years ago. In *The Wealth of Nations* (1776) there is a lengthy discussion as to whether maintaining political control of the British colonial empire, with its accompanying exploitative trade monopolies, worked to the advantage of the Great Britain. Smith concluded: "Under the present system of management . . . Great Britain derives nothing but loss from the dominion which she assumes over her colonies . . . Great Britain should voluntarily give up all authority over her colonies. . . . Great Britain would not only be immediately freed from the whole annual expense of the peace establishment of the colonies, but might settle with them such a treaty of commerce as would effectually secure to her a free trade, more advantageous to the great body of the people [of Britain] . . . than the monopoly which she at present enjoys."[13]

In any exploitative relationship, the expense of maintaining control can be reduced if the exploiters are able to psychologically manipulate the exploited so as to make them feel helpless or accepting, even deserving, of their subordinate position. This is the basis of one of Karl Marx's most important insights, the concept of "false consciousness."[14] This concept can be extended to an even more effective method of maintaining control: getting subordinates to identify with the very system that is exploiting them. If appeals to patriotism (in the case of a country) or loyalty to the "Emperor" (in the case of an empire) succeed in making people proud to be part of such a powerful institution, they may not only accept but also actively support a system that is in fact exploiting them. The majesty of empire, the glory of the nation, the reputation and power of the firm can be compelling, and identification with them can raise the self-esteem of even their lowliest members. But false consciousness doesn't necessarily work forever. Eventually, those disadvantaged by a relationship may come to feel the discontent and disaffection that continued exploitation produces, and see the possibility and desirability of change.

If it is true that exploitation is counterproductive in the long run even for the exploiter, then why do so many of us continue to believe that we are best off if we are dominant in a relationship? I think there are two main reasons. The first and most obvious is myopia. Human beings seem much more easily able to calculate the short-term effects of their actions than they can long-run consequences. This is not just because of uncertainty about the future: the long run somehow does not seem as real to us as the short run. For the most part, what will happen in twenty or thirty years as a consequence of what we do today often seems too abstract to be weighted as heavily as more immediate effects. Even when it is well understood that a behavior is counterproductive in the long run, if the short-term effects seems desirable, it is uncommonly difficult to get people—or their nations—to reject it. Cigarette smoking and substance abuse come easily to mind as examples of such behavior for individuals. People often act as though they have a very high rate of discount for the future.

The second reason may be even more compelling. We come to know virtually from birth that we must depend on others for much of what we want or need in life. Our growth from infancy to adulthood is largely a growth from total dependency to greater self-reliance. Yet even in adulthood we remain intellectually, emotionally, and physically dependent on others for their guidance, interaction, praise, and support, as well as for the material goods and services we want and need. This creates a degree of insecurity that comes from the fear that those on whom we must depend may not do what we want or need them to do. In part, we have learned to deal with our insecurity, with our fears of each other, through a paradigm of domination. If we are in a position of control, we can force anyone who won't go along voluntarily to give us what we want or need.

There is much in the human experience, as individuals and as nations, to support the idea that those who dominate often live at a higher material standard of living, at least in the short run. It is much harder to see that enjoying a higher standard of living does not necessarily translate into a higher quality of life—or a greater level of happiness—for those individuals, even in the short run, when all of life's critical intangibles (such as love, self-respect, and feelings of fulfillment) are taken into account.[15]

In international affairs, the paradigm of domination may never have been optimal, but it has become increasingly dangerous. The machines and institutions of total war are the logical and inevitable creations of this paradigm. They are the ultimate coercive threat for dominating others, and the ultimate counterthreat to frustrate the attempts of others to dominate us. As long as we continue to think of security primarily in terms of domination, the weapons of mass destruction that support the ultimate coercive threat will be widely seen as a prize worth having. Those who already have them will continue to nurture their arsenals, and their proliferation to other nations (or subnational terrorist groups) will continue. Such a world will never be secure.[16]

Soft Power

When it comes right down to it, threat or use of force is actually a less effective, higher cost way of getting others to do what you want them to do than that of building positive, friendly relationships. It is an obvious lesson of everyday life that we fail to apply to the realm of international relations because our thinking has become so narrowed. For example, suppose you are annoyed at your neighbors, who have been playing loud music at night. You could go to their home, pound on the door, and threaten to beat them or have them arrested if they don't stop the noise. If you do this, it is possible they will stop. But it is more likely that they will get angry and either make the music louder or find some other way of annoying you. Suppose instead you wait until an appropriate time, invite your neighbors for coffee and take the time to try to establish a more friendly relationship. If you do this, it is possible they will continue to play music even louder after you ask them to cut down on the late-night noise. But it is more likely that they will turn down the volume. It is even possible they will do this as soon as they become aware that it is bothering you, without your asking. And if you do succeed in establishing a friendly relationship with them, they are likely to try to avoid creating disturbances in the future.

Of course, not everyone is reasonable, and it is not always possible to build more friendly relations. There are circumstances in which coercion is required. But when it is possible to establish friendly relations, such an approach is much more likely to be effective than threatening or actually using force. Friends do not have to be forced to do what you need them to do.

Joseph Nye's concept of "soft power" is useful here. According to Nye, in the international arena soft power is the power to attract and persuade, to get others to want to do what you want them to do because they admire your values, your culture, your economic achievements, and the political nature of your society (for example, its openness, freedom, and democracy). Soft power reduces the need to rely on "hard power," that is, military force. As Nye puts it, "If I can get you to want to do what I want, then I do not have to force you to do what you do not want to do."[17] Of course, friends are even more likely to do things that benefit each other and less likely to threaten or inflict harm on each other than are those who are just admirers. They are more closely tied together, more concerned with each other's well-being. Friendship conveys even more soft power than admiration does.

If such reasoning seems too simplistic to be relevant to the hard-nosed realities of international relations, consider once more the example I offered in Chapter 1. During most of the Cold War, both the French and the British had nuclear arsenals sufficient to do grievous, perhaps terminal, damage to the United States. But our attention, our fears, and our military planning were focused on the nuclear arsenals of the Soviet Union and, to a lesser extent, China, with which we had a relationship filled with hostility and distrust, not on Britain or France, with which we had strong friendly relations.

Nye's concept of building soft power is not quite the same as the idea of fostering friendly relations, but it is similar. It is possible to have a degree of soft power without having a particularly warm relationship, but it is not possible to have much soft power in the face of hostility. Nye argues, "Soft power arises . . . from our values. These values are expressed in our culture, in the policies we follow inside our country, and in the way we handle ourselves internationally."[18] Our culture and the policies that we follow inside our country may have something to do with our ability to build friendly relationships with the governments and people of other countries, but "the way we handle ourselves internationally" is absolutely critical. Nye goes on to say, "The arrogance, indifference to the opinions of others, and narrow approach to our national interests advocated by the new unilateralists are a sure way to undermine American soft power."[19] I agree. Arrogance, indifference, and a narrow, self-interested approach have never been a great way to build friendships—interpersonally or internationally.

Nye claims that "economic power has become more important than in the past, both because of the relative increase in the costliness of force and because economic objectives loom large in the values of postindustrial societies."[20] If: 1) economic power is increasingly important; 2) economic achievements are a source of soft power; 3) soft power is an effective way to get others to want to do what you want them to do without coercion; and 4) soft power derives in part from "the way we handle ourselves internationally," it is logical that establishing a network of balanced, mutually beneficial international economic relationships should be an effective way to build soft power and therefore to reduce the need to rely on the threat or use of military force.

Balanced Decision Making

Even when gains are balanced (both in volume and relative to contribution), if the process involved in making key decisions relative to a relationship is unbalanced, those with less input and control in the decision process are likely to feel that they are unduly dependent on the good graces of the others. Believing that the terms of the relationship are subject to arbitrary, unilateral change creates insecurity and weakens commitment. When decision-making power is more equally shared, everyone involved has ownership in the relationship. It is their property, not simply a gift someone has bestowed upon them and can just as easily withdraw. Every participant will therefore be motivated to nurture the relationship, to ensure its continuation and success. This cannot help but strengthen the incentives of all participants to find peaceful ways of settling their conflicts with each other.

This may seem more like psychology than economics, but it is actually a central tenet of free market economics. It is the reason so much emphasis is placed on the institution of private property. Because property is an asset that can provide continuing economic benefits, owners of private property have a strong incentive to maximize the flow of those benefits by caring for it properly and using it efficiently. That incentive works greatly to the benefit of the society as a whole. Similarly, because a balanced economic relationship is an asset that can provide continuing economic benefits, "owners" of the relationship have a strong incentive to maximize the flow of benefits by caring for it properly. In either case, that incentive would be dramatically weakened if decisions that affect the flow (or distribution) of benefits from the asset were subject to change as a result of arbitrary decisions over which the asset's owner had no meaningful control.

When decision power is balanced in a relationship, all participants have a greater sense of security because they know they will be directly involved in any decision to change the rules or character of the relationship.[21] This will not necessarily prevent all changes that at least temporarily reduce the gains or increase the costs of any particular participant. But it will assure them that no changes will occur without their input and, perhaps (depending on agreed decision rules), their consent. It is easier for anyone who has been a full partner in deciding to make a change to accept it without undue hostility, even if it hurts. Painful change that is coerced or imposed is an entirely different thing. Once again the American Revolution offers a clear example. After all, the revolutionary slogan was not "No taxation," but rather "No taxation without representation."

There are then three aspects of balance in international economic relationships that are relevant to Principle I: 1) balance of benefits; 2) balance of trade volume; 3) balance of decision power. Balance of benefits relative to contribution is the most important to the power of international economic relationships to keep the peace. The lack of this kind of balance is virtually the definition of exploitation. Balance of decision power is probably next in importance, since it is what makes participants in these relationships see themselves as partners, rather than as subordinates. Balance of trade volume is least important though it has played the largest role in empirical investigations of the connection between international economic activity and matters of peace and war. The fact that most statistical studies have ignored other measures of balance has biased the case against the liberal's hypothesis that international economic relationships play a positive role in preventing war. Consequently, it is even more impressive that the preponderance of empirical evidence still supports the liberal view.

The European Union

The effectiveness of mutually beneficial, balanced economic relationships in keeping the peace is illustrated by the development and growth of the European Economic Community (EEC), forerunner of today's European Union (EU). The EEC began as the European Coal and Steel Community, which was formed by six nations in 1952 with the explicit goal of trying to build economic bonds (especially between France and Germany) to make the outbreak of another war among them less likely.[22] By the mid-1980s, the dozen nations that belonged to the EEC included Belgium, France, Germany, Great Britain, Italy, the Netherlands, Portugal, and Spain. These nations had not only fought countless wars against each other over the centuries (including World Wars I and II), most of them were also major colonial powers that militarily dominated and exploited much of the rest of the world. Yet today, if you were to ask the leaders (or the citizens) of any of these countries the odds of their countries fighting a war with each other over the next fifty years, they wouldn't even consider it a sensible question.

These nations have not lost their interest in military matters or their willingness to engage in warfare. France has intervened militarily in Africa more than once since the 1970s (most recently in the Ivory Coast). Britain fought a war with Argentina over the Falkland (Malvinas) Islands in the early 1980s. As members of the NATO military alliance, all of these nations were directly or indirectly involved in NATO's bombing of Kosovo in the late 1990s and subsequent ongoing occupation.[23] And troops from Britain, Italy, the Netherlands, and Spain were part of the U.S.-led invasion and occupation of Iraq that began in 2003.

The fact that many EU nations are members of NATO does have something to do with their reluctance to fight each other, although that that did not stop Greece and Turkey (both in NATO, but neither in the EEC at the time) from fighting over Cyprus in the mid-1970s. But the great military threat against which NATO was created—the threat of the Soviet Union and its allies in Eastern Europe—largely evaporated decades ago. It is clearly not fear about disrupting an alliance protecting them against an awesome military threat that continues to make war among the nations of the European Union so remote.

It is also not as if these countries no longer have conflicts with each other. They have many, economic and otherwise, some of them quite severe. In recent times alone, there were serious disagreements over the banning of British beef by other EU member states because of mad cow disease in Britain; sharp splits over the 2003 war in Iraq (with the governments of Britain, the Netherlands, and Spain strongly in support and those of France, Germany, and Belgium strongly opposed); and ongoing squabbles over the single European currency (the euro), including major disputes over the matter of financial rescue packages for the eurozone's economically weaker governments in 2010.

When Dutch voters rejected a new, more politically integrated constitution for the EU on June 1, 2005, following a similar rejection by French voters three days earlier, the *New York Times* reported, "The double blow could prove fatal to the European charter, which . . . would shift more power away from national governments."[24] In fact, the French vote had already made the constitution a dead letter, since the shared-power balanced decision process in the European Union required that it could be adopted only if approved by all twenty-five nations that then belonged to the EU. The *Times* went on to report, "Some are calling it a divorce; others, a disenchantment. . . . There is a disaffection, perhaps even a rebellion, against the political elites in France, Germany and Italy."[25] But despite all this strong talk, even in the midst of this political "rebellion" no one seriously suggested that the governments or people of France and the Netherlands— or for that matter of any EU nation—wanted to tear apart the *economic* web that binds them together.

The EU nations understand that the network of balanced, mutually beneficial economic relationships they have created gives them a strong stake in finding ways to manage, if not to resolve, the conflicts they have with each other. They simply have too much to lose to let their disagreements get out of control. So they debate, they argue, they shout. But they no longer threaten, or even think about threatening each other militarily, let alone actually going to war. With all its problems, the EU is a clear piece of evidence that building a peace economy is an eminently practical and achievable enterprise.

Principle II: Seek Independence in Critical Goods

As long as economic relationships are balanced, the liberal strategy of maximizing interdependence seems like an effective approach to preventing war. But the realist concern that high interdependence creates security-reducing vulnerabilities is also legitimate. Potential opponents within the web of relationships may deliberately use a nation's dependence on foreign sources of supply as a lever to gain the upper hand.[26] Dependence increases the probability of suffering unintentional harm at the hands of other nations that are simply pursuing their own objectives, without any desire or intention to cause pain. It is also possible that the mere fact of vulnerability may be read as a sign of weakness, increasing the chance that rivals will be tempted to engage in provocative, security-reducing behavior. These fears may be exaggerated or they may be justified, but the insecurity they generate is very real. It can easily lead to defensive, belligerent behavior, increasing the strain on the international system and offsetting some of the benefits of the increased strength that interdependence produces.

The prospects for preventing war would therefore be better if it were possible to create an international economic system whose actors are at once both independent and highly interdependent. The key is to reduce interdependence in those areas of economic interaction in which vulnerability to disruption is most frightening, while increasing it in all other areas that have potential for mutual gain. Heavy dependence on outside sources of supply is more troubling the more critical the good or service in question is to the nation's well-being. A nation is more exposed and vulnerable if it must rely on foreign suppliers for critical elements of its food supply than if it is a large net importer of television programs.

This concept of "critical goods" is similar to the realists' concept of "strategic goods," except that realists tend to put greatest emphasis on goods that are most important to hard power, rather than economic health. Strategic goods are those on which the nation's offensive and defensive military capabilities depend, while critical goods are primarily those most important to the population's material well-being. Which goods and services are vital to economic well-being depends in part on the nature and level of development of the nation's economy. Reliable supplies of steel are more important to an industrialized country than to one that is mainly agricultural; reliable supplies of tractors and harvesting machines are more important to a highly developed agricultural nation than to either one that is mainly industrial or one that is agricultural but less developed. Some categories of goods, though, are critical everywhere.

Potable water is vital to the health of every human being. Yet the World Health Organization (WHO) estimated that, in 2004, about one billion people were without access to clean drinking water, and two and a half times that many did not have adequate sanitation facilities. According to WHO, 88 percent of the disability-adjusted life year "global burden of disease" is related to the lack of access to clean water, sanitation, and hygiene.[27] Contaminated water is the primary cause of the death of children in the developing world.[28]

Difficult-to-substitute foods that are central to the population's diet are also critical goods. Energy is a critical resource for every economy, although the amount and type of energy on which the economy depends differs from country to country. And virtually every economy requires continuing supplies of certain key raw materials.

If a nation were independent of foreign suppliers for all critical goods, it would certainly be much less vulnerable, and therefore more secure. It would not have to worry about other nations sending shock waves through its economy—maybe even causing its economy to collapse—by disrupting access to critical supplies. But can a nation, especially a highly developed nation, ever conceivably attain complete independence in critical goods?

The answer is, probably not—at least not unless the public is willing to forgo the considerable benefits of international specialization according to comparative advantage. But most nations could certainly be much less dependent on foreign sources of supply of critical goods, particularly less stable foreign sources of supply, than they currently are without seriously compromising the economic well-being of their people. Complete independence is not required. A substantial reduction in critical goods dependence should be enough to significantly reduce the strains on the international system that could lead to war.

Reducing Critical Goods Dependence

Three practical strategies substantially reduce critical goods dependence, any one of which can be pursued alone or in combination with the others: 1) domestic production, 2) diversification of foreign suppliers, and 3) "contingent independence." Domestic production is straightforward enough. It means trying to supply as much of the country's requirement for critical goods as possible from sources within its political boundaries. Diversification of foreign suppliers prevents overdependence on any particular nation. "Contingent independence" involves forgoing independence in favor of interdependent trade patterns in normal times, while at the same time doing what is necessary to make independence possible if and when a trading partner tries to exert pressure by cutting off vital supplies. Approaches to *implementing* these strategies will be discussed in the next chapter. But it is possible to briefly illustrate how the strategies themselves might work here, considering each of the key categories of critical goods in turn.

Water

Most of the world's nations have access to sufficient supplies of water within their territory to satisfy the minimum essential needs of their populations. Even in the less developed world, the problem is rarely the threat of external disruption of water supplies as such, but mostly that there is not enough potable water. Water fit for human consumption is not sufficiently available, especially to the poorer parts of the population. The lack of access to potable water is not a technological problem. We know how to build treatment facilities to purify water and sanitation systems that keep human and chemical waste separate from the water supply. It is a problem of insufficient infrastructure investment, a problem of economic development priorities. We will return to the issue of development shortly.

Food

Most of the world's countries have the physical capability to produce sufficient basic food supplies within their political territory to meet the minimum nutritional requirements of their population, although some are increasingly hard-pressed to do so because of insupportably high rates of population growth. This does not imply that they either can or would want to produce domestically the full range of even the major categories of foods their people are used to eating. All that is required to meet security concerns is that they maintain a large enough flow of food to keep their own population going indefinitely at a time when normally available external sources of food supply are threatened. That is a much more modest and achievable goal. The problem created by the time lag between planting and harvest can be overcome by maintaining a stockpile of key foods sufficient to meet the population's minimum nutritional needs at least until the next harvest.

It is also possible to reduce a nation's vulnerability to disruptions of food availability by diversifying its external sources of supply as much as possible. Overdependence on any one nation for vital food supplies puts the importing country at risk of coercion at the hands of its supplier. Making use of the economist's understanding of coercive monopoly power and the value of competition in breaking that power, a strategy of spreading food imports across a diverse group of suppliers should prevent any one of them from being in a strong enough position to intimidate the importer simply by threatening to cut off supplies, or even to increase their price substantially. This does not eliminate the possibility that a militarily stronger country could block the transportation channels through which all of the nation's food suppliers have to send their produce. But diversification could help solve this problem as well *if* the importing nation deliberately included in the group of its suppliers countries that were either powerful enough or influential enough to make potential antagonists reluctant to interfere with their shipments.

Under a strategy of diversification, the logical reaction to a threat to cut off supplies would be to try to make up the difference by reallocating imports among the existing mix of suppliers, or by adding suppliers to the mix. A strategy of contingent independence would involve preparing to make up the difference by shifting productive resources within the country to replace the embargoed goods through domestic production. The time lag inherent in making this shift would be bridged once again by (presumably larger) stockpiles of critical foodstuffs.

While contingent food independence is not a particularly easy or pleasant strategy to activate, it is neither impractical nor unduly expensive. During the Cold War, both Switzerland and Sweden made use of this approach. In the mid-1980s, Swiss-born economist Dietrich Fischer briefly described the Swiss program:

> During peacetime, Switzerland imports nearly 50 percent of its food consumption. In case of a cutoff of imports, food would be immediately rationed, requiring about a one-third reduction in daily caloric intake. Meat consumption would be drastically reduced to arrive at a more efficient calorie conversion factor through a more vegetarian diet. . . . Grassland would be converted gradually, in three yearly phases, into cropland. In the meantime, the food deficit would be bridged with reserves of nonperishable food, which are constantly being renewed in peacetime. Similar programs exist for fuel, certain minerals and other vital commodities.[29]

Sweden's program, like that of Switzerland, was also integrated into its national concept of defense, and as Fischer pointed out, "Sweden's 'economic defense' expenditures for the stockpiling of food, various strategic materials, fuel and heating oil comprise no more than 2 to 3 percent of its total defense budget."[30]

The diversification and contingent independence approaches also have some proactive deterrence value. Even a major supplier of critical goods, knowing either that the importing nation can easily shift to other reliable suppliers or that it has a workable, fully developed, contingent independence plan in place, would see little point in mounting the "attack" (i.e., cutting off supplies) in the first place. There is thus reason to believe that if a diversification or contingent independence strategy is designed and implemented—and advertised—well enough, it could reduce vulnerability without ever having to be activated.

Energy

The history of the advance of technologies of production and consumption is a history of substituting nonliving sources of energy for that of humans and animals. Energy is the lifeblood of modern economies, both more developed and less developed. It is so much a part of our world that disruptions in supply, from power failures to oil embargoes, have direct and immediate effects on nearly all aspects of our daily lives. These days, especially in more developed countries, when the power system fails it isn't just a matter of having to forgo television and read by candlelight.

When the lights went out for fifty million people in eight states in the U.S. and Canada in August 2003, so did the water supply in Cleveland and Detroit, air conditioners, elevators in high-rise buildings, traffic lights, ATM machines, mass transit systems, gas pumps, many telephones, countless computer-related systems, and so on. Because we have come to rely so heavily on a continuing flow of energy, our dependence on centralized, interconnected energy systems has made us unduly vulnerable to their breakdown. Modern society is increasingly at risk of disruption by technical problems, criminal sabotage, terrorist attack, or deliberate withholding of crucial energy supplies by exporting nations trying to apply coercive pressure.

When the OPEC oil embargo of 1973 drove oil prices through the roof, there were those in the U.S. who argued that increased domestic production of fossil fuels was the solution to overdependence on foreign oil. In fact, the U.S. does have enormous fossil fuel reserves.[31] It also has such a voracious appetite for fossil fuels that, every year since 1994, the country has imported more crude oil than it produced.[32] A domestic fossil fuel production independence strategy would at best be a very temporary (and expensive) solution to energy vulnerability.

Beyond establishing a buffer against short-lived disruptions in supply, stockpiling fossil fuels in the service of a contingent independence strategy is also impractical. The U.S. maintains the largest emergency oil stockpile in the world.[33] But the entire 2003 reserve, for example, represented only a little more than two months' supply.[34] At the February 2010 price ($74/barrel), the petroleum alone in a reserve equal to one year's imports at the current rate would exceed $230 billion.[35]

The most pragmatic approach to greater energy independence is shifting to a combination of domestically available energy sources and more efficient energy use practices and technologies. If it is done intelligently over a reasonable time span, shifting energy sources is not nearly as difficult or as costly as it might seem. Consider electric power, at the same time one of the most important forms of energy, one of the major users of energy, and a leading cause of industrial air pollution. There are many alternative ways of generating electricity, more than one of which is likely to be domestically available in almost every country. Some of these ways also have the advantage of potentially being much less centralized, and thus

much less vulnerable to widespread blackout for reasons of technical failure or intentional sabotage than the present system of large fossil fuel
generating plants and nuclear power reactors. Possibilities include biomass
fuels and such natural sources of energy as wind, solar, water, hydrothermal,
geothermal, tidal, and wave power. Many decades ago, the U.S. electrified
the rural South with wind power. Today, wind power farms in Texas are providing the electricity that supplies my house and tens of thousands of other
households in the state. Although some have cooked up schemes to generate
electricity with huge, centralized fields of solar collectors, one advantage of
solar power is that it is naturally distributed widely. Solar arrays on individual
buildings would therefore seem to make more sense, minimizing the cost of
and energy loss in transmission and distribution systems.

It is sometimes argued that renewable energy sources must be at least
economically, if not technically, impractical or they would have already
emerged as major competitors for fossil fuels and nuclear power in the
"real world" of the U.S. commercial marketplace. But the fact is, we have
spent many billions (possibly hundreds of billions) of dollars subsidizing
and thus biasing the market in favor of fossil fuels and nuclear power. Beginning to level the playing field by eliminating those subsidies, let alone
by transferring some of them to renewable energy, would greatly encourage the further development and deployment of ecologically benign, domestically available energy sources.[36]

Even the U.S., the world's largest energy consumer, could move decisively toward substantially reduced dependence on foreign sources of supply
by using a variety of domestically available renewable and nonrenewable
energy sources in a diversified mix. What would take us the rest of the
way? More than thirty years ago, I analyzed in my book *The Conservation
Response* many small changes in the way we design and operate energy using systems that, combined, would save 30-50 percent of the energy used
in the U.S. without negative effects on the American standard of living.[37]
Taking practical energy conservation measures, together with step-by-step
moves toward greater use of renewable energy, would make us all more
secure. We would be much less vulnerable to reliance on oil from politically unstable areas of the world that repeatedly draw us into costly—and
dangerous—military adventures.

Raw Materials

Whether it is possible for a nation to achieve independence in the supply of critical raw materials through a strategy of domestic production depends on the nature of its economy (which determines what raw materials
are the most critical to its system of production), and the extent and character of its natural resource endowment. While every nation has access to
at least some form of renewable energy within its political boundaries, not
every nation has access to sufficient lumber, iron ore, bauxite, copper, etc.,
to support its economic needs. If its resource endowment is clearly nowhere near sufficient, as is certainly true of Japan, for example, supplier
diversification and contingent independence are still potentially viable
paths to raw materials independence.

It is obviously wise for a nation highly dependent on external sources of
critical raw materials to rely on multiple suppliers, preferably in nations
that are geographically dispersed and not too closely aligned with each
other. A contingent independence strategy, on the other hand, is also useful. Stockpiling of critical raw materials would certainly be a key component of such a strategy, though again this may be most practical as a buffer
against *short-term* supply disruptions. It is a workable way to reduce pressures for an immediate "hard power" response by buying time for diplomacy and negotiation or for arranging alternative sources of supply.

The U.S. has had a critical materials stockpiling program for decades.
By the end of September 2002, the so-called National Defense Stockpile
included fifty-seven different critical materials, worth $1.9 billion, nearly
three-quarters of which were metals, minerals, or ores (such as bauxite,
beryllium, chromium, cobalt, lead, manganese, and silver), the remainder
being classified as agricultural (such as vegetable tannin) or "other."[38] The
act authorizing the National Defense Stockpile is quite explicit as to its
motivation and purpose. Section 2, paragraphs (a), (b), and (c) of the Strategic and Critical Materials Stockpiling Act (50 U.S.C. section 98 *et. seq.*)
reads as follows:[39]

(a) The Congress finds that the natural resources of the United States in
certain strategic and critical materials are deficient or insufficiently developed to supply the military, industrial, and civilian needs of the United
States for national defense.

(b) It is the purpose of this act to provide for the acquisition and reten-
tion of stocks of certain strategic and critical materials and to encourage
the conservation and development of sources of such materials within the
United States and thereby to decrease and preclude, when possible, a dangerous and costly dependence by the United States upon foreign sources
for supplies of such materials in times of national emergency.

(c) The purpose of the National Defense Stockpile is to serve the interest
of national defense only. The National Defense Stockpile is not to be used
for economic or budgetary purposes.

Despite the language of paragraph (c) above, which seems to preclude using the stockpile for "economic" purposes, paragraph (a) makes it clear that
it is intended to help supply "industrial and civilian needs" as well as those
of the military. In any case, the contingent independence strategy (of which
critical materials stockpiling is a key component) is precisely a strategy for
national defense.

The contingent independence approach also involves conservation. In
the case of energy, though, conservation mainly implies efficient use. For raw
materials, recycling is just as important as, if not more important than,
efficient use.

While reducing critical goods dependence helps to meet the legitimate
security concerns that realists have raised, maximizing economic interdependence everywhere else is key to achieving the full security benefits that
liberals argue derive from drawing nations together in a binding web of
economic relationships. What is needed is thus a careful balance between
working to establish independence in critical goods and encouraging high
levels of interdependence for the wide range of goods and services that do
not fall into that category. There are many useful and desirable goods and
services that are very much in demand, goods and services whose absence
would be keenly felt, that could not reasonably be characterized as critical.
For interdependence to play its role in increasing the strength of the international system most effectively, it cannot be restricted to goods that are
marginal to the economies involved. A flourishing trade in trivial goods
will do little to bind nations together because the mutual benefits it provides will be minimal.

It is best if the economic interdependence in noncritical goods and services involves multiple sources of imports and multiple markets for exports. Vulnerability to economic coercion may be greatest in the case of critical goods, but it is not irrelevant for noncritical goods, many of which may still be considered important or highly desirable. That is especially true if the interdependence is unbalanced. It is too easy for this kind of situation to degenerate into one that will increase hostility and insecurity rather than positive incentives for maintaining the peace, particularly if one of the trading partners is more economically developed than the other. It is also true that a web of multilateral dependence will tie nations more closely together than a set of disconnected bilateral relationships. The continued economic health of each nation within a multilateral web of economic relationships will come to depend not only on the well-being of its own trading partners, but also on the welfare of those nations that do business with its trading partners. This will broaden and strengthen the economic incentives for peacefully resolving any conflicts that might arise.

If each nation had multiple sources of supply and multiple markets for its products, it would be harder for any single nation to impose effective sanctions on any other nation. Though this may seem to deal a crippling blow to the usefulness of economic sanctions as a tool for enforcing accepted international norms of behavior, it is actually an advantage. When sanctions are applied multilaterally, they will be more powerful economically, politically, and psychologically because they represent a consensus of a broad group of nations. Furthermore, the need to convince other nations to go along will help prevent serious economic sanctions from being applied too casually and too often.

Principle III: Emphasize Development

The poverty and frustration of so many of the world's people is a fertile breeding ground for violent conflict. There have been more than 150 wars since the end of World War II, nearly all of them fought in the less developed world.[40] People in desperate straits tend to reach for extreme solutions. They are much more easily manipulated by demagogues and seem easy, tempting prey to aggressors. Even noted neoliberal Robert Keohane admits that liberalism may be appealing "to satisfied modern elites and middle classes . . . , but it is not likely to be as appealing to the oppressed or disgruntled."[41] The peacekeeping benefits that balanced economic interdependence promises to produce are that much more difficult to achieve under conditions of deprivation and marginalization.

It is important to distinguish between two major subcomponents of the very broad concept of development: economic and political. By economic development, I mean a process that raises the material standard of living of the vast majority of the population. This includes increasing the quantity and quality of their housing, food, clothing, transportation, medical care, and the like. By political development, I mean a process that provides the members of society with expanded civil liberties such as freedom of speech, freedom of organization, and freedom of the press, and that respects their individual human rights. But I also mean a process that facilitates access to full participation in the political process, to choosing those who will govern them, to having their voices heard and their grievances and opinions taken seriously.

Joseph Nye argues that, in "postindustrial societies" (countries at higher levels of development), "the foundations of power have been moving away from the emphasis on military force and conquest."[42] He contends that there is a relationship between the level of a nation's development and its readiness to tolerate the use of force: "Roughly speaking there are three types of countries in the world today: poor, weak pre-industrial states, which are often the remnants of collapsed empires; modern industrializing states such as India or China; and the post-industrial societies that prevail in Europe, North America and Japan. The use of force is common in the first type of country, still accepted in the second, but less tolerated in the third."[43]

Development is important to keeping the peace because people in good economic condition who can meaningfully access the political process are much less likely to support violent revolutionary change. They have a strong vested interest in avoiding serious disturbances in, let alone risking destruction of, the system of economic, political, and social arrangements under which they are doing well. Whether interpersonal or international, violence and the disruption it brings is more threatening to them because they have so much more to lose.

Economic Growth and Economic Development

Although the terms are often used interchangeably, it is important to distinguish between economic growth and economic development. Economic growth is merely expansion in the size of an economy, the increase in its volume of activity. Measured by the rate of change of an indicator of national economic size (typically Gross Domestic Product [GDP] or Gross National Product [GNP]), growth leaves out far too much to be a useful indicator of overall development by itself. It is silent on important issues of structural economic change (such as diversification of the mix of goods and services produced, and changes in the type and character of work). It ignores the quality of the goods and services produced. Perhaps more important, economic growth says nothing about how the gains of expanding economic activity are distributed among the population.

Since the economy is the part of the social system that is focused on providing material well-being, the performance of an economy must ultimately be judged by considering how well it achieves that purpose. The object of development is to improve the economic status of the whole population and the range of economic options available to them. A nation's economic development therefore depends on much more than how quickly the overall size of its economy is growing. It is a complex, nuanced concept that requires attention to more than just how much is produced. It also depends on what is produced, how it is produced, how it is distributed, and, most importantly, the extent to which all this activity has succeeded in raising the material standard of living of the broad mass of the population. A rapidly expanding one-commodity economy in which 5 percent of the population owns nearly all the material wealth may be growing fast, but it is not developing.

An accurate empirical assessment of development requires considering a constellation of indicators of the quantity and quality of a range of key aspects of development (such as housing, transportation, income distribution, communication, education, and health), each of which captures only a piece of the overall picture. In short, while growth means only that the economy is getting bigger, development means that it is getting better—becoming more structurally sound and raising the material well-being of the vast majority, if not all, of the population.

Development and Conflict: Why Development Matters

Because there are many reasons for the eruption of violence, both interpersonally and internationally, there are few grounds for believing that, by itself, even a great improvement in everyone's material well-being would put an end to war. But encouraging inclusive and widespread development is important to giving the largest possible part of the world's population a direct, obvious, and personal stake in avoiding disruptive explosions of violent mass conflict. Furthermore, although growth may be sufficient to increase the stake in peace of the more powerful economic and political elites within a nation (excluding those whose livelihoods depend on the prospects for military conflict), development can bring them even greater long-term benefit. It may benefit them directly by diversifying and strengthening the overall economy, thus reducing risk and increasing returns to domestic investment; and it may benefit them indirectly by reducing internal tensions and thus stabilizing the society. Both these effects should serve to make keeping the peace more attractive to those who are most influential in society. Moreover, because of its breadth, development causes the number and size of influential economically elite groups that have a strong vested interest in avoiding war to grow over time. Looked at through the perspective of Boulding's "chalk theory" of war and peace, development helps keep the peace by strengthening resistance to the outbreak of war, as well as reducing one source of strain that can directly or indirectly lead to war—the frustration and hostility of those who continue to be economically deprived and politically marginalized.

If the advocates of the democratic peace argument are even mostly correct—and the vast majority of evidence is on their side—political development is important to keeping the peace among nations. As democratic governance and freedom spread, the tendency of democracies to avoid going to war with each other will reduce the prospects for interstate war. Just as important, political development will also help to keep peace within nations because it moves societies in the direction of providing sufficient information and access to the political process to make nonviolent pathways available for effectively altering the direction of public policy and private conduct. Political and economic grievances can be aired, heard, and addressed more readily; dissenting views can be expressed and widely disseminated more openly; and alternative ideas of appropriate social (and private) behavior can be presented and subjected to public debate more easily. With a variety of effective nonviolent avenues widely accessible, even those who do not ultimately get what they want will be more likely to accept that outcome (or continue the struggle) without turning to violence. Of course, there may still be those who do resort to violence to accomplish their objectives, but they should become fewer and farther between.

Economic development is also a useful strategy for discouraging civil as well as international war. As we saw from Paul Collier's global, cross-national statistical analysis (Chapter 2), "Economic agendas appear to be central to understanding why civil wars start."[44] This conclusion is reinforced by the fact that "rapid economic decline" is the only category of "grievance" that his empirical work shows to be a statistically significant cause of civil war.[45]

Both Collier's findings and those of Indra de Soysa[46] indicate that a strong relationship exists between the reliance of an economy on exports of "lootable" primary nonrenewable resources and civil war. Collier concludes, "If only the international community can change the economic incentives for [civil] conflict[s], it can substantially reduce their incidence, *even in societies riven by long-standing hatreds.* . . . How can international policy reduce the economic incentives for conflict? . . . by diversification of the economies of those societies that are most at risk" (emphasis added).[47] Exports of primary products such as minerals and agricultural produce tend to loom large in the economies of countries at lower levels of development, but are much less important in more developed countries. Greater economic diversification is one hallmark of higher levels of development.

Development is also key to establishing "positive peace" (Chapter 1), which is at least as important as war avoidance in much of the less developed world. Positive peace includes preventing structural causes of debilitation and death, such as lack of the economic means to obtain nutritious food and clean water, in addition to preventing injury and death caused by war. Michael Renner points out, "Whereas about 300,000 people were killed in armed conflicts in 2000, for example, as many people die each and every month because of contaminated water or lack of adequate sanitation."[48]

According to the UN Development Program, more than a billion of the earth's people still live on the equivalent of less than $1/day. Even if it had nothing to do with keeping the peace, striving to improve the material conditions of life of these desperately poor people, and working to raise the standard of living of the billions more who struggle every day to provide a decent life for their families and themselves, would be an inherently worthwhile enterprise. The fact that economic development can also play an important role in creating an incentive system that can help prevent interstate and intrastate war should further strengthen our resolve.

There is yet another reason to do what we can to encourage development: It will facilitate following Principle I. It is difficult to establish balanced mutually beneficial relationships among countries at low levels of development. If their main exports, for example, are natural resources that are useful mainly as raw materials, they will have little to trade with each other, since they lack manufacturing sectors that require such resources as inputs. If their main exports are similar agricultural products, they will likewise have little to trade with each other. It is also difficult to build balanced and mutually beneficial economic relationships among countries that are at radically different levels of development. It takes greater effort and commitment because of the very different economic bargaining power they bring to the market. It is much easier to establish balanced mutually beneficial relationships between the U.S. and Japan or between France and Germany than between the U.S. and Haiti or between France and Chad. Countries at higher and more equal levels of development have more to offer each other in variety, quantity, and quality. And they come to the bargaining table with more equal economic power.

Paths to Sustainable Development

In order to create the economic conditions and incentive structure required to maximize resistance to the outbreak of war, it is necessary for development to be more than a temporary improvement in a nation's material standard of living—even if "temporary" is taken to mean a few decades, rather than just a few years. Following a path to development that is not viable over the long run may eventually make violence more likely by whetting people's appetite for living at a higher level of material well-being than that path can continue to provide. It may therefore predispose the nation to engaging in coercive, even aggressive and violent, behavior to obtain the means to maintain or continue to improve the level of material well-being that its people (especially its elites) have come to expect. The public may become more willing to support military adventures that they believe can protect their improved material way of life. At the same time, the buildup in national wealth created by the short-term burst of development increases the nation's ability to finance a buildup in its military capabilities. Unsustainable development may also lead to violent conflict within the nation, since in an environment of economic stagnation or decline the only way for one group to continue reaping the economic gains it has come to expect is to take what they can away from others. Recall Collier's finding that rapid economic decline is a significant cause of civil war.

A temporary spurt of development has demonstrably different impacts, implications, and consequences from development that has staying power. I will use "sustainable development" to mean development that is both economically and ecologically viable for the indefinite future. A particular activity is economically viable if the sum of all the benefits it provides is greater than or equal to the sum of all the costs of keeping it going. A development path is therefore economically viable if, taken as a group, the activities it encompasses are economically viable. A development path is "ecologically viable" if the natural environment is capable of providing the resources it requires and coping with the wastes it generates into the indefinite future.

Fostering sustainable economic and political development is critical to creating an international economy that can help keep the peace. There is still considerable debate among economists as to the most effective ways of achieving economically sustainable development. It is a complicated multidimensional problem. Yet there is some agreement on key substrategies (such as the buildup of human capital and physical infrastructure), as well as on some important obstacles that must be overcome (such as corruption and unproductive use of resources). More will be said about this in subsequent chapters. A number of strategies for effectively achieving the ecological dimensions of sustainable development are discussed in the following section.

Principle IV: Minimize Ecological Stress

Competition for depletable energy and mineral resources indisputably generates conflict. The desire to gain (and if possible monopolize) access to raw materials was clearly one of the driving forces behind the colonization of much of the world by the more economically and militarily advanced nations in centuries past. This competition continues to bring nations, and sometimes subnational groups, into conflicts of the most dangerous kind—those in which at least one party believes that the continued economic well-being, political sovereignty, even the survival of its people are at stake. While historically less important as a source of interstate war, increasing competition for critical renewable resources, most notably water, has certainly exacerbated tensions in the past and has the potential to trigger more violent confrontations in the future.

There is little doubt that conflicts in the Middle East would be much less likely to lead to military action by the major powers if it were not for the region's vast supplies of easily extractible oil. The slow and relatively weak reaction of those powers to slaughter in Cambodia, genocide in Rwanda, brutal war in Liberia, aggression in Bosnia, and political and economic disaster in Zimbabwe stands in stark contrast to their swift and strong reaction to the Iraqi invasion of Kuwait and readiness to subsequently invade and occupy Iraq. The difference may have a variety of causes, but the presence or absence of rich deposits of oil is certainly one of them.

Pollution can also be an important source of conflict. Environmental damage knows no political boundaries. The air and the water do not recognize the artificial lines that we have drawn on the earth to separate ourselves from each other. That is clearly illustrated both by acute environmental disasters such as the nuclear power accident at Chernobyl and by chronic environmental problems such as acid rain. Transborder pollution itself may not lead to war, but it has already generated considerable conflict and may yet generate much more. Since every additional source of tension contributes to the strain on the international system, it raises the likelihood that other sources of conflict will lead to the eruption of violence.

Competition for Resources

In 1994, Thomas Homer-Dixon reported on the results of a three-year research project on environmental scarcity and violent conflict that was sponsored by the American Academy of Arts and Sciences, involving thirty researchers from ten countries: "Our research showed that environmental scarcities are already contributing to violent conflicts in many parts of the developing world. These conflicts are probably the early signs of an upsurge in violence in the coming decades that will be induced or aggravated by scarcity."[49]

For hundreds of years, when the economically viable deposits of nonrenewable resources to which they had ready access were depleted enough to be insufficient to their needs, major powers have used force outside their borders to ensure continued access to abundant supplies elsewhere. Whether in the form of colonization or, in more modern times, forceful coercion aimed at bringing about a change in policy or in regime, the central purpose has remained the same. It is easy enough to understand the motives behind such behavior when nonrenewable resources are involved, yet competition for renewable resources can also play a significant role in generating conflict.

In the first place, it is possible to deplete renewable resources too by harvesting them at a rate that exceeds the rate at which they naturally replenish themselves. Growing population and increasing economic activity can easily cause the rate at which the resources are demanded to exceed the rate at which they can be perpetually supplied. Perhaps the most obvious example is the depletion of fisheries in various parts of the world by overzealous exploitation of that otherwise permanently available food source. Many millions of hectares of otherwise naturally renewable forest have also been lost due to a combination of wanton destruction to claim land for other uses (often unsustainable agriculture) and excessive rates of harvest.[50] Renewable resources can also be destroyed or despoiled by pollution or other forms of environmental damage. The same volume of water may continue to flow in the river, but if the water has been contaminated, it may no longer be available at reasonable cost for the range of purposes it previously was able to serve.

Access to and control over forests, croplands, and water can be an important source of intergroup conflict within nations and tensions between nations. If there were going to be conflict, violence, and even war over a renewable resource, it would most likely be over water, the resource most vital to life. While Aaron Wolf et al. argue that "no states have gone to war specifically over water resources since . . . 2500 BC,"[51] they point out that, in the numerous violent confrontations between Israel and its Arab neighbors since the 1950s, "water was an underlying source of political stress and one of the most difficult topics in subsequent negotiations. . . . [E]ven though the wars were not fought over water, allocation disagreements were an impediment to peace."[52] More than half of Israel's water supply comes from aquifers, and, although they drain into Israel, two of the three major aquifers on which that nation depends lie mainly beneath the West Bank.[53]

Rivalries over water, especially river and lake water, have been going on at least since humans settled down and began cultivating food some eight thousand to ten thousand years ago. Homer-Dixon reports: "Our research suggests that the renewable resource most likely to stimulate interstate war is river water. . . . Conflict is most probable when a downstream riparian is highly dependent on river water and strong in comparison to upstream riparians."[54] There are issues of quantity (overuse or diversion by those upstream) as well as quality (contamination by those upstream can spread water-borne diseases, poison fish stocks, and generally make the water less usable by those downstream).

Homer-Dixon predicts that violence will surge in coming decades as a result of growing environmental scarcity, and that it will be "persistent, diffuse, and sub-national." But he goes on to argue that, in effect, the violence will not necessarily stay subnational: "Countries experiencing chronic internal conflict because of environmental stress will probably either fragment or become more authoritarian. Fragmenting countries will be the source of large out-migrations. . . . Authoritarian regimes may be inclined to launch attacks against other countries to divert popular attention from internal stresses."[55] Large transborder out-migrations are often a source of tension and conflict between sending and receiving countries, whatever their cause. They are also frequently associated with hostility against and exploitation of those people swept up in the flow, whether their migration is triggered by natural disaster, human disaster, or simply a desire for a better life. Authoritarian regimes may be more likely "to launch attacks against other countries to divert popular attention from internal stresses," but democratic governments have also been known to use this tactic. For example, while Argentina's unilateral military action in reclaiming the Falkland/Malvinas Islands off its coast in the 1980s provided the formal reason for the British to attack, it is likely that the swiftness and harshness of the British military response was in part a (successful) attempt to reverse the sharply diminished popularity of the Thatcher government.

Pollution

For most of history, human-induced pollution wasn't capable of causing widespread ecological harm, although it certainly did cause considerable localized damage. That began to change with the industrial revolution in the eighteenth century. As economic growth accelerated and population grew, the environment became progressively more polluted. In the first few decades of the twentieth century, particularly after 1920, the rate of environmental pollution—and resource depletion—began to increase sharply. The primary reasons were neither simple economic growth nor population growth, but rather the technology-driven change in the kinds of materials used, the nature of the products produced, and the techniques used to produce them.

More and more, synthetic detergents, fibers, fertilizers, pesticides, and the like displaced their natural counterparts, adding substances to the environment that did not fit into any of the many natural recycling mechanisms that had evolved slowly over millions of years. On June 15, 1998, chemists announced the creation of the eighteen-millionth artificial chemical. While less than 0.5 percent are actually used commercially, that still leaves between fifty thousand and a hundred thousand artificial chemicals in commercial use.[56] According to Anne McGinn, "All of us now have about

500 anthropogenic chemicals in our bodies—potential poisons that did not exist before 1920."[57] Many of these are persistent organic pollutants (POPs), toxic synthetic compounds that tend to accumulate as they move up the food chain, can travel long distances from their source, and are extremely durable. "Even where these chemicals have been banned for 20 or more years . . . they persist in soil, water, and body fat. Many health problems can be traced to chemical releases that ended long before the victims were born."[58]

At the same time the new technologies of production and consumption dramatically raised our standard of living, they enormously increased our appetite for energy, most of which came from fossil fuels. The combustion of fossil fuels, along with rampant deforestation and other ecologically damaging practices, helped to unbalance the earth's oxygen–carbon dioxide cycle, leading to a buildup of atmospheric carbon dioxide. Combined with other greenhouse gases (GHGs), such as methane, nitrous oxide, and water vapor, the buildup of carbon dioxide began to raise the average temperature of the earth. The climate change resulting from this human-induced global warming is a classic example of the transboundary nature of so much of both pollution and its environmental impacts. It has become a globally chronic problem with periodic and potentially disastrous acute manifestations.

Current average global temperatures are now about 0.8°C (1.4°F) above what they were in preindustrial times. The 2001 Intergovernmental Panel on Climate Change (IPCC) projected that the rise in average temperature by the end of this century (2100) is likely to range from 1.4°C (2.5°F) to 5.8°C (10.4°F).[59] That doesn't sound like much. The problem is that this small average global increase does not represent a slight uniform change everywhere, but rather much greater changes in individual temperatures and their variation from place to place and over time. For example, a year that was only a few degrees warmer than usual might be a year with many more extremely hot summer days, along with some winter days than were much colder than normal. Averaging temperatures across the whole earth hides a substantial amount of variability. Because of this, even small average changes in climate can have dramatic effects on the physical environment (e.g., wind patterns, rainfall, storms) that in turn have powerful impacts on the biological environment. By way of comparison, the change in global average temperature between the peak of the last ice age twenty-five thousand years ago and today was only on the order of 5°C (9°F),[60] a change that is within the range of the 2001 IPCC projections.

Climate change can directly affect human health by increasing the rate of heat- and cold-related illnesses and death, and increasing the frequency and/or intensity of violent storms and other extreme weather events (such as floods and drought). It can also affect human health indirectly through its impact on food supply and patterns of disease.

The World Health Organization has argued that changes in the geographic range and seasonality of certain infectious diseases will be among the first climate-related impacts on human health. This includes illnesses borne by organisms that carry disease from one host to another (such as malaria and dengue fever), and food-borne illnesses (such as salmonellosis), both of which tend to be more common in the warmer seasons.[61] Although the effect on the populations of less developed countries will be greater, these problems will surely not bypass more developed countries, with potentially large effects on public health costs.

There is so much movement of people and goods in this globalizing world that disease can spread almost before we know what has happened. The SARS virus, for example, contracted in China in 2003 rapidly became a threat to the health of people living in Europe and North America. According to the World Health Organization, more than thirty new diseases have emerged since the mid-1970s, along with new drug-resistant forms of old diseases, such as tuberculosis, we once thought we had completely under control.[62]

Global warming also affects many aspects of the global water cycle: cloud characteristics, rainfall, soil moisture, patterns of snowfall and snowmelt, the rate at which water evaporates from the Earth's surface, and the rate at which it is released to the atmosphere by plants (transpiration). The ocean absorbs about a third of the twenty-five billion metric tons of carbon dioxide released into the air by burning fossil fuels each year, according to a report by Britain's leading scientific organization (the Royal Society). It is making ocean water more acidic, damaging plankton and disrupting the food chain.[63]

It is by now well accepted that higher global temperatures will cause increased melting of glaciers, and that will lead to a rise in sea level. The third IPCC assessment projected that storm surge flooding (of the sort Hurricane Katrina brought to New Orleans in late August 2005) will affect double or triple the number of people in the next century.[64] A large and increasing fraction of the U.S. population lives near one or another coast. By 2003, there were already 153 million people—more than half the American population—living in the coastal counties of the U.S.[65]

Rising sea level is a serious threat to many island nations as well as to continental nations with heavily populated low-lying coastal plains. Among the more developed countries, the densely populated Netherlands, much of which is already below sea level, is one of the most physically threatened. On the other end of the economic spectrum, so is low-lying, densely populated Bangladesh, one of the world's poorest nations, already subject to frequent, devastating floods.

Researchers studying western Siberia have found that an area of permafrost the size of France and Germany combined has already begun to melt—for the first time in eleven thousand years. The entire sub-Arctic region of western Siberia is one gigantic peat bog, and as it thaws it could release billions of metric tons of methane into the atmosphere. (Methane is a much stronger GHG than carbon dioxide.) It would most likely take many decades for the Siberian permafrost to thaw, and therefore for all that methane to be released. But climate scientist Stephen Sitch and his colleagues have calculated that even if it took one hundred years, it would still add seven hundred metric tons of carbon to the atmosphere each year. That's about as much carbon as is released each year from all the world's wetlands and agriculture. By itself, it could increase global warming by 10–25 percent.[66]

In February 2004 David Anderson, Canada's minister of the environment, was quoted as saying that "global warming poses a greater long-term threat to humanity than terrorism because it could force hundreds of millions from their homes and trigger an economic catastrophe."[67] Although we cannot gauge the literal accuracy of Anderson's threat assessment, it clearly reflects the concern and anxiety that an increasing number of people are beginning to feel over the security effects of this form of global pollution. The people of virtually every nation have contributed and are continuing to contribute to this problem. Some, in richer countries such as the U.S. and Japan, and in faster growing countries such as China and India, burn large amounts of fossil fuels; some, in developing countries such as Brazil and Indonesia, destroy more and more of the earth's forests and practice unsustainable agriculture. They are all adding to the stress in the international system, yet many are reluctant to take bold action to undo the damage, fearing the negative short-term economic consequences.

Though it is unlikely that war will break out over greenhouse gas emissions or the destruction of forests and other natural greenhouse gas sinks, all of the stresses generated by trying to cope with the negative effects of global warming add to the strain on the international system. Just as individuals under stress tend to become more irritable, less accommodating, more prone to bursts of irrationality, and less able to cope with additional stress from other sources, so raising the level of stress on nations is not likely to help them to manage conflict well.

Even greater tension and stress are generated when nations that are clearly major contributors to global environmental threats refuse to join other nations in taking decisive action to mitigate them. Probably the best example is the widespread international hostility to the U.S. that resulted from the Bush administration's unilateral decision to abandon the Kyoto accords, which the U.S. had helped negotiate and signed under the Clinton administration. To many of the more than 150 nations that signed the Kyoto accords—especially those that had agreed to bear substantial costs in a serious collaborative effort to mitigate this global threat to security—-U.S. withdrawal was seen as something of a betrayal. It did not sit well that the world's then largest contributor to the problem seemed poised to free ride on the mitigation efforts of others.

Because the threats posed by transboundary pollution and resource depletion cannot be solved without international cooperation, they create an opportunity to encourage mutually beneficial problem solving that can help strengthen the peace, both within nations and between them. Conca, Carius, and Dabelko have argued, "As a peacemaking tool the environment offers some useful . . . qualities that lend themselves to building peace and transforming conflict: environmental challenges ignore political boundaries, require a long-term perspective, encourage local and nongovernmental participation, and extend community building. . . . [W]here cooperation does take root, it might help enhance trust, establish cooperative habits, create shared regional identities around shared resources, and establish mutually recognized rights and expectations."[68] Active international cooperation in meeting environmental challenges can thus be one more way to help build balanced, win-win relationships that strengthen positive incentives to manage conflicts without resort to violence, reinforcing Principle I. At the very least, such cooperation should help short-circuit some of the negative effects of environmentally generated stresses on the international system.

Are the Peacekeeping Principles Compatible and Cost-Effective?

Each of the four principles underlying the idea of a peacekeeping international economy has the potential to contribute to increasing the strength and/or reducing the stress on the international system. Each therefore has its own contribution to make to creating a set of conditions and incentives that reduce the probability of violent confrontation and war. But that by itself does not establish the peacekeeping effectiveness of the system as a whole, even in theory. Two important questions remain: 1) Are the peacekeeping principles at least compatible with each other, if not mutually reinforcing? and 2) Is there reason to believe that the costs of operating an economic peacekeeping system will not be excessive or even prohibitive?

Compatibility

The most obvious compatibility problem has already been discussed—that between Principle I, which implies expanded economic interdependence, and Principle II, which calls for some version of independence in critical goods. The best approach to dealing with this problem is to maximize independence in a very restricted set of critical goods and maximize interdependence everywhere else. The second most obvious compatibility problem is that between the expanded global economic activity implied by both Principles I and III (balanced interdependence and enhanced development, respectively) and the need to minimize ecological stress (Principle IV).

Expanding Economic Activity While Reducing Ecological Stress

Many believe that the expansion of economic activity itself is inconsistent with maintaining environmental quality, that modern production techniques and consumption activities generate an unavoidable degree of ecological stress. There is a certain amount of truth to this. Still, I contend that it is possible to maintain or improve the economic well-being of the people of the more developed countries and extend that well-being to the people of the less developed nations, without doing intolerable damage to the environment—perhaps even with lower than current levels of environmental damage. Accomplishing this feat requires: 1) much more attention than is currently being paid to the efficient use of natural resources; 2) the development and extensive use of pollution-abating technologies and procedures; and 3) a substantial shift toward qualitative, rather than quantitative, economic growth, particularly on the part of the more developed countries.

In many ways, those of us in the more developed world have been so profligate in our use of natural resources that there is potential for efficiency gains great enough to sharply reduce the ecological damage we are doing without any real sacrifice in our present standards of living. The efficient use of natural resources involves more intensive and widespread recycling of nonrenewable materials, efficiency improvements in the design and operation of energy using systems, and greater use of ecologically benign renewable energy and material resources. Recycling of nonrenewable materials dramatically reduces the rate of their depletion, transforms solid wastes into useful material, and saves energy. Off-the-shelf and soon-to-be-available technologies, combined with more intelligent operation of energy using systems, are capable of delivering enormous reductions in the amount of energy we need to accomplish the same tasks. Together with greater attention to recycling, these technologies would allow for the maintenance and improvement of material standards of living while reducing both the rate of depletion of energy resources and the environmental damage associated with their extraction and use. The detailed, sector-by-sector analysis of the major energy using systems in the U.S. I did more than three decades ago led me to estimate that a combination of improved design and changes in the operation of these systems could reduce energy consumption in the U.S. by 30-50 percent without sacrificing living standards.[69] And of course, the further development of renewable resources will provide supplies of energy and materials that can sustain economic activity indefinitely.

In fact, not only are the goals of enhanced productive economic activity and reduced environmental stress compatible, they have the potential to be mutually reinforcing if the proper paths are chosen. Nowhere is the combination of environmental benefit and economic potential clearer than in the area of renewable energy. Wind power generation, for example, has been the fastest growing power source, growing by some 20 percent per year (through 2003). Given the energy market share projected for wind power by 2020, it should be producing sales of $150 billion to $400 billion worldwide by then, according to a study prepared for the United Nations Environmental Program (UNEP). The same study projects that global sales in the market for all forms of renewable energy will reach close to $2 trillion by 2020.[70]

After thoroughly analyzing thirteen independent reports and studies on the economic and employment impacts of clean energy in the U.S. and Europe (and developing their own model), Kammen, Kapadia, and Fripp of the University of California conclude, "The renewable energy sector generates more jobs per megawatt of power installed, per unit of energy produced, and per dollar of investment than the fossil fuel-based energy sector." Comparing a scenario using renewable energy to meet 20 percent of U.S. electricity demand with a "fossil fuels only" scenario, they estimate that renewables would create between two and three times as many jobs by 2020—close to a quarter million jobs.[71]

Renewable energy tends to create more jobs in manufacturing than in services or operations and maintenance. Construction industries would also be boosted by movement toward creating a more renewables-oriented energy infrastructure, as would agriculture. The flow of benefits to agriculture (particularly important in the developing world) would be particularly strong to the extent that biomass becomes a more important energy source.[72] But wind farms can also help to reinvigorate rural communities. As the Council of State Governments pointed out in 2003, "Wind farms may extend over a large geographic area, but their actual 'footprint' covers only a very small portion of the land, making wind development an ideal way for farmers to earn additional income."[73]

The economic benefits of stimulating the less ecologically stressful renewable energy industry would not be the preserve of only a few nations, or regions within nations. In the U.S., for example, every state has some form of renewable energy resources that can be developed. It is estimated that forty-six of the fifty states have some sort of developable wind resources.[74] A large area of the U.S. receives an average of 3.5 kilowatt-hours or more of solar energy per square meter per day, enough so that a living room–sized collector should be sufficient to power a typical American house.[75] The potential for solar energy is even greater in the less developed nations, many of which are in latitudes where sunshine is more intense and more consistent.

The second requirement for enhancing the compatibility of Principles III and IV—the development and use of pollution-abating technologies and procedures—involves better filtration, waste treatment, and other after-the-fact cleanup. But it also involves the development and use of production and consumption technologies that pose less of a threat to the environment in the first place. For example, in the mid-1990s, I served as a consultant to the Los Alamos National Laboratories on a project intended to reduce toxic chemical wastes by bringing scientists from the labs together with scientists from the chemicals industry to work out ways to eliminate toxic chemicals from key production processes.

Finally, to conceive of economic growth mainly in quantitative terms is foolish and unnecessary. Standards of living are also raised, sometimes more effectively, by improving the quality of goods and services rather than by producing ever larger quantities. Shifting attention to qualitative growth will allow the more developed nations to reduce their insatiable appetite for nonrenewable resources, making their own continued economic growth indefinitely sustainable. It will also reduce environmental pollution and create space for the quantitative expansion of goods and services that is still required to raise living standards to decent levels in many less developed nations.

Having said all of that, there is no doubt that expanding economic activity along the paths the more developed countries have followed in the past—and using these same practices to try to dramatically raise living standards in the less developed world—is a prescription for economic failure and environmental disaster on a grand scale. China is a case in point. Its torrid pace of economic growth is primarily based on the use of the same industrial techniques that have generated so many environmental problems elsewhere. The result has been an ecological mess of heroic proportions—in air and water pollution, and in the nation's growing contribution to the rapid depletion of nonrenewable resources. China's enormous appetite for fossil fuels helped to drive oil prices to unprecedented heights in 2008, and led it to overtake the U.S. in total greenhouse gas emissions that same year.

For most of human history our economic activities could do very intense localized damage to the environment, but until perhaps fifty to a hundred years ago, we did not have the power to do such damage on a global scale. Now, if we continue to behave as we have been behaving, we will not be able to avoid it.

We must change the way we view economic growth and the strategies that are effective in achieving real improvement in material standards of living. What can bring the necessary changes about? The market will help. For example, as resources become scarcer and the demand for them rises, they become more expensive, and that will help induce both conservation and the search for alternatives. But because so many environmental costs do not naturally fall on those who produce them (they are "externalities"), the market will not solve these problems by itself. At the very least, it will be necessary for government to establish rules of the game (such as "pollution taxes" or "cap and trade" systems) that force those who create environmental costs to bear them, and thus to pay attention to them.[76] Consumers also have a critical role to play. By changing their purchasing patterns, people who have become aware of the need to move toward more ecologically sensible economic approaches to production and consumption can take action, using the market mechanism to push for these changes, affecting sales in a way that private sector producers will not be able to ignore.

By maximizing energy efficiency, developing ecologically benign renewable energy and material resources, recycling to conserve depletable minerals and energy resources, and shifting to a less purely quantitative, more quality-based concept of economic growth, we will not only improve the quality of the environment, but also increase material well-being in both the developed and developing nations. It is therefore perfectly possible to remove much, if not all, of the apparent conflict between Principles I, III, and IV.

Does Establishing Independence in Critical Goods Interfere with Encouraging Development?

It is clear that Principles I and III are not only compatible, but also mutually reinforcing. Abandoning exploitative economic relationships in favor of expanding balanced, mutually beneficial relationships (Principle I) will greatly improve the prospects for success of every nation engaged in the process of development (Principle III). The more successful that nations are in raising their level of development, the easier it will be to establish and maintain economic relationships that are truly balanced, and the greater will be the mutual benefits those relationships provide. But there does seem to be a significant compatibility problem between Principles II (which seeks critical goods independence) and III (which emphasizes development).

The attempt by the more developed countries to become independent in critical goods seems to imply reductions in the earnings of the nations that export those goods. Since critical goods include food, subsoil energy resources, and raw materials, all of which are major primary product exports of many developing countries, the attempt to achieve critical goods independence could have a strong negative impact on their development. Furthermore, the attempt by developing countries to become more independent in critical goods themselves could divert limited resources and attention from other productive investments that might have a greater payoff in terms of development.

There is no question that a substantially diminished trade in primary products would interfere with the development of some less developed nations in

the short run. It is less clear that it would interfere with long-run development prospects. To the extent that this state of affairs applied pressure to
developing countries to move away from reliance on primary products (especially easily extracted primary products) and diversify their economies and
thus their export offerings, it could conceivably improve their long-term development prospects.[77] The question is, even if they had the public and private sector expertise and quality of governance necessary to promote such a
shift, would they be able to marshal the investment resources necessary
in the face of diminished primary export revenues?

More hopeful is the fact that only one of the three strategies available for
reducing critical goods dependence—increased domestic production—is
likely to reduce the overall volume of trade in primary products. The other
two, diversification of suppliers and contingent independence, would not.
By itself, supplier diversification would at most just change the distribution of suppliers providing any particular nation with the critical goods it
needs. Contingent independence would have little effect on the volume of
trade in critical goods, unless and until there was an attempt to cut off supplies to a country using that strategy. In fact, if countries working toward
contingent independence decided to build up national stockpiles of critical
goods as part of that strategy, it would actually increase the volume of
critical goods trade in the short run.

The reality is that many countries will not be able to achieve independence in critical goods purely through increased domestic production, and
most of those who have the potential to do so will decide not to bear the
additional costs involved. In any case, it is important not to forget that
for any country only certain nutritionally and culturally important foods
would be considered critical. There will also be some difference in the
definition of which raw materials are critical from country to country.
Trade in all those primary goods not defined as critical (including a great
many foods and raw materials) would be unaffected by an attempt to achieve
critical goods independence through increased domestic production. The
main threat would be to export earnings based on nonrenewable energy
resources (such as oil and coal, which might be displaced by domestically
available renewable energy sources) and, to a lesser extent, depletable min-

erals. However, the growing pressure to reduce consumption of fossil fuels as a means of mitigating human-induced climate change—and the value of increased recycling of minerals as part of the response to that pressure—make the economic diversification of nations dependent on exports of fossil fuels and recyclable minerals an important issue independent of peacekeeping economic principles.

Attempts by developing countries to become independent in critical goods through increased domestic production would most likely center on food, water, and energy. For water, the crucial issue for most developing countries is the need to build up their water and sewage treatment infrastructure, something that is very important for them to do for development purposes, apart from any consideration of critical goods independence. As far as food is concerned, development programs in many poorer countries have shifted the focus of agriculture from domestic production of basic foods for the local population to specialty agricultural produce for export, with seriously negative impacts on the nutritional well-being of their own people. To the extent that moving toward critical goods independence helps undo that pattern, it will encourage rather than interfere with real development. Finally, although Brazil has radically reduced its dependence on foreign sources of fuel by producing vast amounts of ethanol from domestically grown sugarcane, the best hope most developing countries have of achieving energy independence through domestic production is to make much greater use of the abundant renewable energy embodied in sunshine, wind, and flowing water. Moving toward renewables will simultaneously produce benefits in both security and development.

Is It Possible to Reduce Critical Goods Dependence While Reducing Ecological Stress?

As in the case of apparent conflicts between other principles, whether or not working toward lower critical goods dependence is compatible with reducing ecological stress depends very much on the paths chosen. Focusing attention on energy efficiency, renewables, and recycling makes it possible to move strongly toward energy independence without invading and destroying the last remaining wildlife refuges, polluting the oceans and coastlines, and decapitating mountains in a frantic attempt to find additional domestic supplies of fossil fuels. It also makes it unnecessary to construct a new generation of very expensive nuclear power plants with their multi-thousand-year legacy of dangerous nuclear wastes and vulnerability to determined terrorist attack.[78] Reducing dependence on external sources of supply of critical foods is also not inherently damaging ecologically, especially when it is conceived in terms of contingency independence, stockpiling, and—particularly in the less developed world—the displacement of *some* of the production of specialty crops for export by greater local production of basic foodstuffs for local use.

Raw materials present more of a problem. Reducing dependence on foreign supplies of critical minerals might create pressure to develop inferior domestic deposits, which are more expensive and could be more ecologically damaging. Extensive recycling can help, but if the minerals are subsequently exported in the form of manufactured components or products, they will not be available for domestic recycling. If possible, a shift to alternative, domestically available renewable materials would be useful. Interestingly, developments in nanotechnology may ultimately trigger a revolution in materials that makes such a shift much more feasible in the future than it is today.[79] For the foreseeable future, though, it seems that a diversified supplier network offers the most promising path toward reducing insecurity-producing critical raw material dependence on any one or small group of external suppliers, without exacerbating environmental damage.

I do not argue that it is possible to erase all significant conflict among the four peacekeeping principles. As always, there will be some choices to be made, balances to be struck. But I do insist that, by choosing the right strategies, it is possible to minimize these compatibility problems, and to relegate them to the status of a side issue, a marginal concern.

Cost Effectiveness

Economics teaches us that real cost is always relative. Therefore, any costs associated with a peacekeeping international economy must be considered in light of the human and financial costs of continuing to rely as heavily as we currently do on the threat or use of military force for our security. A full and detailed accounting of all those costs is beyond the scope of this analysis. But it is possible to get the beginnings of an idea of the expense of the present military security system by considering some basic data on military expenditures.

In the fifteen years after the end of the Cold War, the nations of the world spent a cumulative total of just under $14.1 trillion (inflation-adjusted) on their military forces. To begin to appreciate the enormity of this sum, consider that a printing press turning out $1,000 every second would have had to be running continuously for close to 450 years to print that much money—thirty times as long as it took to spend it. (It would have printed about $5,000 in the time it took to read the previous sentence.) By itself, the U.S. spent over $5.9 trillion during that period, more than 42 percent of the world total. Even the nations of Africa, living in the economically poorest continent on earth, managed to spend close to $200 billion on their military forces over those same years.[80]

These figures represent only the direct financial costs of the present military-oriented system of security as a whole. Looking at one single military adventure, the 2003 U.S.-led invasion of Iraq enabled Linda Bilmes of Harvard University and Joseph Stiglitz of Columbia University to do a more thorough cost accounting. Their estimate included direct and indirect expenditures "such as lifetime healthcare and disability payments to returning veterans, replenishment of military hardware and increased recruitment costs," among other things. They estimated that if all U.S. troops returned home by 2010, the total costs of the war would exceed $1 trillion; if the troops stayed until 2015, "the true costs would exceed $2 trillion."[81] It is important to note that even the Bilmes-Stiglitz estimates included only the monetary costs to the U.S. They did not include the costs to the other nations that provided troops to the invasion and occupation of Iraq, or, most importantly, the costs to Iraq of destruction of infrastructure, disruption of economic activity, and injury and loss of life.

The economic tradeoffs involved in military spending can be viewed in many different ways. For example, the funds allocated to military expenditures can be considered a pool of financial capital. In that regard, it is interesting to note that total U.S. military spending in the fifteen years leading up to 2003 was roughly equal to the total cost in the U.S. in 2003 alone of all existing equipment, software, and structures owned by every private firm involved in manufacturing, mining, construction, transportation, health care, educational services, wholesale trade, and retail trade combined. In other words, just fifteen years of military expenditures represented a capital fund large enough to repurchase the entire net stock of fixed assets owned by all of the firms in all of those eight major categories of industry at their current cost.[82] Another way of looking at the same basic issue of financial capital is to compare military spending with corporate profits, on a year-by-year basis. For the U.S., from 1999 to 2003, for example, average annual military spending was more than 6 percent *greater* than the average annual *before* tax profits of all domestic private business firms in the U.S. in those same eight categories of industries combined.[83]

More to the point, while military expenditures have some value in political and security terms, they do not directly contribute to providing material well-being (the goods and services that constitute what we call the "standard of living") and thus have little or no economic value, as I will argue in much more detail in Chapter 7. Therefore, from whatever positive value military spending makes to security must be subtracted the burden it imposes on the economy—most importantly, the opportunity cost of the productive economic resources it consumes—the famous "guns vs. butter" tradeoff. Since a peacekeeping economy relies most heavily on providing security through encouraging productive economic activity (such as enhanced trade and investment in products that do contribute to the material standard of living), the (positive) economic value it produces is logically added to, rather than subtracted from, the value of whatever positive contribution it makes to security. While that does not theoretically guarantee that a peacekeeping economy will provide greater total net value than a security system that relies primarily on military force, it creates a reasonable presumption that a peacekeeping economy is more cost effective.

The costs of establishing and operating a peacekeeping international economy in all its dimensions depend on the particular strategies chosen. The cost of trying to sharply reduce critical goods dependence by relying heavily on a strategy of domestic production will be more economically and ecologically expensive for at least some countries than using a strategy of supplier diversification. Similarly, trying to minimize ecological stress through a series of regulations that require producers to use particular fuels and install particular equipment is likely to be more expensive than enforcing emissions caps that give producers the flexibility to use the most cost-effective approaches they can find.

Transitional costs are also an important issue (Chapter 8). There can be a very big difference between the short-term, transitional costs of establishing a peacekeeping international economy and the long-term costs of keeping it going. For example, minimizing the ecological damage done by the way producers and consumers use energy, and by the type of energy they use, is likely to involve substantial short-term investment in new equipment and facilities, as well as in training workers and consumers in proper operation and maintenance. Many of these changes may pay off well enough to at least balance their cost in the long run. A U.S. Department of Energy study in 2001 argued that a combination of measures, such as increased research and development, wider use of cogeneration, and greater use of renewable energy, could have reduced carbon emissions to 13–17 percent below "business as usual" scenarios by 2010 *without any net cost* to the U.S. economy.[84] The IPCC estimated that reductions in equivalent GHG emissions of about 30 percent of current levels could be achieved by 2020 by taking measures that would save enough energy to actually produce *net economic benefits, rather than costs.*[85] But even though many of these changes will cover their costs and perhaps generate a handsome financial and environmental long-run return, there is still a need for financing mechanisms to overcome the short-term hurdles (discussed in Chapter 5). Of course, even in the absence of attempts to reduce stress on the international security system these changes will eventually have to be made for compelling environmental reasons (including but not limited to the need to mitigate global warming). So the costs of making them should logically be spread over both sets of benefits, not just taken to be costs of the security system.

There may also be considerable short-term transitional costs involved in reconfiguring international economic relationships and the institutions that support them to make them more balanced. Once these costs have been borne, though, the balanced economic relationships that have been created will be much less costly to maintain than the more exploitative relationships they have replaced. As I have earlier argued, balanced, mutually beneficial relationships are self-supporting, even self-enhancing, while exploitative relationships require continuing and often costly efforts to maintain dominance.

Reconfiguring these relationships, as well as making many of the other changes required to fully establish a peacekeeping economy, will also produce some losers. For example, those firms engaged in lucrative exploitative relationships with foreign producers, enforced by coercive international intergovernmental arrangements and threats, will at least temporarily lose some ground.[86] When Adam Smith argued (*The Wealth of Nations*, 1776) that Britain should end its exploitative colonial relationships in favor of more balanced free trade, he claimed that would be "more advantageous to the great body of the people," not that it would be more advantageous to everyone.[87] There were clearly some who gained from the colonial relationships Great Britain had established, even some in its colonies. Nevertheless, Smith insisted that the "great body of the people," not merely in the colonies but in Britain itself, suffered because of the unbalanced relationships, and therefore stood to gain substantially if those exploitative relationships were replaced by balanced trade. That is still true today. There are bound to be short-term redistributional effects when dramatic changes are made, even those—such as establishing a peacekeeping economy—that stand to produce very large net benefits for many in the short run, and for nearly everyone in the long run.

Are the Peacekeeping Principles Relevant to Preventing Civil Wars?

We have focused primarily on the peacekeeping principles as they relate to international economic activities and the prevention of interstate war. Because national governments, which have the formal authority to mobilize an entire nation's human and economic resources, initiate and direct interstate wars, they are generally fought with larger, better-equipped forces and more destructive weaponry than are wars within states. International war also poses a greater risk of drawing more nations directly into the conflict, although civil wars often attract support from countries or other foreign forces that have a stake in which of the combatants eventually prevails. Finally, international wars are also subject to greater escalation in terms of the deployment of increasingly powerful forces and destructive weaponry.

Most wars in the late twentieth and early twenty-first centuries have been wars within countries (or what used to be countries), and they have taken an enormous toll in human suffering. They have crippled life-supporting economic activity, taken countless lives, and forced multiple millions of refugees into political no-man's lands in which they have little choice but to depend on the often meager kindness of strangers. The question naturally arises, "Can a peacekeeping economy based on the principles we have been discussing address the problem of preventing or short-circuiting civil wars, or is it only relevant in the international arena?"

This question breaks down into two subquestions: 1) would the establishment of a peacekeeping international economy create incentives that could help prevent the outbreak of civil wars? and 2) could the likelihood of civil war be reduced by applying the peacekeeping principles within national economies?

There is significant evidence that many civil wars, particularly in developing countries, are driven by greed rather than grievance (Chapter 2). It has been argued that the expansion of international economic activity, which is certainly not discouraged by a peacekeeping international economy, increases the opportunity for making profits by forcefully seizing control of valuable extractive resources, whether they be diamond mines or oil fields. Balancing relationships by shifting more benefit to supplier nations exploited in the past (according to Principle I) might perversely make the profit potential of controlling extractive resources in those countries even greater, and thus strengthen the incentive to seize them by force in a civil war.

But trading with those who forcibly seize control of such economic assets for the purposes of enriching themselves and a relatively small number of their trusted followers is a clear and strong violation of the call to emphasize development (Principle III). It is inherent in the very definition of economic development, and in its distinction from economic growth, that engaging in activities that enrich a small fraction of the population at the expense of the rest is the antithesis of development. To encourage real economic development, it is necessary to take steps to ensure that the gains of balanced trade, as a whole, are more widely distributed in the society. It is worth noting that that is very different from an extreme socialist egalitarian viewpoint that everyone in the society must share equally in the gains. We are talking about market economies in which some are likely to gain significantly more than others. But it does mean that development is not furthered when a very small economic or political elite captures all or nearly all of the gains. Allowing the gains of trade to be concentrated in the hands of what amounts to a few thugs and bandits who have seized "lootable" resources is also the antithesis of political development, which is also part of Principle III.

Considerable civil strife has been generated by economic activities that "rape the land," causing environmental costs that are often borne by those who live in the areas where ecologically damaging extractive (and other) activities have been carried out and did not share in the earnings those activities generated. This has certainly been an issue in the oil rich areas of Nigeria, for example. To the extent that such activities raise the level of conflict within national boundaries, minimizing ecological stress (Principle IV) would help to reduce these tensions as well.

Taken as a whole, the principles that guide a peacekeeping international economy clearly have something to offer in creating conditions that reduce the likelihood of civil, as well as interstate war. Can that effect be strengthened by applying them within nation-states—by creating peacekeeping national economies? It is difficult to see what it means to seek independence in critical goods within a nation (Principle II). It could be thought of as an argument for more emphasis on local economic activities, such as buying more food from local producers rather than depending on producers in distant parts of the nation. But it is unlikely that would contribute significantly to reducing civil strife and preventing intrastate war. On the other hand, establishing less exploitative, more balanced economic relationships (Principle I) within the borders of the nation would certainly make a significant contribution to reducing sharp economic inequalities that can and do breed civil strife. The value of establishing balance in decision power and in the distribution of benefits of economic interactions within nations applies to groups, as well as to individuals. Such groups are potentially important sources of conflict generation or resolution that could lead to or prevent the eruption of violence. Again, absolute equality is not necessary, but essential balance between groups could be important in reducing violent conflict within nations. Similarly, at the very least emphasizing development (Principle III) is important in overcoming the economic marginalization of the least powerful groups in society, whose marginalization is a recipe for trouble. And since the air and water cross political borders with impunity, minimizing pollution generated within the country is likely to be a key part of minimizing ecological stress internationally (Principle IV).

In short, the answer to both subquestions is yes. Establishing a peacekeeping international economy should contribute to reducing the likelihood of civil as well as international war. And it is reasonable to expect that creating "peacekeeping national economies" (based on Principles I, III, and IV) should make the outbreak of civil war less likely still.

On Positive and Negative Incentives

I have argued that incentives can be at least as effective—and in most cases ultimately more effective—than the threat or use of violence in inducing behavior that keeps nations and their people secure. Even so, it is worth considering whether positive incentives (such as opportunities to increase economic well-being) or negative incentives (such as economic sanctions) are likely to work better.

It is actually more difficult to distinguish positive incentives from negative incentives than it would at first appear. The difference between the two depends in part on the point of reference of the person (or nation) to whom they are applied. If a person is offered a bonus as a reward for doing his or her job well, that bonus appears to be an unambiguously positive incentive. But if that person becomes accustomed to receiving that bonus each year and comes to expect it, the possible loss of that bonus becomes a negative incentive. The goal of the incentive is exactly the same—to elicit good work performance—but the perception is quite different. Similarly, if someone who expects to receive a $5,000 bonus is given a $2,000 bonus instead, that person may feel as though he or she has lost $3,000 and is being punished rather than rewarded.

In the late 1970s, Daniel Kahneman and Amos Tversky developed an approach to decision making under risk called "prospect theory" as a challenge to the then widely accepted theory of "expected utility."[88] While expected utility theory treated gains and losses as essentially symmetrical, prospect theory did not. Among the best known tenets of prospect theory are that: 1) people do not think in absolute terms so much as they think in terms of gains or losses from their current position; and 2) losses have a greater psychological impact than equivalent gains—a person who loses $1,000 will feel more anguish than the person who fails to win $1,000. People are therefore ready to take greater risks to avoid or recover losses than they are willing to take to make gains. As Robert Jervis points out, "If people are risk-averse for gains and risk-acceptant for losses, they will work to maintain what exists but will take fewer chances to bring about a better situation. As long as existing arrangements are satisfactory, people are prone not to break them to make gains."[89] This has interesting implications for the practical problem of trying to create and then maintain a peacekeeping economic system.

The idea that people are strongly oriented to avoiding losses implies that once the peacekeeping economy is in place, it should work well. Since the benefits created by establishing a widened network of balanced mutually beneficial relationships will be lost if the relationships are disrupted, there will be strong pressure to avoid losses by not allowing conflicts to escalate to the point of war. (This is also true of loss of the benefits resulting from the other peacekeeping principles.) Given the bias to avoiding losses rather than making gains, that is likely to be true even if a particular military adventure seems to offer the prospect of significant short-term gains.

On the other hand, if people feel less strongly about taking the risks that might be necessary to achieve gains, it might seem that they would be less willing to take what they perceive as the risks involved in "changing existing arrangements" by setting up a peacekeeping economy in the first place. But any "risks" involved in setting up a peacekeeping economy can be minimized by putting it in place step-by-step, which is, practically speaking, the only way it is likely to happen anyway. And after all, one important part of the "gains" of a peacekeeping economy is precisely avoiding or reducing the losses associated with a primarily military-centered approach to security. These losses certainly include the financial and wider economic costs of building and maintaining large military forces (Chapter 7), as well as the destruction of property, human suffering, and loss of life that will occur in the event those forces are ever put into action.

Incentives, especially positive incentives, work better than violent threats most of the time, especially in the long run. For one thing, positive incentives don't just encourage the desired action; they produce good feelings, which create conditions that make future cooperation easier. Violent threats (and, to a lesser extent, negative incentives), even if they succeed in coercing desired actions now, are more likely to generate hostility that makes future cooperation more difficult.

Furthermore, the kinds of positive incentives built into the structure of the peacekeeping economy are not gifts or even rewards in the traditional sense of payments for good performance. They are overwhelmingly opportunities instead—opportunities for people to increase their own standards of living by participating in a more sustainable, widened process of production, trade, and investment that creates new wealth and more vigorous economic development. The difference between gifts and opportunities is that the gains achieved by taking advantage of opportunities must be earned by active, ongoing effort. They are not a simple present or prize that someone else decides to bestow. Because they are earned by continuing effort, they produce a greater sense of accomplishment, a greater sense of ownership. As I have argued in the case of balanced decision making in relationships, the incentive to nurture and sustain the system is stronger when all parties feel a greater sense of ownership.

Finally, the positive incentive systems embedded in the peacekeeping economy grow the "pie" of benefits and ensure that all participants receive an equitable share of the gains. Security systems that rely on such incentives are cheaper to operate than those that depend on negative incentives or threats. They are self-reinforcing and generate net benefits rather than costs, while security systems that depend on negative incentives can be sustained only by bearing a continuing net burden. Negative incentives, such as economic sanctions, invariably inflict losses on those who impose them, as well as on the target countries or firms (Chapter 5). Building and maintaining the forces required to make credible military threats, let alone using them, imposes heavy costs and is also subject to the cost increasing "security dilemma": the buildup of military forces by one state to increase its security reduces the security of other states, leading them to strengthen their military forces that undo any initial advantage. Trying to regain the advantage by further military expansion raises costs even more. This is the stuff of arms races, which, historically speaking, are not only very expensive, but also futile in terms of increasing security. They nearly always end in war.

Conclusion

At first glance, the four basic principles—establish balanced mutually beneficial relationships, seek independence in critical goods, emphasize development, and minimize ecological stress—may look like an idealized, disconnected, even incompatible progressive agenda. But in fact they are key elements of an ideologically eclectic yet consistent attempt to harness a number of seemingly disparate forces that can be integrated to help achieve both security and prosperity. International economic trade and investment relationships that are balanced in benefit, volume, and decision power maximize the extent to which self-interests become compatible and mutually reinforcing. This turns the pursuit of self-interest that drives free market capitalism into a potentially powerful binding force among nations, creating strong positive incentives to manage conflict without resorting to violence. Maximizing independence in critical goods while maximizing interdependence everywhere else provides reassurance that blunts the conflict-generating fear of the vulnerability that excessive dependence can create, while allowing the considerable benefits of competition, specialization, and trade to flow freely.

By increasing the material well-being and strengthening the political voice of those who live in the less developed world, emphasizing development strengthens their stake in peace. Development is a powerful force for reducing persistently high levels of inequality, as well as the economic and political marginalization that can so easily give rise to violent conflict. With a better, more prosperous material life and a greater chance to meaningfully participate in the political process comes an increased sense of personal dignity and a stronger resistance to extreme solutions. Furthermore, the kind of balanced economic relationships that foster peace are much more easily established among countries at higher and more equal levels of development. The more developed and prosperous all the parties to such economic relationships are, the greater the benefits that flow in all directions, and hence the stronger the incentives to avoid disruptive, violent confrontation.

Despite the huge technological advances we have made, the natural environment still provides many of the basic resources and services on which our lives and our economies depend. From filtering and recirculating the air we breathe and the water we drink, to serving as a source of raw materials and energy, to carrying away or recycling the wastes we generate, the environment is the critical context within which all economic activity must operate. Economists often refer to environmental factors as "external" to the economy, but they are only external because our systems of measurement and accounting are so deeply flawed. The environment, broadly construed, is actually a central component of economic activity, the ultimate shared resource. The damage that any one of us does to the environment becomes a cost for everyone else. On the one hand, we cannot succeed in effectively reducing the damage done by global pollution without working together, and working together on this mutual problem may actually help strengthen the peace. On the other hand, those of us who continue to add substantially to the problem while standing apart from the cooperative efforts to solve it will generate understandable hostility that will make it more difficult to keep the peace. Furthermore, to the extent that our economic activities put us in competition with each other for nonrenewable natural resources, that competition can, as it has all too often in the past, lead to violence and even war. Carrying on our economic lives, while minimizing reliance on virgin depletable resources, is therefore not just a nice thing to do. It is essential if we are to have both economic progress and peace.

The basic principles underlying a peacekeeping international economy are interconnected in many different ways. We will have a very difficult time if we attempt to balance the whole range of our international economic relationships without paying serious attention to development, and—if the track record of the past fifty years is any guide—development will be much more difficult to achieve without a great deal of balanced international investment and trade. At the same time, if we allow all considerations of independence to be swept aside by a rising tide of interdependence, we will find ourselves susceptible to politically motivated manipulation that can deliver powerful shocks to our economic system, and make it difficult to maintain the web of interdependent relationships we have established. Finally, if we do not attend to reducing the appetite of the more developed world for nonrenewable economic resources as well as to reducing the global burden of pollution, we will have a great deal of trouble in both achieving widespread development of the world's less developed nations and continuing the high levels of material well-being the more developed countries have achieved.

Once they are in place, the four principles underlying the peacekeeping economy will not only be compatible with each other, they will in many ways be mutually reinforcing. There are also compatible, even mutually reinforcing approaches available for putting the core principles into place. Using these approaches will not completely eliminate tradeoffs among them, but it will hold them to a minimum. While the peacekeeping economy may not entirely replace reliance on military power, it is a cost effective security system that has the potential to sharply reduce the size of the military forces required and thus the economic burden involved in maintaining, let alone using, them.

By adopting the peacekeeping economic principles as a guide and putting them jointly into action, it should be possible to create a web of international economic relationships that not only serves our material needs, but also provides strong positive incentives to make and keep the peace. Rather than a world of deepening inequality and growing insecurity, we can use them to build a world that is at once more equitable, more prosperous, more sustainable, and more secure.

But principles and general approaches are not enough. We must also try to work out the kinds of implementation strategies, organizations, institutions, and structures that can be used to build and maintain a functioning peacekeeping economy. That challenge is taken up in the next two chapters.

4

Making It Happen
Building a Peacekeeping Economy
in the "Real World"

IT IS ONE THING TO PROPOSE a set of principles on which a new paradigm for achieving international security can be built; it is quite another to design practical approaches that can be used to build and maintain it. Though that is very important, it is not possible to fill in all the details of such an enormous project here. Instead, in this chapter I will try only to illustrate a set of practical approaches that can be used to implement the principles, and in the next to give examples of the kinds of new or modified institutions and structures that could make an economy based on peacekeeping principles a working reality.

If it is true that the four principles are really as compatible with market capitalism as I have argued, then it is reasonable to begin by asking why capitalism hasn't already created a peacekeeping international economy. The first part of the answer is that much of what is needed to make a peacekeeping economy work *is* already in place. The principles are not the basis for an alternative to capitalism. They are designed as guidelines to help correct some of the most serious conflict-generating tendencies of the present international economic system, while greatly enhancing the positive incentives that system already creates to keep the peace within nations and among them. They are about improving the existing system, not replacing it.

The greater part of the answer is that the narrow short-term interest of those who run market enterprises often diverges from what is in the short- and long-term interest of the wider society. For that matter, it is often different from what is in the firm's own long-term interest as well. This can lead to the adoption of practices that run counter to the peacekeeping principles. For example, establishing unbalanced exploitative economic relationships with suppliers in other countries (in violation of Principle I) serves the short-term interests of the firm by allowing it to pay less for the resources it requires, and to make a greater short-term profit. The fact that this exploitation might generate hostility counterproductive to the security interests of its home country does not necessarily enter into the firm's decision-making process. In an economist's terms, it is a "negative externality"—a side effect of the actions of one party that imposes an unintended cost on another.

The destructive logging that leads to deforestation and the failure to reduce excessive transborder pollution both violate the principle of minimizing ecological stress (Principle IV). They are examples of other practices that might increase short-term profits, but have negative security—and environmental—externalities. The narrowly self-interested decision makers of economic theory do not take externalities into account because they are not directly affected by them. Externalities are one classic example of "market failure," situations in which the normal operation of markets does not lead to a socially optimal result (which free markets are ordinarily presumed to achieve).[1]

It is also possible that continuing exploitative relationships or environmentally destructive behavior will lead to continued higher profits for the firm in the long term. But it is at least as likely that such behavior will create hostility and do reputational damage to the firm that may provoke disinvestment, boycotts, or other actions that might reduce profits or foreclose profitable opportunities in the future. If the managers making decisions are more focused on their own short-term interests than on the longer-term interests of those who actually own the firm, it is quite possible that they will persist in making decisions that convey a fleeting advantage to them or to the firm at the expense of its long-term profitability or even survival.[2]

For these and other reasons, we cannot simply rely on the ordinary, unrestricted operation of the market system to create forces that will ultimately lead to the evolution of a highly effective peacekeeping economy. But neither do we have to unduly interfere with the forces of self-interest that propel the market system forward and give it its creativity, flexibility, and vigor. Instead we have to try to create the right context by finding ways to establish and encourage adherence to "rules of the game" that allow for the motivational advantages of self-interested economic activity, while embedding the peacekeeping principles that lead naturally to the development of a full-blown peacekeeping economy.

The Role of Government in Implementation

The proper role of government in a market economy is to provide the basic legal infrastructure needed to facilitate investment and exchange, and to ensure that the cumulative effect of the actions of private firms actually do benefit society as a whole. It is neither efficient nor appropriate for government to get involved in the detailed internal operations of private sector firms. This is not a matter of ideological preference; it is a matter of information, knowledge, and incentive.

If, for example, privately owned factories producing different products in different ways are polluting the air, it is appropriate for the government to take action in the interest of society to clean up the air by reducing pollutant emissions. But it makes little sense for the government to do this by telling each firm what kinds of fuels or materials to buy or exactly how to change its production process so that less pollution will be emitted. It does not have enough information about each factory's operations, nor enough knowledge about producing each of the varied products to figure out, anywhere near as well as the managers of individual firms can, what is actually the most cost-effective way of reducing emissions. It would be more sensible for the government to create a profit-based incentive for the firms to reduce their emissions, say by establishing a heavy fine for releasing more than an allowable level of pollution (along with a system for monitoring the emissions). Faced with a strong incentive to take action, firms can work out for themselves how they are going to reduce the amount of pollution they are releasing. This way, the social benefits of cleaner air will be achieved at a much lower cost.

The same basic argument can be made as to the appropriate role of government in implementing the four principles that underlie a peacekeeping economy. The idea is for government to create rules of the game that align private interests with the public interest, not to interfere in the microdetails of private sector economic operations and relationships. Implementing the principle of minimizing ecological stress is often a matter of internalizing externalities, as in the pollution example above. Private decision makers ignore externalities in their cost-benefit calculations only as long as they are not directly affected by them. If they can be made to bear the cost that they are imposing on others in the case of negative externalities (or to capture at least part of the benefit in the case of positive externalities), the "externalities" are no longer external. They will become part of the private decision-making process. The same logic applies, for example, to those whose private dealings substantially compromise critical goods independence or those who engage in significantly unbalanced, exploitative economic relationships, both of which impose serious negative security externalities on the people of their home country.

Governments and, for that matter, the private sector as well can also cooperatively create international organizations that serve as effective multilateral tools for implementing the four principles. The character and operation of these institutions will be discussed in more detail in Chapter 5.

It is also possible to create new international institutions or modify those that already exist so that they are better structured and positioned to establish and enforce new rules of the game of international economic relations. The closest thing that now exists to such an intergovernmental institution is the World Trade Organization (WTO). The WTO serves not only as a forum for creating rules that encourage free trade by dismantling trade barriers, but also as an adjudicator of charges of violations and an enforcer of those rules. If some of the more telling criticisms leveled against it were addressed, a modified WTO could be far more effective in reinforcing peacekeeping economic principles. This will be discussed in more detail in Chapter 6.

Finally, governments can create institutions within their own jurisdictions that reinforce incentives that promote the four principles. After all, this is not a situation in which countries following these strategies benefit only if everyone else is following them too. Any nation whose economic relations with other nations are balanced and mutually beneficial, whose

supplies of critical goods are assured, whose policies encourage and facilitate the development of other nations, and whose practices are more ecologically benign will be more secure and prosperous than it would otherwise
be, even if very few other countries are following that path. At the same
time, the more nations, firms, and individuals join in supporting such
practices, the greater the security gains and long-term economic benefits
to all of them will be.

The Free Rider Problem

It might be argued that, as in so many collective action situations,
there is a free rider problem here. If enough other nations undertake
economic peacekeeping, security and economic benefits will accrue to all
nations, even those that do not participate in the peacekeeping economic
regime. So it might seem logical for any particular nation to refuse to
participate, to sit back and let the others bear the costs, while it enjoys the
benefits.

But no nation can take full advantage of the long-term *economic* benefits
that flow from establishing balanced mutually beneficial relationships
without participating in them. Furthermore, as I have already argued, it is
not at all clear that there are large net economic costs involved in following
the principle of balanced relationships. There are more likely to be large
net benefits, especially in the long run (Chapter 3). Furthermore, though it
is true that every nation will become more *secure* to the extent that others
follow this principle, the security gains of any particular nation will be that
much greater if they are not seen as outsiders—and outsiders are easy to
identify. There is thus little if any real incentive to free ride.

Unlike creating balanced relationships, achieving critical goods independence is likely to involve additional economic costs. The extent of those
costs depends on which particular strategies are used to achieve that goal.
But since no nation can gain the security benefits of becoming more independent in critical goods without participating in that strategy, there
should be no significant free rider problem here either.

Encouraging development could involve significant short-term economic
costs, although again that depends on the approach used to implement this

principle. "Trade, not aid," for example, is likely to be less expensive than pouring large sums into designated aid projects. To the extent that the trade is nonexploitative, it will be more effective as well. While the security and long-term economic gains that come from encouraging development will benefit richer countries that do not participate as well as those that do, outsiders are again relatively easy to identify. Because of considerations of goodwill and gains to early market penetration (in the case of trade-based policies), the benefits to participants are likely to be substantially greater than the gains to those that stand apart.

Finally, outsiders are also easy to identify when it comes to collective efforts to reduce environmental stress. Their failure to participate generates hostility that may bring economic and political pressures to bear on them. This is especially true to the extent that outsiders continue to generate noxious and obvious forms of transborder pollution. For certain kinds of collective environmental action, it may well be that there is a net gain to nonparticipation, and hence a free rider problem. For others, nonparticipation may impose its own costs in terms of damage done to the local environment. On balance, then, though there may be some limited elements of a free rider problem involved in building a peacekeeping economy, they are not nearly as strong as they might at first seem.

Implementing Principle I: Establish Balanced, Mutually Beneficial Relationships

Simply put, the basic problem here is that private firms want to pay as little as possible for whatever they buy, and, where they have sufficient power, that tends to lead to exploitative relationships. How, then, can we ensure that trade is balanced and mutually beneficial?

Where there is balanced economic (and political) bargaining power, as between two large multinational corporations (MNCs), there is no problem ensuring that each of the trading partners reaps substantially equal benefits from the transaction. The market will handle it. Where there is a serious imbalance in economic (or political) bargaining power, as, for example, between large multinational corporations and local producers in developing countries, exploitation is very likely unless something is done to balance power across the transaction. There are a number of power-balancing strategies available.

Countervailing Power

Standard microeconomic theory predicts that market transactions taking place under the (extremely unrealistic) conditions of perfect competition will produce a variety of socially beneficial results.[3] These derive from limitations on the power of producers that result from intense competition with those on the same side of the market—other producers. In the early 1950s, economist John Kenneth Galbraith argued that something close to the benefits of perfect competition can be achieved when those on the *other* side of the market are strong enough to prevent large producers that have considerable market power from exercising it. He called this the theory of "countervailing power."[4]

Galbraith went on to argue that the strategy of developing concentrations of power on one side of the market to offset the power of already powerful players on the other side of the market could be used to prevent exploitation and balance the gains between transactors: "The fact that a seller enjoys a measure of monopoly power, and is reaping a measure of monopoly return as a result, means that there is an inducement to those firms from whom he buys or those to whom he sells to develop the power with which they can defend themselves against exploitation."[5]

Put simply, then, where it is not feasible to break up concentrations of power on one side of the market, one alternative strategy is to create a concentrated power on the other side of the market. The most obvious way to do this in the case at hand is to organize the less powerful to act jointly to balance the power of the more powerful. Encouraging developing country producers to organize marketing cartels might be one way to ensure that they have enough bargaining power to get a fair price for their product. The Organization of Petroleum Exporting Countries (OPEC) is a case in point. Although it has been painful to consumers used to the benefits of cheap oil—more so in the developing countries than in the developed—there is very little reason to believe that the handful of large multinational oil companies any longer have the degree of power to hold crude oil prices to artificially low, exploitative levels that they had before the OPEC cartel came into its own in the 1970s. Unfortunately, OPEC is also an example of one of the biggest problems with this approach to balancing relationships. When it comes to "lootable resources" like crude oil, it is not at all clear that the ordinary people of the countries exporting those resources necessarily receive anything more than minimal benefit from the "fair" prices at which the resources are traded.

Balancing the market power of producers by increasing the market power of their suppliers might actually disadvantage consumers that ultimately buy the final product. It is one thing to ensure that valuable resources are traded at prices that reflect their value; it is quite another if firms and their suppliers decide to collude with each other to set monopolistic prices that "exploit" consumers. That is by no means guaranteed to happen, but it is possible when powerful customer and supplier firms are on either side of a market transaction, or when a powerful firm faces a powerful labor union. That this could happen certainly does not invalidate the "countervailing power" strategy, but it does call for exercising caution in implementing it.

It is unlikely that that the powerful economic forces concentrated in the private sectors of the more developed countries will become much weaker and less organized in the foreseeable future. Therefore, better organizing developing country producers to increase their economic power has its problems, but it may be one of the most practical strategies for achieving a greater balance in international economic relationships.

Government Pressure

Another approach is to have government put pressure on firms not to engage in economic relationships that are clearly exploitative. There is considerable precedent here. Within many countries, especially higher income countries, there are "fair labor practice" and "fair trade practice" laws that constrain the power of firms to do as they please in their dealings with their employees in the first case, and their competitors, customers, and suppliers in the second. The purpose of these laws is not to subordinate business to government or to deny firms the freedom of action they need to make profits—even very large profits—in a dynamic market economy. It is rather to prevent large and powerful firms from using their market power and deep financial pockets abusively to exploit the individuals who work for them, the weaker firms that sell to them or compete with them, or those who buy their products. How well such laws are designed, implemented, and enforced aside, they are about promoting fairness and preventing exploitation.

In the rarified theoretical world of perfect competition, such laws would be redundant. The power of producers, and therefore their ability to behave abusively, would be limited by the intensity of competition with their rivals. But in the real world, the world in which there are lopsided markets and great concentrations of economic power, they are at least as important in promoting economic efficiency as they are in ensuring a greater degree of social equity.[6] Government action to establish and enforce rules to keep the free market game honest, from antitrust laws to workplace safety regulations, is key to making self-interest work in practice to the general benefit of society. Because economic and political power are fungible, keeping the free market game honest is important to supporting political freedom and democracy as well.

There are also the equivalent of "fair trade practices" laws in the international arena. One example is antidumping legislation, the economic rationale for which is to prevent foreign competitors with deep financial pockets (or subsidies from home governments) from selling their product below cost (which benefits consumers in the short run) in competition with domestically produced goods. Again the object is to prevent "unfairness," in this case, competition that unfairly disadvantages domestic producers. While charges of "dumping" brought under such legislation are sometimes trumped up by inefficient domestic producers trying to get protection against more efficient foreign competitors, real dumping can be a serious anticompetitive practice.

Presumably home country governments of large and powerful multinational firms could establish "fair trade practices" regulations to put pressure on those firms to avoid at least the most egregious exploitative behaviors in their international economic dealings, without unduly interfering in the microdetails of the firms' business. For example, governments could pass laws that prevent or heavily tax the import of goods or components produced by slave labor, child labor, or labor working under extreme sweatshop conditions.[7] This would pressure large and powerful domestic retail firms not to deal with foreign suppliers that massively exploit their employees. It would also pressure large domestic manufacturers not to buy components from such foreign suppliers or operate the company's own component-supplying foreign subsidiaries exploitatively.

While national governments could independently decide to establish such regulations, this might not be the most effective approach. There are likely to be too many ways around the rules in a patchwork quilt of ad hoc regulations. Government action would be much more effective in moving international economic relationships toward greater balance if it were coordinated through international trade laws and institutions such as a modified WTO.

There are, however, two important questions about the desirability and practicality of using government regulation to balance economic relationships between private firms. First, are such regulations consistent with what government should do? Second, is it realistic to expect that governments would ever pass *and enforce* laws that work against the interest of large, economically powerful (and therefore politically influential) firms based in their own country?

Though there is a great deal of disagreement across the political spectrum as to the proper role of government in free market economies, there is little disagreement that it is the business of government to provide for the nation's security. The impetus for undertaking to establish these regulations is not to control commercial business, but precisely to increase national security by helping to build one component of an international economic system based on peacekeeping principles. If balanced and mutually beneficial international economic relationships do indeed create strong incentives to keep the peace, as I have argued, there is no doubt that government action to encourage such relationships contributes to the nation's security, and so is consistent with the proper role of government.

As to the second question, in addition to fair trade practice and fair labor practice laws and regulations, which already exist in many countries to restrict private sector business in the service of social equity and economic efficiency,

there already are laws and regulations that restrict private sector business dealings explicitly in the name of national security. There are, for example, restrictions on the sale of militarily useful technologies or facilities to those viewed
as current enemies or potential future military adversaries. Furthermore, in
February 2006, when the shareholders of the British firm P&O, which operated terminals at six major ports in the U.S., voted in favor of acquisition by
Dubai Ports World (DPW), a company owned by the government of Dubai
(one of the United Arab Emirates), a political outcry arose in the U.S. that led
to threats of congressional action to block DPW from managing the ports on
grounds of national security. The political furor (which arose because of concerns about potential terrorist threats) and the pressure it produced ultimately
resulted in an agreement by DPW to sell off the entity that managed the U.S.
ports to an American firm.

Although a British firm was involved in this case, there is little doubt
that the reaction would have been essentially the same if P&O had been
an American firm. Objections on grounds of national security (though not
terrorism) raised in the summer of 2005 had already prevented a Chinese
company, the China National Offshore Oil Corporation (CNOOC), from
acquiring American-owned Unocal, an oil firm with reserves mainly in
Asia.[8] As with Dubai Ports World, national security concerns seem to have
been the main source of political opposition that stopped this ordinary
business transaction between two large multinational enterprises.[9]

Encouraging Trade Among Less Developed Countries

In 2001, only about one-quarter of less developed countries' (LDCs')
$658-billion worth of exports were to other LDCs.[10] Yet balanced, mutually
beneficial trade (and investment) relationships are easier to establish
among parties of more equal economic and political power. Greater economic cooperation among the LDCs should also help to break down the
debilitating patterns of dependency and "colonial mentality" that are the
legacy of the subordinate role played particularly by those LDCs that were
colonies during the age of empire.[11]

I am not suggesting that all LDCs are able to exert comparable economic
and political power, or even that they are at comparable levels of develop-

ment. That is simply untrue. By any reasonable measure, the idea of two separate homogeneous groups of nations doesn't begin to represent the spectrum of levels of national development that actually exists. But those countries commonly designated as LDCs (or "developing countries") are, on average, closer to each other in terms of economic development than they are to the more developed countries (MDCs). Furthermore, though there are exceptions, on the whole the paradigm of dominance is not as historically entrenched in interactions among LDCs as it is in MDC-LDC relations. For both these reasons, it should be easier for LDCs to establish with each other rather than with MDCs the balanced, mutually beneficial relationships compatible with a peacekeeping economy.

One counterargument is that countries at lower levels of development may produce more similar products and therefore have less to trade with each other. That is especially true of countries whose economies are structured around one or two similar primary products. Two countries whose main export is coffee, or bananas, or sugar cane, might have limited prospects for trade with each other. Countries that export crude oil or minerals that are important to countries whose economies are based on manufacturing would have less to trade with countries that are not significantly industrialized. Yet this argument can be taken too far. Even though two countries are both primary agricultural product exporters, if they do not export the same agricultural products, they may still have much to trade with each other profitably. Similarly, crude oil–exporting LDCs may benefit from buying primary agricultural products from other LDCs. They may also find profitable investment opportunities in other developing countries, even those that are also crude oil exporters.

With varying degrees of success, a number of regional preferential or free trade zones have been established by developing countries to promote trade among them. In 1960 five nations formed the Central American Common Market (CACM), which disbanded in the 1970s because of political differences but was then resurrected in the late 1980s. In 1975, fifteen countries with a combined population of about 124 million established the Economic Community of West African States (ECOWAS) to encourage development through economic integration. In September 1986, a nonaggression pact entered into force among its member states. The original agreement was expanded in the late 1970s–early 1980s to allow ECOWAS to intervene in the internal affairs of member states. In fact, Article 4 of the agreement *requires* ECOWAS to intervene in "internal armed conflict within any Member State engineered and supported actively from outside likely to endanger the security and peace in the entire Community."[12]

In 1977, the Association of Southeast Asian Nations (ASEAN) established a preferential trading arrangement among the countries that had originally formed the Association in 1967 (Indonesia, Malaysia, Philippines, Singapore, and Thailand). ASEAN launched an initiative in 1992 to strengthen previous trade agreements and create an ASEAN Free Trade Area (AFTA).[13] In 1991, the Mercado Comun del Sur (Mercosur) was established in South America between Brazil, Uruguay, Argentina, and Paraguay. Mercosur established free trade areas with Bolivia and Chile in 1996, and a Dispute Settlement Court in 2003.[14] In 1995, the South Asia Association for Regional Cooperation Preferential Trading Arrangement (SAPTA) was established, which includes India, Pakistan, Bangladesh, and Sri Lanka. That same year, the Common Market for Eastern and Southern African States (COMESA) was also established, successor to the Preferential Trade Area for Eastern and Southern African States (PTA), established in 1982. COMESA became more integrated in 2000.[15]

In 1985, development economist Michael Todaro wrote, "Third World countries at relatively equal stages of development, with similar market sizes . . . stand to benefit most from . . . economic integration. . . . In any event. . . . without cooperation and integration, the prospects for sustained economic progress are bleak."[16] In 1997 he added,

> The lessons of the past 30 years . . . revealed to the Third World nations . . . their need to make every effort to reduce their individual and joint economic vulnerabilities. One method of achieving this goal is . . . greater collective self-reliance within the context of mutual economic cooperation. Though not denying their interdependence with developed nations and their need for growing export markets, many developing countries now realize that in the absence of major reforms of the international economic order, a concerted effort at reducing their current economic dependence and vulnerability is essential to any successful development strategy.[17]

It would certainly not advance the cause of economic development or international security for the developing countries to try to break away from open economic trade with the more developed countries. But a greater degree of economic integration among the LDCs would not only lead to increased balance, it would also put them in a position to strike a better bargain in their economic relationships with the MDCs. That would support both the first economic peacekeeping principle (establishing mutually beneficial balanced relationships) and the third principle (encouraging development).

There are good economic reasons, aside from the peacekeeping advantages, why broadening trade between the LDCs seems like a good idea. LDC producers should understand better than MDC producers the context and limitations of other societies operating at lower levels of development. They should be more attuned to manufacturing products whose design, economic characteristics, operation, and maintenance requirements are more suitable to LDC markets.

Consumer and Investor-Based Pressure

Thus far, we have considered the possibility of creating more balanced mutually beneficial relationships by encouraging the least powerful economic transactors to coordinate their marketing activities by using the power of governments to push the more powerful transactors to engage in more equitable trade relationships, and by increasing the extent to which those with relatively less market power trade with each other. Yet it is also possible to improve fairness by mobilizing the power of investors and those who buy goods and services to put pressure on powerful economic actors to pay more attention to balance in their business dealings.

Probably the best-known example of investor-based pressure in the service of economic, political, and social equity was the international campaign to promote disinvestment in South Africa. The decades-long campaign began in the 1970s, with the goal of bringing down the deeply entrenched apartheid system of race-based economic and political oppression that was enshrined in South African law from 1948 until inclusive constitutional democracy was finally established in 1994. Here the inequity was internal and the source of inequity was the government, not business.

But the campaign was aimed at the white South African business establishment, on the theory that if they felt enough economic pressure, they would ultimately change their own behavior and force the government to end apartheid. By the mid 1990s, apartheid was gone. The disinvestment campaign was not the only reason; a complex of causes brought apartheid down. But the pressure created by disinvestment was certainly one of them. It is one useful piece of evidence proving that it is sometimes possible to organize a successful campaign against businesses for the purpose of achieving greater equity.

Nongovernmental organizations (NGOs) may be more effective (and more appropriate) organizers of disinvestment campaigns than governments. Among the range of strategies available to NGOs to successfully promote such campaigns the shareholder resolution is one of the most interesting: an NGO purchases stock in a company that has investments in a country whose government or private sector supports or directly engages in economically exploitative practices; once the NGO is a shareholder, it can introduce shareholder resolutions urging the company to disinvest. The Interfaith Center for Corporate Responsibility (ICCR), an American association of more than 250 religious denominations established in the early 1970s, has been particularly active in using this approach. ICCR shareholder resolutions have been credited, for example, with playing an important role—some would say a primary role—in making South African apartheid a major issue in the U.S. in the 1980s.[18]

This approach has also been used to pressure companies to end their own exploitative practices or those of the other firms with which they do business. ICCR has introduced hundreds of shareholder resolutions on a wide variety of social responsibility issues, only some of which involved disinvestment initiatives.[19] Although these shareholder resolutions almost never come close to passing, they do provide an opportunity to make other shareholders, as well the public, aware of the company's complicity in the exploitative system being targeted. That can help pressure the company to change its behavior. For example, a shareholder resolution concerning company environmental and human rights policies was filed with Shell Transport and Trading in the U.K. in 1997. The resolution, which referred specifically to the company's operations in Nigeria, was supported by only 10.5 percent of shareholder votes cast. Yet the company ultimately adopted and implemented most of the recommendations contained in the resolution in the months following the vote.[20] According to Karen Ballentine, "Shareholder activism had been a central determinant in making individual companies more accountable and in compelling them to end problematic investments."[21]

The movement for so-called socially responsible investment —investment only in companies that uphold certain principles of socially responsible corporate behavior—has grown from a curiosity to a substantial force in the world of finance. Goldman Sachs, the mainstream Wall Street investment bank, produces reports on the environmental, social, and management performance of companies parallel to more standard analyses of financial performance; it sends out a weekly e-mail letter on "sustainable investing" to hundreds of contacts at eighty institutions around the world.[22] By one estimate, the market for socially responsible investment had grown to some $2.7 trillion worldwide by the early twenty-first century.[23] According to the Social Investment Forum, about 10 percent of the professionally managed investment assets in the U.S. fall into this category.[24] Even more important, "The divide between socially responsible investing and 'mainstream' financial investing has been diminishing as more companies take SRI [socially responsible investing] on board."[25]

Consumer boycott of the products of companies that engage in economically exploitative behavior is yet another way of pressuring those companies to move toward more equitable business dealings. Boycotts are more common than disinvestment campaigns, and often seem more effective.[26] They can be enforced by formal government action, in which case they are called "trade embargoes." But they can also be organized by NGOs as voluntary, coordinated consumer actions. It may seem that strictly voluntary boycotts would be ineffective against any company of size unless they succeeded in enlisting an enormous number of consumers. In one sense, that is true. But it is not necessary to enlist enough consumer support to drastically reduce company sales. Most companies will notice and take seriously anything that shaves a point or two off the company's sales or even sales growth.

In the past, voluntary international boycotts have been effective in changing the behavior of even very large multinational firms whose products are sold to ordinary consumers. In the 1970s and 1980s, a boycott of Nestlé, the multinational food products firm, triggered by serious concerns as to the health implications of its aggressive marketing of infant formula in Third World countries, ultimately resulted in the company agreeing to make major changes in its practices in 1984. In 1990, a boycott of canned tuna targeted the practice of catching tuna in nets that also killed dolphins. Within a short time Heinz, the owner of the StarKist brand, announced it would buy only tuna that was caught in ways that protected dolphins. Its two biggest competitors, Chicken of the Sea and Bumble Bee, immediately agreed to follow suit.[27] In 1989, the Roper polling organization reported that nearly a quarter of the people it surveyed indicated that they had personally supported consumer boycotts of at least one product.[28]

During the 1990s, a number of organizations called for a large-scale consumer boycott of Nike, the major multinational sports shoe and apparel manufacturer. Their reasons differed, and it would be an exaggeration to say that the groups constituted a real coalition. But most of the organizations calling for a Nike boycott, such as Global Exchange, were concerned about the operation of sweatshops by the company (and its subcontractors) in LDCs where workers, including children, were said to labor in unsafe and unhealthy conditions for very little pay. On May 12, 1998, after years of battling with the boycotters, Nike's CEO Phil Knight agreed to meet many of their demands in a public speech at the National Press Club in Washington, D.C. Knight made six specific commitments, including: 1) U.S. Occupational Safety and Health Administration (OSHA) standards would be met in all Nike shoe factories; 2) No workers younger than eighteen would be hired in Nike shoe factories, and none younger than sixteen in other apparel factories; and 3) Nike would allow NGOs to monitor its factories for compliance and would make their reports public.[29] In short, Nike made a dramatic public commitment to stop operating sweatshops and to require adherence to a code promoting safer, healthier, less exploitative labor practices by its LDC suppliers.[30]

The pressure exerted on companies by boycotts, threats of boycotts, and even the unfavorable publicity that results from "naming and shaming" those firms that are behaving badly should not be underestimated. Widely publicized "naming and shaming" by advocacy NGOs was, for example, crucial in convincing the wealthy and powerful De Beers diamond cartel and other diamond companies to support the Kimberly Process, a certification system aimed at curtailing the trade in so-called conflict diamonds, diamonds being looted and sold by violent groups to enrich themselves and to finance the ongoing violent conflicts in which they engaged.[31]

Demand side actions by the ordinary public are naturally more powerful in pushing consumer-oriented firms to change their behavior than in affecting the behavior of producers that sell mainly to other firms. Even very large firms that sell to the general public are quite sensitive to such pressures. With patience and persistence, it is possible to influence them to change their ways of doing business in the service of greater sensitivity to social costs and benefits. On March 27, 2007, Burger King, the world's second largest chain of hamburger restaurants, announced that it would finally accede to a six-year campaign by animal welfare advocates and begin buying pork and eggs from suppliers that did not confine their animals in crates or cages.[32] In April 2007, Home Depot, the world's largest buyer of construction material, announced that it would display a new "Eco Options" label on the products it sells that promote energy conservation, sustainable forestry, and clean water. It agreed to encourage sales of these products through an aggressive marketing campaign, and by giving them prominent shelf space in its 2,000 U.S. stores. This new program was in no small measure the ultimate result of nearly a decade of repeated protests against environmentally questionable company practices. Two years earlier Walmart, the world's largest retail firm, had made a commitment to reduce energy use in its stores, improve the fuel efficiency of its truck fleet, and minimize packaging, after many years of pressure from environmentalists.[33]

It is difficult to organize effective voluntary boycotts against exploitative business practices, but history shows it is certainly possible when the behavior of the company in question is sufficiently egregious to offend the sense of ethics and morality of large numbers of people. Voluntary boycotts take a long time to organize and grow to sufficient size to put significant pressure on the firms involved. They take still longer to produce the desired change in company behavior, and success is by no means guaranteed. Even if boycotts do succeed, continued monitoring is required to ensure that the companies do not return to those or other equally unfair practices when they are no longer in the spotlight.

It is probably a good thing that it is not easy to organize a large-scale effective boycott. If it were, that could be unduly disruptive of the flow of business. A plethora of boycotts could easily result, including many "dueling boycotts" in which different groups were boycotting the same company's products and demanding that it take contradictory actions. After all, many different people might object to one or another practice of many companies for any number of reasons. At the same time, privately organized consumer boycotts are an important manifestation of freedom and democracy in the marketplace. They can be an important tool with which the public can push companies to engage in more equitable business practices—including those that support Principle I—without the intervention of governments.

Although it often takes a lot of time and effort to pressure companies into changing their business policies and practices, it may well turn out that the managements of companies that do move in the direction of greater corporate social responsibility are rewarded by the market, and not just by good feelings for having done the "right thing." For example, there is significant evidence that corporate charitable contributions pay off handsomely in terms of the company's bottom line. By one estimate, an average growth of six dollars in future sales is associated with every dollar of contributions the company makes to charitable causes.[34] There is every reason to expect that other socially responsible corporate behavior could easily produce similar rewards.

The combination of external consumer and investor pressure, reinforced by internal pressure from employees and managers, has even led to the recent growth of what some have called the "fourth sector," made up of organizations driven by both social and financial goals that fall somewhere between what we think of as conventional companies and what we think of as charities. These organizations are also called "for-benefit corporations." For example, Altrushare Securities, a brokerage firm that buys and sells stocks and provides research on companies to investors, is owned mainly by two charities. According to Peter Drasher, its founder, "What makes us different is our nonprofit ownership and our mission, which is to support struggling communities with our profits." Heerad Sabeti, co-founder in 2005 of Trans-Forms, a wall decorations company with sales of close to $2 million, put it this way: "We want social responsibility to be completely embedded in everything we do, not something that occurs as sort of a sideline."[35]

In 1993, Coen Gilbert founded the $200-million shoe company "And 1," which provided a variety of work-life enriching perks to its employees and hired an independent auditor to monitor compliance by its suppliers to And 1's requirement that they refrain from sweatshop labor practices. The company also contributed 5 percent of its profits to charity. Earlier examples of firms famous for their commitment to various "socially responsible" business practices were the Body Shop and Ben and Jerry's. It is worth noting, however, that the owners of all three of these companies ultimately sold out to conglomerates, some of which have continued some of these practices while others have not. Yet other significant socially responsible companies, such as Patagonia, have refused to sell out. There is clearly more support today among investors and consumers for companies to take a longer term and broader view of what is good for the company as well as for the wider society than there was during the era in which the Body Shop and Ben and Jerry's evolved.[36] Over the long term, pressure from consumers and investors has begun to create the context for a sea change in the way business is viewed and conducted, a sea change that could help facilitate movement to a norm of balanced economic relationships.

It is best to think of these varied approaches to implementing Principle I as mutually compatible alternatives, each partially effective, each with its own advantages and drawbacks. Taken together, they constitute a package in which the government, the private sector, and the public at large all have parts to play in creating the more balanced, mutually beneficial economic relationships that are a key element of an international peacekeeping economy.

Implementing Principle II: Seek Independence in Critical Goods

It is in the area of critical goods that the concerns of the realists/neorealists about the vulnerability produced by interdependence are most salient. Accepting this, critical goods are the sole exception to the more general strategy of encouraging broad-based interdependence. Establishing independence in critical goods can be difficult and expensive. Just how difficult and expensive it is depends on a considerable variety of political, social, cultural, and economic factors.

The purpose of critical goods independence is to reduce vulnerability to supply cutoffs in emergency situations. It is therefore not necessary to be fully and continuously independent of external sources of supply; it is important only to have enough capability and flexibility to ride out extended interference with normal trade in critical goods. There are a number of reasonable approaches available, but since critical goods independence is an artificial political goal imposed on the economic system by security considerations, all of them require some sort of government action. In keeping with the argument that the most effective and appropriate role for government is to set rules of the game that align private interest with public goals, all but one of the approaches involves restructuring the incentive system, rather than direct intervention.

Tariffs on Critical Goods

Imposing tariffs on imports of critical goods reduces the attractiveness of these imports to domestic consumers, raising prices and creating greater profit-based incentives for domestic producers to increase their output. By arbitrarily increasing the prices of foreign products to domestic consumers, tariffs reduce the pressure of competition, the most important force driving efficiency in a market economy. It is therefore not surprising that they do not have a lot of support among economists. Why, then, recommend them here?

There are two ways of looking at the case for tariffs on imports of critical goods as a viable and sensible policy for working toward critical goods independence. The first is to accept the argument that tariffs do inevitably produce inefficiencies and interfere with the benefits of trade, and yet to argue that the security benefits of critical goods independence outweigh these economic costs. The second is to argue that, if it has created dependence on very few foreign sources of supply, free trade in critical goods has had a serious negative security impact on the wider society. This "security externality" causes a gap between the narrow private cost-benefit calculations of consumers and firms, and the broader calculations of society-wide costs and benefits. By better aligning the two sets of calculations, critical goods tariffs increase social efficiency through the market. Either way, although tariffs on critical goods increase the immediate costs of these goods to domestic consumers, they are not difficult to justify.

Taxes on imports of critical goods cannot increase the domestic physical availability of the resources needed to produce those goods. But by raising the prices of critical goods, they increase the *economic* feasibility of exploiting less readily accessible resources. If, for example, drought has rendered water in short supply, no tariff will increase rainfall or the flow of river water. But by increasing the cost of water, a tariff will create incentives to: 1) develop water sources that were always available but previously too expensive to utilize, such as deeper underground aquifers; 2) use and improve new and existing but more expensive technologies to produce potable water, such as desalinization; and 3) use and recycle available water more carefully. By analogy, with higher prices there will be a greater incentive to increase food production on the same land by using more costly but more technically efficient and intensive agricultural practices.

Similarly, the availability of domestically produced energy can be increased by shifting to new sources, whether renewable forms of energy that may be more expensive (or involve transition costs) or lower grade deposits of fossil fuels. As it turns out, even the United States, the world's largest energy consumer and a huge importer of fossil fuels, has enough available ecologically benign renewable sources of energy to supply a great deal more if not all of its energy needs. As I discussed in the previous chapter, there are, for example, developable wind power resources available in forty-six of the fifty states; solar energy is also abundant. The commercial exploitation of these resources would certainly be encouraged by the higher prices that would result from tariffs on imported energy. So would more attention to efficient energy use.

There are a number of important cautions here. The first and most com-pelling is that using tariffs in this way requires that great care be taken to protect the poorer parts of the population against the increases in the prices of critical goods these tariffs will create, precisely because we are talking about *critical* goods, basic necessities of life. Any policy that raises the cost of basic necessities of life has the potential to be economically dev-astating, even life-threatening to the poor. Common decency, along with considerations of political and economic stability, requires that such poli-cies be coupled to some form of subsidy that will cushion the poor, espe-cially in the less developed countries. If we have learned nothing else from the disasters the IMF has repeatedly precipitated with its poorly designed "conditionalities" programs, it should be this.[37]

Second, it is important not to be too facile about the assumption that domestic producers in every country will rapidly increase production to fill the gap created by raising the cost of imported goods. In part, that depends on the market structure of the domestic critical goods supplying indus-tries. If these industries are monopolistic, they may simply take advantage of the added market power that the reduction in foreign competition gives them to restrict available output further and drive prices up (especially because critical goods are likely to be price inelastic). The more competi-tive these industries are, the less likely this is to occur. So it may make sense to couple critical goods tariffs with some appropriate form of regula-tory or antitrust policy. The ability of domestic producers to expand pro-duction also depends on the nation's technological capability as well as the availability of capital to finance the necessary investments. Even where the technology and the capital are available, it may take some time to construct the physical facilities required to expand domestic production of critical goods (e.g., new power generating plants and water treatment facilities), and perhaps also to train the required workforces. In economic terms, do-mestic supply may not be all that elastic in the short to medium term even if it is in the long term, so this policy requires a longer-term view.

Finally, not every country has the resources required to make it feasible to produce all of the critical goods it needs on its own, especially if cost con-siderations are taken into account. Critical goods tariffs do not change this basic fact of life.

Subsidies to Domestic Producers

Like tariffs, subsidies are intended to give domestic producers an advantage over foreign producers, encouraging the development of domestic sources of supply. The difference lies mainly in who bears the cost of providing domestic producers with this artificial competitive edge. In the case of tariffs, the burden is borne by those who directly or indirectly buy the critical goods being taxed.[38] Since lower income people spend more of their income on critical goods, price increases created by the tariffs will fall more heavily on the poor. In the case of subsidies, the burden is borne by those who provide the government with the money required to finance the subsidies, typically the taxpayers. Whether lower or higher income people bear the largest relative burden in financing subsidies depends on how regressive or progressive the general tax system is.

The argument for subsidies to domestic producers of critical goods is essentially the same as the argument for tariffs on imported critical goods. It will encourage domestic producers to expand their output, even where doing so requires that they exploit more expensive resources or use more expensive techniques of production. Again, we can look at this either as a cost that is justified by the security benefits critical goods independence would provide, or as a means of correcting the failure of the market to account for the negative security impacts of relying on a few foreign sources of supply for critical goods.

Similarly, pretty much the same cautions apply here as in the case of tariffs, especially the importance of taking into account the impact of the policy on the nation's lower income population. It is certainly possible to blunt the impact of production subsidies on the poor by financing the subsidies with a deliberately progressive tax. That may prove to be politically and administratively easier to implement than handing out money to the poor to compensate them for the higher prices that tariffs have induced.

Government-Funded or Subsidized Technology Development and Adoption

Government has historically been an important facilitator of the development and deployment of new technology. As a joint report of the U.S. National

Academy of Sciences, National Academy of Engineering, and Institute of Medicine pointed out in 1992, "The U.S. government played an important role in facilitating investment, stimulating R&D and technology generation, and promoting technology adoption in sectors [of the civilian economy] such as commercial aerospace, agriculture, energy, and health care. . . . Indeed, in aircraft, high performance computers, and agriculture, the federal government had a direct role in the creation of industries that today dominate world commerce and generate export surpluses for the United States."[39] Government encouragement of the development and adoption of new technologies aimed at creating critical goods independence can fit neatly into this historical pattern.

In addition to funding key research at government laboratories and universities throughout the country, governments can apply regulatory pressure to private sector producers to encourage directed technological progress. For example, by 2006 a number of state governments in the U.S. had established a regulatory mandate that all producers of electricity operating within the state had to have a specified fraction of their electricity generating capacity or sales derived from renewable energy resources (such as wind power, hydropower, and solar energy). This approach, instituted mainly for purposes related to climate change mitigation and pollution control, has had some real success at encouraging the adoption of renewable energy technologies in the short to medium term, which is by itself bound to stimulate the further development and thus adoption of these technologies in the long term (as a result of cost reduction and technological advance).

The government can also facilitate the development and deployment of new critical goods technologies simply by providing a "seed market," a market that gives private sector producers a place to ease into an important, potentially profitable new market that might otherwise seem too risky to enter. A seed market can also give risk-averse customers a chance to see how well the new product works in practice, so that they feel comfortable entering the market as buyers. As Alic, Mowery, and Rubin remind us, "Government procurement during World War I transformed an infant aircraft industry that had produced a cumulative total of only a few hundred planes; by the war's end, U.S. firms had manufactured some 14,000 planes, with much concomitant learning."[40]

Government procurement, as well as R&D support, has also been critical to the creation and extended predominance of the U.S. computer and semi-conductor industries. According to the 1992 National Academy report: "In the 1950s and early 1960s, government military purchases of semiconductors . . . aided the development of the U.S. semiconductor industry. Through R&D and procurement programs, federal assistance to private R&D projects helped to lower production costs through subsidization of manufacturing test and production facilities. . . . The federal government [also] played an important, direct role in the commercial development of the computer in-dustry. . . . [G]overnment procurement practices . . . helped insure a[n] [early] market for products."[41]

Whether through direct funding, regulatory pressure, or seed markets, if government is successful in encouraging the development and deploy-ment of new, more efficient critical goods technologies (such as new ap-proaches for desalinizing seawater, improved technologies for using domestic renewable energy sources, or enhanced agricultural techniques), it can dramatically lower the cost of achieving critical goods independence and thus enhanced security. Realistically, this approach will probably require a considerable financial outlay in the short to medium term. But that outlay should be thought of as an investment, not an expenditure. There is a real prospect that it will result in a very large return in the long run in the form of reduced cost of providing critical goods.

Paradoxically, this approach may also increase trade, at least during the transition to the new technologies, as producers in those countries that have developed the most efficient, lowest cost versions of these technolo-gies (and/or the devices that embed them) sell them to customers in other nations. Interestingly, unlike arms sales, which to some degree cancel out the security advantages of having developed a technological edge, the dif-fusion of technologies that are useful in achieving critical goods indepen-dence may make everyone more secure by eliminating conflict-generating vulnerabilities.

Stockpiling Critical Goods

It is clearly harder to stockpile certain categories of critical goods. Goods or materials that are highly corrosive, toxic, explosive, or otherwise very physically unstable are dangerous and expensive to store (and safeguard) in large quantities. Fortunately, relatively few truly critical goods fall into that category. However, many critical goods are difficult or expensive to stockpile in large enough quantities to provide a long-term buffer against supply disruptions because they are perishable (or otherwise degrade in quality over time) or because they have low value compared to their volume or weight. Both potable water and many kinds of food fall into this category. Although it is perfectly possible for governments to create stockpiles of food and water that could protect their population against disruptions of external supplies that persist for a weeks or months, other approaches must be used for longer-term independence. The same is true of oil, especially for an economy as dependent as the U.S. on external sources of supply.[42] Stockpiling oil has some value in protecting against short-term supply shocks, but it is clearly impractical as a more enduring energy independence strategy.

Stockpiling makes sense for a few key, high value raw materials. Which raw materials fall into this category is sensitive to the nature of the economy in any particular country. The U.S inventory of what it defines as "strategic and critical materials essential to military and industrial requirements in time of national emergency" includes materials such as bauxite, chromium, lead, manganese, palladium, platinum, silver, titanium, tungsten, and zinc. The combined total value of these inventories is far below the value of the strategic petroleum reserve.

In general, it is probably best to think of government-funded stockpiling as a useful, specialized, short-term adjunct to a broader program of critical goods independence.

Supplier Network Diversification

While diversifying networks of foreign suppliers is not a path toward critical goods independence in the literal sense, it does reduce dependence on any particular source of supply. The nation is made more secure because it is less vulnerable to manipulation by threatened or actual disruptions by any one supplier. It is still vulnerable to the economic pressure that can be generated by broad multilateral boycotts imposed by the coordinated action of those nations that are part of its current or potential network of suppliers, but that is probably a good thing. It means that though the nation may be protected against arbitrary pressure from one or two key supplier nations with which it may have come into conflict, it is still subject to the discipline of economic sanctions if its behavior is bad enough to cause a large enough group of nations to agree on joint action.

Of course, diversification of supply networks does not prevent another, more militarily powerful nation from imposing a unilateral military blockade and trying to interdict incoming shipments of critical goods from all suppliers. In that sense, this approach does not offer as much protection as do strategies aimed at expanding domestic production. Still, interdicting shipments from all suppliers by all routes is no simple matter, except in the most extreme cases (e.g., a small island nation blockaded by a great naval power). And having a broadly diversified supplier network guarantees that unless the behavior that triggered the blockade was particularly egregious, the nation instituting the unilateral action would come under pressure from a whole group of supplier nations to lift the blockade and stop interfering with their commerce.[43]

The normal operation of the market does not necessarily lead naturally to a broad diversification of suppliers. There may, for example, be economies of scale (resulting from economies of production, reduced transactions costs, etc.) or technological advantages to dealing with one or a small number of suppliers that make it cost-effective to have a more concentrated supply network under normal conditions. If so, implementing this strategy may require a degree of government intervention. There could be government regulations that require those firms or government entities dealing with key categories of critical goods to limit their reliance on suppliers from any one nation to a specified percentage of their purchases. Or the government could offer positive incentives to diversify through tax credits, for example, to those firms that have achieved a specified level of supplier diversification.

The problem with all of this is that it can easily become too arbitrary and heavy-handed. Although government does have a compelling interest in providing security, undue interference in the normal operation of business will impose excessive cost on an otherwise well-functioning market economy. The lightest touch that will achieve the objective is therefore the best. For example, the national security interest in foreign critical goods supplier diversification does not require that every firm dependent on foreign sources of critical goods have a diversified supply network, only that the firms in any given critical industry taken as a group do. Furthermore, though there may be cost or technology-based incentives to have a more concentrated supply network, there are also natural economic incentives for firms not to be wholly dependent on a narrow supplier base. That is especially true where there is a real possibility that political hostilities may cause their supplier's home government to shut down that trade. It may be enough for the government to offer periodic advisories about the political risk of interference with critical goods supplies from any given nation to get businesses to take this risk seriously and diversify.

Implementing Principle III: Emphasize Development

There has been a long-standing debate, among politicians as well as those who specialize in studying development, as to whether "aid" or "trade" is more effective at stimulating substantial, broad-based improvements in material well-being. It is an important question.

Those on the "aid" side of the argument believe that technological backwardness and the lack of financial and physical capital are the most important obstacles to development. If the MDCs rich in capital and technological knowledge would transfer sufficient quantities of these resources to the LDCs as foreign aid, the logjam would be broken and the LDCs could make real progress in closing the gap. Those on the "trade" side of the argument do not doubt that the lack of sufficient capital and technological resources in the LDCs interferes with their development, but they believe that increasing trade in a growing world economy is the most effective path to providing LDCs with the wherewithal to acquire the needed resources and the incentives to use them efficiently. They do not believe that simply transferring the resources is effective, no matter how well intentioned it might be. There is some truth to both sides of this argument.

Aid

It is first important to differentiate between aid as a humanitarian gesture and aid as an adjunct to development. The difference between the two is analogous to the difference, as the old saying goes, between "giving someone a fish" (which feeds them for a day) and "teaching them how to fish" (which feeds them for a lifetime). Humanitarian aid is intended to meet immediate needs in an emergency situation. When disaster strikes, whether in the form of earthquake, tsunami, or war, there is no substitute for direct aid to those who are most threatened or damaged. They must live through the crisis before they can do what is necessary to rebuild their lives. But as critical as it can be, this kind of relatively short-term aid has very little to do with development. Development aid is intended to build the capacity of aid recipients to meet their own needs. Its goal is therefore to put itself out of business. The success of development aid can be measured by how quickly, completely, and permanently it eliminates the need for further development aid.

There is considerable evidence that development aid has not generally been effective in the past.[44] For example, focusing on Sub-Saharan Africa (SSA), Farahnaaz Khakoo writes,

> In the post-colonial era, SSA was identified as one of the most poverty-stricken regions in the world, likely to sink into further deprivation without some sort of assistance from industrialized countries. Foreign assistance in the form of grants, concessional loans, and technical assistance was to be a primary development tool to combat poverty and under-development. . . .
>
> Five decades and over $400 billion in grants and loans later, SSA is still one of the most impoverished regions in the world. . . . One in two people live on less than $1/day, one in three children do not complete primary school, and one in six children dies before the age of five.[45]

On the other hand, the $12–$14 billion of foreign aid that the U.S. poured into the nations of Western Europe between 1948 and 1951 under the auspices of the so-called Marshall Plan was spectacularly successful in helping those nations to rapidly rebuild their war-ravaged economies.

There are, of course, many important differences between post–World War II Western Europe and Sub-Saharan Africa. Yet there may be something useful to be learned from the very different impacts of foreign aid on development in these two situations. First, this disparity is clear evidence of the critical importance of investment in human capital. Although the physical capital of Western Europe had been terribly damaged during

World War II and millions of people had died, the pool of available human capital (skilled and educated labor) was much greater in Europe than it has been in Africa. All over the world, when skilled and educated people are provided with the incentives, financing, and the physical equipment and material they need, rapid economic progress follows.

Second, aid is most effective when it is designed and implemented cooperatively, with the active participation of both recipients and donors. Many African aid projects have been completely (or nearly completely) donor-driven. The Marshall Plan was not. U.S. Secretary of State George C. Marshall pushed hard for the nations of Europe to decide what they needed to rebuild their own economies, so that the financial and material aid the U.S. was providing could be better integrated into a broad, coordinated program of economic renewal. Khakoo's work on Sub-Saharan Africa provides some evidence that aid (at least in the form of technical assistance) became more effective in encouraging development in the late 1990s and early 2000s, when donors began to emphasize more cooperative approaches, than it had been in the previous twenty years when they did not.[46] Foreign aid can be an important stimulus to development if it is properly designed and implemented.

Making aid more effective also requires institution building. But Mary Shirley argues that those who administer donor aid programs often have neither the incentives nor the tools to foster institutional change needed in recipient countries to make aid more effective. They are more absorbed by the process of approving projects than they are by evaluating and improving project performance.[47] In poorer countries for which aid is a significant part of the budget, the government may become so focused on managing aid projects that non-aid-funded projects that address important domestic problems are shortchanged. Impressive looking but ill-conceived projects, backed by the authority of high status donor organizations and governments, direct the attention and resources of recipient governments away from projects that might look less impressive but that are actually far more important to development. As Everhart and McNab put it, "Aid can take away time from adequate production and put time into acquisition of skill and knowledge in obtaining a share of foreign aid."[48] Recipient governments can get "caught in a cycle of attracting aid, managing aid, and creating environments for more types of aid. As a result, domestic issues such as education, health care and sanitation are often put on the back burner."[49]

The effectiveness of aid delivery also commonly suffers from inadequate donor understanding of the political, economic, social, historical, and cultural contexts of recipient countries, which are so important in determining aid outcomes. This problem is exacerbated by the all-too-frequent use of "high profile," short-term "fly-in, fly-out" development consultants who understand neither the local context nor the context of the wider society to which their therefore less-than-appropriate advice is directed. Furthermore, the fact that such consultants are too often not held accountable for the effects of what they have done—or even for the accuracy of what they claim to have achieved—greatly diminishes any incentive to correct this behavior.[50] All of this further highlights the importance of the active collaboration between donors (who command the necessary resources and perhaps the missing technical and economic expertise) and recipients (who at the very least understand the context of their own societies) in designing and implementing development aid.

Similarly, the ability of aid to stimulate real gains in development can be undercut by "resource diversion"—the use of productive economic resources for economically unproductive purposes (Chapter 7).[51] In the case at hand, diversion of resources tends to take two main forms: 1) corruption; and 2) excessive military expenditure. Corruption has been a central issue in the international development community since the late 1990s, when the World Bank and other international organizations launched anticorruption missions worldwide.[52] Corrupt government officials have been known to divert aid money to projects other than those for which it was intended, and perhaps even more commonly to personal accounts. But corruption originating in the practices of the MDCs has also interfered with the progress of less developed countries.[53]

The economically unproductive nature of military expenditures means that the diversion of valuable economic resources to military-oriented activity burdens any economy, rich or poor. As with any other economic deadweight, LDC economies are more damaged by an excessive military burden because they can less afford to waste what resources they do have. During three potentially critical decades for development, from 1960 to the end of the Cold War in 1990, the LDCs of the world spent well in excess of $2 trillion on their militaries, a staggering total. To understand the enormity of this expenditure, consider that it would take a continuously operating press printing $1,000 every second starting on January 1, 2011, until the middle of the year 2074 to print this much money. In 1960, the LDCs accounted for about 8 percent of worldwide military spending; by 1990, their *share* had more than doubled to 17 percent.[54] This same basic pattern continued even after the Cold War ended. According to data from the highly regarded Stockholm International Peace Research Institute (SIPRI), from 1991 to 2005 the LDCs spent roughly an additional $2.5 trillion (in constant 2003 dollars) on their militaries, accounting for an average of roughly 20 percent of the world total.[55]

Finally, there is the problem of "enclave economies," economies characterized by pockets of production—typically mining, oil and gas production, and "estate agriculture"—disconnected from the rest of economic activity within the country. Foreign aid provided to governments in countries with enclave economies has in the past often helped to sustain these disjointed economies, rather than encouraging real development. Worse yet, Leonard and Strauss find that such aid actually increases the likelihood of conflict and instability.[56]

Trade

While targeted, well-designed, and properly implemented foreign aid can help break through critical roadblocks to development, balanced, mutually beneficial trade is probably more important than foreign assistance in the long run. Many empirical studies of less developed countries from the 1970s to the beginning of the twenty-first century seem to indicate that exports and development are strongly positively related.[57] Unless trade is confined to enclaves detached from the wider economy and society, revenue from export earnings is quite important in facilitating development. With the right institutional context, strong export markets can encourage the growth of private sector businesses and provide a source of profits that can be used to finance the investment necessary to sustain that growth. Taxes on export revenues, in the case of private sector production, or export revenues themselves, in the case of government-owned produc-

tion, can also be an important source of finance for government development initiatives.

Even if foreign aid is successful in building the capacity of LDC economies to produce more and better products, there has to be a solid market to
mobilize their increased capacity or they will not be able to provide a growing standard of living for their people. It is true that that market could be
domestic as well as foreign, but experience shows that it is faster and easier to
accelerate development by at least initially aiming at existing well-developed
markets abroad. In poorer countries, because they are poorer countries,
domestic markets for most products are small. Small markets do not generally provide sufficient incentive for the scale of investment necessary to
get the economy moving, while bigger, more profitable markets abroad are
inherently more enticing, especially to the private sector. Of course, the
goals of economic development cannot be achieved unless the gains in
wages and other incomes created in the process of servicing export markets are sufficiently well distributed among the population. Widely distributed increases in incomes will broaden domestic markets and make them
stronger over time. Otherwise, there may be growth, but there will not be
development.

Stimulating Trade

One of the most effective ways of stimulating LDC exports is by eliminating trade barriers against them, particularly in the MDCs. While the
various rounds of trade negotiations under the auspices of the World Trade
Organization and its pre-1995 predecessor (GATT) have been quite successful in reducing trade barriers against the kinds of goods and services
produced by the MDCs, they have been much less successful at reducing
restrictions on trade in goods that constitute a key part of LDC production.
This is especially true of agricultural produce.

To be fair, even putting considerations of critical goods independence
aside, reducing agricultural trade barriers does present a particularly difficult domestic political problem for MDCs because of the disproportionate political strength of the agricultural sector. This problem is particularly
obvious in the U.S., where Senate approval is required for trade pacts and
each state has two senators, regardless of its population. The considerable

number of more sparsely populated states whose economic base is largely agricultural translates into a power bloc that has historically tended to be less than overjoyed at the prospect of throwing open the doors to competition from agriculture abroad. Nevertheless, progress has recently been made in the direction of lowering at least some agricultural trade barriers. More will be said about this in Chapter 6.

Reducing or eliminating MDC trade barriers against LDC products may stimulate greater trade flows, but it is not enough to ensure that that trade will be balanced and mutually beneficial. If huge multinational agricultural production, processing, and distribution firms control the MDC side of this trade, it is unlikely that it will be balanced. If large landholders and monopolistic private marketing organizations control the LDC side of this trade, it is unlikely that the gains will be broadly enough distributed to generate meaningful progress in development. So, a serious amount of antitrust activity (coupled with a degree of regulation, if necessary) might be required to keep the game honest. Because stimulating trade will lead to real development only if the resulting trade is balanced and mutually beneficial, much of the discussion related to implementing Principle I applies here as well.

If growing international trade stimulates a wide range of economic activities that involve the bulk of the population, it will be very important in generating economic development. But there is a danger (though by no means a certainty) that export-oriented development strategies will stimulate production that is not really integrated with the rest of the domestic economy and consequently enriches only a small portion of the population. *If* this becomes a problem, there are two main ways of ensuring that the economic gains from increased export activity spread broadly enough to trigger real development.

The first is for the government to collect tax from the enterprises and/or individuals who gain from the unbalanced growth that is created by the expansion of exports, and redistribute the wealth after the fact. This redistribution does not have to be in the form of welfare payments. It would make more sense for the government to invest the bulk of the tax money it collects in activities that increase economic opportunity for those initially left out of the export boom. These should include investments in education, health, and nutrition that create productive jobs now while increasing human capital and thus improving the society's future economic capability. It should also include investments in what used to be called "public works"—transportation, communication, water supply, and power generation infrastructure—to create still more productive jobs in the short run and build the critical economic base needed to support further development.

The second way is for the government to create incentives that encourage private business to develop new lines of economic activity that spread the growth to other economic sectors and geographic regions. This might be done through tax breaks, seed capital, short-term subsidies, and the like, the whole range of levers available to government to shape and stimulate private sector investment. Again, the government should not micromanage these projects or make the incentives too specific and directed. It is important to leave room for entrepreneurial talent and creativity to operate. In fact, the kind of government investment in human and infrastructure capital advocated above may, in the medium to long run, be among the most effective incentives that government can create for private sector investment to branch out and thus "spread the wealth."

Increasing the Effectiveness of Development Aid

As with trade, there are so many complexities to the problem of designing and delivering effective development aid that it is the subject of much ongoing discussion and debate. So as with trade, I will focus only on a few key elements of this problem I have mentioned earlier: 1) the importance of understanding the political, economic, social, historical, and cultural contexts of recipient countries; 2) the value of donor-recipient collaboration; and 3) the need to minimize resource diversion in aid-receiving economies.

The Importance of Context

Most economists, especially those with a neoclassical bent, tend to systematically underestimate the importance of societal context in determining aid outcomes. They are working with a "black box" model of economic behavior in which people are the equivalent of rational, utility maximizing machines. While they formally recognize that different individuals do, in general, have different preferences for goods and services (as well as for labor and leisure), they nevertheless believe that in reality people react in a similar ways to the same changes in the objective conditions facing them. It is therefore perfectly sensible to apply the same model of behavior and to advocate the same type of policy to achieve the same goals across different societies. They do not sufficiently appreciate the importance of culture, historical experience, and social norms in causing people to interpret the world differently and thus react differently to what might appear to an outside observer to be the same objective change in circumstance. And, except for institutional economists, they also tend to underappreciate the extent to which different political and economic institutional contexts can radically alter the effects of the same economic policies.

For example, in the early 1990s, Western (chiefly U.S.) economists advocated that Russia adopt the so-called shock therapy approach in transitioning from centrally planned socialism to free market capitalism. They thought the best way to move away from an economic system that suffered from excessive bureaucratic control and the lack of individual motivating incentives was to get rid of those oppressive controls, establish property rights, and increase individual freedom of action as quickly as possible. Yes, they argued, there would be some pain as the prices of necessities rose from subsidized to market levels and as unemployment rose because privatization of business gave the new owners the right to fire unnecessary workers. But with private property and increased economic freedom of action, the market system would soon do in Russia what it does in the more developed market economies—trigger an outburst of entrepreneurial activity, competition among producers that leads to increases in product quantity and quality, greater investment, and rising productivity. The result would soon be higher incomes, reasonably stable prices, and general economic prosperity.

There are a number of reasons why these expectations were not realized, except for the pain, which was deeper, more widespread, and more prolonged than predicted. Among them was the lack of such basic economic institutions as commercial banks, securities exchanges, insurance companies, and contract law. As a consequence, there was no way for independent would-be entrepreneurs to raise capital to fund their business ventures, manage ordinary business risk, or establish and enforce arm's length contracts with suppliers and customers they did not personally know and were not linked to by family ties or friendship networks. Even more telling, after more than seventy years of centrally planned economy, there was no one in Russia with any real experience in operating private market-driven enterprises, aside from the criminals who had been engaged in black market activity. There was also a deeply entrenched culture of corrupt, personalized economic relations and well-established patterns of working around official rules to get what was wanted and needed.

It is not therefore all that surprising that the process of privatizing the nation's economic assets turned into what the Russians came to call the "Big Grab," with those who were well placed in the existing power structure taking over control of public assets at bargain basement prices. Nor is it surprising that criminals and their gangs came to control much of the Russian economy. Furthermore, because the Soviet (especially Stalinist) era economy was characterized by huge enterprises and large-scale plants, privatization turned state monopolies into private monopolies rather than stimulating the kind of competition responsible for the efficiency and resource allocative advantages of a market economy. An economy of private monopolies is no one's idea of an efficient or equitable market system. The point is that what (we will assume) was perfectly well-intentioned development advice, delivered by intelligent and highly educated Western advisers, created a major disaster from which Russia may only now be slowly emerging, because that advice was totally insensitive to institutional, historical, and cultural considerations.

There are all too many examples of aid to less developed countries that have followed a similar pattern. The lesson of these unfortunate experiences is clear and compelling: whether the donor organization or government is providing funding to finance specific aid projects or merely advice, it will be only an accident if aid is effective in the absence of specific attention being paid to these critical issues of context.

The Value of Collaboration

There are three main reasons why donor-recipient collaboration is a key element determining the effectiveness of development assistance. First, the issue of societal context we have just discussed makes it critical that people with deep knowledge of the culture, history, politics, etc., of the recipient country be involved in designing any serious development project and in working out the details of how it will be implemented. Although it is true that not everyone who lives within a society understands it equally well, and it is possible that outsiders who have studied that particular society long and hard may know it better than most insiders, in general it is much more likely that those who live in the recipient country will have greater knowledge of its inner workings. On the other hand, if they are intelligently chosen, outsiders selected by donors to design and implement the project will have the technical expertise required in addition to access to the requisite resources, both of which are likely to be in short supply in-country. Working together, outside experts and recipient country personnel combine the knowledge, experience, and understanding necessary to maximize the likelihood that the project will actually help those it is intended to help.

Second, if the goal of the development assistance is really to make life materially better for those living in the recipient country, it is wisest to learn from those being helped what they think would be most helpful. They know better than anyone else what they want and need, what would make them better off in their own eyes. Since there are almost certain to be different opinions within varying factions of the country as to what the nation's most pressing needs actually are, it is important to work out a reasonably inclusive process to decide on project priorities. It is possible that what those in the recipient country most want may be different from what the donors are willing to assist in doing, and donor priorities and cultural sensitivities also matter. The best way to work out a solution that everyone can accept is precisely by negotiation among a collaborative donor-recipient project team.

Finally, as I argued earlier, relationships in which decision power is more balanced are stronger because both sides feel greater "ownership" in the relationship. That same principle applies here as well. If donor personnel call all the shots, recipient country participants will have little invested in the project, and will tend to be less willing to do what is necessary to watch for and cope with the unexpected problems that inevitably arise. If they do not think of the project as theirs, recipient country officials might see such problems as a demonstration that donor country officials and their surrogates are not so expert as they claim, and perhaps as proof that their own ideas should have been taken more seriously. That is just human nature. If they do play an important role in designing and implementing the project, recipient country personnel are more likely to see failures of the project as their own failures, and therefore do whatever needs to be done to prevent or overcome them. Here, too, there is no doubt that self-interest is a powerful motivator.

Minimizing Resource Diversion

Both corruption and excessive military spending are responsible for diverting large quantities of resources that could otherwise be used to stimulate development. They are both difficult problems to solve. Corruption is so entrenched in the fabric of many societies that those who exercise public power do not hesitate to use that power for their own personal benefit. In the case of police and low-level officials, salaries are often so low as to encourage corruption, at the very least providing a convenient rationalization for corrupt behavior even in the absence of extraordinary greed or arrogance. In the case of leaders, raiding the public treasury or accepting large private contributions from those who want favors can come to be viewed as an effective way of maintaining elite political support, if not as an outright prerogative of power. Therefore, it is very difficult to root out corruption once it is well established, and, once corruption has been excised, it is almost as difficult to prevent it from reestablishing itself. But while there is no human society free of corruption, widespread, large-scale corruption that undermines development can be defeated. There is no easy way to accomplish this, and certainly no universally effective way, yet increasing transparency and accountability within government is an important part of any lasting solution. The kind of anticorruption program that will work best in any particular society, however, will depend on the nature of that society and its cultural context.

It is critical for poorer countries to carefully husband and direct all of their limited resources to meet the current needs of their populations and to build their capacity to improve future economic conditions. They are therefore especially weakened when they use the resources they do have unproductively. In recent years, there has been greater recognition of the importance of lightening the military burden to successful development. There has even been some movement toward attaching conditions to development-oriented lending requiring reductions in military budgets. It is still a politically sensitive area, and progress has been slow. Nevertheless, without serious attention to reducing this drain of national resources, development assistance has little chance of overcoming the economic drag that excessive military spending creates, let alone propelling the country forward. Fortunately, the very fact of working toward a security strategy based primarily on economic peacekeeping principles should help to make significant reductions in military budgets easier to accomplish.

Human Capital Investment

People are at once the focus of development and the most important means for achieving it. A physically vigorous, mentally sharp, highly skilled, and motivated population is an enormous asset in creating a productive and prosperous economy. If such a population is given half a chance, their ingenuity and creativity will drive the economy to new heights.

When Japan, which had been devastated by the terrible destruction of World War II, was provided with development assistance, its economy rapidly rebounded to become one of the most prosperous and powerful in the world in less than thirty years. To be sure, both the new democratic political order and the postwar prohibition against high military spending removed important obstacles to development. They permitted greater freedom of action and allowed the nation to focus its available resources on productive economic activity. But even with these important changes and copious financial aid, in the absence of a highly skilled and educated population, the Japanese economy would never have grown so strong so quickly.

Investment in human capital takes two main forms: 1) activities that increase the quantity and quality of education; 2) and activities that promote physical and mental health. Education involves more than acquiring particular factual knowledge and skills; it involves learning how to use one's mind to find solutions to meaningful problems. This is a critical skill for fostering development, where there are a plethora of problems requiring creative solutions. Education of this sort requires going beyond textbooks, beyond memorizing facts and predigested answers. Similarly, health involves more than just the absence of definable disease; it involves physical vigor and mental clarity. Health is not just a matter of doctors and medicine; it also depends on adequate nutrition, proper exercise, and the quality of both the physical and psycho-sociological environment. None of this is cheap. It cannot be produced on the scale required without a strong social and political commitment. But it has long been a key element in building a nation's economic capacity, and is likely to be even more important in the globalizing, higher technology future.

Having said this, I should point out that simply pouring resources into human capital investment clearly is not enough. Experience has shown that if investment in education, for example, is not accompanied by the chance to put newly acquired skills and training to productive use, the result can be very disappointing to the individuals directly involved as well as to the broader society. Increasing the ranks of the "educated unemployed" does nothing to achieve economic goals. Furthermore, because education inherently raises expectations of a better job and a better life, the lack of opportunity to fulfill those expectations can be both personally disheartening and socially disruptive. To reap the full return to investment in education, there must also be some attention paid to a host of other issues relevant to development, from building infrastructure to encouraging entrepreneurship. Development is never reducible to one magic bullet.

Foreign Direct Investment

Since low productivity economies do not generate much surplus beyond what is needed to meet current needs, they tend to invest relatively little. But low levels of investment perpetuate low levels of productivity, trapping these economies in a circle of poverty. One way out of this trap is to attract investment capital from outside the country. If foreigners with capital can be encouraged to invest enough of it directly in the country, the circle can be broken. It might even eventually be turned into a self-sustaining spiral in which growing productivity generates greater investable surplus that can be used to raise productivity still further.

It is interesting to consider the very different paths with respect to foreign direct investment (FDI) taken by India and China, the two largest developing countries in the world, both of which have been growing rapidly since the 1980s. Although foreign direct investment has long been allowed in India, it was not particularly encouraged (many would say it was actively discouraged), and India did not make comprehensive moves toward liberalization until 1991.[58] China only began to permit FDI in 1979,[59] but it has been actively encouraged since then as an integral part of China's economic "opening."

According to the World Bank, net FDI was $79 million in India in 1980; by 1989, it was still only $252 million. While FDI was insignificant in China in 1980, by 1989 net FDI was $3.4 billion. As India began to shift its policy, FDI accelerated from $237 million in 1990 to $2.2 billion in 1999. Still, FDI flows into China remained much higher, rising from $3.5 billion in 1990 to $38.8 billion in 1999.[60] Essentially the same pattern has continued in the 2000s.

In 1980, real Gross Domestic Product (real GDP) per capita was 37 percent higher in India than in China ($228 vs. $167); by 1990, it was 8 percent higher in China than in India ($350 vs. $324); by 2002, it was more than 90 percent higher in China than in India ($944 vs. $493).[61] Both countries had shown impressive gains from 1980 to 2002, but in China the percentage growth in real GDP per capita was four times what it was in India (465 percent vs. 116 percent).[62]

These are interesting numbers, but by themselves they certainly do not make the case for FDI as a boon to development. First of all, while real GDP per capita is not meaningless, it is a very flawed and incomplete measure of development. Second, it is necessary to control for the impact of variations in the many other factors important to a nation's development before any meaningful statement can be made as to the contribution that FDI may have made. A simple comparison is insufficient; more sophisticated statistical techniques and/or qualitative analysis are required.[63]

Finally, there is the very important question of how LDCs can use foreign direct investment to provide the sustained stimulation their economies need to get themselves going without becoming overly dependent on FDI in the long run. It is easy to become addicted to large, economy-boosting flows of foreign capital, but it is also important to remember that foreign investors are not engaged in a charitable enterprise. They are out to make money, not to support the country or encourage national development per se. They may decide to leave whenever they choose for reasons of their own. As Adam Smith succinctly put it, "A merchant . . . is in a great measure indifferent . . . from what place he carries on his trade; and a very trifling disgust will make him remove his capital, and together with it all the industry which it supports, from one country to another."[64] Neither Smith nor I mean to imply that FDI is to be avoided, or even that it is not an important, perhaps critical, stimulus to development. I am simply arguing that it is not healthy for an economy to become permanently addicted to foreign capital; at some point a nation needs to develop its own homegrown investment capacity.

Development is a complicated phenomenon that transforms not just economies but whole societies. Much of what a nation itself should do and what interested outsiders can do to best stimulate it is a matter of ongoing controversy and debate. Yet despite the limits of our knowledge and the complexity of the problem, we cannot allow ourselves to be deterred from doing what we can. The economic progress of the world's developing nations is too critical to building a global peacekeeping economy that works.

Implementing Principle IV: Minimize Ecological Stress

Both environmental pollution and competition for depletable resources stress the ecology of the planet in ways that can and do generate human conflict. But, for centuries now, environmental pollution has been an unavoidable byproduct of the production of goods and services, and the use of depletable resources (like coal and oil) has been an integral part of the development path we have followed. Implementing Principle IV without undermining Principle III requires that we reduce or remove these environmental stressors while at the same time maintaining or improving the material well-being of those in the more developed countries and extending the benefits of MDC living standards to the people of the developing world. The key to doing this is: 1) relying more heavily on renewable

natural resources; 2) improving the efficiency with which we use all resources (depletable and renewable); and 3) shifting toward a more qualitative as opposed to quantitative concept of economic growth.

Increasing Reliance on Renewable Resources

There is probably no arena in which shifting from reliance on nonrenewable to renewable resources would be more effective in reducing both
conflict and environmental pollution than that of energy supply. There is a
great variety of naturally occurring ecologically benign renewable energy
sources available, among them wind, sunshine, tides, waves, falling water,
biomass, geothermal activity, and ocean thermal gradients. The whole ecology of the planet is driven by natural energy flows. There is nothing new
about relying on renewable energy. People have always used it. For many
millennia, we had no choice. Our technology had not developed enough to
allow us to do otherwise. Now we do have a choice. As we finally come to
realize that our addiction to nonrenewable fossil fuels threatens our security and is neither physically nor environmentally sustainable, we can
shift back. We can put our enormous economic and technological capabilities into action and get down to the business of working out the most
efficient ways of powering modern economies with ancient sources of
energy.

Some renewable energy technologies are already up to the task. Wind
energy and hydropower are now being used to feed considerable electricity
into power systems around the world. Biomass has been used for years to
produce ethanol for automotive use, most notably in Brazil. Techniques for
using passive solar systems to improve the energy performance of buildings are available off the shelf. But there are also many areas in which additional technological progress would go a long way to making renewables
more useful and economically attractive. For example, although they have
made substantial progress and are already economically feasible for some
uses, active solar technologies would benefit greatly from further development. And, the fact that many ecologically benign renewable energy sources
are intermittent (the wind, tides, sunshine, etc.) means that their technical
usefulness and economic feasibility would be greatly enhanced by serious
progress in the technologies for storing energy (such as batteries).

This kind of technological development can be encouraged by both positive and negative incentives. Positive incentives include providing funding for R&D (especially to university researchers and government labs), offering prizes that carry prestige and/or monetary reward, and providing effective protection of intellectual property (through patents, for example) so that successful private sector inventors and university researchers can profitably exploit their inventions. Negative incentives involve putting pressure on companies or researchers to achieve particular objectives. For example, many U.S. states have established "renewable portfolio standards" that require electric utilities to get a minimum fraction of the electricity they sell from renewable energy sources. This encourages the search for new technologies to make generating electricity from renewable energy sources more efficient.

As I pointed out in the discussion of the implementation of Principle II (critical goods independence), government has historically played an important role in stimulating and directing technological development, for better and for worse, even in market economies. Besides directly funding key research and applying regulatory pressure, government has facilitated technological development by serving as a market that gives private sector producers a less risky place to explore potentially profitable product ideas and risk-averse customers a chance to see the new products in action.

In the U.S., sixteen states had some form of "green purchasing" program at the state or local level by 2003.[65] Some include requirements for more energy efficient and/or environmentally benign design of the facilities and equipment they purchase. Considering its past success in providing seed markets and the magnitude of current federal civilian procurement, a federal government equivalent of these state and local green purchasing programs in the U.S. would create a market large enough to encourage the private sector R&D and investment necessary to achieve the scale of operations and experience that would help make renewable energy products attractive in price and quality to ordinary nongovernment customers.

There are therefore a number of practical ways in which government can further advance the technology, economic feasibility, and customer acceptance of renewable energy: 1) It can provide adequate funding of relevant R&D and consumer purchase incentive programs; 2) It can apply enough regulatory pressure to stimulate private sector creativity through such means as renewable portfolio standards; and 3) In some cases, it can serve as a critical seed market or "purchaser of first resort."

A cautionary note is required here. While the idea of encouraging R&D has a great deal to recommend it, it is important to beware of the "technological fix" mentality. It is foolish to think that we are likely to find new technologies that free us from the need to pay attention to how we are using the world's resources and what we are doing to the global environment on which all of our lives literally depend. Technological progress is likely to play a very important part in finding a solution to the problems of human-induced environmental pollution and resource depletion. But we must avoid the temptation of pouring all our efforts, resources, and attention into chasing after the politically appealing chimera of the technological "master stroke." More than once we have thought we could find a technological fix to our problems only to find that it either did not work or created as many problems as it cured.[66] Technological progress is very powerful and very important, but it is not magic.[67]

Improving the Efficiency of Resource Use

Using natural material resources and energy more efficiently reduces environmental pollution at the same time it reduces the intensity of competition for depletable resources and extends the life of available natural materials and nonrenewable energy inventories. Improvements in the design of products from automobiles to office towers can conserve materials and energy, making it easier to do more with less during the lifetime of the products, and to recycle the materials of which they are made when their useful life is over. The advance of technology has a potentially important role to play here too. The strategies discussed above to stimulate renewable energy technologies can therefore be applied to this purpose as well.

The Importance of Paying Attention

Attention is one of those scarce resources that most economists tend to overlook. But the reality is, no one can pay attention to everything at once.[68] That is one of the reasons why government rules and regulations aimed at the private sector can actually increase efficiency, rather than interfering with it, as economists and private sector actors so frequently argue. Government regulations can force those in the private sector to pay attention to issues they have been ignoring, but they are not the only thing that can refocus the attention of the private sector and help them see possibilities they were previously overlooking. Changes in the marketplace, especially those that dramatically increase the price of resources they buy, will also catch their attention.

When energy prices first skyrocketed in the mid-1970s, it suddenly seemed to make sense to pay more attention to how much energy we were consuming. Once our attention was focused on the issue, we began to see changes that could have saved a significant amount of money even before energy prices took off. For example, in that era of rapidly rising energy costs, the architects designing a new office building for Toledo Edison were instructed by their client to make it as energy efficient as possible. One of the possibilities they considered was using fairly expensive, specially coated double-glazed windows to save energy. They then realized that using those windows would allow them to reduce the size of the building's heating, ventilating, and air conditioning (HVAC) system. That meant that the space needed for the air ducts could then be reduced, allowing them to make the building smaller and to use a lot less steel and other construction materials without reducing the amount of useable interior space. As it turned out, the money saved by using a smaller HVAC system and less material in the structure was greater than the extra cost of the more expensive energy conserving windows. In addition to saving tens of thousands of dollars a year in energy costs, the newly designed building actually cost less to build. It would therefore have made sense to build it that way even before energy became so expensive. But neither the architects nor their clients thought of that until soaring energy prices refocused their attention.[69]

Such a situation is not as rare as one might think. As Lawrence Goulder of Stanford University pointed out with respect to environmental pollution, "Several studies indicate that, in many circumstances, firms fail to minimize their private costs by overlooking *pre-existing* zero or negative cost opportunities for emissions reductions. . . . A public policy intervention can stimulate 'discovery' of costless emissions reduction opportunities that, in a sense, were already there for the taking."[70] Though it is unlikely to be enough, we should always go after such low-hanging fruit first.

A Few Rules for Conserving Energy and Material Resources

An energy conservation effort comprehensive enough to bring about a very substantial reduction in environmental pollution while maintaining high standards of living requires basic changes in our approach to the design and operation of energy using systems. A great deal of energy can be saved by relatively simple and cheap changes in how we do things. Other changes are more complex and expensive, but still both technically feasible and economically viable. A few broad rules of thumb could take us a considerable part of the way.[71]

Rule 1: Think Simple. Often the simplest and most straightforward approaches are the most effective, reliable, and economical. For example, one particularly simple solar heating and cooling system design consists of "ponds" of water sealed in clear plastic and lying on a metal roof lined with a layer of black plastic. Above the clear-plastic-sealed ponds is a layer of movable insulation. In cold weather, the insulation is moved away during the day, allowing the roof ponds to be heated by the sun. Some heat passes through the metal roof to warm the interior. At night, the insulation is moved over the ponds, preventing heat from dissipating into the night sky, and maximizing heat radiation from the ponds to the inside of the house. In hot weather, the process is reversed. Such a system, operating in Phoenix, Arizona, for a full year, maintained an indoor temperature between 68°F and 82°F (with supplemental heat or cooling required on only a few days) in the face of external temperatures ranging from subfreezing to 115°F.[72]

Rule 2: Avoid Overdesign. Overdesign involves making everything bigger, stronger, harder, brighter, or more powerful than necessary. Sometimes it is done to ensure that the system being designed meets performance requirements with enough margin for error to avoid the additional work needed to more carefully evaluate what is needed to meet the demands the system will actually face. It is easier to use a brute force approach than to look for creative, ingenious ways of meeting requirements more efficiently. But overdesign nearly always results in systems that waste energy and/or materials. For example, a plant manufacturing jar lids was using an over-sized six-foot tall, seven-foot wide natural gas oven to cure the sealing compound in lids as they passed through the bottom of the oven. Nearly 95 percent of the heat was being absorbed by the belt and the walls or going up the stack. When this monster oven was replaced by a smaller oven whose heat source was much closer to the lids, more than 90 percent of the energy used was saved.[73]

Rule 3: Recycle. There are basically two forms of recycling: reuse and reprocessing. Reuse means that the product is used again after its first use, either for the purpose for which it was originally designed or for another purpose. Reprocessing reduces the original product to scrap and uses it as raw material. Both sharply reduce the rate at which virgin supplies of raw materials are depleted, and recapture the materials and energy already embodied in the product.

Policies for Encouraging Efficiency

When social costs and benefits substantially diverge from private costs and benefits, the actions that private decision makers choose to take in their own best interest will not necessarily be in the interest of the wider society. In market economies, the most effective way for governments to realign public and private interests is to create incentives that close the gap. Therefore, actively encouraging more efficient use of energy and materials is primarily a matter of designing and implementing policies that create the right incentive structure.

Probably the simplest way to encourage more efficient use of nonrenewable energy and materials is by making them more expensive. Although quite a few governments already have energy taxes, it is often politically difficult to make them high enough to make maximum energy efficiency a primary objective of both businesses and consumers. Unless there are reasonably priced alternative forms of energy and higher efficiency energy using devices readily available, simply increasing energy prices is inequitable and impractical. It would be more realistic to gradually phase in a tax on nonrenewable energy, along with policies to encourage the expansion of economically viable renewable energy supplies and increase the availability of much more energy efficient processes and devices.

Put forth as a means of mitigating pollution, the cap-and-trade approach also creates positive and negative incentives for more efficient use of non-renewable energy, as well as wider adoption of ecologically benign renewable energy sources. The approach puts a ceiling on allowable pollution emissions, then issues permits adding up to that ceiling that can be freely bought and sold. It is also especially sensitive to differences in both the technical difficulty and the financial cost of taking the actions the policy is trying to encourage. As a result, it has the right incentive structure to achieve policy goals at the lowest possible cost.

Like the energy tax, this approach leaves it up to those who know best how to work out the most cost-effective path to follow, the companies themselves. But it is even better at encouraging innovation, because firms have both positive and negative incentives to find better, cheaper ways of meeting the target. Those spending money to buy extra pollution permits can save that money if they can find technological advances in energy efficiency and renewables that reduce their emissions; those selling pollution permits can earn more money by selling more of them if they can do the same. Cap-and-trade is also flexible enough to be implemented country-by-country or, if it is possible to get wider agreement, regionally or even globally. Finally, if it turns out that stronger action is required, issuing a smaller number of permits the following year is a simple way to increase the pressure.

High taxes on the sale of virgin nonrenewable materials would certainly make them less attractive as opposed to recycled scrap. So would high taxes on the disposal, as opposed to the recycling, of solid waste. They would also create an incentive for recycling or reuse. Such negative incentives would be much more palatable and effective if combined with positive incentives, like subsidies for recycling or tax credits for using recycled materials.

Qualitative Growth

The primary purpose of economic activity is, and always has been, to enhance material well-being. That goal can be achieved by increasing either the quantity or the quality (or both) of available goods and services that add to material well-being. For politicians, journalists, and even most economists, the rate of growth of GNP (Gross National Product) or its first cousin, GDP (Gross Domestic Product), has become the most prominent measure of economic success. Yet both GNP and GDP are quantitative measures of the total amount of goods and services produced; neither is increased by improvements in product quality.

It does not take much reflection to realize that, once we have enough of the basic necessities of life, our standard of living depends as much on the quality of goods and services as it does on their quantity. Still we remain fixated on the sheer volume of output and the rate of its growth. This fascination with quantity is not just a regrettable quirk; it is economically counterproductive and environmentally problematic. Quantitative growth more rapidly depletes nonrenewable material and energy resources, reducing their availability and driving up their relative prices, with potentially negative long-run effects on the standard of living. It also generates higher levels of air, water, and solid waste pollution, degrading the environment and further reducing material well-being.

Most of us who live in the more developed world could dramatically reduce the amount of damage we are doing to the global environment without compromising our living standards simply by shifting our focus from quantitative to qualitative growth. Building safer, more comfortable, more energy efficient, higher performance, less polluting cars rather than just more and bigger cars, for example, would make us better off economically without causing nearly as much ecological stress. It is generally true—though not universally true—that higher quality products and the production processes required to manufacture them are less environmentally damaging than is producing more, lower quality products. This is particularly obvious if we include environmental criteria (such as energy efficiency) in the definition of quality, as we should. After all, ruining our lungs by breathing in pollutants generated by the exhaust of an ever-increasing number of big, energy inefficient automobiles can hardly be thought of as a net gain in material well-being.

It has been said that most of the human-induced ecological damage is done by the richest billion and the poorest billion of the world's people.

While that maybe true, it is equally true that the richest billion are in a far better position to do something about it without compromising their survival. For the poorest billion, quantitative economic growth is still vital. For the richest billion, qualitative growth makes far more sense. And for the billions in between, some combination of the two is more materially beneficial than the fetishism of quantity alone.

It would not be difficult to concoct an array of economic policies that could be used to discourage our continued myopic and counterproductive focus on quantitative economic growth, some combination of taxes to penalize the production and purchase of "more" and tax breaks and subsidies to reward the production and purchase of "better." But the reality is, this change of focus is not so much a matter of pure economics as it is a matter of psychology and sociology. What is really needed is a mind shift. People with access to enough goods and services to have at least a reasonably comfortable standard of living—the richest billion, for example—need to be convinced that having more and bigger stuff is not nearly as important to their material well-being *or their social status* as having better stuff. Straightforward appeals to logic and strictly economic incentives are less likely to be successful in this than first rate advertising and public relations campaigns.

Conclusion

There are many possible approaches to implementing the principles that underlie a peacekeeping international economy. I have tried to analyze some of the most important implementation issues and suggest a series of pragmatic policies that seek to address them. I make no claim to having been comprehensive. I have merely tried to illustrate that building a strong peacekeeping economy is not just a nice, blue sky idea, but a practical, achievable project.

Still, the political process is such that even the best policies are unlikely to be taken up or persistently and effectively applied unless the right organizations, institutions, and structures are in place to support them. Though many of the policies that require governmental action can be implemented by existing national governments (and some even by state and local governments) within their own jurisdictions, it is likely that (except for Principle II) the independent actions of national governments will not produce as practical or effective a peacekeeping economic system as would more coordinated intergovernmental activity. It is to the question of building broader, coordinating international organizations, institutions, and structures that we now turn.

5

Making It Stronger
Organizations and Institutions

IT MAY BE TRUE, as Douglass North reminds us, that "the process of change is overwhelmingly an incremental one."[1] But creating progressive change requires more than just an incremental approach. It requires a combination of both vision and pragmatism: a vision of a working reality that *could* be, and a practical plan for getting from here to there. Without a broader vision to guide it, it is an accident if incremental pragmatism ever leads us anywhere we really want to go. Without a practical plan, the most appealing and achievable vision remains a distant dream. It was motivational and not just moving when Martin Luther King Jr. said, "I have a dream," precisely because we knew that he also had a plan.

In Chapter 3, we developed four basic principles underlying a vision of a world in which economic relations play a much larger role than the threat or use of military force in keeping the peace within and between nations. The peacekeeping economy is a realistic vision based on the hard currency of self-interest, which, as we already know from massive experience, is a powerful driver of human behavior.

In Chapter 4, we looked more closely at some practical approaches to implementing the basic principles on which the structure and operation of a peacekeeping economy rests. Now we consider the types of organizations and institutions that might help to coordinate and facilitate these approaches to implementing the principles, further buttressing a security system that does not fundamentally depend on military force.

It may be tempting to begin by conceptually throwing out all existing organizations and institutions so that we can start with a clean slate to design those that would be ideal for a peacekeeping economy—in the same way the Brazilian government invited architects and planners to start from scratch when it decided to create the new capital city of Brasilia from whole cloth in the middle of the rain forest. But that is not how the world ordinarily works. If serviceable organizations and institutions already exist, it is more practical to concentrate on how they might be modified or enhanced with new complementary structures to better support a peacekeeping international economy.

Douglass North defined institutions as "the humanly devised constraints that shape human interaction . . . perfectly analogous to the rules of the game in a competitive team sport. That is, they consist of formal written rules as well as typically unwritten codes of conduct that underlie and supplement formal rules."[2] Though North carefully distinguishes between institutions (as "rules of the game") and organizations (as "players"), he does argue that they both influence and shape each other.[3] At first glance, the four peacekeeping principles might seem to be proposed "rules of the game" and thus institutions in themselves by North's definition. But rather than rules as such, they are more like strategies for mobilizing the basic force of self-interest within the institutions of capitalism to create both prosperity (which we know capitalism can create) and security (which, I have argued, it is capable of creating under the right conditions).

Political scientist Robert Keohane and others use the term "institutions" more broadly than does North, encompassing both rules and organizations. They argue that international institutions play an especially important role in coordinating cooperative activity in the international arena, where there is no overarching coercive political authority (analogous to a world government) with the capacity to enforce any particular set of rules on nations, firms, or individuals. Interestingly enough, this is precisely the context in which the market system was designed to operate, and in which it operates most efficiently. There is no "strong sovereign" that forces the parties involved in economic transactions to interact with each other. The market system is a network of voluntary interactions that take place cooperatively. The system is held together by an incentive structure that plays on self-interest. While there is no compulsion, there are norms of behavior that can be usefully reinforced by agreed institutions. Some of these supporting institutions (such as contract law) can be enforced on subnational actors (such as firms) by national governments;[4] others may require recourse to supranational or international intergovernmental bodies.

The market system is analogous to a continuing game with many iterations. As empirical experiments based on game theory have taught us, cooperative strategies are realized more easily in a game that is iterated than in a single play game. In a single play game, the violation of norms of behavior is tempting since it might lead to a significant one-time gain. In a continuing game, any short-term gain from bad behavior is likely to be more than offset by the subsequent longer-term losses that will result from withdrawal of cooperation by other players. The short-term gains that might, for example, be achieved from breach of contract or failure to repay loans can easily be more than offset by the costs that will result when suppliers refuse to provide future services or lenders refuse to grant future loans. While it is far from perfect, the threat of withdrawing cooperation works reasonably well to deter bad behavior in any ongoing game.[5]

Thus, if it is true, as Keohane argues, that institutions tend to increase interaction among the parties, they would by that means alone deter bad behavior and increase cooperation, because they are in effect increasing the number of iterations of the game. If it is also true, as Keohane argues, that they facilitate information sharing, reduce transactions costs, and provide mechanisms for joint decision making and dispute resolution, properly designed institutions can be that much more valuable in supporting the establishment and ongoing operation of a peacekeeping international economy.[6] The fact that there is no overarching international political authority with the capacity to compel nations, firms, and individuals to adhere to the basic peacekeeping principles is therefore not an insurmountable obstacle to eventually accomplishing their widespread adoption.

Keohane also argues, "Governments must be persuaded; they cannot be bypassed. This means that international institutions need to be constructed both to facilitate the purposes that governments espouse in common and gradually to alter government conceptions of self-interest in order to widen the scope for cooperation."[7] The "commonly espoused" and strongly desired goals of prosperity and security certainly give plenty of scope for garnering the support of governments and other powerful transnational actors to construct and operate international institutions aimed at achieving these goals. Over time there is no reason why these institutions could not gradually widen "government conceptions of self-interest." To the extent that self-interest can be mobilized, then, by an appropriate incentive structure buttressed by the right kinds of supporting institutions, the same cement that holds the market system itself together should make it feasible to enlist the cooperation of governments in making the incremental changes necessary to build a peacekeeping international economy.

It is possible to conceive of a variety of institutions, organizations, and supporting structures that together should help to facilitate this process by enhancing incentives for, and removing obstacles to, this kind of collective action. They will give strength, substance, and vigor to the peacekeeping economic system that can be fashioned from the already existing complex of international economic and political relationships. It is far too ambitious a task to try to lay out here the full suite of modifications to the present set of institutions and organizations that could usefully perform this function, let alone to blueprint the process of reform. I will instead try merely to describe a handful of specific examples to illustrate the character and feasibility of the institutional changes that would be most helpful.

Organizations

Of all the currently existing intergovernmental organizations, the three that have the greatest global reach are the United Nations, the World Bank, and the World Trade Organization (WTO). All three were created in the aftermath of the thirty-two fateful years between 1914 and 1945—years that saw the rise of communist and fascist totalitarianism and genocide, a devastating worldwide Depression, and two terrible world wars that took the lives of fifty-sixty million people and spawned the age of nuclear weapons that came to threaten our very survival. By the middle of the twentieth century, all this had dramatically raised the attention given to issues of national and international security, both physical and economic. It was in this climate that, at the urging of the U.S. (unquestionably the most economically, politically, and militarily powerful nation of the time), the nations of the world began to form a series of organizations to ensure that military and economic disasters of this magnitude never happened again. The United Nations and the World Bank came into being in 1946. The following year, the General Agreement on Tariffs and Trade (GATT) was born, the organization that was ultimately to be transformed into the WTO.

Each of these organizations was given a central mission that directly relates to the problem at hand. The UN was to provide a forum for settling international disputes that could erupt into war, and to take action when necessary to prevent aggressor nations from succeeding. The World Bank was to provide funding and technical expertise in the service of encouraging economic development. The GATT/WTO was to increase the free flow of international trade by working to remove tariff barriers and other impediments. There have been many calls for reform of all three of these organizations, but it is not my intention to deal with comprehensive organizational reform here. Instead, I will suggest a few specific proposals to illustrate the kinds of practical changes in the structure and behavior of these organizations that would better support the building and operational effectiveness of a peacekeeping international economy.

The United Nations: A Council on Economic Sanctions and Peacekeeping

Economic sanctions are the main form of negative economic incentive used to influence international political behavior.

In 1990, Gary Hufbauer, Jeffrey Schott, and Kimberly Elliott published an update of their extensive analysis of the use of economic sanctions in international relations since World War I.[8] Applying a consistent set of criteria, they scored each case of sanctions. Not surprisingly, the degree to which sanctions succeeded was related to the nature of the foreign policy goal that caused them to be implemented. Overall, they judged economic sanctions successful in 34 percent of the 116 cases studied—not an overwhelming endorsement of sanctions as a policy tool, but strong evidence against the often-stated opinion that sanctions do not work.

There are three basic categories of economic sanctions: trade embargoes, financial boycotts, and freezing assets abroad. Trade embargoes range from the erection of high, punitive tariff barriers to a total ban on exports to, and imports from, the target country. Financial boycotts include divestment of the securities of the target country or firms from the target country, withdrawal of foreign investment in infrastructure or plant and equipment, and denial of foreign aid. If the target nation has substantial physical or financial assets abroad, those might be frozen. Although the assets still remain the property of the offending nation, it would lose access to the assets or the earnings they generate until it came into compliance with the conditions specified by those initiating the sanctions.

There are two questions involved in the issue of whether sanctions work. The first is, are they effective on their own terms? For example, are trade embargoes really able to cut off trade or can the target country get around them by shifting trading partners? The second is, are they successful? Do they ultimately have the desired effect on the behavior of the target nation? The answers to these questions are interrelated: sanctions that are not effective are unlikely to be successful; but even very effective sanctions could fail to bring about the desired change, if the leaders and/or people of the nation in question believe they have enough at stake, and so are willing to suffer the punishment rather than give in. Clearly, the ultimate criterion of the how well sanctions work must be success, not effectiveness.

Although it is wisest to emphasize positive economic incentives, the international economic system will be more successful at keeping the peace if can also effectively apply economic sanctions when some coercive pressure is needed. Hufbauer, Schott, and Elliott's analysis indicates that sanctions generally work best when they are: 1) multilateral rather than unilateral; 2) imposed by a large enough group of trading partners to cost the target country a serious fraction of its GNP; 3) imposed on target countries that are much smaller economically than those imposing the sanctions; 4) much more costly to the target than to the imposers; and 5) applied quickly and in full force. All of these conditions (with the possible exception of quick action) are easier to fulfill when sanctions are instituted by a broad-based intergovernmental organization, such as the UN.

The Security Council is currently responsible for debating and deciding on the imposition of sanctions through the UN organization. There are a number of problems with this arrangement. For one thing, the membership of the Security Council is limited, and it would be better if the body that imposed economic sanctions were more inclusive. For another, the small size of the Security Council, combined with the absolute veto power of its five permanent members, creates a very unbalanced decision process that has the flavor of the few imposing their will on the many. Sanctions are more likely to be effective if fewer nations feel alienated by the way in which sanctions decisions are made, and are thus less likely to engage in overt or covert sanctions-busting.[9] Finally, the Security Council has many other important functions; the task of imposing, monitoring, and enforcing sanctions is large and complex enough to justify creating an entity wholly focused on doing these functions well. Furthermore, housing these functions in a body that is separated from that which has the power to authorize military action (the Security Council) would underline the commitment of the community of nations to a less-military-oriented style of international relations.

Though its activities would certainly have to be coordinated with those of the Security Council, it would make sense to establish a separate UN Council on Economic Sanctions and Peacekeeping (CESP). Ideally, every (or nearly every) country that belongs to the UN would be eligible to be a member of CESP, and none would have a veto. However, while that has the advantage of being the most inclusive, broad-based structure possible, it immediately raises questions about voting procedures. If every member nation had one vote, and none had a veto, the large number of relatively smaller nations in the UN would dominate the Council's decisions and override the will of the world's largest and most powerful countries. That is both undesirable and completely unrealistic. Some sort of equitable weighted voting scheme would have to be created. For example, each nation might be given a number of votes more or less in proportion to its economic size. Using some reasonably objective measure like GNP, a number of rough categories of economic size could be established. Each nation in any particular category would have the same number of votes as every other nation in the same category. Those that fall into larger size categories would have more votes than those in smaller size categories. Using comparatively few categories—defined by broad ranges of size, with some reasonable relative number of votes assigned to each category—would prevent any large country (or small group of countries) from completely dominating the Council's decision making.

The second question is how sanctions resolutions would be initiated. Certainly, the Security Council should have the power to ask CESP to institute sanctions. Beyond that, it might be best to require that at least a specified number of member nations agree to cosponsor a sanctions resolution before CESP would take up the request. As long as the number was kept relatively small, say six to ten, this would help to avoid "frivolous" resolutions without putting undue restrictions on any nation's ability to bring important grievances before the Council. After all, a resolution that could not garner that limited a number of cosponsors would have virtually no chance of succeeding anyway.

Certain acts could also be objectively defined in advance as so unacceptable that sanctions would automatically be imposed against any nation committing them. It could be agreed, for example, that any nation (or group of nations) that invades or launches a serious military attack against the territory of another nation would be subject to an immediate and total trade embargo by all other member nations. The embargo would continue until the attacks ceased or the forces were entirely withdrawn and a UN peacekeeping force deployed to monitor compliance with the ceasefire or withdrawal. Only participation in UN-authorized military actions (including those set in motion to stop a genocide or to help an attacked nation repel the attack or invasion) would be exempted from this provision. Of course, any nation against which a sanctions resolution was proposed would have the right to present arguments and evidence in its defense before CESP. It might also be a good idea to establish an ex post facto appeals procedure.

The debate and vote on sanctions should always be in two stages: first, whether or not to impose sanctions; then, if yes, what sanctions are to be imposed? The initial sanctions resolution should include a clear statement about what behavior the target nation would have to change to cause CESP to lift whatever sanctions it was imposing. In the case of trade embargoes, the second vote should specifically consider whether basic items of food and medicine should be exempted from the boycott, and if so, how they should be delivered to the people of the nation being sanctioned. This two-step procedure is analogous to the practice of having a innocence/guilt phase and a punishment phase in capital murder trials. Separating the condemnation of the offending behavior from the debate on sanctions helps avoid situations where the parties are so far apart on punishment that they become deadlocked and do nothing at all. Delaying a clear joint condemnation of the behavior—a matter on which they might all strongly agree—would weaken the potentially effective "naming and shaming" impact of a widely supported sanctions resolution.[10]

Once CESP agrees to institute sanctions, it must have means available to monitor them. One way, but certainly not the only way, to do this is to create a second new UN agency to which CESP would have direct, priority access. Call it the "UN Monitoring Organization" (UNMO), and it should include a range of specialists, from those skilled at gathering and interpreting economic data on financial and trade flows to those able to operate, maintain, and interpret data from special dedicated UN-operated satellite surveillance systems. UNMO would be the internationally controlled equivalent of the headquarters of a national intelligence-gathering agency, minus the secrecy (and minus any covert action operations).

UNMO could perform additional functions that are also of vital interest to the world community. For example, it could help monitor compliance with certain types of arms reduction and disarmament treaties, as well as ceasefire and other agreements, reducing the costs of monitoring and increasing the costs of violations. It could also provide economic data for research, planning, and development; advanced warning of severe weather events; and useful ecological, geological, and geographic information. If the more technically sophisticated and space-capable members of the UN refused to support the idea of establishing a truly capable UNMO, more conventional means of monitoring compliance could be found.

For example, information gathered by the national military intelligence and surveillance systems of member governments could be made voluntarily available to help in monitoring movements of planes, railroad trains, truck convoys, and ships, a step that is critical for sanctions that involve trade embargoes. The problem is that nations understandably guard both their intelligence gathering capabilities and the information they gather closely. Combined with the possibility of bias in favor of or against the target nation in any particular sanctions situation, it is more problematic to depend on voluntary sharing of information gathered by national intelligence systems than on an independent, internationally operated organization such as UNMO.

One of the most important reasons parties to international law or treaty agreements continue to comply is the fear that violating an agreement will cause it to collapse, and the benefits they have been getting will then be lost. This may seem a weak force, but it can be strong enough to achieve compliance. Some international treaties, like those governing the mails, have been extremely successful. Others, like the law of the seas, are violated all too often but are still obeyed much more frequently. And after all, with all their enforcement mechanisms, domestic laws are violated on a daily basis in virtually every country on earth. The fact that enforcement is far from perfect does not mean that it is completely ineffective.

Having an organization like CESP engaged in enforcing established norms of international behavior makes sense precisely because it is of great mutual benefit to the nations of the world. The multilateral CESP sanctions approach to world order and global security is more democratic, less dangerous, much cheaper, and more stable, just, and effective than continuing to rely so heavily on the brute force of national militaries applied unilaterally or by small numbers of countries in alliance. As always, of course, the real test of the strength of any member's belief and commitment will come when CESP votes to do something with which that particular member's government strongly disagrees. The question then becomes, will it accept the cost of complying with such a decision in order to retain the ongoing benefits of keeping CESP strong?

The answer to that question depends primarily on just how beneficial CESP is believed to be by the government in question, and how likely a refusal to comply is to impose serious costs, including the opportunity costs of weakening or destroying the agreement. For example, when the U.S. was charged with violations of trade rules under the provisions of the WTO in the 1990s and it lost the cases, it complied with the WTO decisions. The U.S. did not want to undermine the WTO and thus reduce the economic advantages it provided.

There is no question that military and police forces can be important in enforcing trade embargo sanctions. It is perfectly possible that national governments would agree to a set of sanctions that private profit-seeking interests or subnational political groups would then try to violate. After all, most of the enormous amount of smuggling in this world is not a government enterprise. Naval blockades, "no-fly zones," and other forcible interdictions of the movement of people and goods might well be necessary. Military and police forces are certainly useful and perhaps indispensable here.

Partial boycotts are more difficult to enforce than total boycotts. It is easier to stop all ships from entering target country ports than it is to permit certain types of cargoes to pass through while stopping others. Total boycotts do not require boarding and inspection of cargo, but partial boycotts do. The only way to get around this is to have the UN itself, or some other appropriate international group (say, the Red Cross) put together shipments of the goods that are not being interdicted (like food or medical supplies) and deliver them in vehicles over which they have total control. Even so, there would have to be some way to stop the movement of other vehicles, by force if necessary. Military forces could be very useful for this.

All military or police forces involved in enforcing CESP sanctions should always be clearly identified as UN forces. They should fly UN flags and use UN decals and the like so that they do not even appear to be the forces of any particular nation. If it were possible to organize such a thing, a flotilla of UN-flagged ships blockading the harbors of the offending nation would have a very different psychological impact than ships flying the colors of any nation or group of nations. It would be a clear and unmistakable symbol of the world community's condemnation of the acts that led to the imposition of trade sanctions in the first place.

The type and magnitude of military forces useful as an adjunct to other means of enforcement of trade sanctions does not require maintaining anything like present day arsenals of the major military powers. To begin with, nuclear, chemical, or other weapons of mass destruction are of no value for this purpose. Long-range offensive forces are similarly irrelevant. What is needed is the capacity for comprehensive border patrol. And since CESP actions would be very multilateral by definition, the forces of many nations would be potentially available to put together the combined military capability required.

Like every other approach to dealing with violations of the norms of decent national and international behavior, economic sanctions will not always succeed. While it is difficult to specify how long sanctions should be allowed to operate before they are declared unsuccessful, they are a tactic that requires patience. Clearly economic sanctions rarely work quickly. They are not a tool for quickly achieving total surrender; they are a means for applying strong, sustained pressure to move the target nation increasingly toward compliance. Economic sanctions should always be used jointly with continuing attempts at diplomacy and other nonmilitary means of conflict resolution. Unless the offending behavior is so dramatic and difficult to reverse as to compel more drastic approaches—as would be the case, for example, where the offending nation is engaging in genocide—sanctions should be given at least a year, if not a few years, to produce reasonable progress.

Sanctions should be lifted immediately once CESP certifies that the offending nation has met the required conditions, as specified in the original sanctions resolution, or has met subsequently negotiated modified conditions. At the same time, CESP would evaluate whether the target nation has directly done significant damage to another nation (or readily defined subnational group) in concert with its offending action. If the nature and extent of the damage is judged sufficient to warrant consideration of reparations, CESP should refer the case to the International Court of Justice for final judgment.

The threat of economic sanctions is an important negative incentive in the overall structure of mainly positive incentives on which the peacekeeping economic system depends. Sanctions can be used to enforce a variety of norms of international behavior, including those that are directly relevant to the peacekeeping principles.[11] By changing the organizational locus of the imposition and enforcement of multilateral economic sanctions from the UN Security Council to an organization like CESP, it is possible to make the decision process more balanced and democratic, and the sanctions more effective.

The World Bank: Operational Change in the Service of
Sustainable Development

There are four main lending agencies in the so-called World Bank Group, the largest and best known of which is the International Bank for Reconstruction and Development (IBRD), which is generally called the World Bank. Its primary mission is to grant loans and other aid to further the economic development of less developed countries.

More than 180 nations are members of the World Bank. In 2009, it provided $46.9 billion for 303 development projects throughout the LDCs.[12] Though IBRD charges lower interest rates than commercial banks on the loans it makes, it operates like a commercial bank, making loans based on credit worthiness of the borrowers and its judgment as to the economic soundness of the projects to be undertaken. But it is not always bound to use strictly economic criteria. For example, in 1996 it ran some programs to help Bosnia's shattered economy; set up a program to create jobs in the West Bank and Gaza to further the Middle East peace process; and used some of its net revenues to help reduce the balances owed to the International Monetary Fund by the world's most heavily indebted nations.

The World Bank and the International Monetary Fund (IMF) have both been criticized for often attaching painful conditions to their loans. The IMF has been more enthusiastic about doing this than the Bank has been, sometimes requiring that the borrowing nation take drastic measures that include: removal of government subsidies or price controls on such basic items as food and fuel; dramatic cutbacks in government-sponsored social programs; devaluation of currencies that sharply raise the price of imports; and severe import restrictions. Recipient countries see these so-called conditionalities as an undue compromise of national sovereignty. They undoubtedly inflict a great deal of economic pain on the poor, which is counter to the whole point of development. In some situations, these conditionalities can even create dangerous political instability. Furthermore, rather than curing the underlying economic problems, they sometimes make things worse. In the words of Joseph Stiglitz, former chief economist and senior vice president of the World Bank (from 1997 through 1999),

I personally believe that conditionality . . . is a bad idea; there is little evidence that it leads to improved economic policy, but it does have adverse political effects. . . . Some defend conditionality by saying that any banker imposes conditions on borrowers, to make it more likely that the loan will be repaid. But the conditionality imposed by the IMF and the World Bank was very different. In some cases, it even *reduced* the likelihood of repayment.[13]

In addition, the World Bank has been criticized for its voting structure (as has the IMF). While apportioning voting power in a donor organization in accordance with financial contribution is logical—one might even argue that it is equitable—consequently five developed countries—the U.S., U.K., France, Germany, and Japan—together have more than 40 percent of the vote. Though that does not give them a majority, it does allow them to dominate decision making in this development-oriented organization, of which most members are less developed countries. Some allege that this makes the organization more responsive to the agendas of the "big five" MDCs than to the pressing needs of the LDCs.

The World Bank has also been criticized for paying far too little attention to the environmental and social costs of the projects it finances. To its credit, the Bank has taken these criticisms seriously enough to investigate them. In 1994 it issued a report that concluded that dams and other projects the Bank funded had displaced 2.5 million people from their homes between 1986 and 1993, turning them into "development refugees." In 2000, another World Bank report estimated that up to one hundred million people had been displaced by infrastructure development projects over the course of a decade.[14] As is the case with the UN, there is considerable scope for constructive change in the World Bank's structure and operation to focus it more effectively on promoting environmentally sensible and economically sustainable development, in support of peacekeeping Principles III and IV.

Debt and Alternate Forms of Financing

In recent years, there has been an increasingly successful campaign to relieve the most heavily indebted nations of the huge burden of debt they had accumulated. From 1990 to 2004, eighteen of the highest income countries forgave nearly $56 billion in bilateral debt.[15] Since 1996, the World Bank and the IMF have jointly overseen the Debt Initiative for Heavily Indebted Poor Countries (HIPCs) as a specific mechanism through which bilateral and multilateral creditors could provide debt relief. In 2005, the so-called G8 (Group of Eight)[16] agreed to entirely cancel the debts owed to the World Bank and IMF by the eighteen countries that completed the HIPC Initiative.[17]

Debt relief has made a difference for the least developed countries. From 1990 to 2003, their total debt service as a percentage of Gross Domestic Product (GDP) fell by 25 percent (from 2.8 percent to 2.1 percent).[18] It fell more than 50 percent as a percentage of exports and net income from abroad (from 16.2 percent to 7.5 percent).[19] But, after all of this, the developing countries as a whole still had an enormous $2.5 trillion in outstanding debt.[20] Sixty-seven developing countries were identified by the three British NGOs spearheading the civil society campaign for debt relief as needing immediate debt cancellation in order have any hope of achieving the Millennium Development Goals by 2015.[21] Their combined outstanding debt was on the order of $820 billion.[22]

The burden of debt service is not just a financial problem for low income countries. Trying to pay off this debt puts enormous pressure on their governments to cut back other forms of government spending. Often, spending on education, health care, food and fuel subsidies, and other social programs on which much of the welfare of the population depends is cut back the most. Yet ironically the lending that led to the accumulation of debt that induced these painful cutbacks, especially that of the World Bank, was intended to increase the material well-being of the population, not reduce it; to stimulate development, not inhibit it.

Once a person, a business, or a country has accumulated an unmanageable burden of debt, those to whom the money is owed come to have uncommon control over what were previously autonomous decisions. The extraordinary accumulation of debt by low income countries that cannot pay it off has seriously compromised their national sovereignty. It has understandably, whether or not justifiably, led to resentment and cries of neocolonialism.

Borrowing money and being in debt is not inherently a problem. The system of lending and borrowing is a crucial economic mechanism for transferring funds from those who have excess capital to those who have productive ways to put that capital to use. Those who borrow become debtors, but if they put the money they have borrowed to productive use, they can pay off their debts with the new wealth their projects generate. Lenders get a good return on the loans they have made, and borrowers will continue to reap returns from the projects that they could not have gotten off the ground without the borrowed money. Borrowing and being in debt becomes a problem when the money is put to uses that are not economically productive. With no newly generated wealth to pay back the money borrowed and interest due, the debt must be paid out of existing wealth. This can be very painful. After all, if the borrower already had enough preexisting wealth to pay back the loan easily, it would not have been that necessary to borrow money in the first place. The key determinant of whether or not borrowing money and being in debt is a problem is neither the amount borrowed nor the amount of debt accumulated, but rather the way in which the borrowed money is used.

Although debt forgiveness may be a crucial means of removing an unsupportable burden from the world's poorest countries in the short term, it does not make sense to continue lending money to countries that do not, and perhaps cannot, use it productively enough to pay it back out of newly generated wealth. To the extent that very low income countries need to invest in basic projects that do not have a readily capturable return in order to get development going, those funds should be provided in the form of grants, not loans. Loans should be reserved for financing projects that are productive enough to generate sufficient capturable return to pay back the borrowed money, with interest.

Development loans should continue to be provided at low rates of interest over long periods of time. But the World Bank should emphasize equity financing for development projects that have profit potential. In return for its funds, the Bank would receive the equivalent of nonvoting preferred stock in the project. If the project became profitable, the Bank would receive dividends on its investment up to a preset maximum before anyone else received a share of the profits. This kind of equity financing arrangement would give the Bank a stronger incentive not only to evaluate projects more carefully initially, but also to do whatever is necessary on an ongoing basis to ensure that a funded project succeeds. They would get no return, and would stand to lose their initial investment, if it failed. At the same time, unsuccessful projects would not create a continuing financial burden for the developing country, and successful projects would not see a disproportionate share of their return continuing to leave the country. The LDC's downside risk is limited without unduly restricting the profit-based incentives of any private investors or LDC government agencies that have also put their own money into the project.

While Stiglitz is clearly right in arguing that the kind of conditionality imposed by the World Bank (and IMF) has not been a good idea, there are two conditionalities that would make sense: 1) the requirement to introduce strong culturally adapted anticorruption measures; and 2) reductions in excessive military spending. Both inhibit large, economically unproductive diversions of funds. The Bank has pursued anticorruption initiatives of one sort or another since 1996. Anticorruption measures are important; development cannot be advanced by funds that have been diverted from needed programs to the personal use of those in authority.[23] But there are relatively harmless practices common in one culture that appear corrupt when seen through a different cultural lens.[24] Anticorruption programs must therefore be designed and implemented carefully to inhibit serious diversions of needed development funds without being seen as culturally insensitive and insulting.

The World Bank has already recognized that military spending looms large among economically unproductive expenditures.[25] Since it is clearly counter to the purpose of any form of development assistance to stimulate developmentally unproductive activity, it makes sense to require reductions in military spending as a condition of receiving aid. It is also important to introduce transparency and accountability mechanisms to ensure that development aid is not even indirectly being used to sustain or enhance economically unproductive activity. Monitoring how development funds are spent is not enough; it is necessary to ensure that this aid increases social and economic development spending in the recipient country beyond preexisting levels.

Greater Donor-Recipient Collaboration

The World Bank appears to have been paying more attention to the issue of collaboration over the past decade or so. But there is room for substantially expanding this "partnership" view of development assistance. Since real development requires improving the material well-being of the broad mass of the population (especially the poor), it makes sense to include the input of representatives of a broad socioeconomic spectrum in defining project priorities and implementation strategies. The more diverse the society, the more important this is. A more ongoing, interactive process of consultation and collaboration is also useful in making effective "mid-course corrections" to deal with unforeseen contingencies that arise after the project is under way.

Adjusting the Scale of Projects

Some twenty-five years ago, economist Masaki Nakajima, who headed Japan's Mitsubishi Bank, proposed the establishment of a special global infrastructure fund, a proposal that was supported by Saburo Okita, the former foreign minister of Japan. This "global Marshall Plan," to be financed primarily by the MDCs running substantial trade surpluses, would make $25 billion per year available as seed money for funding massive infrastructure projects "that would have worldwide impact but are too costly to be undertaken by a single nation, such as massive water projects to 'green' the world's deserts."[26] The chief problem with the Nakajima proposal was its focus on large-scale "macro-engineering" projects that were more likely to have positive economic impacts on the MDC construction firms that built them than on the LDCs in which many of them would be located. The environmental impact of such grand projects is also questionable. I do not doubt the good intentions of this proposal; but I do believe it was ill conceived.

Although they have not been on the massive scale of the Nakajima proposal, the World Bank has also tended to favor large-scale projects. It is understandable that those of us living in the MDCs, seeing the extensive gaps in development in the LDCs, would think in terms of massive projects that could sweep aside these deficits with one grand stroke. We long ago came to appreciate the real and considerable benefits of economies of scale. Huge hydroelectric dams produce massive quantities of electricity at a much lower cost per kilowatt-hour than do small-scale generating plants, large-scale diversion of river water irrigates otherwise parched farm land at a lower cost per acre-foot than do more limited irrigation systems that rely on water drawn from small wells, and so on. Mass production is the key to driving down unit costs. But there are at least three reasons why smaller-scale projects may be more appropriate and more efficient under the conditions that typically prevail in LDCs.

The first is that mass production is cost-effective only if sufficient market demand exists for the product. Large-scale projects typically have high fixed costs, such as the high cost of building a huge dam for power generation. In LDCs, markets are often small. Even when, aggregated across the country as a whole, demand is large, that demand may be fragmented into much smaller, largely disconnected local or regional markets. If only a small market exists for the product that the large-scale project produces, that high fixed cost is averaged over a small number of units, leading to a very high cost per unit, much higher than if the product were produced with techniques better suited to the size of the market. A few large-scale development projects may look very impressive, but they are often less practical and less useful than undertaking many smaller-scale operations.

The second reason is that large-scale projects are much more likely to cause substantial social dislocation and environmental damage, neither of which is easy for a highly developed country to handle, let alone a country at a substantially lower level of development. When Hurricane Katrina slammed into the Gulf Coast of Mississippi in late August 2005, hundreds of thousands of people were forced to evacuate, and much of the city of New Orleans was devastated. Years later, in one of the richest and most powerful countries on earth, not only was much of the city still in need of reconstruction and repair, but the massive social dislocation caused by the storm had still not been fully resolved. There are many differences between the devastation caused by a ferocious storm and the social dislocation and environmental damage caused by a huge development project such as China's Three Gorges Dam. But there is also one important similarity: it is difficult for any society to deal equitably with the political, economic, and social problems caused by disruption of the daily lives of very large numbers of ordinary people as a result of major dislocations of population.

The amount of involuntary dislocation caused by large-scale development (particularly infrastructure) projects is much larger than most people realize. In the earlier referenced World Bank volume, published in 2000, Michael M. Cernea and Christopher McDowell wrote, "Development programs that are supposed to widely improve living standards have also brought, under the wings of progress, the forced displacement of millions and millions of poor and vulnerable people in many of the world's developing countries, inducing impoverishment and hardships. The number of persons involuntarily displaced and re-settled by infrastructural development projects during the last 10 years is between 90 and 100 million."[27] This massive problem has not gone unnoticed by development aid donors:

> Responding to the international concerns about the world's growing numbers of forced resettlers and refugees, many governments and international organizations have strengthened during the last decade their policies and assistance programs in this area. All 29 developed country members of the Organization for Economic Cooperation and Development (OECD) have adopted the same set of unified policy guidelines regarding the involuntary resettlement of people under their aid agencies' projects. . . . In turn, the World Bank, after having formulated the first international policy on resettlement (1980), has strengthened this policy with new provisions.[28]

It is good that aid donors are now more sensitive to the rights of those displaced. But rather than just focusing attention on smoother resettlement, does it not also make sense to consider reducing the scale of the projects themselves and trying to avoid creating so many "development refugees" in the first place? Doing many small-scale projects may not always result in less social dislocation and environmental damage, but it will do so often enough to justify thinking long and hard about alternative smaller-scale routes to the same development objectives.

Finally, large-scale projects are not only expensive to build but also expensive and technically difficult to operate and maintain. It may therefore be more cost-effective and more useful to undertake many smaller projects that are cheaper and easier to operate and maintain. Digging a thousand small wells close to where people live may be a better route to improving the water supply than building a huge, technically sophisticated water treatment plant with extensive, complex piping systems for distribution. Building many hundreds of miles of simple roads may extend the benefits of improved transportation to a much larger part of the population than building a few multilane superhighways around the capital. The history of development assistance is littered with examples of well-intentioned donors providing complex, technically sophisticated products to people without sufficient skill or financial wherewithal to keep them operating properly. As a result, things are more likely to break down, and when they do, the first rate equipment provided by the most well-intentioned donor turns into a useless pile of junk.

Facilitating Microlending

Lack of access to capital is one important barrier that prevents poor people from acting on whatever entrepreneurial impulses they may have. Microlending is an attempt to break through that barrier to economic self-improvement by making very small loans, at reasonable rates of interest, to poor people so that they can start up very small enterprises. The loans range from a few dollars to a few hundred dollars, depending on the economic context of the country involved. Microlending makes sense for some of the same reasons that paying more attention to smaller-scale projects makes sense. It is a way of providing development assistance directly to those who need it the most, and spreading economic opportunity more broadly. Putting a little capital, and the responsibility to repay it, in many different impoverished hands can go a long way toward overcoming the obstacles to economic development created by lack of access to the means of self-investment, lack of self-confidence, and lack of hope. Microlending programs are likely to work better when they also incorporate an element of education to convey to borrowers the skills they most need to take advantage of the economic opportunity that access to capital has given them.

One of the best-known and most successful examples of this approach is the Grameen Bank of Bangladesh, begun in the mid-1970s by Muhammed Yunus (former Chittagong University economics professor and winner of the 2006 Nobel Peace Prize), with an initial capitalization of less than $50.[29] By 2003, it had more than 1170 branches serving more than two million clients, 94 percent of whom were economically disadvantaged women. Even more striking, though it lent money to people so poor that it had always been assumed they were bad credit risks, Grameen achieved an enviable loan repayment rate greater than 90 percent.[30] This was the result of deliberately incorporating a deep understanding of Bangladeshi culture and society into the design and implementation of the bank's lending programs.[31]

The lessons of the Grameen Bank's success do not lie so much in the specific ways in which the Bank carried out its lending and educational programs. The lessons are that microlending is an effective way to help the poor take some control of their own economic development, and that the rules of the microlending game have to be harmonized to the particular cultural environment in which they are applied. This is especially true of the procedures chosen to ensure responsible use of the funds and ultimate repayment, which are likely to be very culture-dependent. Consequently, those with a deep and personal knowledge of the cultural environment in any particular application of microlending should play a key role in designing the system.

It is not wise for an organization as large as the World Bank to get directly involved in microlending itself. The most effective role the Bank can play in encouraging this approach to poverty reduction lies in helping to guide the design and fund the creation of multiple microlending institutions within a wide range of developing countries. It is also important to use a collaborative donor-recipient approach, and to ensure that both transparency and the inclusion of corrective feedback systems are part of the design and implementation of the program.

There is no reason why a version of microlending cannot be put to effective use in addressing tenacious pockets of poverty within more developed countries. After all, lack of access to capital can be a barrier to the very poor in richer countries as well.[32]

Social and Environmental Impact Statements

Beginning in the 1980s, NGOs related to the environmental movement, among others, became increasingly critical of the World Bank for funding projects that caused large-scale social and environmental damage. For example, the Bank financed a 1,500-kilometer highway (and related feeder roads) in the northwest Amazon region in Brazil. Completed in three years, the road triggered a rapid expansion of the population in the area over the next six years that far outran the provision of support services, particularly health care. Consequently, thousands died of malaria. The project also promoted extensive logging, with considerable attendant damage to the Amazonian environment. In the late 1980s, after the U.S. Congress voted to withhold funding for a Brazilian dam project on environmental grounds, the Bank created an environmental department to integrate environmental considerations into its project lending. It also consulted with NGOs on assessment practices.[33]

It is important to evaluate the broader environmental and social consequences of alternative designs of development projects before they are under way. Requiring social and environmental impact statements—and opening them up for public view and comment—make it more difficult to unintentionally overlook or intentionally ignore these issues. Taking social and environmental issues explicitly into account in the choice among development projects also helps avoid repeating some of the more regrettable mistakes of the past.

Given the will, there is little problem preparing social and environmental impact statements or in integrating them into the development assistance process in a meaningful way in an organization as technically sophisticated as the World Bank. But is the preparation of such statements a good idea in national development programs in general? Since preparing social and environmental impact statements will absorb some of the funds that presumably would otherwise be used for development purposes, it is worth asking under what conditions these statements are actually likely to matter. The fact is, most impact statements are beyond the ken of the average citizen, even in countries where citizens really do have input into the political process, and the best analysis will do no good gathering dust in some forgotten archive. The answer to making this exercise meaningful, I believe, lies in the presence of an active and vital civil society.

Grassroots NGOs are an important mediating force between powerful governmental institutions and the reams of paper they produce on the one hand, and the general public on the other. Where there is an active and vital civil society, when the social and environmental impact statements are made available, NGOs mobilize nongovernmental expertise to interpret the sometimes nearly incomprehensible language that is common in such documents, distill the essence of the analysis, and present the key points in it in a way that any reasonably educated person can understand. Then, crucially, the relevant NGOs can use these "translations" to inform the general public, build support for or opposition to the projects, and bring the issue back to government decision makers with the force of organized public opinion behind it.

Although it is a good idea to prepare both social and environmental impact statements for every project the World Bank undertakes to finance, it is particularly important to do so for whatever megaprojects the Bank continues to fund. At the very least, they provide advanced warning about the magnitude and type of problems the projects are likely to create, so that ameliorative measures can be incorporated into the project design.

Creating a More Effective Global Environmental Fund

In 1990, France and Germany recommended that the World Bank take the lead in establishing a financing mechanism to help low and middle income countries undertake projects with worldwide environmental benefits. Set up as an independent financial organization, that mechanism is called the Global Environmental Facility (GEF). The World Bank is the dominant partner, but GEF projects are jointly managed by three agencies: the Bank, the UN Environment Program (UNEP), and the UN Development Program (UNDP). The original motivation for the GEF was to allay the concerns of developing countries that they would be obligated to undertake and pay for expensive projects they could ill afford if they signed on to a number of international environmental agreements supported by the more developed countries.[34]

More than 170 nations are members of the GEF, which remains an important financing mechanism today. It supports six major international environmental priorities: 1) maintaining biodiversity; 2) mitigating or reversing climate change; 3) reversing the environmental deterioration of international waters; 4) preventing and controlling the degradation of land and land-based environmental resources (primarily in the form of desertification and

deforestation); 5) protecting the earth's ozone layer; and 6) reducing or eliminating persistent organic chemical pollutants.[35] From 1991 to 2004, the
GEF provided $6.2 billion in grants and "generated over $20 billion in cofinancing from other sources" in support of 1,800 projects in 140 developing
or transitional countries. Biodiversity and climate change projects accounted
for the largest part of GEF funding by far over that period (30.5 percent and
28.1 percent, respectively), followed by projects on international waters,
ozone depletion, persistent organic pollutants, and land degradation.[36]

The GEF's self-stated mandate is to provide "grants to developing countries for projects that benefit the global environment and promote sustainable livelihoods in local communities," which is certainly compatible with
both Principles III and IV of the peacekeeping economy. Yet there are a
number of ways in which the GEF could be strengthened and made more
effective. The most obvious of these is to substantially increase the funding
made available for grants in support of projects aimed at addressing these
important environmental issues. There is no question that $6.2 billion is a
lot of money. But when you consider that this was the cumulative amount
of funding over a fourteen-year period, that means an average of only about
$440 million a year was made available to address these pressing environ-
mental issues worldwide. It is clear that the scale of this effort is far too
small. As Zoe Young points out, "GEF funds constitute less than 1 percent
of total international aid flows to the South and offer the equivalent of one
day's global spending on military 'defence' for each year of protecting the
global environment."[37]

In the long run, sustained economic development has little chance of
succeeding unless attention is paid to its environmental consequences. Just
as an athlete who takes dangerous drugs to enhance immediate performance will do long-term damage to his/her body, a country that spurs its
economic development by clear-cutting its forests or engaging in mining
practices that pour toxic chemicals into its waters will ultimately find its
development stalled and the material well-being of its people deteriorating.
Even if it did not seem true in the past, it is undeniable given the present
condition of the global environment that long-term economic development
can be achieved only within ecological constraints. There is simply no
choice. But though it is more challenging, even short-term development

can be achieved within ecological constraints. We need not fear that a call to devote more resources to dealing with the kind of ecological issues that the GEF addresses in the developing world will inherently drain resources away from vital projects encouraging economic development, provided we design and implement both the environmental and development projects carefully.

The GEF claims that its efforts have generated more than three times as much cofinancing for projects than GEF itself has provided. That leveraging seems like an unmitigated advantage, but it is important to ask in what form the cofinancing was provided. Since many projects to mitigate environmental damage may not in themselves generate substantial new money wealth, to the extent that the financing was in the form of loans, the additional debt burden can be economically and even environmentally problematic. Indeed, heavy debt burdens have been part of the reason highly indebted low income countries felt pressed to engage in ecologically damaging but short-term profitable exploitation of natural resources (such as clear-cutting forests) in the past. Grants are an entirely different, and much broadly beneficial, form of financing.

The environmental issues that constitute the main mission of the GEF are of undoubted global importance. But there are other regional forms of transboundary environmental pollution that also have the potential to generate international stress and conflict. Production or consumption activities occurring in one nation may result in ecological damage that has a more significant impact on another country in the region than it does on the nation in which the activities originated. Acid rain is one example: sulfur oxides ejected high into the air from the tall industrial smokestacks of one country combine with atmospheric hydrogen to produce sulfuric and sulfurous acids which then rain down on another country, damaging its forests and lakes.

This is a classic problem of negative environmental externalities. In such situations, substantial improvements in the environmental quality of Nation R (the recipient of the pollution) could be achieved if Nation S (the source) either halted its pollution generating activity or instituted measures to reduce its emissions. But if S gets net economic benefits from the activity that also generates the pollution, while R bears the penalty without getting any benefits, S has no short-term, self-interested reason to take costly measures to reduce the pollution it is generating. If S does take action to reduce the pollution associated with the activity, it bears the cost and gets little or no benefit, while R gets the benefits of pollution reduction without incurring the costs. The disincentive to take action is that much stronger if Nation S is a less developed country whose access to pollution control technologies is limited and whose resources are already stretched to the limit, and Nation R is a more developed, technologically advanced country in relatively good economic condition.

Often the richer nation on the receiving end of the pollution can do little within its own borders to mitigate the damage the pollution is doing to its environment that is anywhere near as cost-effective as what can be done within the borders of the poorer, pollution-generating nation. It therefore makes sense for the receiving nation to reimburse the poorer source nation's costs of pollution control (and perhaps transfer the relevant technology as well). In theory, this could be done bilaterally. But there is often political resistance to making such agreements. Perhaps this is because they seem too much like the victim rewarding the offender; perhaps it is because there are other tensions, political or otherwise, between the countries involved. Either way, it may be easier to accomplish the same objectives through the intermediary of an international grant-making fund like the GEF. Making grants for such purposes is certainly compatible with the GEF's other activities, as well as with economic peacekeeping principles. And it would help to broaden its mission in ways that meet some of the criticisms that developing countries have leveled at the GEF in the past.[38]

An expanded GEF would provide more grants to less developed countries for improved sewage treatment facilities, air pollution control, protection of endangered species, and preservation of increasingly rare environmental assets, such as hardwood and rain forests. Where it is culturally and ideologically acceptable, it could also buy land in less developed countries and hold it as an environmental preserve; where that is not acceptable, it could provide "perpetually forgivable" loans to governments or private indigenous groups to buy the land and protect it. Repayment of such a loan would be due at the same time every year, but would be postponed another year if the area remained environmentally intact. As long as the area was a well-protected environmental preserve, the loan would never actually have to be repaid.

Clearly the GEF and, to a lesser extent, the World Bank, modified as suggested, are not set up as classic profit-making financial institutions. They are not sustainable in the absence of continuing external support. Rather these organizations become mechanisms through which the more economically prosperous countries can provide aid to the less developed countries on a multilateral basis. While potentially valuable, bilateral aid has too often been used to bribe corrupt officials or to buy political favors. With broader participation among the more developed countries, and a governing board structured to avoid domination by a few of the richer countries, it is easier for multilateral organizations to reduce and perhaps completely avoid some of the more blatant political manipulation and abuse that has so often accompanied bilateral government aid in the past, abuse that has rendered it less than effective in stimulating either economic development or environmental sustainability.

What incentives do the MDCs have to offer such aid? One incentive, primary to our focus on building a peacekeeping international economy, is that this would be a far more effective and much cheaper way of buying security than continuing to pour huge amounts of money into maintaining or expanding large military forces. In 2008, the nations of the world spent close to $1.5 trillion dollars on their militaries, more than $600 billion of which was spent by the U.S. alone.[39] A small fraction of this amount, even 1 percent, would make available some $15 billion extra a year—more than twenty-five times the average amount the GEF has been spending per year to date. A few percent more could substantially increase the scope of multilateral development aid. If properly spent, these funds could go a long way toward stimulating (or at least removing some of the obstacles to) development and cleaning up the global environment. These are matters important to the health, economic well-being, and security of people in both the donor and the recipient countries.

The ultimate goal of global development should be to eliminate the Third World as an identifiable entity. While it is unlikely that international differences in living standards will ever completely disappear, there is no reason why there must continue to be a permanent economic underclass of nations. Given this ultimate goal, some of the organizations that might be useful to help in building a peacekeeping international economy—in particular the World Bank and the GEF—should be considered as transitional, rather than permanent. In a sense, their success can be measured by how quickly and completely they render themselves obsolete.

Trade Organizations

The 1950s and 1960s saw a proliferation of regional trade arrangements. A few of them succeeded; many others had little or no success. The next decades saw an increased focus on global, rather than regional, trade arrangements, followed by a resurgence of regional agreements in the 1990s.[40] The growth of regional and global multilateral trade agreements and the organizational structures that support them is clearly a key component of (though not sufficient for) creating the broadly interdependent network of balanced economic relationships critical to enhancing the peacekeeping capabilities of the international economic system.

Analyzing or even describing the structure and functioning of these arrangements and organizations in any detail, let alone how they might be shaped to service the needs of a peacekeeping economy, is too big a task to be profitably undertaken here. They have already been the subject of many books, and are likely to be the subject of many more. But it is useful to briefly consider the character of key trade organizations and the possibility of creating others that might help to balance as well as expand international trade.

Lessons from the European Union On May 9, 1950, Robert Schuman, then foreign minister of France, announced a plan to put "the whole of Franco-German coal and steel production under a common High Authority, within the framework of an organization open to the participation of the other countries of Europe."[41] Thus began the formation of the European Coal and Steel Community (ECSC), which gave rise to the European Economic Community (EEC) that subsequently became known as the European Community (EC) and ultimately evolved into the European Union (EU) in 1993. The original ECSC was intended to stimulate economic growth in post–World

War II Europe. But, as discussed earlier, it was also explicitly designed to use economic cooperation and cohesion—in two industries that had been key to the war effort—as a deliberate strategy for securing the peace. Today, with all its contentious disagreements, the European Union remains one of the best working models in the world of a peacekeeping international economy, albeit one restricted to a relatively small (but growing) group of countries.

The EU's central institutions derive much of their power from the national governments, which still dominate the decision-making processes of the EU member states. The member states are, in effect, pooling and sharing sovereignty rather than transferring it to a higher level. The central institutions have full jurisdiction over external trade; they try to coordinate some other aspects of foreign policy, but there is much (including defense policy) that they do not control at all.[42] Nevertheless, in a number of ways, the EU has managed for the most part to avoid the pitfalls of narrow nationalism and take a broader and longer-term perspective. One of the most important of these is its recognition of and methodical attempt to reduce the disparities in income and economic opportunity that exist among not only its member states, but also its regions.

Even before the enlargement of 2004, which added ten new member states with incomes from 35 percent to 72 percent of EU average, GDP per capita in the ten most prosperous regions of the EU was almost three times as high as in the ten least developed.[43] The EU consciously tries to reduce such disparities by transferring resources to improve conditions in its lower income, lower opportunity regions without compromising the economic well-being of those that are more prosperous. The four "structural funds" that support this policy have paid out serious money, an estimated €213 billion between 2000 and 2006, roughly one-third of total EU spending. About 70 percent of the funding has gone to regions where the GDP per capita is less than 75 percent of the EU average, with another 11.5 percent to areas experiencing structural economic decline. This is not charity. These are development funds intended to finance improvements in transportation and environmental infrastructure, stimulate business investment, and create productive jobs.[44]

The EU contends that the gap between its richest and poorest regions and nations has narrowed over the years. Just how much the EU's regional and national disparities have actually been reduced is still a matter of some debate in the academic literature. There is even more debate as to whether the "structural funds" are responsible for whatever narrowing has occurred or whether it is simply the result of the general economic benefits of being part of a prosperous and dynamic free trade zone.[45]

More central to the matter of building a broader international peacekeeping economy is the question of what has motivated this group of sovereign states, particularly those that are richer, to engage so seriously in this policy of deliberately trying to reduce the economic disparities among them by promoting economic development in the poorer states and regions. "The two words, solidarity and cohesion, sum up the values behind regional policy in the EU: *solidarity* because the policy aims to benefit citizens and regions that are economically and socially deprived compared to EU averages . . . *cohesion* because there are positive benefits for all in narrowing the gaps of income and wealth between the poorer countries and regions and those which are better off."[46] Understanding the importance of reducing disparities to solidarity and cohesion, and the importance of solidarity and cohesion to both prosperity and security, seems critical to binding nations together in the kind of enlightened self-interest that can make a peacekeeping international economy a working reality.

In that respect the EU, with all its limitations and imperfections, is still a great source of encouragement. On the theory that anything that has already happened is possible, the fact that the nations of the EU (many of which were historic enemies) not only held such values but acted boldly upon them is further evidence that the enterprise of building a peacekeeping economy is a practical and achievable endeavor.

LDC Primary Product Marketing Cartels In the previous chapter, I discussed the possibility of strategically applying John Kenneth Galbraith's "theory of countervailing power" to improve balance in the trade relationships between more developed and less developed countries. While this is not necessarily the preferred approach, the idea is that it may be possible to offset the leverage of MDC companies, particularly those with considerable market power and global reach, by forming LDC-based marketing cartels. With more equal bargaining power across the market, it should be possible to strike a fairer price for LDC products, one that better reflects their true value. According to the theory, when monopoly power on one side of a market is countervailed by monopoly power on the other, a price is likely to result that more closely approximates that which would emerge in a bilaterally competitive marketplace. This may be especially important for LDC primary products.

What economic and political conditions would allow the LDCs to form effective primary product marketing cartels? First, the product being cartelized must be sufficiently important to its purchasers; second, there should be no other readily available commodities that purchasers consider close substitutes for the product at hand. (Taken together, these conditions mean that demand will be relatively price-inelastic.) Cartels operate to drive up prices by restricting supply. If the product is important enough to consumers that they don't want to do without it and there is no close substitute to which they can easily switch, higher prices will not reduce the quantity demanded very much. Suppliers will sell nearly the same amount of product at higher prices, and as a result have higher revenues (income).

Another important condition is that the cartel organizers must be able to draw enough producers into the cartel to control the marketing of sufficient product so that they can drive its price up by restricting its availability. Since the best substitute for any product is always the product itself, if there is too much of the same commodity available from suppliers who are not part of the cartel, the cartel will have little power. In practical terms, if there are too many LDCs that produce substantial amounts of this same product, it may be difficult to get enough of them to agree to join the cartel to make it effective. This is a serious collective action problem. Another serious collective action problem is that of ensuring adherence to the cartel agreement. Cheating is the Achilles' heel of cartels.

Generally speaking, the more members there must be in the cartel for it to have enough market share to be effective, the more difficult it is to organize the cartel in the first place, and the harder it is to police the agreement and avoid cheating after the cartel has been formed. When countries and not merely companies are involved, contentious political differences may be added to these economic issues.

Assessing the situation in the mid-1970s just *before* the Organization of Petroleum Exporting Countries (OPEC) initiated its infamous oil embargo, C. Fred Bergsten wrote,

> Four countries control more than 80 percent of the exportable supply of world copper. . . . Two countries account for more than 70 percent of world tin exports, and four countries raise the total close to 95 percent. . . . Four countries possess over one-half the world supply of bauxite [aluminum ore], and the inclusion of Australia . . . brings the total above 90 percent. . . . OPEC had to pool twelve countries to control 80 percent of world oil exports, but fewer countries are usually involved in the production of other primary products.[47]

Bergsten's implication is clear: more OPECs are certainly possible.

There are two main ways to structure intergovernmental cartel-style agreements intended to raise commodity prices. One is to negotiate agreements restricting the amount of the commodity each producing country can export. The other is to establish an intergovernmental joint marketing agency, which buys up all of the primary product in question from the LDC producers at a "fair price" and serves as the sole seller of the product to MDC importers. The International Coffee Agreement was of the first type. It broke down in 1973 over market sharing conflicts. OPEC is a much more successful example. The subsidiary of De Beers called the Central Selling Agency is a classic example of the second type. It has been quite successful, establishing and maintaining a virtual monopoly on the sale of diamonds worldwide for many years. For a number of reasons, it has always been more difficult to operate primary product cartels of either type for agricultural than for nonagricultural primary products. Among other things, it is harder to prevent overproduction of agricultural products and to store them.[48]

Since the idea is to use primary product cartels to reduce exploitation and help create more balanced international trade relationships, it is important that the actual LDC producers of the products—for example, the farmers and the miners, and not just corporate agribusinesses or mining companies—actually get a proper share of the benefit from the higher prices being paid by MDC importers. Shifting the source of the exploitation from MDC importers to LDC mining companies or marketing cartels does not accomplish the goal of building an economic system that reduces or eliminates the outbreak of violent conflict.

In a world where, for various reasons, only a minority of primary products could be cartelized or jointly marketed effectively, the negative impacts on the larger group of "outsider" LDCs would be much more profound than they would be on the richer countries. This was certainly the case when the OPEC actions of the mid-1970s more than tripled the price of crude oil within a few months. The sharp rise in price caused considerable economic trouble in the developed countries, but that was nothing like the pain it caused in the oil-poor LDCs. Therefore, if a policy of better organizing primary product producers in the LDCs is put into action, it is especially important that some mechanism be created (other than accumulating unsustainable levels of debt, as in the case of OPEC embargo) to ease the impact of these price rises on other low income countries. Failing to do this will offset at least some of the peacekeeping economic effects of this policy.

Fair Trade NGOs A number of nongovernmental organizations around the world have taken a completely different and more progressive approach to establishing mutually beneficial balanced international trading relationships. One of the more interesting of these is a nonprofit U.S.-based organization called Transfair USA. Transfair, which bills itself as "the only independent, third-party certifier of fair trade products in the U.S.," sees its mission as building "a more equitable and sustainable model of international trade that benefits producers, consumers, industry and the earth." It tries to achieve that mission by signing legally binding agreements with manufacturers and importers in the U.S. that allow them to display a "Fair Trade Certified" label on products, in exchange for producing or purchasing products that have been produced in accordance with strict Fair Trade Standards. Transfair was established in 1998 and began certifying products the following year. By 2006, it was certifying at least some of the agricultural products of five hundred American companies, including coffee, tea, herbs, cocoa, chocolate, fresh fruit, sugar, rice, and vanilla.[49]

Transfair is one of twenty members of a broader group called Fairtrade Labeling Organizations International (FLO). FLO develops and reviews international Fair Trade Standards and certifies producer groups adhering to those standards (currently including over one million farmers and farm-workers) in close to sixty countries in Africa, Asia, and Latin America. Both Transfair (for U.S. manufacturers and importers) and FLO (for developing country producers) have active audit processes to ensure that those companies whose products they certify continue to abide by the rules.[50] Just what are these rules?

The Fair Trade Standards begin with a "fair price" requirement. Developed country importers guarantee that they will pay Third World producers at least an agreed minimum floor price. An additional premium is paid for certified organic products. Farmer groups are also eligible for preharvest credit financing. But Transfair's standards go far beyond this to require: 1) direct trade with developing country producer groups (eliminating unnecessary intermediaries) as a strategy for "empowering farmers to develop the business capacity necessary to compete in the global marketplace"; 2) democratic organization of farmer groups, with living wages, safe working conditions, and freedom of association for workers, and no forced child labor on Fair Trade farms; 3) investment of Fair Trade social premiums (for example, currently an additional five cents per pound for coffee) in development projects, such as scholarships, health care, and training to improve product quality; and 4) farming methods that are environmentally sustainable and protect worker health.[51] Clearly, all of these standards, and not just those that directly relate to balanced trade, are compatible with the underlying principles of a peacekeeping international economy.

Transfair is not the only NGO working along these lines. The Rainforest Alliance certifies farms producing bananas, coffee, cocoa, citrus, flowers, and timber. Their certification process focuses on ecologically sustainable farm management practices and worker protection. Like Transfair, it is intended to improve prices for developing country producers in the market, but its agreements do not include minimum price guarantees. The Fair Trade Federation, on the other hand, is an organization of companies that have expressed a commitment "to providing fair wages and good employment opportunities to economically disadvantaged artisans and farmers." It does not actually certify products or companies.[52] World of Good is an example of an organization that belongs to the Fair Trade Federation. Its mission is to "create opportunities for hundreds of artisan communities around the world . . . by serving as a bridge to the U.S. retail market. We . . . assist artisans by providing access to fair wages, safe working conditions and long-term economic sustainability."[53]

To the extent that fair trade NGOs are able to help smaller LDC producers strike a fairer bargain for their primary products, they are helping to deliver on the economic promise of free markets to the developing world. Primary products constitute a very large part of the current export capacity of many of these countries. The value of NGO efforts in this arena is especially high for agricultural products since, as I have argued, it is generally more difficult to organize effective agricultural product cartels or joint marketing organizations. Nevertheless, in principle there is nothing to prevent fair trade NGOs from being more helpful in working toward more balanced trade in craft or manufacturing products, and even in services.

Although some of the producers, manufacturers, importers, and other companies participating in one way or another in the fair trade movement may be involved out of moral concern, it is a virtual certainty that most if not all of them see it as a practical and profitable business strategy. That is encouraging for two reasons. First, it is a clear indication that a large and growing number of companies see enough consumer support for the concept of fair trade to believe that following fair trade practices will give them a competitive advantage in a segment of the market. Second, as the option of buying fair trade products becomes more widely available, it empowers ordinary consumers to express support for fair trade in ways that will create powerful incentives for these and other companies to expand their fair trade practices. To the extent that the public can be made to see the multiple benefits of balanced mutually beneficial trade, they will have an effective method of taking personal action to move the economy in that direction.

It is important to appreciate the limits of NGO action in achieving the objective of fair trade. To date, Starbucks Coffee has been one of the most prominent companies that have actively engaged with Transfair in promoting Fair Trade Standards. From 2000 through 2005, Starbucks imported some 20,343,000 pounds of fair trade coffee, more than half of which (11.5 million pounds) was imported in 2005 alone. Yet even its 2005 imports represented only 3.7 percent of Starbucks coffee sold that year.[54] Its fair trade business is merely a drop in the bucket (or, in this case, a drop in the cup).

LDC–LDC Trade Organizations Three decades ago, referring to the developing world as the "South" in the terminology of the time, Mahbub ul Haq advised, "The weakness of most proposals for South-South Cooperation has been that they tended to build grand designs on the basis of an aggregated, mythical South. . . . It may be far more productive to follow up on avenues of cooperation on a regional or sub-regional level and in certain specific areas of action."[55] This is good advice. While there is certainly room for globally based "grand designs" in the arena of trade (and investment), that is already taking place in the more inclusive WTO system, to which both developed and developing nations belong. There may not be all that much additional net gain in forming a parallel world trade organization for LDCs alone. But a number of benefits can be achieved by more restricted regionally based trade organizations.

None of the benefits of expanded LDC–LDC trade discussed in Chapter 4 are substantially reduced by creating LDC trade organizations that are regionally, rather than globally, oriented. Properly designed regionally based organizations should be easier to form and operate effectively because the commonly encountered collective action problems should be less severe. There will be fewer nations involved and, although there are plenty of exceptions, social, political, and cultural differences among those nations and their peoples are likely to be smaller than they would be for a globally based trade organization. It should also be less difficult and costly to monitor the agreement, an especially important matter when lower income nations are involved.

Teresa Nelson has argued that regional trade organizations might be more effective in supporting the peacekeeping economic principles if they followed the example of the fair trade NGOs and worked to eliminate unnecessary (and largely unproductive) intermediaries by connecting producers to buyers as directly as possible. This would allow producers (especially small producers) to receive a more equitable share of the gains of trade. Cooperation between, or more direct combination of, trade organizations and financial institutions engaged in microlending also makes sense. It could help the benefits of increased regional trade (and investment) to penetrate national economies more deeply to reach the poor, not as charity, but as payment for the product of their labors. Very small loans might be the key to greatly increasing the opportunities for those who have been locked in poverty to become active participants in a growing pool of intra-LDC trade, and therefore to share in its benefits. By helping to mitigate the extremes of economic inequality within countries, as well as to balance trade among them, these approaches would reduce the stress that can and does lead to the eruption of both internally and externally generated violent conflict.[56]

In practice, successfully forming effective international trade organizations requires serious attention to resolving the many conflicts that inevitably arise in negotiation—conflicts on the rules of trade, and conflicts on the rules for resolving present and future conflicts. This process has been playing itself out for more than half a century on a global scale in the various rounds of negotiations underlying the building of the GATT and its offspring, the WTO. Resolving the first type of conflict is critical to creating the organization; resolving the second type of conflict is critical to its longevity and effectiveness once it begins to function. Fortunately, the negotiating parties can embed in their trade agreement a variety of mechanisms that can keep it viable by resolving disputes that arise after the agreement takes effect.[57]

Successfully building economic cooperation through regional trade organizations is also more likely to lead to other forms of economic cooperation. Once these trading relationships are well established and perceived as mutually balanced and beneficial, these same organizations can work toward more rational regional patterns of other economic activity, including investment in development-enhancing infrastructure. Economies of scale that are difficult to achieve country-by-country may be easier to achieve regionally, without being overwhelmed by the task of trying to coordinate such activities on a global basis. It may also be easier to address some types of serious environmental problems regionally than either intranationally or globally. And as we have seen with the European Union, if things work well and the will is there, what begins as a regional trade organization can evolve over time into much broader forms of economic and political cooperation.

Institutions

Having considered a few types of organizational change that would be useful in enhancing the peacekeeping properties of the international economic system, it is time to consider some potentially useful institutions (in North's sense of the word) as well. The "rules of the game" they incorporate may or may not be promulgated or enforced by specific international organizations, but they nevertheless share the property of supporting one or another of the peacekeeping economic principles. As in the discussion of organizations, I have chosen the particular collection of institutional arrangements discussed below because I believe them to be particularly important to economic peacekeeping. But, as in the case of organizations, this list is illustrative, not comprehensive.

International Regulation of Multinational Corporations

Multinational corporations (MNCs) play a much greater role in the global economy today than they did in the 1960s and 1970s, when their activities became a matter of increasing concern. According to the UN Centre on Transnational Corporations, by the late 1980s, these firms already employed seventy million people around the world and produced 25 percent of all manufactured goods.[58] In a very real sense, MNCs represent an evolution of business beyond the evolution of political systems. They are capable of operating an integrated, centrally controlled organization on a truly global scale. Their ability to coordinate financing, investment, production, and marketing activities worldwide takes them beyond the reach of any single political authority.[59]

To some, MNCs are among the most dangerous and exploitative forces in the world today; to others, they are the greatest force for encouraging development and the kind of ongoing, mutually beneficial international economic relationships that build trust and understanding around the globe.

In any case, there is no doubt that they have revolutionized the conduct of international business within a remarkably short period of time.

Multinational business has already created a vastly more integrated and interdependent international economy, and is capable of carrying the process much further. That is potentially a good thing. The problem is that much of this integration has been shaped by decisions made in pursuit of corporate goals that emphasize the growth in the size and power of the corporations, rather than the economic, social, or political benefit of the wider society. Although decisions made on this narrow basis won't inevitably be in conflict with the broader and longer-term goals that characterize a peacekeeping international economy, there is also no reason why they should be compatible. It cannot be blithely assumed that they would produce the same sort of global economic system that would result from the direct, conscious pursuit of peacekeeping economic goals.

The extent to which MNCs encourage or discourage economic development, for example, is still a matter of dispute. It is clear that some of the past actions of MNCs have interfered with development directly and/or tacitly or have explicitly supported repressive governments that have been more interested in law and order than in justice or development. But what has been the *net* effect of MNCs on development? On balance, do they contribute additional capital, train more indigenous personnel, and transfer useful technologies to LDCs? Or do they mainly divert the limited capital available in LDCs from local entrepreneurs, preempt already skilled workers, and either prevent meaningful technological transfer or perhaps transfer only technologies that make local operations more dependent on MNCs and have little positive effect on local economies? These are important empirical questions to which we still do not have clear and definitive answers. Nevertheless, whether MNCs have net negative or positive effects on development, it is important to understand that those effects are incidental to their primary goals. These corporations are not in the business of encouraging or discouraging development, they are in the business of making money. That is not an innately bad or good thing. It is simply the reality. But it does have important policy implications.

To the extent that MNCs are operating at cross purposes to the principles of a peacekeeping international economy, rules of the game must be established that will give them strong incentives to shift to more desirable behaviors, without directly intervening in the details of their operations. But in the absence of an overarching political authority such as a world government, who can effectively change the rules of the game for corporations whose operations routinely transcend national political boundaries?

It is perfectly possible to change the rules of the game for MNCs through the international cooperation of nation-states in establishing mechanisms such as a generally agreed convention on the conduct of multinational business. Comparable international agreements already effectively govern the conduct of international air travel, postal service, and behavior on the high seas. Like every other set of laws, these agreements are sometimes violated. But on the whole, compliance is reasonably good. Enforcement of a code intended to regulate the behavior of MNCs could be achieved through a combination of domestic legal arrangements in each signatory country, the equivalent of international extradition treaties, and economic sanctions instituted by a multilateral organization like the Council on Economic Sanctions and Peacekeeping (CESP), discussed earlier in this chapter. Economic sanctions are a particularly useful enforcement tool here. They are even more likely to be effective against economic enterprises than they are against renegade governments. But perhaps the most logical organization to deal with the details of regulating MNCs is an appropriately modified version of the WTO, redesigned to be more equitable in its structure and operation. I will say more about the WTO next chapter.

Setting up clear and socially responsible rules of the game for international business is hardly a new idea. There already have been a number of efforts to promulgate codes of conduct for multinational corporations, most of which include some combination of issues of workplace and worker rights, environmental responsibility, human rights, appropriate conduct in conflict zones, ethical behavior, and wider social impact. Some have been championed by intergovernmental organizations, such as the UN's Global Compact, the more narrowly focused UN Norms on the Responsibilities of Transnational Corporations and Other Business Enterprises with Regard to Human Rights, and the Guidelines for Multinational Enterprises of the Organization for Economic Cooperation and Development (OECD).[60] Others come from financial institutions, such as the Equator Principles, launched by a group of international private sector banks in June 2003, which "established a framework for addressing the social and environmental issues surrounding lending to controversial projects"; and the Hermes Principles, put forth in 2002 by the company that manages of one of the biggest pension funds in Britain, a central principle of which holds that "companies should behave ethically and have regard for the environment and society as a whole."[61] Still others, such as the Principles for Global Corporate Responsibility: Benchmarks for Measuring Business Performance (launched in May 2003), were developed by NGOs and faith-based organizations. French president Jacques Chirac reportedly had planned to propose that the G8 leaders endorse a Charter of Principles for a Responsible Market Economy at the June 2003 summit he was hosting in Evian, but abandoned the idea because of U.S. and British opposition.[62]

Investors have a potentially powerful impact on corporate behavior because of their leverage as stockholders of, and/or lenders to, MNCs. The market for socially responsible investment was estimated to be nearing $3 trillion worldwide early in the twenty-first century.[63] Furthermore, "The divide between socially responsible investing and 'mainstream' financial investing has been diminishing as more companies take SRI [socially responsible investing] on board."[64]

Since the Interfaith Center for Corporate Responsibility (ICCR) was one of the founding organizations of the movement for corporate social responsibility, it is interesting to briefly take a closer look at the fairly comprehensive code of corporate conduct that they participated in developing. Principles for Global Corporate Responsibility addresses workplace conditions, calling on corporations to respect the International Labor Organization's core labor rights, such as freedom of association, the right to organize, nondiscrimination, protection of the rights of children, paying a "living wage," and providing a work environment that is healthy and free of harassment. It addresses environmental concerns, calling for firms to reduce pollution, protect biodiversity, and take responsibility for the life cycle environmental impact of their products and processes. It also provides contract supplier guidelines, calls for attention to the sustainability of local

communities, and strongly advises that "the company by policy and by practice does not commit or engage in activity which leads to the abuse and violation of internationally recognized human rights standards, nor does it
assist in abuses or violations committed by others. . . . [W]here it operates
in post-conflict and/or oppressive situations [it] seeks to implement existing
policies of reconciliation where they are in place."[65]

It may seem too softheaded to insist that hardnosed businesspeople and
the enterprises they run adhere to principles of ethics and social responsibility. But capitalism minus ethics equals Enron, and Enron is not a viable
model for a market system that works. This and other styles of unaccount-
able, no-holds-barred capitalism will not produce the considerable economic advantages that give capitalism its legitimacy, let alone create the
prosperous and peaceful world we'd like to see. In no small measure,
anything-goes financial capitalism played a key role in precipitating the
worldwide financial crisis of 2008 that brought so much economic dislocation and pain to so many. At the same time, for a code of conduct to set out
"rules of the game" that could serve as a practical basis for the global
regulation of business, it must leave firms plenty of flexibility to carry out
their operations in ways that are profitable enough to be economically viable. That is a prerequisite for the regulatory process to make economic
sense, as well as for having the slightest chance of being taken seriously
politically. It is also a prerequisite for it to serve the interests of building
and sustaining a peacekeeping economy. We need not, and should not try
to, turn profit-making business enterprises into angels, any more than we
should let them do whatever is in the short-term interest of the corporation
without any regard for its broader and longer-term social and political consequences.

It has become a commonplace to claim that any meaningful attempt to
constrain the behavior of business through regulation is bound to impose
substantial economic costs, and that these costs undercut the ability of the
companies affected to compete against rivals that are not subject to these
burdensome regulatory requirements. More stringent environmental regulations in the U.S. put American firms at a disadvantage relative to their
competitors in China, where environmental rules are much less stringent.

Because this argument seems so straightforward, it is often accepted uncritically. But in the first place, the costs imposed by regulations are not always anywhere near the burden or the handicap that those who oppose them like to contend. For example, industry groups in Europe have claimed that the EU's proposed rigorous new chemicals safety and environmental regulations (known as REACH) will be prohibitively expensive. Yet Frank Ackerman and Rachel Massey have calculated that if the entire €3.5-billion cost of these relatively expensive regulations were fully passed on to customers, it would raise the average price of chemicals produced by European industry by only about one-sixteenth of one percent (0.0006), hardly a lethal blow to European competitiveness.[66]

Secondly, a set of globally imposed regulations, such as a seriously enforced uniform code of conduct for MNCs, could not put any given industry or firm at a competitive disadvantage because all its rivals would be subject to precisely the same set of rules.

Regulation of International Trade in Hazardous Materials and Products

Trade in hazardous materials raises both environmental and political concerns. Transportation and storage accidents can pose a real threat to public health and safety. Furthermore, some of these materials can be used to manufacture products, including military weapons and terrorist weapons, whose actual or even threatened use can compromise national well-being and international security. Hazardous materials are a cause for serious concern when they are traded wholly within a nation. But accidents with or intentional use of dangerous goods shipped in from other nations have a still higher probability of generating or sustaining violent conflict.

Because of differences in health and safety regulations, it is not all that rare for producers to sell unsafe or at least questionable products internationally that can no longer be legally sold in their own home country. Pesticides and pharmaceuticals, for example, banned within some developed countries, have been sold by MDC producers for use in economically less developed countries whose health and safety regulations were also less developed. Yet there is not a shred of evidence to indicate that the people in the

LDCs or the environments in which they live are less susceptible than those in the MDCs to the medical or ecological dangers that caused those products to be severely restricted or banned in the first place.

If such trade is allowed to continue, it sends a clear message that those in the MDCs believe that the health and well-being of people in the LDCs are somehow less important. That is not only profoundly immoral, it is exactly the type of message that is bound to generate the international antagonism and conflict that a peacekeeping economy must seek to avoid. It is foolish and counterproductive in other ways as well. For one thing, pollution knows no national boundaries. An ecologically damaging substance that has been banned in MDCs but is then sold to LDCs may well find its way across borders to MDCs. Even if the substance itself does not, the environmental damage it causes might. Furthermore, when MDCs import LDC products that have been produced with the banned substance, they may import the dangers as well. Fruit, for example, that has been grown with the use of a pesticide banned in the MDCs because it has been found to be carcinogenic may be imported to the MDCs, even the same MDC whose producers sold the banned pesticide in the first place. The MDC's consumers are therefore exposed to the very danger from which their own country's regulations were intended to protect them.

Conceptually, the easiest way to begin to deal with the problem is to negotiate an agreement in which each nation undertakes to write into its own legal code a law that prohibits the export of any product or material that cannot legally be sold within its own boundaries. Such a law could be written to include the activities of firms operating outside the nation's political jurisdiction that are subsidiaries of firms based within its jurisdiction.

There is also a large and flourishing trade in an even more important category of hazardous material—weapons, both large and small—and the equipment, components, and materials critical to building them. Over the period 1980–2005, more than $700 billion worth of major conventional weapons systems (in 1990 dollars) were bought and sold (or otherwise transferred) on the international arms market. More than $340 billion of that trade occurred after 1989, the putative end of the Cold War. More than two decades after their Cold War rivalry ended, Russia and the United States are still the largest suppliers of arms to the world. From 2001 to

2005, each had about a 30 percent share of the global market for major conventional weapons, with France, Germany, and the U.K. next in line at 9 percent, 6 percent, and 4 percent, respectively.[67] While this large and once again growing market in weapons may or may not contribute to outbreak of war, it certainly has made the wars that do break out far more destructive.

Because there are so many valuable civilian uses for so much of the industrial machinery and equipment that can also be used for weapons manufacture, it is doubtful that much can or should be done to try to restrict trade in any but the most specialized types of equipment and the most dangerous technologies and materials. Trade in fissionable materials and the equipment for concentrating them, along with the knowledge critical to the development and manufacture of nuclear weapons, clearly fall into the latter category.

An active black market in nuclear materials has existed for decades. A British documentary that aired in the late 1980s, *Dispatches: The Plutonium Black Market,* claimed that an illicit trade in nuclear materials had centered on Khartoum, Sudan, since at least the 1960s, allegedly involving Israel first, and later Argentina, Pakistan, and South Africa.[68] In 1987, the Sudanese prime minister reportedly briefly acknowledged (and then denied a few months later) the existence of such a black market when Sudan's government seized four kilograms of enriched uranium that had been smuggled into the country.[69] In the 1990s, there were a series of reports of nuclear and other dangerous materials smuggled out of the former Soviet Union.[70] And then there were the nuclear black market activities of Pakistani scientist A.Q. Khan, father of his nation's nuclear arsenal, which were apparently begun no later than the mid-1990s. In March 2005, the *New York Times* reported that Khan's network was believed to be selling "not only technology for enriching nuclear fuel and blueprints for nuclear weapons, but also . . . the hard to master engineering secrets needed to fabricate nuclear warheads." According to the report, North Korea, Libya, and Iran had all done business with Khan's network, though it is not known exactly what each of them had bought.[71]

It is not clear how much, if any, of this black market material and know-how may have reached the hands of terrorist groups. But even if none of it yet has, it would be foolish to assume that this will continue to be true.[72] Of course, we must be similarly concerned about trade in the other, nonnuclear materials and technologies of mass destruction (such as nerve gas and virulent biological weapons). Though there will never be a foolproof means of trade restriction, there is a compelling case for developing the most effective system possible for stemming trade in this brand of extremely hazardous products.

At the same time, there is also a strong case for limiting the international flow of small arms. Though they are not as frightening or dangerous as the technologies of mass destruction, they have fueled the many smaller-scale civil wars around the globe and made them more deadly. The fact is that much of the killing in organized conflicts in this world is carried out with small arms. Early in the twenty-first century, by some estimates more than one million people died in three years alone as a result of the trade in small arms.[73] Instead of a patchwork of arms embargoes based on the nature of political relations between pairs and among small groupings of nations, a more systematic and inclusive approach is required. Such a system should certainly put a substantial part of the responsibility for keeping track of small arms and ammunition on those who manufacture and sell them, and not rely solely on customs officials and the like. Modern record-keeping technologies, along with identification devices from bar codes to chemical taggants to RFIDs, are certainly up to the task.[74] The problem is no longer so much one of technology as it is one of political will.

Since the early 1990s, various efforts have attempted to develop principles and codes of conduct to regulate international traffic in conventional weapons. Recurring themes in these proposals include banning arms sales: 1) to nondemocratic regimes; 2) to regimes that are likely to use the weapons to commit violations of human rights; 3) when the sale of such arms will fuel ongoing internal or external conflicts; and 4) where arms sales could undercut development and exacerbate poverty.[75] During the 1990s, the U.S. established an arms trade code of conduct that prohibits arms transfers to nations that do not promote democracy, fail to respect human rights, or are engaged in armed aggression. However, the code allows the president to declare exceptions for what he or she considers reasons of national security or the existence of an emergency, and Congress requires a two-thirds vote to override the president. The European Union also introduced a code of conduct for arms exports in 1998, pretty much embodying the four principles above. Although both codes appear to be a step forward, there are still far too many ways for determined arms exporters to avoid or evade them. For example, arms producers can license the right to produce their weapons to foreign companies operating in areas with weak arms export controls; brokers can establish shell companies and shipping agents to transfer arms; exporters can engage in corrupt practices, such as using fraudulent end-user certificates for weapons sales, and can avoid punishment because of insufficient monitoring and oversight.[76]

On October 26, 2006, the first committee of the United Nations General Assembly voted overwhelmingly in favor of a resolution "calling for the establishment of a treaty to stop weapons transfers that fuel conflict, poverty and serious human rights violations." Some 140 countries voted in favor, 24 abstained (Russia, China, India, and Pakistan did not participate in the voting), and only one country—the United States, the world's largest arms exporter—voted no. The vote came after three years of negotiations by diplomats and, it is worth noting, a global campaign by NGOs involving 170 countries and more than one million people.[77]

It may be impossible to design systems and negotiate agreements that regulate trade in hazardous products as thoroughly as would be ideal from the perspective of a peacekeeping economy. Nevertheless, international agreements and regulatory mechanisms for enforcing them can certainly be made more restrictive and less porous than they are today. The arms trade increases not only the level of damage done when war does erupt, but also the likelihood that nations that supply critical arms to the combatants will somehow be drawn into the conflict—if not directly, then perhaps indirectly as targets of terrorist acts initiated by those angered by the arms supplying nation's role. Trade in the most hazardous products is too dangerous and provocative to be considered a legitimate part of the broadening of trade that is key to a peacekeeping international economy.

The Spread of Liberal Democracy

The combination of representative democracy (in which those who govern are chosen in free and fair elections by the governed), constitutional checks and balances, and commitment to the rule of law has come to be known as "liberal democracy." With the benefit of hindsight and more than two hundred years of experience, it is even clearer in the twenty-first century than when it was advocated by James Madison in the eighteenth century that this approach was basically sound. Liberal democracy is the best guarantor yet developed of government driven by the will of the majority but protective of the rights of the minority, even the rights of a minority of one.

A truly liberal democracy includes broad civil liberties guarantees not only built into the constitution and laws of the society, but also enshrined in its norms of daily behavior. The basic freedoms of speech, the press, association, belief, and the like, as well as equality before the law and equality of opportunity, are key to respect for the dignity and potential of each human being. As a result, they are also key to the creation of a decent society capable of solving its problems effectively, resolving its conflicts peacefully, and providing the political context necessary for a high quality of life. To the extent that the emphasis on political liberty in liberal democracy carries with it emphasis on freedom and equality of opportunity in the economic arena, it will encourage initiative and provide strong incentives for increasing productivity and innovation as well, helping to create material prosperity and facilitate the establishment of balanced, mutually beneficial domestic and international economic relationships.

Going back at least to Immanuel Kant, it has been a tenet of political liberalism that republics in which individuals have fundamental civil rights are less likely than autocratic forms of government to go to war, and thus that the spread of liberal democracy is a force for peace. The modern variant of this idea has come to be known as the "democratic peace" argument (Chapter 2). Advocates of democratic peace do not generally argue that liberal democracies are less likely to go to war because they are in some sense less conflictual, more peace-loving societies. Rather they argue that liberal democracies are unlikely go to war *with each other* because of shared norms of, and working internal mechanisms for, nonviolent conflict resolution. When confronting other democracies, it is also much more difficult for a democratic government to argue for violent regime change by claiming that the government of the opposing country does not represent the will of its own people.[78] Democracies are not necessarily all that hesitant about going to war with authoritarian nations, as we have repeatedly seen. In fact, often enough the leaders of liberal democracies explicitly use the authoritarian nature of nations against which they have decided to take hostile action, up to and including military invasion, as part of their argument to build support for going to war among their own people. The Bush administration's 2003 invasion of Saddam Hussein's Iraq is an obvious case in point.

There is considerable power to the democratic peace argument. Functional liberal democracies are theoretically and empirically less likely to go to war with each other than with nondemocratic nations, or than nondemocratic nations are to go to war with each other. Functional liberal democracies are also less likely to experience serious eruptions of civil war and rebellion, not only because of their norms of peaceful conflict resolution, but also because they have better *mechanisms* more widely available to their own people for expressing political opinions and getting grievances heard, as well as for peacefully resolving conflicts.

The idea of democratic peace and the principles of economic peacekeeping are more than compatible; they are mutually supportive. The spread of liberal democracy creates fertile ground for the establishment of a peacekeeping economy. At the same time, the implementation of economic peacekeeping principles, especially the first principle of broadening and balancing international economic relationships, also plays an important role in supporting the spread of liberal democracy. The school of thought that Susan McMillan characterizes as "sociological liberalism" emphasizes the importance of connections among people that form in the course of commercial relationships. According to this concept, the communication and cooperation that those ongoing links imply will increase people's knowledge and appreciation of each other and of their customs and culture.[79] Part of the knowledge and appreciation of culture that is likely to grow as a result of positive commercial experiences is knowledge and appreciation of political culture. As the network of balanced economic relationships between liberal democracies and nondemocratic states expands, the normal ongoing interactions among business people and their friends and families help to convey democratic ideas to people living in more authoritarian countries. To the extent that the ideals of liberal democracy are appealing, this process will slowly build a solid base for the evolutionary, if not revolutionary, replacement of authoritarianism with more democratic forms of governance by the people of those countries themselves. This is likely to be a far more effective way to spread workable forms of democracy than attempts by foreign governments to impose democratic systems through the force of arms.[80]

Together, the nonviolent spread of liberal democracy and the building of a peacekeeping international economy help reduce the likelihood of both civil and international war more than either process could by itself.

The Role of Religion

Samuel Huntington argues that the end of the Cold War produced a multipolar world characterized by what he calls a "clash of civilizations." This clash is most importantly characterized by "fault lines" between Eastern Orthodox and Western Christians, Western Christians and Muslims, Muslims and Hindus, and Hindus and Chinese. Huntington sees a world of endless conflict across these fault lines, occasionally punctuated by spasms of violence and war, especially between Muslims and non-Muslims.[81] Religion clearly plays a central role in this pessimistic and paranoid worldview.

There is certainly a connection between religion (or at least religious identification) and conflict in today's world. Reflecting on the nature of then current conflicts in 2001, John Ullmann wrote, "The largest group of . . . conflicts is religious. Some originate with events long past that are treated as if they happened yesterday, such as the battle of Poitiers in 732 that halted the Arab incursion into Europe, the final split between the Catholic and Orthodox churches in 1054 that set Serbs against Croats in Yugoslavia, the battle of Kosovo in 1389 that established the Ottoman empire and Islam in the Balkans, and of course that hardy perennial, anti-Semitism."[82]

It is impossible to deny that religion has been an important driver of war and other forms of violent conflict. Millennia of human history provide more than ample evidence for this proposition. But at the same time, religion has also indisputably been an important disseminator of the idea that the pursuit of peace is a lofty and moral goal, and a key motivator of movements for social justice. Although there is considerable variation among religious traditions in the emphasis given to one or another of these roles, it is important to note that no particular religion has had a monopoly on any of them.

Within the realm of organized religion today and for the foreseeable future, the most critical distinction between traditions that are and those that are not likely to generate war, terrorism, and other forms of violent confrontation (and thus interfere with the building and goals of a peacekeeping international economy) does not lie across the broad categories of religion on which Huntington focuses. What matters is not the difference between Muslims, Christians, Jews, Hindus, Buddhists, and the like; rather, it is the difference between fundamentalist religious fanatics of all faiths and the vast majority of their other adherents.

The fanatical religious fundamentalists within any broad category of organized religion see themselves as utterly distinct from those fundamentalist fanatics of any other religious stripe, but the fact is that they have much in common. As Ullmann has put it,

> Whatever their mutual hatreds and claims as the only sources of wisdom and salvation, fundamentalists of all faiths may be said to share three doctrines. First, life is better in the hereafter, so there is every reason to get there for the cause. Second, they are much given to establishing careful rules for sexual behavior that ultimately boil down to tyranny over women. Third, they espouse cultural "purification," meaning censorship and tight control.[83]

I want to be clear that I am not arguing that all those who believe in a strict interpretation of their own religious tradition, and so might legitimately be called "fundamentalist," fall into this category of religious fanatic. It comes down to a matter of tolerance and respect. No matter how committed one may be to his or her own faith, no matter how deeply that person believes that it is the only "true path," if that individual respects the right of others to believe and openly practice differently without harassment, interference, or recrimination, then he or she may be a fundamentalist but not a fanatic. Whatever the doctrinal and ritualistic differences, to the extent that the institutions of organized religions emphasize the necessity of tolerance and respect for other beliefs, they are not inherently in conflict with the goals of a peacekeeping economy.

In fact, religion has historically had much to say on a number of subjects central to, consistent with, and supportive of the building of a peacekeeping international economy. Many religious traditions embrace some version of the Golden Rule ("Do unto others as you would have them do unto you"), which amounts to a call to engage in relationships that are balanced and mutually beneficial, rather than in those that dominate and exploit. The moral imperative of taking actions that will help those who are disadvantaged (economically and otherwise) to improve their condition is another common thread. Religion also typically has something to say about the relationship between humans and the environment, though some traditions see humans as holding dominion over the nonhuman world, while others see the human role as one of stewardship and caretaking, and still others see people as simply a thread in the complex web of life. Finally, issues of violence, brutality, and war—and the ascendancy of peace as an ultimate goal—are core elements in virtually all major religious traditions.

The Peacekeeping Economy: Who Gains, Who Loses

Douglass North has argued, "Institutions . . . are created to serve the interests of those with the bargaining power to devise new rules."[84] If he is right, then judging the prospects for actually establishing new organizations and institutions—or modifying or expanding those that already exist—to better support a peacekeeping economy requires an assessment of whose interests would be furthered and whose interests would be contravened. Only the most general assessment is possible here. But it is too important a question to ignore.

The sampling of supportive organizations and institutions we have discussed in this chapter includes: 1) a UN Council on Economic Sanctions and Peacekeeping; 2) a modified World Bank more effective at promoting sustainable development; 3) a more effective Global Environmental Fund; 4) LDC primary product cartels; 5) fair trade NGOs; 6) LDC-LDC trade promoting organizations; 7) more effective international regulation of multinational business (including corporate codes of conduct); 8) stronger regulation of international trade in hazardous materials and products (including weapons); 9) nonviolent spread of liberal democracy; and 10) increased emphasis on the peace-oriented commonalities of varying religious traditions (including mutual tolerance and respect).

It is tempting to argue that the most obvious powerful interest contravened by these changes—and for that matter, by the very construction of a peacekeeping international economy—would be that of the world's military establishments. While that is largely true, it is not entirely true. The success of a peacekeeping economy and its various adjunct organizations and institutions in forestalling the outbreak of war in all of its forms would substantially reduce the need for and the emphasis on military forces. That in turn would correspondingly shrink the flow of resources to the world's armed forces, an outcome that is not likely to be greeted with wild enthusiasm by military establishments. But the need for military forces would not be entirely eliminated. Instead their function would be changed to that of being the option of last resort for protecting their country or securing the most vital legitimate interests of their people after every other alternative has failed. That is still a proud and patriotic mission. As it used to be said in the pre–World War II U.S., "The military should be on tap, not on top." More than a few military officers around the world, particularly those who have seen the real face of war, could not only accept but might well prefer such a mission.

Still, the military establishments of the world are unlikely to be happy about the prospect of a dramatic loss of power and resources. Nevertheless, I believe the strongest, most dogged opposition to the changes I have discussed will come from those businesses (and related institutions, such as government laboratories) with a major focus on producing weapons, weapons technology, and allied equipment for military use. Too much of what they do depends upon a large and continuing flow of funding from the military budget. This group includes not just the owners and managers of such enterprises, but also the people who work for them and the surrounding community that sees them as an economic asset, all of whom can be expected to do what they can to see to it that their piece of military funding continues. It has happened many times before. Removing this major source of economically based political opposition to any changes that would substantially shrink the military sector is important to making progress in directing society toward less military-oriented paths to achieving security. The key is not only providing viable economic alternatives for the managements, workforces, and communities involved, but also working out a smooth and efficient way to make the transition to these new activities. In less developed countries, the actual demobilization and reintegration of those who serve in the military itself is also a first order consideration. The nature of these transitions and the strategies for carrying them out are the subject of Chapter 8.

The economic gains from moving to a far less militarized security system are potentially very large, much larger than the economic losses to those disadvantaged by this change. Those gains are the subject of Chapter 7. The benefits they represent can be expected to flow to civilian-oriented commercial business; the nonmilitary agencies of all levels of government and the programs they support; key nonprofit institutions of society such as public schools, universities, and public hospitals; and the general public. But the mere fact that the gains are much larger than the losses in the aggregate does not guarantee that these changes will have enough political support to be realized. The truth is, smaller but more highly concentrated vested interests often trump even much larger but much more diffuse interests. One of the reasons is that it is easier for more concentrated interests to see that they have a substantial stake in the outcome, which leads them to invest more resources in their cause and be more persistent in pursuing it. This is why raising awareness of what is possible and what is at stake in terms of the wider interest of the society is so important to making progressive change.

There is a great deal at stake in terms of the wider interests of society in building an international security system based more on economic peacekeeping principles than on the threat or use of military force. In these increasingly troubled and troubling times, it is a realistic and practical path to creating a world that is more peaceful, as well as more prosperous and secure.

Before moving on to further analyze the critical issues of gains and transitions, it is worth taking a closer look at the worldwide phenomenon that
provides such an important context for the web of international economic
relationships—the much discussed phenomenon of globalization—and its
relationship to the issue of global security. That is the subject to which we
now turn.

6

Does Globalization Contribute to Economic Peacekeeping?

MUCH HAS BEEN WRITTEN about the ongoing process of heightened worldwide economic, political, and cultural integration that has come to be known as "globalization." Its most ardent advocates claim that it is leading us inexorably toward a world of unprecedented prosperity, a world where borders don't matter and all of us have access to the same opportunities to succeed in life. Its most ardent opponents claim that it is riding roughshod over cultural, political, and social diversity, provoking a "race to the bottom" of the economic barrel for an increasing proportion of the earth's population and, in the process, savaging the global environment. And then there are those who argue that the whole phenomenon is grossly exaggerated, that the world was more economically integrated a hundred or more years ago, and more politically integrated in the Age of Empire.[1]

The purpose of this chapter is not so much to wade into the midst of this controversy as to raise two main questions relevant to the impact of increasing global integration on the prospects for and performance of a peacekeeping international economy: 1) Does economic globalization have the potential to contribute to international security as well as to general economic well-being? and 2) If so, what forms of and paths to economic globalization are most helpful in realizing both those potentials?

The first thing to note is that globalization is neither an inherently elitist plot nor a recently discovered path to nirvana. It is instead the natural outcome of a broad trend of widening and thickening human interaction that has been going on for thousands, if not millions, of years. As the technologies of transportation and communication improved over many millennia of human history (and prehistory), formerly isolated groups have more and more come into contact. They increasingly traded with each other, learned from each other, and, all too often, fought with each other. In the course of doing so, the exchange of goods, ideas, and practices broadened, intensified, and became more important to them. Like the earlier stages of this process, the most recent globalization stage too has been greatly facilitated by improvements in the technologies of transportation and communication that, in this case, had their origins in the late nineteenth century and underwent explosive growth during the twentieth century.

In a sense, some form of globalization was virtually inevitable, given human curiosity, greed, and technological prowess.[2] But that does not presuppose that the particular form of globalization we have today was or is inevitable. We can still change the shape of globalization in any way we choose.

To date, the modern phase of globalization has not in any sense made the world "flat," to use Thomas Friedman's inept metaphor.[3] It may have made the playing field more level in that there is wider, less restricted access to markets, and a more consistent set of rules with which economic rivals must comply. But that does not mean that all hard-working, capable competitors have an equal chance of succeeding in the global marketplace, as the image of a "flat world" implies. The small- to medium-size local entrepreneur does not have anywhere near as good a chance of winning the global competition as does the large multinational corporation (MNC). As Ethan Kapstein puts it, "Libertarian or procedural theorists . . . find justice in the rules and procedures that shape market relationships and transactions. I do not believe such rules are always *sufficient* for establishing a level playing field—a soccer team from a small university hardly enjoys a 'level playing field' in its contest against Real Madrid, even though the ground rules are the same for both teams."[4]

There are still vast inequalities in opportunities as well as in outcomes (such as wealth, power, and income) around the world, though inequalities of opportunity may be less a function of pure geography today than in times gone by. The opportunities available to individuals remain very much a matter of socioeconomic class, and increasingly a matter of skill level. While individuals with comparable levels of skill are in more direct competition across borders than ever before, access to the means of acquiring comparable skill is still far from universal. An engineer in India may be more able to compete with an engineer in the U.S. for a particular piece of work now than in the past, but not every Indian (or American) who has the desire and potential to be an engineer has an equal chance of getting the necessary education.

Does Bigger Mean Better?

Businesspeople and economists long ago discovered that increasing the scale of operations often reduces the cost per unit of the good or service being produced. These "economies of scale" are the result of enabling the use of organizational practices and technologies of mass production that are very efficient when the volume of output is large (and typically very inefficient when it is not). Bigger seems obviously better. But in the first place, merely being bigger is not enough to achieve these efficiency gains—the right practices and technologies must be adopted. Furthermore, there are limits to economies of scale. At some size, growing bigger still may not reduce cost per unit very much ("decreasing returns to scale"), and may even result in higher unit costs ("negative returns to scale"), as information, motivation, and coordination problems raise the cost of operations. Whether these limits on economies of scale become serious within a range of size that is relevant to real world markets is an empirical question. It is unwise to simply assume that they do not.[5]

Still, with the exception of Principle II (independence in critical goods), the expansion and intensification of economic relationships that is a key part of globalization are not only consistent with, but also strongly supportive of and perhaps essential to, building a peacekeeping international economy. In that sense, bigger seems clearly better. Whether that is true or not depends on the conditions and rules of the game under which globalization takes place, as well as on the nature of the most important players.

For purposes of rough comparison, treating gross sales of MNCs as a measure of economic size comparable to Gross Domestic Product (GDP) for nations, the combined size of the top 200 global corporations had already exceeded the combined size of 182 national economies (all but the 9 largest) more than a decade ago.[6] To the extent that large multinational corporations wielding substantial monopoly power dominate globalized markets, even if their unit costs of production are lower they will act to keep prices substantially above costs, as monopolistic firms are wont to do. Prices could conceivably be higher than they would be if less globalized markets were serviced by more localized intensely competitive smaller firms whose costs were higher. Even from the narrowly economic standpoint, then, it is a nontrivial question to ask whether expanding markets to the global scale actually leads to both decreasing costs *and* sufficient competition to force prices down, making goods and services affordable to a wider range of the world's population.

Expanding markets to the global scale also raises political concerns. After all, economic power and political power are in many ways fungible. Large multinational firms are not merely economic enterprises; they also represent considerable centers of potential political power and influence whose actions could affect the outcome of elections (as well as other processes that determine who governs) and distort government policymaking to their advantage. The political process, especially the democratic political process, is likely to work better in the absence of high concentrations of economic power, and very large corporations represent high concentrations of economic power. That globalization can promote the further growth of firms capable of not only affecting politics within their home countries but also reaching across the globe to influence the political process in every country in which they operate is indeed another reason why bigger does not always mean better.

Of course, the fact that large MNCs can and do influence economic and political processes does not in itself mean that they will use their influence in ways that are detrimental to the interests of the broader public. Nor does it mean that their behavior cannot be affected by that public. We have already argued, for example, that NGO boycott, stockholder resolution, and "naming and shaming" campaigns (among other approaches) have demonstrated an ability to pressure even very large MNCs engaged in harmful practices to alter their behavior, and sometimes positively influence the behavior of others (Chapter 4). Even in the absence of such pressures, there is nothing inherent about being a large MNC that prevents firms from behaving in ways that support, rather than contravene, the public interest. But then the same thing can be said of kings, and yet we are undoubtedly better off with elected officials running our governments.

It is perfectly possible, though not particularly easy, for governments to agree to jointly and separately set up "rules of the game" that allow for globalization that does not facilitate the degeneration of the international marketplace into a playground for a relatively small number of dominant firms. Among the most obvious of these is serious antitrust policy, to break up huge firms into smaller, more competitive pieces. Even if there is some loss in narrowly defined efficiency (e.g., lower unit cost) in the process the benefits of ensuring more competition and less economically based concentration of political power are almost certainly greater than the costs.

Globalization dominated by large monopolistic firms is more likely than a less monopolized, more competitive form of globalization to violate Principle I of the peacekeeping economy. It is tempting for large firms with considerable monopoly power to use the disproportionate economic leverage they have to form economic relationships that are more exploitative than balanced and mutually beneficial—especially when they are dealing with local businesses, disorganized and economically depressed workforces, and relatively unsophisticated or corrupt governments. These conditions are more likely to exist in less developed countries, making the economic relationships that large MNCs form with the enterprises and governments of LDCs generally less balanced than those they form with the enterprises and governments of MDCs. Since more exploitative relationships are less likely to stimulate development, globalization dominated by large monopolistic firms is also not particularly supportive of peacekeeping Principle III (emphasize development).

The impact of economic globalization on the ecology of the planet also depends on the rules of the game, the conditions under which it is played, and the nature of the players. If we continue to insist on a simpleminded definition of economic progress as producing ever greater quantities of goods and services, then the growth we associate with globalization will ultimately do intolerable damage to the global environment, compromising our economic, political, and social well-being. If we continue to allow the economic agents who cause environmental damage to escape paying for it, they will continue to ignore the costs that environmental damage imposes on everyone else. Expanding economic activity on a global scale will therefore move us closer and closer to the edge of the ecological abyss. Bigger will definitely not mean better.

In theory, if the CEOs of large, monopolistic MNCs took a long-term view of their trust to operate the firm in the best interest of the stockholders, they would make decisions that might result in less environmental damage than would be done by a host of smaller highly competitive firms. For example, a lumber firm with monopoly control over a forest would have an incentive to harvest the wood sustainably because the company would know that this practice will preserve a valuable, income-generating asset for the firm into the indefinite future. Give smaller, fiercely competitive lumber companies access to the same forest, and they will rapidly cut it down, each company lacking assurance that replanting and/or slowing the rate of harvest would not simply leave more trees for their competitors to harvest. But if the CEOs of large, monopolistic firms believe their tenure at the firm will be relatively limited and that their compensation is closely related to their firms' short-term performance (as is so often the case in the U.S.), they may become more fixated on short-term profitability than on long-term viability. The incentive to carefully husband their firms' resources will evaporate, and the forest will disappear. In the context of globalization, this may be heightened by a frontier mentality—use up the land, then move on.

Furthermore, even in theory, the argument that monopolies will do less ecological damage applies only to sustainable harvesting of well-defined *renewable* resources. They do have an incentive to deplete reserves of *nonrenewable* resources (such as coal and oil) more slowly, but they do not have an incentive to limit the environmental damage they do in the process of extracting those resources. They may, for example, take coal from the land at a more measured pace, while at the same time having few qualms about using an ecologically devastating process (such as mountaintop removal mining) to extract the coal. They also have no incentive to pay any more attention than highly competitive firms do to the pollution they release into the air or water, even though they can more easily afford pollution control. Because large monopolistic firms are in a better position to exert political influence, they are more able than smaller, more competitive firms to shape the structure and enforcement of pollution control laws and regulations to their advantage, avoiding the costs of changing the processes they use to reduce the environmental damage they are doing.

Globalization, whether dominated by more or less monopolistic firms, inherently implies greater reliance on long-distance transportation than would a system of economic relationships that are either locally or regionally focused. The current system of transportation is so reliant on fossil fuels that it is a major source of air pollution in general, and global warming in particular. Unless we move to more ecologically benign transportation technologies, this aspect of globalization will worsen the global burden of pollution.

In summary, if globalization proceeds via a vast expansion in the quantities of goods and services produced and then transported over ever greater distances in a fossil-fuel based system of production and distribution dominated by large monopolistic, short-term-oriented MNCs, it will do increased damage to the global environment and thus run counter to peacekeeping Principle IV (minimize ecological stress), as well as to Principles I and III. But globalization need not proceed in this way.

Alternate, more competitive and balanced forms of globalization, operating under a basically free market ideology bounded by a properly designed set of rules of the game, conditions, and institutions, are not only consistent with but also highly supportive of peacekeeping economic principles. In short, if globalization is done right, bigger really can be better.

Globalization and the Theory of Comparative Advantage

The most recent phase of economic globalization is consciously driven by the liberal ideology of free trade. The idea that uncontrolled, unregulated, and unobstructed trade across national boundaries increases economic well-being had its origins in the eighteenth century writings of

Adam Smith. It was refined and taken to a new level in the nineteenth century writings of economist David Ricardo, who developed the theory of comparative advantage.

The essence of Ricardo's argument is that the labor, capital, and natural resource endowment (including such things as climate and geographic location) of each country is somewhat different, giving it an advantage relative to other countries in producing certain types of goods and services. If each nation specializes in producing those goods and services that it is best at producing, and trades for the other goods and services its people want and need, not only will the largest total world output of goods and services be produced, but each nation individually will also be better off than if it tries to produce all the goods and services its people want on its own.

Although this argument has its intricacies, the basic proposition is easy enough to accept. After all, it is obvious that we are all better off as individuals by being able to "specialize" in doing the things that we do relatively well (our "comparative advantage") and "trade" for the other things we need, than we would be if we each had to do everything for ourselves.[7] If it is clearly true for people, why should it not also be true for nations?

The theory of comparative advantage has been criticized on a number of grounds. First of all, it is a comparative static theory: it doesn't consider that freezing trade flows according to the pattern of comparative advantage that exists at any point in time interferes with structural change that is critical to real economic development, especially in LDCs. Raising education levels, improving the skill of the labor force, and adopting updated technologies are vital to making progress in economic development. Yet they all can change comparative advantage. Investing the time, money, and effort needed to accomplish them will not be encouraged if nations are restricted to producing the same kinds of goods and services they have produced efficiently in the past, and must give up moving into new areas of economic activity in which they will almost certainly not be very efficient at the outset.

Furthermore, those countries whose comparative advantage lies in primary products, such as unrefined minerals, timber, and especially agricultural goods (mainly LDCs), will be at a chronic disadvantage in a purely free trade environment. Primary product markets tend to have unstable prices that are typically low relative to the prices of processed goods and services that primary goods exporting LDCs must buy from other nations. Agricultural products in particular are also subject to wide swings in supply (and therefore in price) because of weather conditions and other factors that are largely or completely beyond the control of farmers in the countries that produce them.

The theory of comparative advantage implicitly assumes that when patterns of production and trade do change, labor will move instantaneously and costlessly from one activity to another within the country. That is simply untrue. Skill-based, cultural, and other rigidities mean that when a country switches from producing a wide array of goods and services to specializing in areas of production where it has a comparative advantage, labor formerly employed in the areas abandoned will not easily find employment in the "new economy." Without specific transitional assistance, the period of unemployment can be long and painful for those displaced and those who depend on their income. (Transition issues are discussed in more detail in Chapter 8.)

It is also assumed that the resource endowment that creates a nation's pattern of relative advantage does not change easily. That is truer of its natural resources than of capital and labor, both of which are at least potentially mobile and changeable. If all capital and labor were perfectly mobile, the only thing left that would be relevant to the theory's foundational idea that countries have durably different comparative advantages would be their endowment of immobile natural resources. In reality, some types of capital are quite fluid, while other types cannot be readily changed or moved from place to place;[8] labor tends to be even less mobile than capital for various political, social, and economic reasons. But neither is fixed in place.

Finally, the theory postulates a world in which economic activity is carried out by firms that are engaged in fierce competition with each other, whereas much international trade today is carried out by large multinational corporations. In fact, a substantial amount of what we call international trade today consists of transfers internal to large MNCs whose subsidiaries are widely dispersed geographically, by some estimates between 30 and 50 percent.[9] It is also noteworthy that "in the 1990s, . . . overseas production by American transnational corporations was more than twice the value of American exports; sales by foreign-owned companies inside the United States were nearly twice the value of imports."[10] This is not the picture of international trade that underlies Ricardo's nineteenth century theory of comparative advantage.

Apart from these theoretical issues, some critics have argued that the idea that protectionism is anathema and free trade is critical to development is simply not supported by historical experience.[11] The growth of the textile industry in the United Kingdom in the seventeenth and eighteenth centuries took place behind a high wall of tariff barriers. Britain had high tariffs on manufactured goods through the early nineteenth century, decades after its industrial revolution began.[12] By the time manufacturing tariffs were eliminated, U.K. manufacturing had developed enough to be able to handle foreign competition on its own. The great industrial expansion in the U.S. from 1870 to 1910 took place in a protectionist environment, when average tariffs on manufactured goods were on the order of 40–50 percent. Even the Smoot-Hawley Tariff of 1930, which is often "credited" with deepening the Great Depression, applied an average manufactured goods tariff of 48 percent, which is within this range.[13] Only after World War II, when U.S. industrial capabilities were already firmly established, was there a steady reduction in tariffs.

More recently, a combination of tariff and nontariff barriers, along with significant government involvement in the economy, accompanied Japan's economic emergence into the ranks of advanced industrial nations. And beginning as an economically impoverished and war-devastated nation in the early 1950s, South Korea became one of the most striking examples of the rapid development of an LDC in modern history without following anything approaching a pure free trade path. From the early 1960s on, government policy protected domestic markets, heavily favored Korean-owned firms, and used state-owned industries to increase national productive capacity in strategic areas. The extent of South Korea's economic achievements are especially impressive when compared to those of North Korea, which remains mired in deep poverty.

Looking at the same issue from a different direction, consider the impact on Mexico of its entry into the North American Free Trade Agreement

(NAFTA) in 1994, a wide-reaching agreement to open trade with both of its more developed neighbors to the north, Canada and the U.S. As Stiglitz and Charlton have written, "If ever there were an opportunity to demonstrate the value of free trade for a developing country, this was it. NAFTA gave Mexico [preferential] access to the largest economy in the world, which was right next door." What happened? Mexico's exports did grow rapidly through much of the 1990s. Foreign direct investment in Mexico also increased substantially, but "growth during the first decade of free trade was slower than it had been in earlier decades [prior to 1980], mean wages at the end of the decade were lower, and some of the poorest had been made worse off as subsidized American agricultural products flooded the market. . . . Inequality and poverty both increased under NAFTA and by the end of the decade, Mexico was losing to China many of the jobs that had been created since the signing of NAFTA."[14] Certainly not the total disaster some had feared, but far from a ringing endorsement of the efficacy of free trade.

There are clear advantages, economic and otherwise, available from a degree of economic specialization combined with wider and less obstructed trade, both domestic and international. But while pointing us in useful directions, the theory of comparative advantage should not be taken as gospel. It does not provide the kind of unassailable argument for unrestricted trade that the most ardent advocates of free trade allege. Even more important, it certainly does not guarantee that globalization through free trade will necessarily generate a win-win situation for all those who live in participating nations.

The Importance of Looking Inside the Box

It is often helpful and convenient to use the nation as the unit of analysis, to talk about what nations do and how nations are affected by one or another set of actions or circumstances. But it is important not to forget that this is, after all, simply a useful rhetorical device, a convenient shorthand. What really matters is what the people who are living their lives within the state are doing and what is happening to them. It is important to remember to look inside the box.

There are interest groups within the state that are strongly but differently affected by any given path to or form of globalization. Consistency with the principles of a peacekeeping economy requires that they be represented in the process that sets the rules of the game by which globalization proceeds, balanced decision power being a key element of Principle I. Within any nation, economic globalization tends to benefit most those groups that dominate the market. Therefore, as meaningful participation in the market is more broadly dispersed, the gains of globalization will likewise be shared more broadly. A business sector that consists primarily of many intensely competitive small- to medium-size firms will spread the benefits of economic globalization more broadly and equitably among the population than one that is dominated by a few very large monopolistic enterprises. A business environment that encourages and facilitates the entry into the market of new small- to medium-size entrepreneurial firms will likewise tend to distribute the economic benefits of globalization more broadly than one in which entry is difficult and expensive.

If the market is dominated by a smaller group that is more politically powerful, as market-dominant groups often are, that group may be able to use its disproportionate influence to ensure that the national government takes an approach to globalization that increases the benefits its members receive relative to the benefits that flow to other groups within the same nation. This can exacerbate whatever internal intergroup tensions may already exist. It is even more likely if the market-dominant group constitutes an ethnic minority.[15] The fact that globalization tends to enrich them relative to the indigenous majority tends to provoke (or strengthen) ethnic antagonisms that can easily erupt into civil violence—a possibility that is certainly at cross-purposes with economic peacekeeping.

We usually think of a globalizing free market economic system and a democratic political system as compatible, if not mutually reinforcing. But Amy Chua argues,

> In the numerous societies around the world that have a market-dominant minority, markets and democracy are not mutually reinforcing. . . . [M]arkets and democracy benefit different ethnic groups. . . . Markets concentrate enormous wealth in the hands of an "outsider" minority, fomenting ethnic envy and hatred among often chronically poor majorities. In absolute terms,

the majority may or may not be better off . . . but any sense of improvement is overwhelmed by their continuing poverty and the hated minority's extraordinary economic success.[16]

Chua goes on to argue that pursuing free market democracy when there is a market-dominant ethnic minority almost invariably results in a backlash—against markets and the wealth of the minority, against democracy itself (by the market-dominant minority), or, most virulently, in the form of ferocious "majority-supported violence aimed at eliminating a market-dominant minority." The genocidal slaughter of some eight hundred thousand Tutsi in Rwanda in 1994 is but one horrifying example.[17]

Kapstein considers economic relationships to be just to the extent they are "*inclusive, participatory,* and *welfare-enhancing.*" But he takes a "statist" approach to economic justice, focusing on "economic relations among states (as opposed to among firms or persons) . . . and the wellbeing of each state within the international system."[18] He contends that fairness and justice in economic relations do matter to international stability and the likelihood of the outbreak of violent conflict, and with that I obviously agree. But I believe the issue of whether or not globalization is "inclusive, participatory, and welfare-enhancing" and therefore "just" must ultimately be judged by its impact on people, not on states. Even if globalization brought about a world of state-by-state balanced relationships in which every nation had the same per capita income and the same growth rate of per capita income, we could not conclude that globalization had necessarily been economically just. Kapstein's conditions for economic justice could be met on the national level at the same time a small elite in every country held nearly all the wealth and everyone else in every country was mired in poverty and politically marginalized. In such a world, the vast majority of people in every nation would be economically and politically excluded, without a voice in the process, and with their welfare reduced. *All* of Kapstein's conditions for economic justice would be met at the level of the nation-state, while *none* of them would be met for the vast majority of the people in every nation. Globalization that led to this state of affairs could not reasonably be considered economically just, and would certainly not be compatible with the principles of a peacekeeping economy.

Furthermore, though the state as an institution may remain the primary unit of governance into the indefinite future, it is important to look inside the box because states do not make decisions, rather the particular individuals who hold key positions of power do. Even in liberal democracies, "the people" have only indirect control over those who make decisions and even less control over, and participation in, either the key decisions that must be made in times of perceived emergency or the detailed day-to-day process of routine governmental decision making. To be sure, the structure and operating rules of the state as an institution are very important. They constrain and condition the behavior of decision makers. But it really does matter which particular individuals hold positions of power. So much of what governments do, what paths they follow, ultimately depends on who holds the reins. Even in liberal democracies, once a particular individual holds the levers of power, he/she can use them to bring the public along for long enough to create a new reality that constrains the ability of others to change it.

The Bush administration's decision to invade Iraq in 2003 is a good case in point. Justified publicly on the basis of what largely turned out to be "faulty intelligence," even five years after the invasion occurred the new reality the administration had created by the decision to invade continued to bind the hands of political decision makers. Despite the fact that both the war and the president who launched it had become very unpopular with a considerable majority of the American public, few national political leaders who claimed that they were opposed to the war were willing to take action to withdraw the support necessary to keep fighting it.

There is much to celebrate in the potential impact of globalization "done right" on the ordinary people who live within nation-states—enhanced economic well-being, greater political participation, deeper and richer cultural diversity, and of course, the many benefits of living in a more peaceful world. Yet there is reason to be concerned about the social and psychological, as well as the economic and political, effects on those same people of globalization "done wrong." If globalization raises economic, social, and political expectations of the vast majority of the public while at the same time substantially exaggerating inequalities, the disjuncture between the benefits most people expect and the reality most people experience will be psychologically painful. Quite apart from the dangers of exacerbating ethnic antagonisms, about which Chua has written, raising expectations of a much better life and then failing to deliver on them is a recipe for personal frustration and heightened social tensions that can rise to the point of violent explosion.

Some have also expressed deep concern that globalization in its present form is paying too little attention to the basic human need to form and hold onto meaningful attachments to places and especially to people, and too much attention to the short-term, personal flexibility, and adaptation to constant change. As Nicholas Carr put it, "Globalization, by creating a world in which we are constantly being asked to . . . reinvent ourselves, think in the short term and stay flexible, sets us all adrift. . . . [W]e don't bond with others; we 'team' with them. We don't have friends; we have contacts. We're not members of enduring nurturing communities; we're nodes in ever shifting, coldly utilitarian networks."[19]

If we are to shape globalization in ways that facilitate the operation and enhance the effectiveness of a peacekeeping international economy, we must pay attention not only to what is happening at the level of nation-states, but also to how globalization affects the economic, political, and social well-being of the individuals who live within them. Only in this way can we ensure that globalization fulfills its potential to contribute to both prosperity and peace.

The World Trade Organization and the Shape of Globalization

The World Trade Organization (WTO) was formally created in 1995 as the successor organization to the General Agreement on Tariffs and Trade (GATT), born in 1947. The organization has grown enormously since its inception. While the original GATT had only 23 member nations, as of July 2008 the WTO had 153, more than three-quarters of which were developing countries or countries in transition.[20] The WTO's members, taken together, today account for in excess of 85 percent of the world's trade.

In general, agreements negotiated though the WTO are lengthy and complex, covering a considerable variety of activities. Nevertheless, the organization claims, "a number of simple, fundamental principles run throughout all of these documents."[21] These include: 1) countries should not discriminate among trading partners, nor favor their own products over those produced abroad; 2) trade should be made freer through negotiations to reduce all forms of trade barriers; 3) foreign companies, investors, and governments should face a stable and predictable trade and investment environment, protected against arbitrary changes in rules; 4) unfair trade practices, such as subsidizing exports and dumping products below cost, should be discouraged; and 5) the agreements should establish an international trading system that is "more beneficial to less developed countries."[22]

At the top of the organization's structure is the Ministerial Conference, which can make decisions on any issue that falls within the scope of any of the underlying trade agreements. Between the infrequent ministerial conferences, a committee called the General Council, to which all members belong, carries on the organization's work. The WTO has the power to enforce its rules and assess trade penalties against violators. When one country charges another with trade violation, a three-judge panel hears the complaint. If the panel finds that a violation has occurred, WTO can assess trade sanctions if two-thirds of the member countries agree (each country has one vote). Under this procedure, *any domestic law of any member country can be disallowed by WTO, if it is found to be a de facto trade barrier.* This has led to fears that WTO will be used as a device by economic and political elites to overturn laws protecting the environment, worker and public health, and safety. This concern has been behind the protest demonstrations held at virtually every major WTO meeting since the famous Seattle protest in the fall of 1999.

The fears of the protesters are clearly not entirely unfounded. In 1998, WTO ruled against a U.S. law that banned importation of shrimp caught by countries using nets that did not protect endangered sea turtles. WTO also ruled against a health related EU ban on U.S. beef from cattle injected with hormones. As of 2005, the United States was a defendant in seventy-one WTO dispute settlement cases that had been resolved. The U.S. lost sixty-eight (96 percent) of these cases, changing domestic law to comply in fifty-nine (87 percent) of them.[23]

The WTO Decision Process

The WTO likes to present itself as a thoroughly, even painfully, participatory democracy:

> The WTO is run by its member governments. All major decisions are made by the membership as a whole. . . . Decisions are normally taken by consensus. . . . [T]he WTO is different from . . . the World Bank and International Monetary Fund. In the WTO power is not delegated to a board of directors or the organization's head. . . . The rules are enforced by the members themselves under agreed procedures that they negotiated. . . . [S]anctions are imposed by member countries, and authorized by the membership as a whole.
>
> Reaching decisions by consensus among 150 members can be difficult. Its main advantage is that decisions made this way are more acceptable to all members. . . . The WTO is a member-driven, consensus-based organization.[24]

The WTO is also careful to present itself as paying considerable attention to organizational transparency. It proclaims that, on its public website, "News of the latest developments are published daily. . . . And those wanting to follow the nitty-gritty of WTO work can consult or download an ever increasing number of official documents, now over 150,000."[25] It claims to be open not only to the public at large, but also to the activist organizations of civil society: "In 2002, the WTO Secretariat increased the number of briefings for NGOs on all major WTO meetings and began listing the briefing schedules on their website. NGOs are also regularly invited to the WTO to present their recent policy research and analysis directly to member governments."[26]

But even the WTO admits that special informal meetings of smaller numbers of delegates, called "Green Room" meetings, held in a less than public setting, are key to carrying out some of the organization's most important negotiations. "No one has been able to find an alternative way of achieving consensus on difficult issues. . . . So, informal consultations in various forms play a vital role on allowing consensus to be reached, but they do not appear in the organization charts."[27] WTO contends that such meetings are critical in allowing members to negotiate more freely, work out bilateral deals, and put together packages of proposals that ultimately give each party enough of what it wants to build the necessary consensus. Critics believe that such closed door meetings are intended precisely to allow the kind of arm-twisting and under-the-table deal making that could not survive public scrutiny because it so obviously serves the interests of business and political elites, rather than those of less influential and less powerful businesspeople and the wider public.

One such critic is Richard Peet, who writes, "The WTO presents itself as a neutral place where governments can make agreements about trade and resolve the disputes that inevitably arise in an equitable way. . . . [But] the WTO does not practice organizational, bureaucratic neutrality. . . . It has a total commitment to a single, well-defined and elaborated, carefully defended ideological position: free trade."[28]

The reality is that the WTO is not a neutral policy analytic or negotiating forum. It was established precisely for the purpose of moving the nations of the world toward a freer, more open trading regime, a mission that is in many ways compatible with the idea of establishing a peacekeeping international economy. But it is compatible only if the decision process by which trade expands is balanced; the established rules of the game discourage exploitation, encourage balanced mutually beneficial relationships, and allow for exceptions to free trade for critical goods; and care is taken to ensure that this widened trade stimulates development and is sensitive to the need to protect the global environment. These are issues of first order importance to economic peacekeeping. Freer, more open trade, by itself, does not guarantee that any of these conditions will be met.

Although on paper the decision-making process could not be fairer or more inclusive, it is clear enough that the economically larger MDCs have had considerably more influence than the LDCs on outcomes. One of the most obvious pieces of evidence is that much more progress has been made in lowering trade barriers against those products that loom large in MDC export portfolios than those that are a large part of LDC exports. WTO has had much more success in reducing tariffs, import quotas, export subsidies, and other barriers to free trade for manufactured goods, services, and even intellectual property than it has had in reducing those same barriers for agricultural products.

The WTO and Development

Reducing agricultural protectionism was one of the central concerns of the so-called Doha Round of negotiations, launched at the WTO's Fourth Ministerial Conference in Doha, Qatar, in November of 2001. In the aftermath of the terrorist attacks of September 11, there was considerable discussion of the possible connection between acts of terrorism and the lack of progress in economic development that had trapped so much of the world's population in deep poverty. Whether a reflection of renewed seriousness in addressing global poverty, excessive optimism, or simply public relations, the negotiations process begun in Doha was labeled "the development round." The negotiations ran into serious trouble almost from the very beginning, collapsing completely on July 24, 2006. Why? In the words of the U.S. Congressional Research Service, "The principle cause of the [indefinite] suspension was that a core group of WTO member countries—the United States, the European Union (EU), Brazil, India, Australia and Japan—known as the G-6—had reached an impasse over specific methods to achieve the broad aims of the round for agricultural trade: substantial reductions in trade-distorting domestic subsidies, elimination of export subsidies, and substantially increased market access for agricultural products."[29]

After decades of successful negotiations aimed at reducing barriers to trade in the products that were most important to them, the developed countries were simply not willing to make the kinds of concessions that would have more fully opened their own markets to the products most important to the developing world. Whatever can be said about the particular positions taken in the Doha negotiations or the probable impact of those positions on the developing (or developed) countries, this state of affairs reflects a serious imbalance of decision power. Furthermore, the lopsided record of WTO agreements to date is not conducive to supporting and encouraging balanced mutually beneficial economic relationships. For both of these reasons, the reality of the WTO, as opposed to the rhetoric, has been less than fully consistent with the principles of economic peacekeeping.[30]

In addition, the WTO's record in encouraging development has been mixed, at best. Certainly progress in development depends on a wide range of factors. The WTO can hardly be given full credit for its successes or blame for its failures. Nevertheless, WTO critics, such as Lori Wallach and Deborah James, argue, "Instead of promised gains, during the WTO decade, economic conditions for the majority have deteriorated. The number and percentage of people living on less than $1 a day in Sub-Saharan Africa and the Middle East have increased while the percentage living on less than $2 a day has increased in these regions, as well as in Latin America and the Caribbean."[31] The developing nation most successful in poverty reduction in recent decades, China, did not even become a WTO member until 2001. Furthermore, China's success was hardly achieved by strictly adhering to WTO-approved practices. "[T]he economic policies that China employed to obtain its dramatic growth and poverty reduction are a veritable smorgasbord of WTO violations: high tariffs to keep out imports and significant subsidies and government intervention to promote exports; an absence of intellectual property protection; government-owned operated and subsidized energy, transportation and manufacturing sectors . . . and government-controlled, subsidized and protected agriculture."[32]

Trade and the Environment

On environmental matters, once more the WTO takes pains to present itself in the most positive light: "The objectives of sustainable development and environmental protection are stated in the preamble to the Agreement Establishing the WTO. . . . At the end of the Uruguay Round . . . , trade ministers from participating countries . . . created the Trade and Environment Committee. This has brought environmental and sustainable development issues into the mainstream of WTO work."[33] From the WTO's perspective, the purview of the committee extends to considering only how the environment, or how attempts to protect the environment, might affect trade, not how trade might affect the environment. Furthermore, if environmental concerns do affect trade, upholding the organization's view of what constitutes free trade trumps those environmental concerns. Justifying its behavior in terms of the rhetoric of fair play: "The WTO agreements are interpreted to say two important things. First, trade restrictions cannot be imposed on a product because of the way it has been produced. Second, one country cannot reach out beyond its own territory to impose its standards on another country."[34] But the effect of these "two important things" is to open a route to undercut attempts by any country to use the positive economic carrot of access to its markets to provide incentives to other countries to behave in ways that better protect the environment. Much of the pollution generated in the manufacture of a product is generated as a result of "the way it has been produced." Taking away the right to restrict the import of products that have been made by "dirty" processes, when other "cleaner" but perhaps more expensive processes are used by other producers, is tantamount to giving a competitive advantage to those producers who do the most environmental damage. Beyond this, if the "dirty" producer is located in a neighboring country, and the pollution it is spewing into the air or water, for example, is directly degrading the environment of the country that wishes to restrict the import of its products, then insisting that the way a product is produced is not permissible grounds for this restriction seriously hampers the ability of the importing country to protect its own environment.

Furthermore, restrictions by a country on imports that are produced in ways that, for example, destroy the rain forest or threaten endangered species outside its own territory are perfectly reasonable. The idea that a country is not permitted to reach beyond its own territory in encouraging environmental protection betrays a misunderstanding of the very nature of the global environment and its human interactions. The air, the water, the flora and fauna do not recognize the artificial political boundaries people have drawn upon the earth. The living and nonliving natural resources provided by the world's environment are a part of the heritage of all people and, in one way or another, affect the well-being of all of us more or less directly. The fact that the Amazonian rain forest, for example, lies wholly within the boundaries of a few South American nations does not mean that its condition has no relevance to the lives of those who live elsewhere.

Of course, the WTO does not prevent, and does not claim to have the authority even to inhibit, the nations of the world from concluding or enforcing environmental treaties that reach beyond their individual boundaries. But when the WTO sees the environmentally related actions of any country or group of countries as restrictions on the free flow of trade with any other member country that chooses to bring a complaint, it does have mechanisms available to enforce its decisions by bringing sanctions to bear that will pressure the violators of its principles to back off from the "offending" environmental protections they have instituted. It not only has such mechanisms; it has repeatedly and forcefully used them.

According to Peet, "When issues essentially of free trade, on the one hand, and environmental regulation, on the other, come into conflict, the GATT/WTO dispute system always found in favour of trade, and against national environmental regulation. . . . [I]n the entire history of the GATT/WTO disputes, the WTO has very tentatively allowed one, single exception that conserves environmental resources."[35]

Reforming the WTO to Better Support Economic Peacekeeping

Much of what the WTO already claims to be generally supports the principles of economic peacekeeping. The problem is that its practice falls far short of its rhetoric. Its decision process has the appearance of inclusivity and transparency, providing equal participation for its members, ready access for the nongovernmental institutions of civil society, and abundant, readily available information to the public at large. But the reality is that much of the key decision making still goes on in unreported informal, closed door meetings. While there is certainly some value in avoiding the obstructive posturing that inevitably goes on during public government bargaining sessions, it is important to expose the results of closed negotiations to wider public scrutiny before they are set in stone. The public must have the chance to have meaningful input into the process while there is still time to modify the results instead of time only to ratify them. Judging by the lopsided outcome of WTO negotiations, it seems clear enough that the economically larger and politically more influential countries—and interests within countries—dominate the process of deciding on international trade rules that have considerable impact on nearly everyone's economic life.

Because the WTO is an organization of governments, it is difficult to avoid the distortions of decision making that result from the disproportionate influence exerted on member governments by powerful business and political interests within their own countries. That is an important limitation of all intergovernmental organizations. Perhaps the most useful counterweight to this influence is to provide stronger mechanisms for more active and consequential participation of the organizations of international civil society, including global environmental groups (such as the World Wildlife Fund and Greenpeace), development advocacy groups (such as Oxfam and Outreach International), and, for issues of immigration and working conditions, human rights groups (such as Amnesty International and Human Rights Watch).

We learned from the tragic impotence of the League of Nations that an international organization established to achieve a widely accepted purpose must somehow be able to enforce its decisions on otherwise sovereign states in a way that they find compelling, if it is to have a chance to succeed. The WTO's enforcement mechanisms are clearly effective and have the advantage of requiring the agreement of a supermajority of members before decisions can be applied. The potential severity of the possible sanctions—and even more important, the value to members of keeping the organization intact and functioning well—also provide a strong incentive to negotiate settlements "out of court."

The disjuncture between the WTO as it currently exists and the kind of WTO most compatible with the needs of a peacekeeping international economy is primarily a matter of the organizational mindset that leads the ideology of free trade to trump all other considerations. Although the rhetoric of WTO and even the language of some of its basic documents provide for exceptions, whenever conflicts arise between the ideology of free trade and alternative human concerns such as environmental protection or workers rights, the deck is stacked heavily in favor of trade. Yet, while expanding (balanced and mutually beneficial) trade is an important element of economic peacekeeping, so too are environmental sustainability and inclusive development that improves the well-being of people, both as consumers and as workers. If the WTO is to shape globalization in ways that help keep the peace, the organization needs to see its mission from a broader perspective.

There is also a pressing need to change the underlying WTO rule that trade restrictions cannot be imposed because of the way a product has been produced, as I have earlier argued. The way a product has been produced is of great importance to both environmental sustainability and human rights. There are many ways to fish, many ways to farm, and many ways to manufacture any given product. Some of them are more protective of the environment than others; some of them are more sensitive to the welfare of workers and the wider public than others. To prevent nations from considering how a product is produced in deciding whether or not its entry into their country should be restricted is to remove a potent tool for pressuring those who use methods that are environmentally damaging and/or disrespectful of workers' human rights to pay more attention to these matters, both of which are important to economic peacekeeping. More than that, it is to give a commercial advantage to those who choose the cheapest methods of production, even when those methods impose very big environmental and human costs on others.

If taken literally, the WTO proscription of a country reaching "beyond its own territory to impose its standards on another country" would disallow the use of economic sanctions to punish violations of the accepted norms of international or domestic behavior by another country. Such a proscription for instance, would have prevented any nation from participating in the disinvestment campaign that finally helped bring down the brutal system of racial apartheid in South Africa.

Given the WTO's dedication to the mission of expanding free trade, it is not difficult to understand the organization's concern that allowing restrictions of trade related to the way a product is produced, and reaching beyond borders to impose local standards on other countries, might be used as backdoor mechanisms for protectionism. The problem is that preventing nearly all such restrictions in practice (while claiming to allow exceptions on paper) makes it far too easy to roll back progress in the key areas of environmental protection, public health and safety, and workers' rights. The best solution to this dilemma might be to require that any restrictions on trade alleged to be due to any of these key reasons be supported by clear and compelling evidence. Together with abandonment of the WTO's apparent organizational mindset that supporting free trade outranks all other considerations, this would help to bring the organization into better alignment with the requirements of a peacekeeping international economy and the underlying goal of improving human well-being. It is easy to argue that tariffs and export subsidies designed simply to offset any competitive advantage foreign producers might have—owing to poor environmental or worker health and safety practices—actually help to level the playing field and increase economic efficiency. If producers in developing countries need technical or other forms of assistance to adopt more acceptable practices, the revised version of the Global Environmental Fund and the World Bank discussed in the preceding chapter should be most helpful.

Rather than simply removing barriers and expanding trade, the WTO's top priority should be making international trade more balanced and mutually beneficial. In part, that will come from paying as much attention to the trade priorities of the LDCs as to those of the MDCs. Beyond some exceptions required to accommodate greater independence in critical goods, trade restrictions and subsidies in primary products that are key to the current comparative advantage of developing nations should be treated the same way as those in manufactured goods and services.

The WTO is not in a position to break up large multinational firms based in the developed countries. Therefore, where such firms face off against developing country suppliers that are much too fragmented to balance their market power, the WTO should encourage and perhaps facilitate the formation of regional or international developing country marketing cooperatives. Although it may seem antithetical to the purposes of the organization to encourage concentration rather than greater competition, its inability to reduce the degree of concentration on one side of the market obviates balancing market power by increasing competition. That leaves increasing concentration of market power on the more fragmented side of the market as a second-best alternative for creating a situation that has a real chance of ensuring that the gains from trade are more equal on both sides of the market.

Admittedly, it will be politically difficult—perhaps prohibitively difficult—to get developed country governments to permit the WTO to take an action that appears to so directly contravene the interests of powerful MNCs based in their own countries. But since achieving more balanced mutually beneficial relationships is key to establishing a peacekeeping international economy that will work, it may be possible to convince these governments that their own security interests require the WTO to move in this direction. If that ultimately proves unsuccessful, the WTO should at least stay out of the way by refusing to use its free trade enforcement mechanisms to interfere with the formation of developing countries' marketing cooperatives on grounds that they constitute unacceptable trade restrictions. Other mechanisms are available to move toward making international economic relationships more balanced and mutually beneficial (Chapters 4 and 5), if the WTO cannot or will not play this role. But the WTO should not be yet another obstacle they have to overcome.

While the World Trade Organization does provide "special and differential treatment" for lower income countries, most often that takes the form of allowing more time or offering additional assistance in complying with WTO requirements. That is all to the good, but it is very different from and not nearly as important as working directly to create more balance in international economic relationships.

The Global Flow of Capital and People

Globalization and Capital Mobility

As a consequence of economic globalization, the volume and speed of the global flow of capital has increased enormously. In the mid-1980s, an average of about U.S.$200 million of financial capital moved around the world each day. Largely because of the deregulation of financial markets and the rolling back or elimination of capital controls (in many countries at the urging of the International Monetary Fund), by the late 1990s that figure had grown to an astonishing U.S.$1.5 trillion a day, or more than U.S.$547 trillion per year.[36]

The fluidity and mobility of this river of financial capital has both advantages and disadvantages. Some argue that through it the market disciplines governments and companies whose policies and practices take a wrong turn.[37] If, for example, a government institutes a policy that the owners of that financial capital believe will interfere with economic growth and the prospects for profitable business activity, that capital can and will rapidly flee the country, throwing it into a serious economic downturn. Capital flight thus serves to punish the country, putting the offending government under enormous pressure to reverse its stand. Even the prospect of such capital flight, it is argued, serves as a deterrent to instituting what the controllers of financial capital see as counterproductive policies. At the same time, a government that institutes policies favoring economic growth and enhancing profitable business opportunities will be rewarded, as a strong flow of foreign financial capital into the country boosts its economy.

The government decisions, policies, and actions that trigger these flows need not be purely economic. A country moving toward greater democracy might be considered to be creating a more favorable climate for entrepreneurial economic activity, and therefore rewarded with large capital inflows. A country moving in the direction of greater internal repression and inequality might be considered to be heading toward political instability and rebellion, thus triggering punishing outflows of capital. Of course, rather than letting the unaided market decide, it is always possible to organize deliberate campaigns to encourage or discourage capital inflows to a particular nation in order to pressure governments to support broader social objectives (Chapter 4), the disinvestment campaign aimed at bringing down apartheid in South Africa being a famous case in point.

Adding to this argument, Gartzke and Li make the case that the global mobility of capital makes violent conflict less likely because "when capital is free to move globally, talk is no longer cheap." In particular, because hostile talk between the leaders of two nations can induce a costly outflow of capital from their countries, "The leader making a threat reveals resolve because of the harm she imposes on her economy. The target of the threat in turn has an incentive to accommodate the demand in order to stem capital outflows [from its country]." Demonstrating resolve by "scaring markets," they argue, is an essentially nonviolent alternative to the more traditional idea of demonstrating resolve by bearing the costs of actually going to war.[38]

There are also those who argue that the hypermobility of financial capital that has accompanied economic globalization has strong negatives. A relatively small group of controllers of financial capital decides where the bulk of the money flows, and their decisions are overwhelmingly influenced by considerations of short-term (sometimes very short-term) profitability, rather than the broader public interest or even what is most economically beneficial in the long run. Capital markets can be driven by rumor, "irrational exuberance," and exaggerated pessimism, making them uncommonly skittish at times. In this era of less regulated global financial markets, problems in one part of the world can quickly be transmitted, magnifying their reach and impact, even to the proportions of a global crisis. For example, when a loss of confidence triggered a rapid outflow of financial capital from Thailand in the summer of 1997, the Thai currency collapsed, marking the beginning of a financial meltdown among the "miracle" economies of East Asia (Indonesia, Malaysia, South Korea, and Thailand) that also created serious problems for Japan, Russia, and Latin America. More recently, the financial earthquake that began in the United States in 2008 had its origins in a crisis in the poorly regulated U.S. sub-prime mortgage market in 2007 and spread throughout the world, shaking investor confidence in markets all over the globe.

Financial capital (money, stocks, bonds, and the like) can easily be exchanged on one or another of the currency, stock, bond, and commodity markets around the world that are part of a globally interconnected financial system which never sleeps. Fixed investment (capital embodied in the actual buildings, machinery, and equipment that firms need to produce their products) is far less liquid, and as a consequence less mobile. Ghemawat argues that capital flows across national boundaries are smaller and less important to this kind of investment than many people suppose: "The fact is, the total amount of the world's capital formation that that is generated from foreign direct investment (FDI) has been less than 10 percent for the last three years for which data are available (2003–2005). . . . [M]ore than 90 percent of the fixed investment around the world is still domestic."[39]

Nevertheless, Gartzke and Li's empirical analysis provides strong evidence for the proposition that the international flow of capital is important to reducing "militarized inter-state disputes" (MID). Their analysis also makes it clear that the flow of foreign fixed capital investment is much more important than that of financial capital. In every statistical model in their analysis in which it appears, FDI is significantly and negatively related to militarized disputes whether or not financial capital is also included. On the other hand, financial capital is significant and negatively related to MID only when FDI is not also included in the same model. When both FDI and financial capital are present together, financial capital shows no significant relationship to MID.[40] Polachek, Seiglie, and Xiang point out that the annual rate of growth of FDI exceeded the growth rate of international trade over the decade from the mid-1990s to the mid-2000s, and broke through the trillion U.S. dollar mark as early as 2000.[41] To see what impact this had on international conflict and cooperation, they looked at some 450,000 international interactions between pairs of countries for the period 1990–2000. Overall they concluded that FDI reduces international conflict and encourages cooperation, finding that a 10 percent increase in FDI leads to on average a 3 percent decrease in conflict.[42] Taken together with Gartzke and Li's results, there is at least some solid empirical evidence that global capital flows can play a role in reducing violent international conflict, particularly if those flows are in the form of fixed investment.

Foreign direct investment creates more of a stake for the investors in the continuity and stability of the economic relationship it establishes. Achieving solid returns on investment in physical buildings, facilities, and equipment requires time. The longer the relationship remains stable and productive, the better the chances of realizing the projected return that led investors to make their investment in the first place. Because it establishes a deeper stake in the longer-term outcome, it is not surprising that investment in cold "bricks and mortar" seems to work better than "hot money" in reducing conflict.

There is, however, still the important matter of whether the relationships established by fixed or financial capital flows are balanced and mutually beneficial. There is nothing inherent in FDI (or in purely financial investment) that makes these relationships necessarily balanced or unbalanced. Companies have historically invested considerable funds in FDI of the most exploitative kind, such as in fixed plant and equipment necessary to extract large amounts of oil or mineral resources from the territory of a nation without anything approaching fair (or well distributed) compensation for the privilege. But companies have also made substantial fixed investments under conditions that were much more balanced and mutually beneficial. Not surprisingly, a relatively greater number of the fixed investments that large developed country multinationals have made in developing countries have been of the first kind, while a greater number of their investments in other developed countries have been of the second kind. Unequal bargaining power and sophistication in negotiating have led to these outcomes in the past, but there are ways to address this disparity (Chapters 3 and 4). If we are to make full use of the security-increasing peacekeeping potential of international economic relationships, we must work toward ensuring that investments made in developing countries are of the more balanced mutually beneficial type.

The Global Flow of People

In the past few decades, both intrastate and interstate violence has forced huge numbers of people to flee their homes. The Office of the UN High Commissioner for Refugees (UNHCR) estimates that, as of June 2007, there were nearly thirty-three million refugees, asylum seekers, or internally displaced persons.[43] There has also been substantial economic migration, but globalization has done much less to open up and encourage the flow of people than it has to liberalize the flow of capital.

Centuries ago Adam Smith argued the importance of a free flow of labor "from place to place" and not just a free flow of capital. But he also recognized that government policies were generally more favorably disposed to the mobility of capital ("stock") than to the mobility of labor:

> The policy of Europe, by obstructing the free circulation of labour and stock both from employment to employment, and from place to place, occasions in some cases a very inconvenient inequality in the whole of the advantages and disadvantages of their different employments. . . . It is everywhere much easier for a wealthy merchant to obtain the privilege of trading in a town . . . than for a poor artificer to obtain that of working in it.[44]

According to Ghemawat, in relative terms long-term international immigration has changed very little over the past century: "Rough calculations suggest that the number of long term international migrants amounted to 3 percent of the world's population in 1900 . . . versus 2.9 percent in 2005."[45] It has been estimated that as of the beginning of the twenty-first century, only about 1.5 percent of the world's labor force were working outside their country of origin.[46] Even in the European Union, which is supposedly committed to the free movement of labor across national borders, less than 2 percent of the workforce was working outside their home country in the mid-1990s, about the same percentage as in the mid-1970s.[47]

At one end of the spectrum of international migrants are millions of skilled and highly paid managers, consultants, engineers, and the like who live and work abroad for a significant period of time (though perhaps not permanently), often in the pay of multinational corporations. At the other end of the spectrum are low-skilled and low-paid workers who cross national borders, many times illegally, in search of basic economic opportunities unavailable to them in their home countries. The former group constitutes a business elite that generally has little trouble moving across national boundaries and lives an economically privileged existence; the latter group must many times take great personal risks to cross borders, and is often subjected to economic and social exploitation and abuse during the process and after arrival. There is little need to be concerned about the fate of elite business migrants whose numbers have been swelled by economic globalization. But there is every reason to be concerned about "low-end" economic migrants, particularly those who are undocumented, since they are so vulnerable to mistreatment on the one hand, and such an easily exploitable potential source of social tensions and political scapegoating on the other.

We often think of this low-end migration primarily as a flow of people from LDCs to MDCs. But the World Bank estimates that 47 percent of this migration (74 million out of 156 million) consists of people moving to poor developing countries from even poorer developing countries.[48] The Bank also estimates that money sent by immigrants to family and friends back home rose from $70 billion to $230 billion from 1998 to 2005.[49] Although this is swamped by other global capital flows, it has become a major source of "hard currency" reserves for the governments of many developing countries. In the Philippines, for example, these remittances have been the third largest source of foreign currency earnings over the past several years.[50] In Mexico, they have been second only to petroleum exports. Yet, this does not mean that the developing countries which exported the labor that is the source of these remittances have experienced a net gain as a result. If they had been able to generate a sufficient quantity and quality of job opportunities through their own development activities to put these people to productive work at home, they might have gained far more, even in foreign currency reserves generated by exporting the goods and services they could have produced.

According to the United Nations, during the 1990s criminal organizations netted about U.S.$3.5 billion a year in profits from the illegal trafficking of migrants for work. By 2006, estimates of profits earned from the illegal trafficking of migrants for the sex trade alone ranged from U.S.$19 billion to U.S.$27 billion.[51] Many illegal migrant workers are subjected to appalling working conditions as well as physical and economic abuse. Saskia Sassen writes,

> Men and women are trafficked for work, with women at a greater risk of being diverted to work in the sex trades. Some women know that they are being trafficked for prostitution, but for many . . . the extent of abuse and bondage become evident only after they arrive in the receiving country. The conditions of confinement are often extreme, akin to slavery, and so are the conditions of abuse. . . . Sex workers are severely underpaid, and their wages are often withheld.[52]

There are essentially two ways to deal with the problems related to low-end international economic migration that are consistent with peacekeeping economic principles. The first is to stem the tide of migration by the only means that is at the same time humane, fair, and respectful of the "inalienable right to life, liberty, and the pursuit of happiness"—by creating equally attractive economic opportunities in the home countries of these potential economic migrants. That in turn involves working hard to raise the level of economic development of low-income countries and ensure access to the opportunities that greater development creates for the vast majority, if not all, of their people (Principle III: emphasize development).

The second is to regularize and facilitate procedures for temporary low-end economic migrants that give them sufficient legal, political, and social status to offer them real protection against at least the most serious forms of exploitation and mistreatment. This could be done most efficiently through the actions of national governments, moved forward under whatever public and international pressure is necessary to move them. The UN's International Labor Organization (ILO) might play a useful role in helping to mobilize pressure on its member nations to take seriously and apply to immigrant workers the four internationally recognized core principles embodied in its eight fundamental conventions: 1) freedom of association and the effective recognition of the right to collective bargaining; 2) the elimination of all forms of forced or compulsory labor; 3) the effective abolition of child labor; and 4) the elimination of discrimination in respect to employment and occupation.[53] More than a decade ago, at their 1996 Singapore Ministerial Conference, the member nations of the WTO identified the ILO as "the competent body to deal with labour standards."[54] Therefore there is a kind of precedent for a more equity-minded WTO to work toward adopting the ILO's core labor principles and applying them to all workers, including international migrants.

Since these two approaches to the problem of low-end international economic migration are entirely compatible with each other, it would make sense to do both. Immigration can be an important source of economic strength and vitality for a society, as well as cultural "hybrid vigor," as long as it is not overwhelming. Doing both would help prevent overwhelming flows of economic migrants, while promoting human rights and allowing the flexibility the global economy needs and the mobility that freedom requires.

When capital is more "stationary," as in the case of FDI, and labor is freer to live in foreign countries, then there are strongly vested interests—the domestic firms that own capital abroad and the families and friends of those living in other countries—pushing against any attempt by the government of their own country to break the peace with any other country in which they are invested. This could also generate pressures against going to war with any country tied in a strong economic network with countries that house subsidiaries of the home country's firms and host many of the home country's citizens, because the disruption of the network would ultimately impose serious economic and political costs on all the nations that are part of it.

Distancing, Homogenization, and Conflict

Those who see globalization as an unabashedly positive phenomenon often go beyond the purely economic arguments to rhapsodize about how it is bringing the whole human community on this planet closer together. It is surely true that the communications- and transportation-based technologies that have been so critical to supporting economic globalization have metaphorically made the world smaller. They have made it possible for millions of people to communicate almost effortlessly with each other over vast distances at reasonable cost on a daily basis, and even to travel across the distances that separate them much more easily and quickly (though not nearly as cheaply or frequently). That has put us in touch with each other in a way that simply has no historical precedent. It is also true that the flow of goods and services itself has made the fruits of the daily work done by people all over the globe part of the daily lives of others who live at great distance from them.

But at the same time, globalization has increased the physical distance between the points of production and consumption for a great many people. That has made it more difficult for those who consume the majority of the earth's bounty to see in their immediate geographic neighborhood the consequences of what producers have done to the environment in less affluent parts of the world in order to supply them with the goods and services they are consuming. It has also made it more difficult to see the conditions under which people have labored to produce those goods and services. The problem is that this kind of physical distancing can encourage psychological distancing that tends to reduce our inhibitions against doing or tolerating violence done to others. It is easier to ignore ecological damage, intolerable working conditions, child labor, and even slave labor when there is greater physical distance separating those who benefit from those who suffer. In spite of all our technological sophistication, TV images, e-mail traffic, and sound bites still do not have the same impact as actually being there. It is much easier for even truly moral people to ignore the moral imperative to take action when they are not physically confronted by the reality of what is being done to others and to the earth in the process of satisfying their economic wants and needs.

To be sure, human cruelty and environmental insensitivity are as old as humanity itself. Long before those of us living in North America and Europe feasted on the produce of South America, Asia, and Africa, poor ecological practices caused entire societies to collapse.[55] Forced labor under appalling conditions was a fact of life. When fearsome ecological damage and inhumane treatment were literally in our own neighborhoods, as they still are in some parts of the world, it did not always move us to action. Instead we invented racism, sexism, classism, and ethnic prejudice to rationalize what we do to each other, to convince ourselves that those being exploited are somehow not as fully human, not as deserving as we are of dignity, respect, and freedom. Why, then, does it matter how much physical distancing globalization creates?

Although we still live in a world that is very far from perfect, in more and more places more and more people have learned to take seriously the rights of other human beings, as well as the fate of the biosphere on which all of our lives depend. We are making progress in the slow spread of democracy and in the idea that various forms of nonviolent action are sometimes more effective than violent confrontation (Chapter 9). There are too many exceptions, but much of the human race is becoming more educated and living life under less physically challenging circumstances than in times past. All this has the potential to move us in the direction of becoming a kinder, less violent species. It would be terrible if the realization of that potential were even partially subverted by the creation of a world in which physical distancing made it so much easier to ignore the costs others were paying for the benefits we receive.

I am not arguing that the physical distancing created by the separation of the points of production and consumption *must* make us insensitive to the health and well-being of workers or the environment, but rather that it is making it *easier* to ignore these problems. It is therefore increasingly important to work hard to find compelling ways through media, education, and activism to overcome the dulling effects of distance and keep these problems in the public consciousness. Their ultimate solution, however, lies in making real all that is embodied in peacekeeping Principles I, III, and IV.

As the cultures of the more economically successful and politically influential countries become more dominant under the force of homogenizing globalization, we are in great danger of losing the enormous accumulation of artistic creativity and adaptive ingenuity that is embodied in the wide range of cultures people have developed over millennia in response to the conditions in which they lived. It is important to understand that loss of cultural diversity, like loss of biological diversity, is not just an aesthetic problem. It represents a loss of ideas, a loss of solutions to problems that have faced us in the past, to problems that face us today and to problems that will confront us in the future. Just as the genetic adaptations of diverse plant and animal species to the challenges they have had to confront have led us to some of our most potent medicines, so past adaptations embodied in the diverse "cultural genes" of our own species may yet have much to offer us. For example, in the 1950s and 1960s, the Israelis reached far back into history to base a modern irrigation technique on the principles of an ancient farming practice known as "runoff agriculture," which had reached its peak during the period from the end of the third century B.C. to the middle of the seventh century A.D. Using the principles of this energy efficient irrigation technique allowed them to grow such crops as peaches and apricots successfully in the parched Negev desert.[56]

In the twenty-first century, we find ourselves struggling to maintain or improve material living standards while trying to meet compelling environmental challenges, such as global warming, that seriously threaten our future. There is an emerging consensus that one of the technically and economically most sensible and effective ways to do this is by dramatically increasing energy efficiency, especially in buildings and transportation. It is likely that part of the solution to the problem of reducing the energy used by buildings lies in applying some of the principles that underlie the set of culturally based building practices known as "primitive architecture." Although no one ever sat down at a drawing board or computer to design them, it turns out that the snow igloos of the far north, the grass huts of the tropics, and the thick-walled, narrow-windowed, terraced structures of low latitude deserts from the Southwest U.S. to Morocco and Egypt are remarkably energy efficient. These and other similar architectural structures around the world developed slowly as part of the cultures of those who built them. They are energy efficient because they were so well harmonized to the environments in which they evolved. Lacking modern machines for heating, ventilating, and cooling buildings, the people who built them had no other choice.[57] Embedding the engineering architectural principles that account for their energy efficiency in modern structures built with modern materials and equipment should allow us to maintain the high degree of environmental comfort we have become used to with much less energy use.

It is of course not just the culturally evolved technical practices in which we may find the inspiration we need to solve our problems, but also in differing culturally evolved social rules for many kinds of human interactions. There may be, for example, something useful for us to learn in our quest for a more peaceful and secure world from better understanding the social relational practices of relatively peaceful cultures as remote from the mainstream of modern society as the !Kung (or Zhun/twasi) people of the African Kalahari.[58] In the end, there may be larger or smaller contributions made to the artistic, musical, technical, political, spiritual, and social relational progress of humankind by any particular culture. But in a rapidly changing world it is very difficult to know in advance which culture will provide the knowledge or inspiration that helps us to solve the next set of pressing problems we find ourselves confronting. The smaller the menu of cultural choices, the less likely we are to find what we need among them.

All of this is true, and yet cultures also can and do embed pernicious attitudes and behaviors that we would be better off without—from dangerous and inhumane primitive practices like female genital mutilation to the hypercompetitiveness of some modern societies that leads to physically and mentally unhealthy patterns of chronic overwork. Racism, sexism, and militarism can also be culturally embedded. Cultures are by no means sacrosanct. We should not feel compelled to accept the validity of all practices, no matter how pernicious, simply because they are culturally embedded. But neither should cultures be routinely and casually denigrated or destroyed.

I do not mean to imply by any of what I have said that globalization inherently requires or inevitably produces economic, political, or cultural homogenization. That is not true. It is not difficult to conceive of a style of globalization that is respectful of all these forms of diversity, yet able to take advantage of the benefits of wider and more intensified economic, social, and political interactions across national boundaries. Such a process of globalization would not provoke the type of resistance—and even violent conflict—provoked by the style of globalization that crushes small businesses, rides roughshod over the rights of workers, assaults the environment, and sweeps away the cultures that some hold dear. Globalization "as if people mattered" (to borrow a phrase from E. F. Schumacher) is not only possible, it is also necessary if we are to make maximum use of the power of international economic relationships to keep us secure and preserve the peace.

Shaping Globalization to Promote Peace

Globalization offers the possibility of movement toward a more unified world political system, perhaps even the evolution of a world government. For some, world government is a much-desired path to sustainable peace, as the interests of disparate nations are subordinated to the good of the whole, and potentially violent conflicts are resolved by the central political authority. Just as the apparatus of the U.S. federal government has long been available to settle conflicts among the states, so a world government would provide mechanisms to settle conflicts and create a more perfect and peaceful union among the nations. For others, world government is the stuff of nightmares, a recipe for abuse of authority and the trampling of civil liberties under the weight of an all too powerful centralized political regime. Even if it is begun with the best of intentions and fortified with democratic institutions, such a concentration of political power can never be trusted. Overly centralized political authority is all too likely to eventually degenerate into one or another form of tyranny. If it offers the promise of peace, it is only the peace of the prison, if not of the graveyard.

There is no reason why economic globalization should lead to world government. That outcome is obviously not necessary because globalization has already proceeded quite far without anything remotely resembling world government coming into being, and there is no barrier yet in sight that would prevent further economic globalization in the absence of world government. It is also not desirable because even the freest and most democratic of governments may from time to time embark on adventures or major policy changes that some of their citizens find troubling. If they find them troubling enough, it is good to have somewhere else to go. Just as with cultural diversity, the diversity of political structures and attitudes represented by different nation-states offers us a richer menu of choices. If at any time we were really able to live in whichever nation we choose, having more available options would mean that we had greater freedom. Even if barriers to immigration complicate movement, it is still better for people to have at least the possibility of seeking refuge from alternative governments if the overriding political authority under which they are living becomes too threatening or too oppressive. That possibility would not exist if it were the world government itself that turned in such pernicious directions.

Economic globalization neither requires nor implies world government. But does it affect how countries operate within their own political borders? Can it, for example, be used as a tool for encouraging nation-states to become more democratic? To the extent that economic globalization does produce real economic benefits for the nations and people who participate in it, the answer is yes. There is at least the possibility of holding out greater access to these benefits as an incentive for nations to move in the direction of greater democracy. Once again, the EU is a useful "real world" example. The EU's considerable economic success has made membership so attractive that nations eager to join have been willing to work hard toward meeting stringent EU entry criteria that include substantially increased democratic practice. If full participation in the institutions and organizations of a more balanced and mutually beneficial version of the globalization process were to be made contingent on moving toward more democratic national governance, there is little doubt that progress could be made. Beyond this, simply by bringing the businesspeople and private citizens of less than democratic nations increasingly into regular contact with their counterparts in freer and more democratic societies, it is quite possible that such a style of globalization would gradually build internal political pressure to move toward greater levels of democracy. Democracy has proved to be a durably attractive form of governance for those who have had the opportunity to experience it, most effectively spread by exposure and example, not by the barrel of a gun.

How can globalization be shaped to enhance the effectiveness of economic peacekeeping, as well as to promote higher material standards of living? For one thing, a serious degree of antitrust activity is required to break the largest multinational corporations into pieces big enough to achieve substantial economies of scale, yet small enough to make much more competitive those international markets that are today dominated by a few monopolistic firms. For another, it is important to establish stronger national and international regulation of financial markets, not to try to micromanage finance, but to prevent short-term, hit-and-run practices and the creation of speculative instruments that divert attention and serious amounts of capital from the critical economic role of finance—productive investment in infrastructure and the facilities and equipment that drive the system of producing real goods and services. Keep in mind that there is evidence that FDI may be more important than purely financial investment in reducing militarized international disputes. Thirdly, there is also a need for stronger national and international rules of the game to encourage responsible labor and environmental practices, particularly by industries engaged in manufacturing, transportation, construction, and natural resource extraction and refining. A World Trade Organization whose reality catches up with its rhetoric could be very important here.

The answer to the question "Does globalization contribute to peace and prosperity?" depends entirely on what form globalization takes. Globalization dominated by the few, built on a series of highly uneven bargains supported by opaque and undemocratic institutions, and based on short-term profitability and a simpleminded quest for endless quantitative economic growth will lead us toward neither long-term prosperity nor peace. Globalization that is inclusive, based on balanced mutually beneficial relationships, supported by transparent and democratic international institutions that encourage equity, and driven by a focus on real economic development, will help lead us closer to the kind of world we seek.

Months before his death, having led the United States through a time of truly extraordinary threats to its people's economic well-being and physical security, President Franklin Roosevelt offered the nation a lesson he had learned about the importance of positive international relationships and interdependence through the experience of those troubled times: "We cannot live alone at peace; . . . our own wellbeing is dependent on the wellbeing of other nations. . . . We have learned to be citizens of the world, members of the human community. We have learned the simple truth . . . that the only way to have a friend is to be one."[59]

PART TWO

THE ECONOMICS OF DEMILITARIZED SECURITY

7

The Economic Promise of
Demilitarized Security

ALTHOUGH BUILDING A PEACEKEEPING INTERNATIONAL ECONOMY will set
us on a more effective and much less violent path toward peace and security, it is unlikely that by itself it will eliminate the need for military forces.
Despite the web of strong positive incentives to avoid violent conflict and
the threat of painful negative sanctions, there may occasionally be bad actors in the international system against whom the threat or use of military
force will still be a valuable tool. But a peacekeeping economy will allow us
to back away from reliance on military force as our primary means to security. That will make dramatically reducing military budgets a sensible and
practical thing to do.

For many years, economists have referred to a nation's military spending
as its "military burden," recognizing that military spending imposes an
economic sacrifice. It seems clear then that there should be real economic
benefits to substantially reduced military spending. Some of these benefits
are obvious and widely recognized. There are financial benefits that flow
from being able to redirect the enormous sums of money currently spent
on national military forces to a wide variety of civilian projects—from improving education, health care, transportation, and environmental quality
to encouraging small business entrepreneurship to putting the money back
into the hands of ordinary households to use as they see fit. There are
benefits derived from redirecting workers, machinery, equipment, factories,
and the like to producing the goods that consumers enjoy and tools that

businesses need. This is the famous "guns vs. butter" tradeoff that is widely found in basic economic textbooks. A society that uses less labor and capital to produce "guns" (military goods and services) can use more of its labor and capital to produce "butter" (civilian goods and services). And there are also much less well-understood long-term benefits in economic strength, vitality, and resiliency that derive from unburdening the economy.

The financial benefits of demilitarization may be widely recognized but they are often understated because we tend to seriously underestimate the full financial cost of maintaining a large military sector, and the cost of the adventures into which military approaches to security periodically lead us. The American invasion of Iraq in 2003 and subsequent occupation is a case in point. While prewar estimates of the cost of the war from the White House Office of Management and Budget (late 2002) were on the order of $50–$60 billion, by 2008 Linda Bilmes and Joseph Stiglitz were estimating the full long-term financial cost of the war at roughly $3 trillion, fifty to sixty times the early estimates.[1] Part of the reason the estimates are so different has to do with having more information on the cost of dealing with casualties and replacement cost of military equipment destroyed after five years of war. But it is also because Bilmes and Stiglitz took care to consider costs that earlier estimates largely ignored, such as the financial costs of caring for thousands of seriously wounded veterans, in many cases for the rest of their lives.

The short-term "guns into butter" benefits of undoing the diversion of productive labor and capital to the military sector are also widely recognized but are generally thought to be substantial and meaningful only when the military budget is large compared to the size of the economy. If poor economies have diverted any significant fraction of their limited economic capacity to military-related activities, they clearly gain when they are able to reclaim those resources. Even rich economies whose military budgets are huge, such as the U.S. during World War II, gain greatly when they shed that heavy burden. But the *long-term* benefits of scaling back on military spending are less widely recognized because the costs imposed on an economy that carries a substantial military burden for a long time are seriously underappreciated. In the long term, the military burden can distort the very foundations of the economy and undermine its ability to function properly.

Because this issue is at once the most fundamental, important, and least well-understood benefit of relieving the military burden, the focus of this chapter (and the next) will be on this longer-term concern. In order to fully appreciate the benefit that derives from reversing the structural costs imposed on the economy by high levels of military spending, it is first necessary to understand how and why carrying an extended military burden interferes with the economy's ability to do what economies are supposed to do. That understanding begins with the most basic of economic questions: what is an economy and what is it supposed to do?

The Purpose of the Economy

Most economists see the economy as defined by the set of money-valued transactions involved in the production, distribution, and consumption of goods and services.[2] This mainstream definition drives the calculation of the GNP and GDP, closely related and widely used measures of economic size. If it is a legal activity for which money is paid associated with producing, distributing, or consuming goods and services, it is part of the economy. It does not matter what the activity is or what it produces. It does not even matter if the activity is useful, useless, or harmful.

On the other hand, any activity for which no money is paid is not part of the economy, no matter how beneficial, even vital it may be. Childcare, health care services, meal preparation, housekeeping, and do-it-yourself projects done without pay in the home are not considered to be economic activity. Because no money is paid for them, they are defined to have no economic value. They are not included in either GNP or GDP. Yet when you consider how many people and how many labor-hours in virtually every household are involved in such activities across the population of any nation, that is a considerable omission. In sum, by this definition, the economy begins and ends with money. It is not the nature of the product that counts; the only thing that matters is whether it is bought and sold.

Of course, this definition, like all definitions, is arbitrary. It is no more correct or less correct than any other. What really matters is whether the definition helps us to understand what we are trying to understand. For many questions economists ask, this definition is perfectly serviceable.

But for the purpose at hand, it obscures rather than illuminates. We need a fundamentally different way of looking at the economy, a way that emphasizes function rather than form.

Let us think of the economy, then, as the part of the society we have created to satisfy a powerful human need, the need for material well-being. Material well-being is important, but it is not all that people need or want. We are multidimensional creatures, with many different types of needs and wants. Because we are inherently social beings, we have created different social structures and institutions to help us satisfy them. The economy is just one of these social creations, but there are others created to satisfy needs other than material well-being. For example, because we need a degree of structure and predictability in our lives, we have created systems of governance that include legislatures, judges, courts, police, etc., to satisfy our need for law and order. Because most of us feel the need for some degree of moral or spiritual guidance, we create churches, synagogues, mosques, temples, and secular moral organizations to help us satisfy that need. Because we need a sense of protection from unwelcome external disruption of our political, social, and economic lives, we create military forces and diplomatic corps (and someday a full-blown peacekeeping economy?) in an ongoing quest for security. These other needs and wants are also important to the quality of our lives. Any given person may consider any one of them more or less important than material well-being. I am not ranking these wants and needs or the parts of the social system aimed at satisfying them. I am merely claiming that they are *different*.

There is nothing abstract or mysterious meant by this phrase "material well-being" or its commonplace equivalent, "standard of living." I mean it in the most straightforward and pragmatic sense. In common speech, when we say that someone is materially well off or has a high standard of living, we mean that he/she has a good quantity and quality of food and clothing, lives in a nice house, drives a good car, has access to health care when needed, can afford to travel, and so on. We do not mean that they are functioning on a high spiritual plane, that they are psychologically healthy, that they are well protected against foreign intervention, or even that they live in a democratic and free society.

Departing from the more mainstream definition, I therefore do not see the economy simply as a set of activities and transactions held together by money. Rather, it is a social system defined by its social function: to provide the goods and services that take care of our material needs, the goods and services that make up the standard of living. It does not exist to provide moral guidance; it is not intended to establish law and order. The economy's purpose is to provide us with food, clothing, shelter, health care, transportation, and the like.

There are striking practical differences between these two distinct definitions of the economy. By the money-oriented definition, money value and economic value are the same thing. But if the economy is defined by its function, any activity that adds to material well-being is an economic activity and therefore has economic value, whether or not money changes hands; any activity that does not add to material well-being is not an economic activity and therefore has no economic value, no matter how much money may be paid for it. Money value and economic value are very different things.

Economically Contributive and Noncontributive Activities

If the economy consists of all activities that add to material well-being, then unpaid housework, home child care, home meal preparation, and do-it-yourself household projects are every bit as much a part of the economy as providing paid architectural services or manufacturing television sets or automobiles. Because they contribute to the purpose of the economy, these and all other activities that add to the standard of living are "economically contributive."

There are two main types of economically contributive activities: those involved in satisfying immediate material needs and wants, and those involved in building up the economy's capacity to satisfy material needs and wants in the future. Producing ordinary consumer goods (such as furniture, clothing, and audio systems) is an example of the first type; producing the industrial equipment and machinery (such as lathes, looms, and plastics molding equipment) that are used to make consumer goods (or other industrial and machinery) is an example of the second. The first type adds to present material well-being; the second type expands the capacity to produce future material well-being. Many economically contributive activities are paid; many others are not.

Activities involved in servicing some purpose other than providing material well-being do not contribute to the purpose of the economy. Religious institutions, systems of governance, military systems may employ a lot of people; they may perform functions that are extremely important in society—for some, more important than the economy's function. Nevertheless, no matter how important their activities are, because they do not add to material well-being they are classified as *"economically* noncontributive."[3]

Like the economy, every social system we have created to satisfy our noneconomic wants and needs requires goods and services to do what it has been designed to do. Religious institutions need bibles, prayer books, pews, buildings in which to hold prayer meetings, etc.; they need the services of priests, rabbis, ministers, imams, and the like. Systems of governance need administrative offices, courthouses, police cars, jails, buildings in which legislatures can meet, etc.; they also need the services of legislators, judges, police officers, and the like. Military systems need uniforms, bases, and weapons, as well as the services of soldiers, pilots, and generals. Producing the goods and services that support economically noncontributive activity requires labor and capital, just the same as producing those goods and services that support economic activity does. In other words, both economically contributive and noncontributive activities make claims on the nation's economic resources.

Most economists believe that there is a basic two-way tradeoff in the allocation of the labor and capital of a society. Either resources can be directed to satisfy immediate needs and wants ("consumption"), or they can be directed to building up the nation's capacity to produce in the future ("investment"). Directing more resources to consumption means a higher present standard of living but slower growth; directing more resources to investment means faster growth, but a lower present standard of living. But there is actually a three-way tradeoff. The nation's labor and capital resources can be directed to (contributive) consumption, (contributive) investment, or economically noncontributive activity.

Allocating more of a nation's resources to contributive consumption has an economic cost (in terms of foregone growth), but it also creates economic value by raising the current standard of living. Allocating more of a nation's resources to contributive investment has an economic cost (in terms of current standard of living foregone), but it also creates economic value by increasing economic growth and thus raising the future standard of living. But allocating more of a nation's economic resources to noncontributive activity has an economic cost (in terms of both the current standard of living and foregone growth) while it creates no economic value. From the point of view of the economy alone, noncontributive activity is a net drain, imposing an *economic* cost by absorbing labor and capital without returning any *economic* benefit.

That certain activities absorb labor and capital without producing economic value is not a new idea. Writing in 1776 in *The Wealth of Nations*, Adam Smith argued, "The whole, or almost the whole public revenue, is in most countries employed in maintaining unproductive hands. . . . Such people who they themselves produce nothing, are all maintained by the produce of other men's labour."[4] Smith went on to specify a few types of labor that were engaged in activities that he thought were particularly "unproductive" from the point of view of the economy: "Such are the people who compose a numerous and splendid court [the governance structure], a great ecclesiastical establishment [religious institutions], great fleets and armies [the military], who in time of peace produce nothing, and in time of war acquire nothing which can compensate the expense of maintaining them, even while the war lasts."[5]

There are important differences between Smith's concept of "unproductive labor" and my concept of "noncontributive activity." But the key underlying similarity is that both concepts reject the idea that the mere fact of paying money for the activity of producing a good or service makes it a positive contribution to the economy. Both concepts also classify military-related activities (as well as governance and religious activities) as being a net drain on the economy, because they impose significant economic costs without producing any economic returns.

While economically noncontributive activities do not have economic value, they may be very important generators of other types of value. Ethics and morality, good governance, and security are clearly beneficial to us collectively and individually. They even indirectly affect economic value, by affecting both the behavior of individuals and the social context within which economically contributive activities must operate. Society taken as a whole is a complex interconnected interactive system. What happens in any part of the social system can easily affect one or more of its other parts. For example, more than a hundred years ago, Max Weber argued that religion can have a substantial impact on the functioning of the economy.[6] Ethics and morality, or rather the lack thereof, clearly played a significant role in bringing down the high flying economic enterprises Enron, Worldcom, and Tyco early in the twenty-first century.

Internal social order and political stability, as well as external security, are also important to the economy. It is difficult to carry out contributive business and economic activities in chaotic and insecure situations. For one thing, the decision to invest depends on the likelihood of reaping a solid return in the future, which is substantially affected by the stability and predictability of the business environment. For another, carrying out the normal activities involved in producing goods and services requires a dependable supply of inputs (including labor, fuels, and materials) arriving in good condition at the right time at the right place. In situations of chaos and insecurity, that dependability may be difficult or impossible to achieve.

If it is true that the social systems we create to provide for ethical and moral guidance, internal "law and order," and external security can have important impacts on the functioning of the economy—and therefore on economic well-being—why are they not also classified as economically contributive? The answer is that affecting critical aspects of the context within which the economic system must operate is very different from being part of the economic system itself. An analogy is useful here. The human body, like the economy, is a complex interconnected interactive subsystem, in this case a biological subsystem, of the ecology as a whole. There are many aspects of the environment, such as the climate, that can and do have dramatic effects on the ability of the human body to function properly. People who live in very cold climates will die if they do not have proper clothing and shelter. But even though clothing and shelter are critical to creating a context that allows the human body to survive in cold climates, we have no trouble understanding that clothing and shelter are not actually part of the human body. As important as they might be to the body's ability to do what it needs to do in the world, they do not actually do what the body does. The same is true of economically noncontributive activities. They create part of the context within which the economy operates, in some ways a critical part, but they are not part of the economy itself; they do not do what the economy does.

The Macroeconomic Cost of Economically Noncontributive Activity

In the long run, economically noncontributive activity does more than reduce material well-being by holding productive labor and capital in uses that have no economic value. It does not simply impose an opportunity cost year by year. If the diversion of productive resources is large enough and persists for long enough, it will throw sand into the gears of the economic machine doing structural damage that will undermine its ability to fulfill its central purpose, providing material well-being. Just how does noncontributive activity undermine the economy?

In virtually all countries, the vast majority of the population earns the largest part of its income in the form of wages and salaries. Relatively few people of working age earn most of their income in the form of rent, interest, or profits. Therefore, in order for the economy to deliver a high and rising standard of living to the broad mass of the population, wages and salaries (including benefits) must be high and rising. But for most producers of goods and services, labor costs are a large part, if not the largest part, of their costs. High and rising wages and salaries mean high and rising labor costs, and rising costs create pressure that eventually forces firms to raise prices. As prices rise across the economy, this "cost-push" inflation erodes purchasing power, undercutting the value of the higher wages and reducing material well-being. When the prices of domestically produced goods rise relative to those of foreign producers, domestic firms become less competitive. If they do not move their operations to countries where labor is cheaper, they will lose markets to foreign competitors and be forced to lay off workers; if they do move to countries where labor costs are low, jobs will be lost in their home countries. Either way, domestic unemployment will rise, causing a further deterioration in material well-being. Keeping wages and salaries down may undo the pressure of rising labor costs on prices, allowing domestic firms to remain competitive, but it will also cause the incomes of the vast majority of the population to stagnate. Their standard of living will be neither high nor rising.

How, then, is it possible to generate a high and rising standard of living for the mass of the population while keeping domestic firms competitive on markets at home and abroad? Wages and salaries can be increased year by year without pushing costs up and making firms uncompetitive if the amount produced per worker (labor productivity) is also increasing at a comparable rate. For example, if a firm gives its workers a 5 percent wage increase, but at the same time is able to achieve a 5 percent increase in its output per worker, its labor cost per unit of product will not increase at all. The rise in productivity will completely offset the higher wages. There will be no labor-cost-based pressure for it to raise its prices. If productivity can be increased even more, the firm will actually experience a drop in labor costs (per unit of product) even though it is giving its workers higher pay. Strong productivity growth will allow the firm to stay competitive while the incomes of its employees grow.

If productivity is increasing across the economy, firms in general will be able to offset the rising cost of labor, paying workers more without being forced by labor-cost-based pressures to raise prices. With prices relatively stable, the purchasing power of the higher wages and salaries will not be eroded, and the vast majority of the population will see its standard of living rise. Domestic firms will remain competitive with foreign rivals and therefore will not be pushed into choosing between moving their operations to cheap labor havens or seeing their market evaporate. Domestic employment will remain high. Living standards will be rising and the nation's economy will be strong.

A rising level of productivity depends primarily on three things: 1) raising the skill and motivation of the workforce; 2) increasing the quantity and quality of the physical capital (machinery, equipment, facilities, and other tools of production) available to and usable by the workforce; and 3) improving the level of product and process technology. All three of these pillars of productivity growth have one thing in common: achieving them requires the dedicated application of a substantial amount of a nation's economic resources. The skill of the workforce cannot be increased over time without using some of the nation's labor and capital resources to educate and train new labor force entrants to a higher level of skill than that of the people who have left because of retirement, illness, or death. When it is done well, education and training take time and considerable resources. Similarly, the only way to increase the quantity and quality of the machinery, equipment, and facilities is to replace those that have physically worn out or become obsolescent by new machinery, equipment, and facilities of better quality. It takes a substantial quantity and quality of labor and capital resources to design and build all this new productive capital. Finally, advances in the technology built into products and in the processes used to produce goods and services do not just happen. They are the result of the dedicated efforts of well-trained engineers, scientists, and technicians focused on finding and applying the knowledge necessary to drive technology forward.

The quantity and quality of capital and labor resources required to support these three pillars on which productivity growth depends, taken together, make a considerable claim on the nation's resource base. An economy that has diverted a large amount of its capital and labor to support a substantial amount of noncontributive activity may not be able to devote sufficient resources to keeping the productivity of its producers growing at a rate that keeps them competitive with foreign producers in economies not bearing as large a burden of noncontributive activity. If that is true only for a relatively short period of time, say, up to a few years, after which many of the resources diverted to noncontributive activity are redirected to supporting productivity growth, it may not be that difficult to regain lost ground. But if the economy continues to divert large amounts of resources for a period stretching into decades, the lag in relative productivity growth will cripple the ability of its producers to increase wages and salaries, offset labor-cost-based pressure on prices, and stay competitive. They will be pushed into the choice described earlier: hold down wages; raise prices and be faced with losing market share; or move operations to places where labor is cheap. This is a recipe for economic decline.

It is difficult to conceive of a good society—one capable of meeting the complex of people's noneconomic as well as economic needs and wants—that would not absolutely require some degree of noncontributive activity. The problem only really occurs when the noncontributive burden is both large enough and sustained for long enough. A simple analogy may be useful here. Suppose we think of the economy as similar to a pot-luck dinner, a social gathering in which everyone invited is asked to bring a different part of the meal. Whatever particular dish they have brought, everybody gets to enjoy the appetizers, main dishes, and desserts that others have brought. Suppose thirty people have accepted an invitation to participate. If, say, ten of the people invited bring no food, but just drop by to say hello, have an hors d'oeuvre and a quick drink, then leave without eating or drinking anything else, the dinner will be smaller than planned, but still successful. But suppose instead that one of the invitees shows up without any food and offers to tell stories as his contribution to the party. The host decides to let him stay and eat a full dinner in exchange for his storytelling. There will still be no problem. Then suppose another invitee shows up without any food but offers to play the guitar as her contribution to the party, and the host decides to let her stay and have dinner too. There is still no real problem. But if more and more invitees show up without bringing any food yet stay long enough to eat a full portion of the food that others have brought, it will soon become clear that there is not enough food to go around. The party may be a success on other grounds, but the pot-luck dinner portion will be a failure. The dinner will not be able to do what it was set up to accomplish—provide enough food to feed all those invited.

In Adam Smith's words, "Those unproductive hands, who should be maintained by a part only of the spare revenue of the people may consume so great a share of their whole revenue and therefore . . . encroach . . . upon the funds destined for the maintenance of productive labour, that all the frugality and good conduct of individuals may not be able to compensate the waste and degradation of produce."[7] Smith's meaning is clear. The economy can still function properly with a small burden of what he called "unproductive labor," but as that burden expands, there will be a shortage of resources needed to keep the economy efficient, a shortage of "funds destined for the maintenance of productive labour." The result will be so much damage to the economy, such "waste and degradation of produce," that nothing else can offset its effects. Translated into present-day terms, this means that a large and ongoing burden of noncontributive activity will undermine the ability of any economy to succeed in that which it is supposed to do: provide the broad mass of the population with a good standard of living.

Military Spending, Productive Efficiency, and Economic Competitiveness

In a sense, the advance of technology is the most basic of the three primary sources of productivity growth. It is obvious that modern economies would not be anywhere near as productive as they are if their workforces were still using eighteenth century tools and equipment (let alone stone-age hammers and chisels), no matter how much of that kind of capital they had to work with. Modern machinery and equipment are so much more productive because of the tremendous advances in scientific and technological knowledge built into them. Much of what workers have to learn to be productive in modern economies is also tied to the changing technologies with which they will be interacting in the workplace. The skills of a first rate nineteenth century factory or office worker would be hopelessly out of date in an equivalent modern day setting, largely because the huge advance in technology has rendered so many of their skills obsolete. Technological progress has historically played and continues to play a critical and fundamental role in driving productivity growth. A strong and continuing stream of contributive technological advance helps keep a nation's producers competitive with their foreign rivals not only in product price, but also in product quality.

Modern military forces are equipped with weapons and related systems that are technology intensive. State-of-the-art fighter planes, bombers, missiles, warheads, tanks, and military ships are high tech wonders, as are the communication, detection, and geographic location devices on which they depend. Because military research, development, and production are so technology intensive, any modern military-industrial sector worthy of the name requires the talents of large numbers of high quality engineers and scientists. Yet these are precisely the people whose talents, when directed to the development of contributive civilian technology, are key to designing better civilian products and more efficient ways to produce them.

When they work to develop contributive civilian technology, engineers and scientists keep productivity growth strong, in terms of both product quality and output quantity per worker. That allows the purchasing power of wages and salaries (and therefore the standard of living) to rise while keeping domestic producers competitive with foreign rivals. But when their talents are diverted from this crucial economic activity, the civilian technological progress that drives productivity slows down. Because they divert the talents of large numbers of highly skilled engineers and scientists, modern military sectors are an especially damaging form of noncontributive activity.

It is often claimed that drawing scientists and engineers into military-oriented research and development (R&D) enhances rather than retards the advance of civilian-oriented technology. The essence of this so-called spin-off argument is that people have always made more technological progress during war or the preparation for war. The urgency of war focuses the technological effort in a determined attempt to achieve a decisive advantage over the enemy in the capability and performance of weapons and other military equipment. The treasure trove of technological knowledge uncovered by the military research effort is then available to spin-off (spill over) to civilian applications. Twentieth century examples, from radar to the Internet to GPS (global positioning satellite) systems, all of which were developed as military projects and later applied to civilian purposes, are cited as proof that spin-off is a real and important technological phenomenon.

Counter to the spin-off argument is what could be called the "technological resource diversion" or the "brain drain" argument. The essence of this argument is that the kind of scientific and technological knowledge developed through the efforts of scientists and engineers is strongly conditioned by the kind of problems they are trying to solve. If they are looking for better ways of shielding a nuclear warhead against the heat and shock of reentry, or ways of making missile guidance systems accurate enough to bring that warhead within fifty feet of the target, they may turn up some information that later turns out to be useful for making better cookware or improving the performance of car audio systems. But most of what they find will be relevant mainly to warhead shielding and missile guidance, not only because that is what's driving the design of their experiments but also because it conditions what results capture their attention. In any case, the technologies that improve cookware and audio systems will come much faster and (key to competitiveness) at less cost if they are sought directly, rather than picked up as unintended technological crumbs from missile research projects.

Clearly both the "spin-off" and "brain drain" effects exist. The economically relevant question is which one is stronger. If the spin-off effect is stronger, the net result of devoting a great deal of a nation's scientific and engineering effort to military-oriented R&D will be to boost the rate at which (contributive) civilian technology advances; if the brain drain effect is stronger, the net result will be to retard the progress of (contributive) civilian technology. A thoroughgoing answer to this essentially empirical question is well beyond the scope of this present analysis, but it is possible to present some general presumptive evidence.[8]

If spin-off were the strongest effect, then it is logical that those nations engaged in massive military R&D efforts should also be leading sources of civilian technology, and inversely those nations that do relatively little military R&D but focus more on civilian R&D should be lagging in areas of civilian technology. During the nearly half century of the Cold War, the developed nation that did the most military R&D was the Soviet Union, and the two developed nations that had substantial R&D efforts but did very little military R&D were Japan and West Germany. Rather than being a source of advanced civilian technology, the Soviet Union lagged far behind, while Japan and Germany came to be leaders rather than laggards in many areas of civilian technological advance. This well established observation gives some credence to the idea that the "brain drain" effect is actually more powerful.

But what of the United States? During all of this time, the U.S. had the world's second largest military R&D effort. During the Cold War somewhere on the order of 30 percent of all U.S. engineers and scientists were engaged full-time in military-oriented activity.[9] And hasn't the U.S. been a continuing beacon of civilian technological advance?

In 1980, Simon Ramo wrote a book with the revealing title *America's Technology Slip*. Ramo, himself a scientist, had advised U.S. presidents on science policy and had been a senior Pentagon official in addition to being one of the co-founders of TRW, Inc., a major industrial enterprise with substantial amounts of military contracts. As a longtime insider to the business of technological innovation and a major participant in the military sector, it is interesting to note Ramo's assessment of the impact of America's focus on military R&D on the overall progress of civilian technology in the U.S.: "In the past thirty years [1950–1980], had the total dollars we spent on military R&D been expended instead in those areas of science and technology promising the most economic progress, we probably would be today [1980] where we are going to find ourselves arriving technologically in the year 2000."[10] In effect, Ramo estimated that thirty years of heavy military R&D activity in the U.S. had created a roughly twenty-year lag in contributive civilian technological progress. It is hard to reconcile this assessment with the idea that civilian spin-off from military R&D is anywhere near large enough to compensate for the "brain drain" or diversion effect, let alone a source of civilian technological advantage.

At the height of the Cold War in 1984, Ronald Reagan convened a special President's Commission on Industrial Competitiveness and charged it with determining why American industry was having so much trouble competing with foreign rivals in an increasingly global economy. To head the commission he chose John Young, the CEO of Hewlett-Packard Company, a company with substantial military contracts that remains a very important player in high tech industry today. Other members of the commission included high level officials in corporations such as Rockwell International and Texas Instruments, major military contractors of the day. After a year of careful study, the Young Commission concluded that the competitiveness problems of U.S. industry were not the result of wages being too high (as early as 1980, the average wage of U.S. manufacturing workers had fallen to ninth in the world).[11] Rather, they were very much the result of the relative weakness of American civilian technological progress: "Roughly half of the total R&D done in the United States is funded by the federal government, which spends most of its money (about two-thirds) on defense and space programs. And in those two areas, commercial spillover is not a prime objective. Thus when we look at what the United States spends on civilian R&D—areas of innovation from which we reap the greatest commercial reward—we find ourselves behind both Germany and Japan."[12] Succinctly stated, one of the commission's four main recommendations was, "Create, apply, and protect technology." They were not talking about military technology. There is little doubt that American military technology was, and still is, the best in the world.

A few years later, I was invited to testify, orally and in writing, at hearings on the "Role and Balance of Federal R&D Support" before the House of Representatives Subcommittee on Science Research and Technology.[13] Testifying in the same session of the hearings were Rear Admiral Eugene Carroll, U.S. Navy (Retired), and Dr. Jerome B. Wiesner. Wiesner, who spoke immediately after me, had been science adviser to President John F. Kennedy, as well as president of the Massachusetts Institute of Technology (MIT) from 1971 until 1980, one of the finest and most respected schools of engineering and science in the world. When he died in 1994, he was described as "a leader for decades in shaping the nation's science and technology policies."[14]

I gave my testimony, arguing that the long-lasting diversion of large numbers of engineers and scientists to military-oriented R&D in the U.S. had produced a substantial slowdown in the rate of American civilian technological progress, and that that in turn had seriously handicapped the competitiveness of U.S. industry. Wiesner then began his testimony by pointedly saying that he agreed with almost everything I had just said, and then proceeded to illustrate this by relating the following: He said he had become increasingly concerned about the competitiveness problems of American industry, but was unsure why domestic U.S. producers were having so much trouble competing internationally. On a trip to Tokyo he had dinner one night with a friend who happened to be the president of SONY Corporation, one of the world's most efficient producers of high quality civilian electronics. Wiesner said he asked him why he thought U.S. firms could not produce a television set good enough in price and quality to compete head-on with the sets that SONY produced. The president of SONY looked at him and said, "Jerry, when is the last time an MIT engineer went to work for a TV manufacturer? You know where they go in your country."

He went on to say that his company had access to the best engineers and scientists in Japan and asked, "How do you expect to compete with that?" How indeed.

When the Cold War ended in the early 1990s, thousands of engineers and scientists were laid off from military-oriented firms and R&D projects in the U.S. They were not eagerly gobbled up by civilian firms, primarily because so much of their training and experience was far more specialized to the needs of the military sector than to the very different needs of civilian industry (see Chapter 8). No program was in place to help them reorient themselves and reshape their skills in ways that would make them more suitable to carry on civilian commercial R&D. It was a difficult and painful time for these highly skilled and formerly highly paid people.

Much of the skill and experience of many of these engineers and scientists was unsuited to the civilian sector, but one thing that was attractive to civilian commercial business was a facility with computers. A few years into the 1990s, we found ourselves in a technology-led economic boom, chiefly involving the computer and telecommunications industries. Then, as military budgets began to rise again in the late 1990s and rapidly escalate after 2000, the technology-led economic boom fell apart. It is possible that this is further evidence that it does matter to the economy whether engineers and scientists are doing military- or civilian-oriented R&D. But it will take considerable careful empirical research to firmly establish the apparent connection between these events.

Engineers and scientists are not the only important productive resources diverted from contributive economic activity by swollen military budgets. A great deal of capital is also diverted, both financial capital and physical capital used to develop new military-oriented technologies and to produce weapons and related systems. As far back as January 17, 1961, in his farewell address to the nation, President Dwight Eisenhower (Supreme Allied Commander during World War II) pointed out, "We annually spend on military security more than the net income of all United States corporations."[15] In other words, the annual military budget of the United States represented a larger pool of financial capital potentially available for productive investment than all of the profits of all U.S. corporations combined. A similar pattern continues into the twenty-first century. As of 2005, total annual outlays for national defense in the U.S. easily exceeded total annual corporate profits not distributed to shareholders and thus potentially available for productive investment.[16]

As for physical capital, in the mid-1980s the book value of the stock of all physical capital directly owned by the military component of the U.S. government was 46 percent as large as the book value of all the equipment, machinery and structures owned by all manufacturing establishments (including military industrial firms) in the U.S. combined.[17] By 1990, more or less the end of the Cold War, the total book value of physical capital directly owned by the Department of Defense alone (including plant equipment, structures, weapons, and related equipment and supplies) had grown to more than 80 percent as large as the total book value of capital equipment and structures in all U.S. manufacturing facilities combined.[18]

Among other things, the diversion of capital is important because investment in new physical capital is often the means by which much of the progress engineers and scientists have made in product and process technology is deployed to the factory floor. A great deal of technological progress is "embodied," that is, physically built into the new equipment. Without the right piece of equipment, it is not possible to take advantage of the new technology. By interfering with the process of capital investment, diversion of both financial and physical capital gets in the way of putting new technologies into action in the service of the economy.

Supporting a full-fledged military-industrial sector is a particularly damaging form of noncontributive activity because it undermines the economy at its key source of strength, the advance *and* deployment of productivity-enhancing contributive technology. The part of the military budget that poses the biggest economic problem is that which directly supports R&D and the procurement of weapons and related military systems. That is what deprives the economy of the engineering and scientific talent needed to drive contributive technology forward and the physical capital needed to put it to use. Although it is a large fraction of the budget, the part that goes to support the salaries and normal operating expenses of those in the military is not nearly as big a problem. The money spent is nowhere near as important as the real resources diverted. Lifting the economic burden of resource diversion by adopting a demilitarized system of security, such as the peace-keeping economy, is therefore an enormous economic advantage.

Countries that have large military budgets but no substantial military R&D programs or military-industrial sectors may still find that military spending diverts sufficient resources to create a significant drag on their economies, especially if their economies are not strong enough or diversified enough to provide their people with good civilian-oriented economic opportunities. This is often the case in developing countries, where, for many who lack alternatives, the military seems the best path to a reasonable standard of living and a degree of status and influence in their society. Under these conditions, the military attracts a disproportionate number of the better educated and more highly skilled people, at least into the officer corps. That will deprive the nation of their potentially critical contribution to developing the civilian economy. Since most less developed countries do not have huge reserves of hard currencies with which they can carry out international transactions, spending a great deal of what reserves they do have to buy weapons and related systems deprives them of the wherewithal to import the machinery, equipment, and civilian technologies they need to build up their economies. For both these reasons, high levels of military expenditures economically disadvantage many countries that do not have large military-industrial sectors. For them too, moving toward a demilitarized security system would provide great economic benefits.

The Long-run Economic Advantages of Demilitarized Security

The United States emerged from the Second World War essentially intact, the only major industrial power that was not physically and economically devastated. It was both inevitable and desirable that this position of nearly total economic and political dominance would not last forever. To its everlasting credit (and tremendous benefit in terms of security), the government of the U.S. helped bring this about with the European Recovery Act, better known as the Marshall Plan. As the war-torn economies of Europe and Asia rebuilt, they were bound someday to reach the point where their industries would once again become forces to be reckoned with by

American industry. But it was neither inevitable nor desirable that U.S. civilian-oriented producers would come to lose contest after contest in the competition with their economic rivals in Europe and Asia, increasingly turning the United States into a second rate industrial power. That was the unintended result of a conscious policy that equated security with the threat and use of military force, and therefore required continually sustaining an enormous military sector in the period since World War II—even during peacetime—for the first time in U.S. history.

Like a runner far ahead of the pack who straps on a heavy backpack that sharply slows his pace, decades of bearing the heavy burden of high levels of economically noncontributive military spending slowed the American economy down and predetermined the decline of American industrial competitiveness. Because we were so far ahead, it took decades for our economic rivals to catch up, but catch up they did. Our historic ability to provide a higher standard of living for each subsequent generation slowly but surely disappeared. In recent decades, we have become a country in which only a small fraction of our population becomes economically better off year by year, while the standard of living of the majority either essentially stagnates or declines. The material standard of living of most Americans is little better today than it was nearly two generations ago. For most, what was long the American economic dream has become an illusion.

No one did this to us. We did it to ourselves.

Nor were we alone in overburdening the nation's economy. The Soviet Union began the Cold War with the U.S. in a much weaker position. Much of World War II (whether measured by lives lost or by property damaged) had been fought within the political boundaries of their country. Their economic system, which lacked the incentives for efficiency that come with competition in the marketplace, staggered under the heavy additional burden of noncontributive military activity. The Soviet Union committed to military R&D perhaps twice the percentage of their nation's engineering and scientific resources that the U.S. did, and gave comparable priority to the military-oriented use of virtually every other productive economic resource.[19] With a command economy so poorly suited to the difficult business of finding and applying ever more efficient production techniques and so focused on military capability, the Soviet Union was never able to produce a high standard of living for its people. By the time Mikhail Gorbachev came along with a serious program for economic and political reform that included substantial cuts in military spending, the country's economy was already in shambles.

If the diversion of productive resources is large enough for long enough it will drag any economy down, capitalist or socialist, developed or developing. This is a virtually universal phenomenon.[20] Consequently, developing an effective security system that is far less dependent on the threat or use of military force has potentially enormous long-term economic advantages. But it is also critical to understand that while removing the military burden frees up key resources for productive economic use, it does not guarantee those resources will be put to such use. Apart from any considerations of political will, there is a substantial and complex, yet clearly solvable, economic transition problem involved in moving resources from military-oriented to productive civilian-oriented activity (Chapter 8). It is important to solve that problem because the economic damage done by the military resource diversion is primarily the result not of what the resources *are* doing (military-oriented activity), but rather of what they are *not* doing (activity that contributes to material well-being). If we move to a less military-centered security system and the resources released from military activity become unemployed (or reemployed in other forms of economically noncontributive activity), they will still not be contributing to material well-being. The economic promise of demilitarized security will remain unfulfilled.

Assuming we handle the transition process well, what kind of economic benefits can reasonably be expected from adopting a less military dependent security system such as a peacekeeping international economy? The U.S. is a large, developed, and resource-rich economy. Taking it as a particularly striking example, there are a number of ways in which moving toward a demilitarized approach to security could provide substantial economic benefits.

For one, it would be possible to move forward on a serious program of rebuilding the nation's debilitated economic infrastructure—without adding to federal budget deficits—with the resources made available as military budgets are substantially reduced. The American Society of Civil Engineers (ASCE) is the main professional organization of those engineers

who have the expertise to design and oversee the inspection and maintenance of a major part of the nation's infrastructure—the physical component
of the basic systems of transportation, water supply, sewage treatment, and
the like on which both producers and consumers depend. In 2001, then
again in 2005, ASCE issued its evaluation, a "Report Card" on the state of
the American infrastructure:

> With each passing day, aging and overburdened infrastructure threatens
> the economy and quality of life in every state, city and town in the
> nation. . . . Congested highways, overflowing sewers and corroding bridges
> are constant reminders of the looming crisis that jeopardizes our nation's
> prosperity. . . . With new grades for the first time since 2001, our nation's
> infrastructure has shown little to no improvement since receiving a collec-
> tive D+ in 2001, with some areas sliding toward failing grades.

The Society's overall evaluation in 2005 was a D (meaning "poor"), lower
than in 2001. None of the fourteen categories of physical infrastructure
ASCE graded in 2005 got higher than a C ("mediocre").[21]

What would it take to put things right? "ASCE estimates that $1.6 tril-
lion is needed over a five-year period to bring the nation's infrastructure to
good condition."[22] That is a considerable capital investment but one, it is
interesting to note, that would require only a little more than half the financial capital that Bilmes and Stiglitz estimated to be the long-term cost
of the Iraq War alone.[23]

Similarly, other pressing issues directly related to the nation's economic
capabilities and its population's material well-being become far easier to
address without adding to the national debt once the tremendous diversion
of resources into the military sector is substantially reduced. Health care is
a particularly interesting case. It is an oft-stated fact that tens of millions of
Americans have little or no health insurance and therefore much reduced
access to good health care when they need it. It is also a well-known and
oft-stated fact that one of the roadblocks to a full-scale national system that
would guarantee the whole population access to quality health care is its
enormous cost. We are repeatedly told that the cost of health care is so high
in part because it is so expensive to develop and produce effective new
medicines and because state-of-the-art medical equipment also comes

with a very high price tag. Clearly there is much more involved with the high cost of health care in the U.S. than this alone. But while there is no purely technological fix, to the extent that the high cost of medicine and equipment is a serious part of what is making quality health care unaffordable, this is precisely the kind of problem that properly transitioned former military sector engineers and scientists could help to solve.

Looking for and finding ways to reduce costs and improve productivity is one of the central economic functions of civilian-oriented engineers and scientists. The infusion of appropriately retrained engineering and scientific talent into economically contributive activity that would become possible after substantially downsizing the military sector would provide the resources needed to carry out a frontal assault on this important aspect of health care costs. The payoff would not come overnight, but with time good health care would become that much more affordable. Properly applied, the substantial financial resources freed from the military budget would also be very helpful in solving this pressing national problem.

The real and present danger posed by global warming and the climate change it produces is another pressing problem that the resources freed from the military sector could potentially help to solve. As in the case of health care, there is no technological fix, but there is a technological component to the solution. Improvements in the technical and economic efficiency of energy using devices, from automobiles to air conditioners to lightbulbs, and reductions in the cost of ecologically benign renewable energy sources (such as wind and solar power) would be extremely helpful in achieving substantially reduced emissions of greenhouse gases without negatively affecting the standard of living.[24] As I have already argued, they would also contribute to energy security and reduce other environmentally based stresses on the international system. And they would save producers and consumers money. This will be much easier to accomplish with an infusion of technological talent currently locked into advancing military-oriented technology.

Without doubt, though, the most important economic advantage of adopting a less-military-dependent security system is that it will make available a whole range of productive resources critical to rebuilding the competitive strength of American industry. As a substantial fraction of these resources previously devoted to economically unproductive military use starts to flow into myriad companies and industries across the economy, the damage done by more than half a century of bearing a heavy military burden will begin to heal. It will not be nirvana; it will not solve all of the nation's economic problems or resolve our social conflicts; and it will not happen overnight. But it is a critical step in restoring the health and vigor of the American economy. It will help create an economy that once again thrives on producing quality goods and services at affordable prices and delivers ongoing improvements in material well-being to the broad mass of the population. The U.S. will become more efficient and more competitive, both of which are key to long-term success in a globalizing world.

Though I have focused on the U.S. as a particularly salient example, every nation whose economy is heavily burdened by military spending can expect real economic benefits from moving toward a less militarized security system. This is especially true of less developed countries (see Chapter 10). With a smaller and often less diversified economic base available to bear the military burden, even those developing countries without any military industry suffer relatively greater economic opportunity cost than do comparably burdened developed nations.

In 1987, historian Paul Kennedy published *The Rise and Fall of the Great Powers: Economic Change and Military Conflict from 1500 to 2000*.[25] Kennedy's central thesis was that, for five hundred years, countries have become great powers on the basis of their economic strength. Their emergence as great powers led them to build up large militaries to protect their interests. Eventually, these oversized militaries so burdened their economies that those countries ultimately receded from the center of the world stage. In this chapter, we have had a brief look at the economic mechanism behind Kennedy's scrupulously documented historical observation: the long-term damage done to productive efficiency by the diversion of key economic resources to noneconomic uses. Clearly, continued heavy reliance on the threat or use of military force as a guarantor of security has a very serious tradeoff in terms of prosperity and—if Kennedy is right—national power and influence as well.

Rather than forcing such powerfully negative tradeoffs, moving toward heavier dependence on a peacekeeping international economy for security creates a positive, self-reinforcing spiral. The greater the reliance on economic peacekeeping for security, the less the need to rely on military force and thus the smaller the military burden; the smaller the military burden (assuming the freed resources are used properly), the stronger and more prosperous the economy; the stronger and more prosperous the economy, the stronger the peacekeeping incentives created by the expanding web of international economic relationships; and the stronger these incentives, the more effective the peacekeeping economy will be in providing the security we want and need.

8

Removing Barriers to Demilitarized Security
Managing the Transition

EVEN IF THE IDEA OF ECONOMIC PEACEKEEPING becomes accepted as an effective primary security strategy, it will still be necessary to overcome political resistance to the change, rooted in the vested interests of those workers, businesses, and communities who believe their economic success—in terms of jobs, profits, and tax base—is closely tied to the military-oriented security system. In the U.S., for example, since the early 1950s the "jobs argument" ("thousands of jobs will be lost if this military project is cut") has been a powerful political obstacle to serious cutbacks in any sizeable weapons program, no matter how ill-conceived or unnecessary. This has been even more true of across-the-board reductions in military spending.

The essence of the problem is that politicians in the Congress have found it extraordinarily difficult to vote against military programs when that vote would cost their own constituents large numbers of jobs, even in the short run. A few brief anecdotes should suffice to illustrate the strength of this problem:

- George McGovern, the progressive senator from South Dakota, ran as the Democratic Party candidate for president in 1972 on a platform that promised a quick end to the Vietnam War and major cutbacks in military spending. McGovern once told me that early in his career he had found himself in the awkward position of having to fight against the Pentagon's decision to close a military base in his home state because it would have cost his constituents too many jobs.

- In the 1970s, while we were discussing an upcoming vote on the B-1 bomber in the office of Rep. George E. Brown of southern California, his legislative assistant told me the congressman believed that the B-1 was expensive and unnecessary to the nation's security. But the congressman was going to vote for it, because there were thousands of jobs in his district at stake.
- During his tenure as chair of the Senate Armed Services Committee (1981–1984), John Tower, the conservative Republican senator from Texas, wrote an open letter to all his colleagues in the Congress, asking those who were talking about cutting back the huge military buildup to send him a list of all the military projects and facilities *in their home district or state* they would like to see eliminated. He reported receiving not a single reply.

If comparable alternative economically productive jobs were available for those who would be displaced by the transition to a peacekeeping economy, along with smooth, effective ways of getting them from here to there, they would no longer be faced with the false choice of military work or no work. That is critical to overcoming the resistance—of politicians, of the workers who would be affected, and of the communities in which they live—to substantial reductions in military spending. It would free the Congress to base votes on particular military projects and on the military budget as a whole on legitimate national security needs rather than on vested economic interests. It is therefore critical to analyze the technical and economic obstacles to shifting resources from military-oriented to civilian-oriented activity, and the ways of overcoming these obstacles.

There is a remarkable precedent for carrying out large-scale military-to-civilian transition successfully. At the end of World War II, the U.S. was faced with shifting a huge amount of the nation's output from military to civilian production. The challenge was met with room to spare by a combination of corporate planning and federal, state, and local government planning. Roughly 30 percent of U.S. output was transferred in one year without the unemployment rate ever rising above 3 percent.[1] Clearly, with the right approach it is possible to efficiently redirect even very large amounts of productive resources from military to civilian activity without unbearable economic disruption. Yet this experience must be interpreted carefully.

During WWII, workers in the U.S. earned high incomes at the same time government rationing severely restricted their ability to buy the goods and services they wanted. This meant that when the war was over and rationing finally ended, war producers could turn to a very large, unsatisfied market for civilian goods and services. Because of the extensive damage done by the war to virtually every other industrial economy in the world, there was little foreign competition to challenge American producers. Even more important, nearly all the companies that produced for the military during the war were basically civilian enterprises that shifted temporarily to military production. While they produced military equipment and materiel for a few years in support of the national war effort, they were civilian market–oriented firms. All their workers knew how to operate in an ordinary commercial market environment. Some modifications had been made to their production facilities and equipment to better support the war effort, but most of it had originally been designed and configured for efficient civilian production. For these workers and the firms that employed them, this was a "reconversion": They had converted from civilian to military production during the war, and now they were going back to business as usual.

The situation is very different today. More than sixty years after World War II, there is no deep well of unsatisfied pent-up demand, and there is fierce foreign competition. Long before the rise of China as a major industrial producer, decades rather than a few years of the burden of high military spending had already made domestic production much less competitive than that done overseas (Chapter 7). Today there are whole generations of military sector managers, engineers, scientists, and production and maintenance workers whose experience includes little or nothing except military-oriented work. Many of today's military-industrial firms have never competed in the civilian commercial marketplace. Even large firms that manufacture both military and civilian products (such as Boeing) have typically kept their military and civilian divisions operationally separate, functioning as wholly owned subsidiaries reporting to the same CEO.

During WWII, both the production processes and the technologies embodied in military goods were still fairly similar to those in the contemporary civilian economy. But over the past sixty years, the physical plant, machinery, and processes involved in producing military and civilian goods have sharply diverged. The technologies built into the products themselves have become even more different. For example, a World War II era bomber was not all that different from a civilian aircraft of the day. But a B-2 Stealth bomber of today could scarcely be more different from a modern airliner or civilian cargo plane. For the major military-oriented producers, moving into civilian commercial markets is no longer a matter of returning to business as usual. It is a movement into new and unexplored territory. It is conversion, not reconversion. That makes the military-to-civilian transition process more difficult. But with some care and the right advanced preparation, there is little question this conversion can be handled smoothly and well.

The Nature of the Transition Problem

Military industry is fundamentally government-oriented, performance-driven, and insensitive to cost. The perception that every increment of performance is crucial to the outcome on a battlefield creates enormous pressure to squeeze out every ounce of performance possible in the design and manufacture of weapons and related systems. Though there are cost constraints, the high priority (and funding) given to the military sector in the U.S. and most other arms producing countries makes those constraints so loose that the cost of the product is no more than a secondary consideration.

Civilian industry may be oriented to the government or to the private sector, but it tends to be much more sensitive to cost, especially if it is operating in a competitive commercial marketplace. There the customer is not a high priority government department with deep pockets and an output ("national security") that is essentially unmeasurable, but an ordinary consumer with relatively limited income or a firm that must sell to such a consumer. If a company servicing ordinary civilian customers is not attentive to keeping cost down, the probability is high that it will be forced out of business by its more astute and efficient competitors.

At the same time, while product performance is important to civilian customers, it is nowhere near as much of a driving force for most civilian products as it routinely is in military industry. Civilian products do not typically have to operate under conditions as hostile and extreme as those of the military sector. They are not usually subject to the kinds of stresses, vibration, shock, etc., that weapons and related equipment must be capable of handling. No one is likely to be shooting at them. They do not have to be designed to work equally well in a low-altitude desert one day and in rain-soaked mountains the next. Nor is achieving every increment of speed, range, maneuverability, and other aspects of performance considered as vital. These differences turn the two sectors into two very different worlds: an extreme performance, cost-insensitive military-oriented world; and a good performance, cost-sensitive civilian world.

Transitioning Engineers and Scientists

Engineers and scientists are critical to driving the productivity gains that are so important to keeping the economy healthy and strong over the long run (see Chapter 7). The prospect of being able to undo the military drain of these technological resources and reinvigorate the industrial economy is exciting, but redirecting these resources requires care. The difference between the military and civilian-oriented worlds strongly affects how engineers and scientists work. Because of the emphasis on maximizing the technical capability of weapons and related systems and the looseness of cost constraints, large teams of technologists are assembled to design, develop, and produce these extremely complex and sophisticated products. The engineers, scientists, and technicians in such teams tend to be highly specialized within very limited areas of expertise, so they can do the difficult detailed work necessary to squeeze every increment of performance out of the resulting product. Since cost is of much less importance, they are also relatively ignorant about the impact of the research and design choices they make on the ultimate cost of the product.

Because successful design for the civilian marketplace requires careful attention to keeping cost down, engineers and scientists in the civilian sector must be well versed in the implications of all aspects of what they do for product cost. Among other things, they should not be extremely specialized. They need to understand the overall design of the product and the interactions of its components so that they can trade off changes in one part of the design against changes in another to achieve good product performance at the lowest possible cost. Keeping costs down enables the firm to increase its sales and profits by keeping its prices at a level that makes its products attractive to ordinary civilian customers.

Because of these differences, the engineers and scientists of military industry must be retrained (given some different skills) *and* reoriented (taught to look at what they do from a different perspective) before they are likely to be successful in civilian R&D. They have a solid base of knowledge on which to build. But a degree of de-specialization and a strong dose of learning to pay careful attention to cost, along with the skills necessary to do that, are required to connect them to the realities of civilian design.

Converting Management

In practice, military weapons producing firms have only one customer, the nation's armed services. They cannot directly sell their products to civilian customers, and they can typically sell to foreign governments only with the direct and specific approval of their own government. In most cases, even the weapons that are sold by military firms to foreign governments were originally designed, developed, and produced for their home government.

This one-customer orientation produces a very different sales and marketing situation from that faced by civilian firms. Managers of civilian commercial firms must know how to advertise effectively in a mass market, how to survey markets for acceptability of new product lines, how to price a product for penetration of a new market or expansion of an existing one, etc., most of which is entirely irrelevant to operating in the military sector. Military industry managers have to know the minute detail of government procurement regulations, how to develop good working relationships with key government procurement personnel, and how to lobby effectively with the legislature and the administration, much of which is irrelevant to operating in the civilian sector.

Beyond this, the military-oriented firm typically sells its product before it is produced. Combined with the possibility of "progress payments" (i.e., payments made by the government as different stages of the design and production process are completed), this puts the firm in a very different (and much better) financing situation than that faced by most civilian manufacturers. They have the advantage of not having to finance as much of their investment in advance. Furthermore, with high priority attached to military procurement and the absence of strong operational incentives for cost control, military firms that run up the cost of products may be more rather than less successful in generating higher revenues, and perhaps higher profits as well.[2]

It is unreasonable to expect managers accustomed to operating in a situation in which financial risk is small, high costs can become a path to higher revenues, and only one well-funded customer needs to be serviced to operate successfully in risky, cost-sensitive, multicustomer civilian markets without substantial retraining and reorientation. The dismal performance of unconverted military industry managements in producing civilian products is one of the most frequently cited pieces of evidence for the proposition that military-oriented enterprises cannot really be converted and must instead simply "downsize" if they lose business. Aside from the fact that downsizing leaves unsolved the basic economic problem of making productive use of a highly skilled workforce, this is an excessively superficial reading of the record. These enterprises never really reshaped themselves to fit civilian requirements. They simply began making something civilian essentially the same way they had always made military products in the past. This is not conversion. And there is little ground in theory or experience for believing this approach would ever work.

Beyond all of this, the management organization will almost certainly need to be reshaped.[3] The special requirements of the military sector typically result in managerial structures that are top-heavy and poorly organized for civilian operations. There are built-in tendencies for management and administrative structures to grow out of proportion to any gains in efficiency that might result from better coordination or control, dragging down the economic efficiency of the enterprise.[4] It may well be necessary to reform and tighten the management structure as part of the process of converting to efficient civilian production.

Transitioning Production Workers and Administrative Staff

Reorientation to the standards of work efficiency required to minimize cost is likely to be necessary for production workers with long experience in the military sector, and may be required for administrative staff as well. It is also possible that some of the more highly skilled workers, being more specialized, may require on-the-job retraining to convert to civilian work, though that will be minimal compared to the retraining and reorientation required for converting engineers, scientists, and managers. Former production workers and administrative staff may also require retraining to reconnect with civilian employment if there is an oversupply of their particular type of labor. They might need to train for areas of work in which more and better job opportunities exist.

Conversion of Capital Equipment and Facilities

Some of the industrial equipment and facilities currently employed in military industry and at military bases are sufficiently general purpose to be directly usable in civilian-oriented work. But others, such as certain types of machine tools with extreme performance capabilities or highly specialized equipment for working with extraordinarily toxic materials uncommon in civilian industry, are not directly transferable. As long as the operating cost of machinery and equipment with excessive capabilities is not too high, it might still be usable for civilian work. On the other hand, those industrial facilities that do not so much possess excess capabilities as the wrong capabilities have to be reconstructed or abandoned. That cannot be properly evaluated until specific plans have been developed for a particular alternative use.

Preparing capital equipment and facilities for the military-to-civilian transition requires a detailed assessment of what changes in layout, equipment, and facilities are implied by the chosen civilian alternative. Given such an assessment, it is not difficult to estimate both financing requirements and the time needed from start to finish for the actual physical conversion. This, in turn, enables development of a financial plan, as well as effective coordination of this phase of the transition process with others.

Strategies for Successful Transition

Given a thorough understanding of the nature of the military-to-civilian transition, it is possible to develop policies that will successfully carry workers and facilities through this complex process. For technical reasons, there are some things, such as the retraining and re-orientation of engineers, scientists and managers, which must be done whatever the particular shape of the transition process. But other things will depend upon whether the focus of conversion is internal or external to the firm.

Internal vs. External Conversion

"Internal" conversion involves the transition of workforce, facilities, and equipment to civilian-oriented activities inside a formerly military-oriented firm (or division of a firm) that is transitioning to the civilian market. "External" conversion involves finding new, civilian-oriented uses elsewhere for workers, facilities, and equipment that are released by a downsizing military-oriented firm (or a closing military base). Since it retains intact as much of the workforce as is economically sensible, internal conversion minimizes the disruption of the lives of workers and their families. It minimizes disruption of the surrounding community as well by maintaining the tax base and the geographic patterns of living, spending, and commuting. There will generally be less adjustment for the affected workforce, because they continue to work at a firm and workplace with which they are familiar.

But some external conversion is unavoidable. Even if all military contractors moving to civilian markets were committed to planning for internal conversion, some of their workforce would have to be externally converted. The engineering intensity and management staff size common in military industry are simply unsupportable in any economically viable, unsubsidized civilian firm.[5] An efficient transition almost inevitably requires some paring of the workforce. External conversion would therefore be needed to retrain and reorient engineers, scientists, and managers laid off from converting military enterprises and reconnect them to civilian firms.

Furthermore, no matter how much care is taken in preparing for and implementing internal conversion, it is reasonable to assume that it will not always work. There are many reasons, not the least of which are the uncertainties of life in the world of business. It is useful to have a mechanism in place to help find new civilian opportunities for the workers (and physical capital) connected to plans that did not work. External conversion planning will also be required because many military contractors, especially major contractors, have historically been extremely resistant to any form of internal conversion planning. When they lose a contract, they simply lay off workers and shrink the company. For many years, these firms have successfully used the threat of large-scale layoffs as a way of coercing government to fund military programs that, in some cases, even the military did not want. This habit is unlikely to die without serious pressure from the government that is their customer.

There is an argument that external conversion is likely to work better because it is easier to get off on the right foot in a new enterprise than to completely reshape patterns of operation within an existing company. It seems to be true that it is harder to change behavior when much of the surrounding physical and sociological environment remains the same. Yet it has become increasingly obvious in this globalizing world that businesses must be flexible enough to reshape themselves when conditions change. There are few ways to get deeper into trouble in business, especially in the long term, than to get caught in a changing game without realizing the game is changing. As we move toward greater reliance on structuring international economic relationships to keep the peace, the game will certainly be changing for many military industrial firms. For the firms, their employees, and the surrounding community, internal conversion is likely to be a better option.

One of the technical advantages of internal conversion is that job retraining programs are much more effective when they are targeted to specific job opportunities. With internal conversion, the job any given worker will be doing after the transition is known nearly as well as the individual's present job. From scientists and engineers to clerical or administrative workers, it is easier to develop a successful program for retraining and reorientation with this knowledge in hand. The length of time required depends on the specific individual involved, the nature of his/her previous education and experience, and the particular pair of activities between which the transfer is taking place. For example, a civil engineer moving between design work on jet fighter aircraft and design work on corporate jets will require less extensive retraining than will one transferring from jet fighter design to bridge building.[6]

Knowing the destination position is such an advantage that it is useful to develop mechanisms to connect workers to future employment before retraining begins, even for external conversion. The government might, for example, sign retraining contracts with potential civilian employers, and then subsidize retraining tailor-made to the needs of the employer if the employer agrees to hire and retain the trainee for a minimum period upon successful completion of the program.

Choosing Alternative Products

When management of military-industrial enterprises begin to think seriously about converting, they tend to try to sell essentially the same military-oriented product they have been making to civilian users. But the peculiar requirements of the military sector tend to shape products in ways that make them awkward and inefficient for civilian use (both technically and in terms of cost), if they are usable at all. It is better to generate the most comprehensive list possible of alternative civilian products that the company could produce, then choose those that make the most economic sense. This process begins with analyzing the "core competencies" of the firm—its workforce and equipment—looking in detail at what particular things they are best at doing. For example, the firm may be expert at integrating electronic and mechanical controls, or it might have considerable experience designing products to operate in highly corrosive environments. Once identified, these core competencies can then be matched with civilian applications that will result in products with a strong and profitable market. It could easily turn out that the best civilian alternative product for an enterprise currently manufacturing components for fighter aircraft is industrial control equipment, rather than components for civilian aircraft. Looking only for the closest matches to existing product lines is not the best way to find the civilian product lines likely to be the most successful.

It is extremely important to distinguish between that which is merely technically feasible, and that which is actually economically viable. It has been a common mistake to think of alternative products as appropriate as long as making them with the workforce, equipment, and facilities available was technically possible. But if the products are not economically viable, the firms will either go bankrupt or need continuing and burdensome public subsidy, neither of which is a necessary or acceptable alternative.

Public/Private Sector Responsibilities

The military-to-civilian transition will work best as a public sector–private sector partnership, specialized according to comparative advantage. Conversion is not likely to work well unless it is highly decentralized. The managements of the enterprises involved in conversion have a strong comparative advantage in looking for and finding productive and profitable civilian activities to replace their previous military mission. Plans for reshaping capital and labor to fit the new activities chosen must be tailored to the details of each facility and workplace. A one-size-fits-all approach is a virtual guarantee that nothing will fit well. Because no one knows the details and capability of the workforce and facility better then those who work there and those who manage the enterprise, they have an enormous advantage in working out transition plans. It would therefore be a serious mistake for the government to try to blueprint facility and workforce conversion. Even close oversight of plant and firm-level conversion by the national government is unlikely to improve the effectiveness of conversion plans and very likely to be inefficient and expensive. Although this is more obviously true of internal conversion, it is important for external conversion as well.

A more appropriate role for the national government is to use its leverage as customer to pressure military-industrial firms to begin transition planning in advance of need. Serious corporate planning for the post–World War II military-to-civilian transition began fully two years before the war ended. So did a parallel process of preparations by the state, local, and national government. Following the precedent of other federal legislation (such as equal employment opportunity laws, which set requirements for federal contract eligibility), the national government could, for example, require military contractors to set up independently funded labor-management "alternative use committees" as a condition of eligibility for any future federal contract, military or civilian. While it cannot be guaranteed that this planning would be taken seriously and done well, with independent funding and both labor and management participating, the probability of triggering effective contingency planning for internal conversion in most military industrial facilities is high.

With all the differences between the reconversion problem that followed World War II and the conversion problem today, the basic division of responsibility that succeeded then still makes sense. Then, the public sector—federal, state, and local—took care of education and training, and planned public works projects to create productive jobs building the nation's infrastructure (such as those in the Obama administration's 2009 economic stimulus package). But the private sector did all of the microlevel corporate planning.[7]

Alternatives to Conversion

Conversion is one of three available policy approaches to smooth the economic transition to the lower levels of military expenditure implied by the adoption of a security strategy more focused on economic peacekeeping. While it is the most comprehensive approach, it is also the most complex and difficult. "Diversification" is a second possibility. Diversification seeks to minimize the economic cost of transition to the firm by reducing the company's dependence on a continuing flow of military dollars. In the U.S., it has been the strategy most commonly embraced by those military-dependent firms that have paid any real attention to the possibility that the volume of their military contracts might someday fall precipitously. They have sought to diversify by operating parallel civilian-oriented product divisions within their own companies or by acquiring other civilian producers to protect the companies financially against possible loss of military business. Financial diversification has worked reasonably well within its narrow scope, but it does little or nothing to protect the livelihood of the firms' military-sector workforce or the tax base of the communities in which the firms' military divisions operate.

When major U.S. military-industrial firms have tried to diversify by producing civilian product lines in their military divisions without doing the retraining and restructuring crucial to conversion, the results have routinely been disastrous for both the companies and their customers. There is a long and depressing history of failure of this type of diversification. A few classic examples:

- The Bay Area Rapid Transit (BART) rail system in San Francisco carried its first passengers in 1972. The prime contractor for the system's electric trains was Rohr Industries, a military aerospace company in Chula Vista, California. The system was years late getting into operation and suffered frequent breakdowns of its rolling stock when it finally did get into service. As is common with military weapons projects, there was also an enormous escalation of costs: the original cost estimate for the fleet of 450 cars Rohr contracted to produce was $62 million; the actual delivered cost of the fleet was $160 million—a 158 percent cost overrun.[8]
- In the early 1970s, Boeing Vertol (now Boeing, Philadelphia) was turning out thirty large helicopters a month for use in Vietnam.[9] To cope with the declining military market in 1973, Vertol signed a contract to produce 175 light-rail vehicles for the Massachusetts Bay Transportation Authority (MBTA) to be used in Boston's mass transit system. The vehicles suffered from many problems, including frequent derailments and breakdowns. By the end of June of 1979, only thirty of them were actually in service: forty had yet to be delivered, seventy were in different stages of maintenance or modification, and thirty-five were in such bad shape they had to be shipped back to the factory. Boeing ultimately paid MBTA $40 million to relieve the company of any further responsibility.[10]
- With the downturn in military aerospace between 1971 and 1974, Vought Corporation (a Texas-based military division of Ling-Temco-Vought, LTV) contracted to design and manufacture "Airtrans," an automated people-mover for Dallas/Fort Worth Airport.[11] Airtrans was designed to carry passengers and employees between the airport's terminals and parking lots. While it was a serviceable system (which I rode many times), its slow speed, many twists and turns, and hills and valleys made it seem more like a slow-motion amusement park ride than an efficient transit system. Its considerable cost overruns and project delays led to a flurry of lawsuits between Vought and the Dallas/Fort Worth airport authority. And more than thirty years after the system was built, it still did not meet all of its original specifications.

These few examples are typical of what happens when military-sector firms (or divisions) try to diversify into civilian product lines without paying attention to the structural changes and the retraining and reorientation of workforces that are essential to internal conversion. Ironically, the predictably dismal record of this kind of product diversification has been cited by some prominent leaders of military industry (such as Norman Augustine, former CEO of Martin Marietta and Lockheed Martin) as proof that internal conversion does not work. Given the compelling contrast in requirements, focus, and operating environment between the military sector and civilian commercial business, it is easy enough to see that this version of the product diversification strategy (as opposed to purely financial diversification) is doomed to failure. But it bears no real resemblance to real internal conversion.

"Community Economic Adjustment" is yet another strategy for dealing with the economic impact of reductions in military spending. Here government provides financial and technical assistance to military-dependent cities and towns to help them surmount the economic difficulties created by base closings, loss of contracts by locally based military industry, or the integration of large numbers of discharged military personnel into the local economy. Sometimes there are direct subsidies to school systems and the like. More often, there is help in developing strategies to attract new sources of economic activity, to replace the money flows being lost and often to diversify the local economic base as well.

In the U.S., this approach to the military-civilian transition has long been favored by the Department of Defense (DoD) as its preferred way of quieting the boisterous local protests that ordinarily accompany its announcement of military-base closings. Rather than supplying much financial help to affected localities, DoD's usual pattern has been to provide limited technical assistance and to offer its services as liaison for the communities with other federal agencies.

Intelligently implemented financial diversification and well-funded economic adjustment programs will be useful in mitigating the financial stresses that military-dependent firms and communities face when military budgets are scaled back as we move toward an international security system less reliant on the threat and use of military force. But only conversion will help displaced military sector workers retool and redirect their skills for civilian employment. There is no reason to accept the personal cruelty and social folly of writing off many thousands of highly skilled military-sector workers because they require reshaping to properly fit into the civilian economy. Only conversion is designed to recover the largest part of the enormous investment society has made in the skills of the engineers, scientists, and other highly trained workers of the military sector. And only conversion considers whether it makes economic sense to reuse military-serving facilities and equipment, with whatever modifications are necessary to do so efficiently.[12]

Coping with Demobilization

Just as the U.S. was remarkably successful in reconverting its war industries back to civilian work after WWII, it was also highly successful in demobilizing millions of soldiers who served in its armed services during the war and reintegrating them into the civilian economy and society. There were a number of reasons why this worked so well, not the least of which was the so-called GI Bill of Rights. Among other things, the GI Bill made it possible for former armed services personnel to enroll in institutions of higher education and get training that would have otherwise been financially beyond their reach. This major national investment in human capital not only eased the economic transition, but also dramatically increased the earning potential of the demobilized soldiers and greatly boosted the productivity and vigor of the postwar American economy.

Generally speaking, the economic and social reabsorption of former soldiers into civilian life that would be associated with movement toward a peacekeeping economy is not likely to be much of a problem in countries with well-developed, relatively intact economies and well-integrated societies.[13] The more developed countries, especially those not engaged directly or indirectly in active warfare, should be able to handle this aspect of the transition without a huge public effort. The shift of money from military budgets to more economically productive forms of public and private expenditure enabled by the change in security strategy will provide a stimulus to the economy through the market just when that stimulus is most needed.

With a handful of notable exceptions (including Brazil, Israel, Pakistan, China, and India), only a few less developed countries have any sizable military-industrial sector and therefore any substantial conversion problem. Thus, while conversion will be the main transition problem for the more developed countries with substantial arms industries, demobilization, not conversion, will be the first order transition problem for most developing countries. Demobilization will ultimately be of great economic, social, and political benefit to developing countries, but it will be a challenge to make it work well. They have fewer resources with which to support whatever public programs may be useful to the demobilization effort. But their biggest problem is the smaller size and relative weakness of their economies, which complicates the absorption of a sudden bulge in the workforce. This is especially true of those developing countries that are emerging from civil wars or long periods of brutal political and economic oppression.

If demobilization is not handled properly, the potential economic benefits of demilitarization will fail to be achieved, and new problems may be created that will further disrupt economic and political development efforts. The experience of Ethiopia offers a useful example. Beginning in the early 1960s, a series of wars of liberation shook the nation.[14] It took a long time, but by 1991 Ethiopian troops had lost control of the territory that two years later became the independent country of Eritrea. When Eritrea's war of independence was finally over, many Ethiopian soldiers were simply released from the military and told to go home. There was no conscious effort to help them integrate into the nation's civilian life. A lot of them had been in the military so long that they didn't know any other kind of life. When they were sent home, they took their guns with them. With guns and without any real civilian skills, they became roving bandits preying on people in the countryside and further disrupting economic life. They managed to do considerable damage before the government finally realized it had to do something to address the problems they were causing. To its credit, rather than simply trying to subdue them by force, the government undertook a variety of programs aimed at retraining and otherwise reintegrating these former soldiers into civilian life. The programs turned the former soldiers into an asset rather than a liability to the nation. It was a painful experience, but an important lesson to learn.

There is by now considerable experience with attempts at demobilization among the developing nations of Africa—in Somalia, Angola, Sierra

Leone, Mozambique, Namibia, and Uganda. Ethiopia alone demobilized on the order of half a million soldiers during the 1990s; Eritrea another 55,000. Not all of this experience was positive.[15] Each demobilization process took the specific shape it did because of the particular socioeconomic, cultural, and political context within which it occurred. Nevertheless, there are some common threads that run through the process of demobilization and connect it to conversion and other types of transition.

As in the economic conversion of military industry, retraining and reorientation of the personnel involved is a critical matter. If they are lacking in useful civilian-oriented economic skills, as many longtime soldiers in the developing world will be, they must be retrained so that they can take advantage of whatever economic opportunities may exist. They must also learn to replace their military way of thinking with a way of thinking more compatible with success in the different context of civilian life. In demobilization, that means changing from a military mindset, in which unquestioned obedience is expected and extreme violence is an acceptable means of achieving the mission at hand, to a mindset that is oriented to individual creativity, initiative, and achieving results by peaceful cooperation. For both conversion and demobilization a major shift in perspective is critical to success, a shift that cannot be assumed to be automatic.

Describing the plight of ex-solders in Africa, Nicole Ball provides a useful insight into the problem of demobilization at least in the world's poorer developing countries:

> The typical veteran is semi-literate at best, is unskilled, has few personal possessions, often has no housing or land, and frequently has many dependents. Some veterans are also physically and psychologically handicapped by wartime experiences. Many find it difficult to take independent initiatives and to cope with the ordinary demands of civilian life. Even when they possess a marketable skill, such as mechanic or driver, ex-combatants tend to have little or no experience in the labor market, having taken up arms at an early age.[16]

Ball suggests thinking of the demobilization process as having four stages: assembly, discharge, short-term reinsertion, and long-term reintegration.[17] First, mainly for reasons of security, soldiers need to be brought to specific assembly areas to be counted, registered, given identification cards, and relieved of their weapons. Assembly areas are often the most cost-effective places to retrain and reorient demobilizing soldiers, and to provide them with needed in-kind assistance and cash.[18] Effective retraining and reorientation is at the same time crucial and time-consuming. Rather than yielding to financial pressures to get them out quickly, a period of assembly stretching over a few years might make more sense, especially when large numbers of former combatants are being processed.

When the former soldiers are ready for discharge, they (and their dependents) should be provided with transportation to the places they intend to settle to ensure that the ex-combatants are dispersed, rather than concentrated in the same place, to avoid future problems. Once they reach their diverse destinations, further reorientation sessions conducted by or at least with people from the local community will help them adjust more quickly and completely to their new surroundings in the short run and the new roles they are expected to play in the long run. Successful long-term reintegration of ex-combatants into civilian life requires that they and their families achieve social acceptance in the communities in which they will be living.

Conclusion

Psychologists tell us that transitions—even good transitions—are among the most stressful life events. They are movements from the known into the as-yet unknown. On a societal scale, the transition from a security strategy centered on the threat or use of military force to one that relies primarily on economic peacekeeping has much to recommend it. But it would be foolish to simply ignore the stresses that even contemplating such a structural shift can create, if for no other reason than because failing to address them adequately may prevent us from building the political will to make the change.

It is ironic, but nevertheless true, that one of the most important sources of stress produced by what would be a greatly beneficial economic change is the uncertainty it creates for those who believe their economic present and future to be tied to the continuation of the current military security system. In this, as in many situations of progressive social change, the vastly greater but more diffuse benefit the change will produce for a majority of the population can be held hostage to the much smaller pain it will produce for a concentrated but politically influential minority. Economists often talk of overcoming this kind of roadblock by having the gainers directly compensate the losers. In this case, it makes more sense to put a mechanism into place that will reassure those who fear loss that they will be protected from that loss, not by a handout but by help in moving efficiently through the change and reconnecting to productive economic activity. Such a mechanism is not only valuable in overcoming political barriers to moving toward a peacekeeping economy, it is crucial to ensuring that we realize the enormous potential economic gains of reconnecting the resources diverted to the military sector to productive economic activity.

In 1977, with my colleague, Seymour Melman I wrote specifications for a piece of federal legislation that embodied one model for a highly decentralized system of private sector planning (encouraged by the public sector) for military-to-civilian transition in advance of need. Among other things, there were two key provisions: 1) as a condition of eligibility for any government contract, all military contractors in the U.S. would be required to set up independently funded alternative use committees composed of representatives of labor, management, and the local community to develop a facility and workforce conversion plan (military bases would have a similar requirement); and 2) a cumulative reserve fund would be established, financed by a small tax on military contracts, to pay for all required retraining and related benefits in the event a conversion plan needed to be activated.[19] Had the bill become law, much of the economic distress the employees of military industries experienced when the Cold War ended would have been prevented by the mechanism the bill would have set in motion. More importantly, it would have helped to undercut the pressures to maintain Cold War levels of military spending after the collapse of the Soviet Union, and therefore perhaps helped to saved the nation billions if not trillions of dollars.

Many economists argue that no such mechanism is necessary to facilitate conversion. The unaided market is fully capable of handling any necessary transition that might result from the decision to move to a new and structurally different security system. In one sense, they are right. Given that decision, market forces will eventually lead us to a new allocation of resources in which military-serving activity accounts for a much smaller share of business. But market forces will not prevent or even mitigate the degree of economic pain inflicted during that unaided transition. Market forces are perfectly willing to sacrifice the talents of an entire generation of military-sector workers and write off much of the huge social investment that has been made in their considerable skills because without modification those skills are unsuited to success in comparable civilian work. For an unnecessarily long time, if not permanently, that will deprive the economy of the considerable potential for repair, regeneration, and revitalization those talents represent. More importantly, without some concrete means of smoothing this transition, it will be much more difficult to overcome the politically powerful vested interests that are arrayed against it. Preparing in advance for military-to-civilian conversion will prevent us from getting stuck in the past, and therefore from failing to realize the reinforcing cycle of prosperity and security that a peacekeeping economy is capable of delivering.

9

Extending Demilitarized Security
Economic Peacekeeping and
Nonviolent Action

THE PEACEKEEPING INTERNATIONAL ECONOMY offers the promise of greater prosperity and security by transforming an international security system based primarily on the threat or use of force into one that relies primarily on strong positive incentives to keep the peace. If conscientiously applied within as well as between countries, peacekeeping economic principles will help to prevent the eruption of both interstate and intrastate violence and war. But what happens if and when the system of positive incentives fails to prevent external war or internal brutality and repression?

There are circumstances in which the use of military force in defense of the nation or the use of violence in the face of barbarism is justified, even unavoidable. But there are also many circumstances in which active non-violent resistance may be a more effective way of fighting, whether to overcome hateful policies, overthrow governments, or deter or repel attackers. The theory and practice of nonviolent action, developed by such noted advocates as Mohandas Karamchand Gandhi and Martin Luther King Jr., has been supplemented in recent decades by a body of academic analysis best represented by the work of political scientist Gene Sharp.[1]

No government can govern without the acquiescence, if not the active support, of the vast majority of the population. From this it follows that if any substantial fraction of the population actively withdraws cooperation and refuses to obey any particular government edict or policy, the government will be unable to enforce it. By extension, if any substantial fraction of the population withdraws cooperation and completely refuses to obey the government in general, that government cannot stand. This sounds humane and empowering, yet hopelessly idealistic and naïve. But a considerable body of evidence has accumulated since the early twentieth century to demonstrate that this approach is not only eminently practical but also remarkably effective.

Starting with his successful campaign of civil disobedience against unjust and discriminatory laws imposed by British colonial rulers in South Africa (1907–1914), Mohandas Gandhi dedicated his life to the principle of active nonviolent resistance. He used that tactic to successfully liberate his native India from British rule by the mid-1940s.[2] A decade later in the United States, Martin Luther King Jr. put Gandhi's insights to work, leading the now famous boycott against racial segregation of buses in Montgomery, Alabama. King became the most prominent of a number of Americans of African descent leading a decades-long nonviolent struggle against the system of legal and de facto racial segregation and discrimination in the U.S. The nonviolent tactics of King and his colleagues were not an unqualified success in ridding the country of racial discrimination. But they did make enormous progress, progress that reached far beyond simply eliminating legally sanctioned racism. By the early twenty-first century, there were a number of symbols of the striking changes that had been brought about by the American civil rights movement: the first black chairman of the Joint Chiefs of Staff (Colin Powell), two sequential black secretaries of state (Colin Powell and Condoleezza Rice), and the first African-American president (Barack Obama).

Thirty years after King led the Montgomery bus boycott, the ordinary people of the Philippines rose up in a nonviolent "people power" revolution, triggered on February 22, 1986, by the defection of a small group of soldiers who were led by the nation's defense minister and the deputy chief of staff. Though the pressure had been building for years, that defection catalyzed the nonviolent revolution, with hundreds of thousands of Filipinos pouring into the streets to protect the rebellious officers with their own unprotected bodies, determined to rid themselves of the repressive authoritarian government of President Ferdinand Marcos. They simply refused to obey the government's edicts any longer and faced down a powerful military force sent to crush the rebellion. Within a few days, without any bloodshed, the Marcos government was swept away.

The mid-1980s also saw the rise of Mikhail Gorbachev to power in the Soviet Union. Intent on making the Soviet system more efficient and democratic, he introduced the policies of glasnost (openness) and perestroika (restructuring). Gorbachev actively sought to end the arms race with the U.S. in an attempt to lift the crushing military burden from his country's economy and redirect resources from servicing military to civilian needs. Within a few years of Gorbachev's ascendance, reformist movements in Eastern Europe became much stronger, ultimately leading to revolutions that overthrew all the region's repressive communist regimes. All but one of these rigid, authoritarian governments were overthrown by completely nonviolent revolutions, as the populations of these countries simply refused to recognize their authority any longer.[3] The Berlin Wall, symbol of the Cold War, was finally opened by the East Germans on November 9, 1989, and torn down by the end of the next year. Once again, nonviolent resistance had been used with remarkable success.

Then, on August 19, 1991, while Gorbachev was vacationing in the Crimea, hard-liners in the Soviet government staged a coup. Tens of thousands of Soviet citizens poured into the streets of Moscow in a massive nonviolent demonstration of their opposition to the coup and determination to prevent the rollback of the freedoms they had been experiencing. By the second day, more than 150,000 people stood between the military tanks and government buildings, urged on by Boris Yeltsin, soon to become president of the Russian Federation. By the end of the third day, the coup had completely collapsed, brought down by the power of resolute nonviolent resistance.

Pushed over the edge by blatant electoral fraud in the parliamentary elections of November 2003, the people of the former Soviet Republic of Georgia staged a successful massive nonviolent uprising, called the "Rose Revolution" (because many demonstrators carried roses), against the government of Eduard Shevardnadze. Shevardnadze had been the first secretary of the Communist Party of Georgia from 1972 to 1985 and the foreign minister of the Soviet Union from 1985 to 1991 before he became the ruler of post-Soviet Georgia in 1992. Popular because of the role he had played in leading the country out of anarchy in the early 1990s, he was elected president in 1995 and again in 2000. Shevardnadze's government was accused of rampant corruption. When the extent of rigging of the 2003 elections became clear, the Georgian people, many of whom were mobilized by a youth group called Kmara (Enough), refused to accept the result or allow the government to stand. They took to the streets of the capital by the thousands in nonviolent demonstrations. The opposition took control of parliament, and Shevardnadze, who was unable to regain control of the country, was forced to resign. Without any blood being spilled, the abusive government was gone and on January 25, 2004, a new president, Mikheil Saakashvili, was democratically elected.[4]

Later that same year, evidence of massive fraud in a presidential runoff election in nearby Ukraine, also a former Soviet Republic, triggered another demonstration of the power of nonviolent resistance. Nonpartisan exit polls taken during the runoff election on November 21, 2004, indicated that Viktor Yushchenko had received 52 percent of the vote. Yet after hours of silence, the Central Electoral Commission announced that Viktor Yanukovych, favorite of the nation's corrupt elite and their powerful ally Russia, had won by 2.5 percent. There was, they claimed, a miraculous last minute upsurge in voter turnout (up to 40 percent higher than turnout in the first round of the election) in areas in which 97 percent of the vote went to Yanukovych.[5]

International observers from the Organization for Security and Cooperation in Europe (OSCE) reported massive irregularities, including acts of intimidation, fraud, and abuse.[6] Hundreds of thousands of people flooded Independence Square in Kiev, the nation's capital. For the next seventeen days, through bitter cold, snow, and sleet, millions of Ukrainians nationwide participated in nonviolent protests against what they regarded as an attempt to hijack their young democracy. As this entirely peaceful "Orange Revolution" (orange was the color of Yushchenko's party) grew stronger, the nation's military and security services began to fragment. On November 27, Parliament declared the runoff election invalid. A few days later the supreme court called for new elections, ultimately held on December 26.

With the media operating more freely and more than twelve thousand election monitors from North America, Russia, and Asia observing, this time Yushchenko was certified as having received 52 percent of the votes and declared the winner. On January 11, 2005, Ukraine's Yushchenko and Georgia's Saakashvili issued a joint declaration thanking the world community of democracies for supporting the struggles in their countries, while at the same time pointing out that it was the nonviolent effort of their own people that had overcome tyranny.[7]

Even these brief and incomplete descriptions make it clear enough that nonviolent noncooperation has an impressive record in securing freedom, independence, and political rights.[8] But it is not magic. No security strategy, including nonviolent resistance (and, for that matter, economic peacekeeping), works all the time. Certainly violent revolutions and security strategies that rely on the threat or use of military force have failed repeatedly, often leaving devastation in their wake. But probably the most spectacular late twentieth century failure of nonviolent protest took place in 1989 in China in Beijing's enormous Tiananmen Square.

The events began with a demonstration by students in Beijing, Shanghai, and other cities in commemoration of the death on April 15, 1989, of Hu Yaobang, a former leader of the Chinese Communist Party who had been replaced after refusing to halt student demonstrations in December 1986. The memorial soon evolved into a far-reaching protest aimed at dramatic political and economic change. On May 4, the students in Beijing read a proclamation in Tiananmen Square "calling on the government to accelerate political and economic reform, guarantee constitutional freedoms, fight corruption, adopt a press law, and allow establishment of privately run newspapers."[9] That same day one hundred thousand students and workers marched in Beijing in support of democratic reforms. Nine days later, some students began a hunger strike in support of their demands. The government did nothing. Over the next days and weeks, tens of millions of citizens took to the streets in peaceful demonstrations in Beijing and many other Chinese cities to demand that the government respond.

A limited dialogue began, and there was great hope in China and around the world that this remarkable, nonviolent pro-democracy movement too might succeed. But the government warned it would take whatever action it thought necessary to put an end to the growing "social chaos." Then protestors demanded the removal from power the country's top leader, Deng Xiaopeng, and other high officials. Finally, on June 4, the government sent the People's Liberation Army to clear Tiananmen Square. Hundreds of protestors and their supporters were arrested. Acting with tremendous brutality, the troops killed hundreds and injured some ten thousand more. Since that terrible day, economic reforms have made great progress in China, but despite some local political reform, the central government remains authoritarian and the democracy movement has, at best, gone deep underground.[10] It remains to be seen if and when it will reemerge.

Nonviolent action does not always elicit nonviolent responses from government and other opponents. People engaged in nonviolent struggle were killed or injured during Gandhi's campaign for Indian independence and during the American civil rights movement, as well as in Tiananmen Square. The most pragmatic advocates of this strategy do not argue that it is "safe," but rather that it is a more democratic, persuasive, moral, and effective means of "fighting"; and that reconciliation of those who were on opposite sides of the conflict becomes much easier when the struggle is finally over.

A violent revolution might have succeeded in liberating India from British rule; it did in what was to become the United States. It is conceivable that violent rebellion might have eventually achieved the goals of the American civil rights movement, although that is much less likely. But even if these movements could have achieved their ultimate objectives through violence, is there any doubt that many more people would have been killed and injured in the process? Or that the legacy of violent versions of these struggles would have been bitter and difficult to reconcile?

The historical record of nonviolent noncooperation clearly establishes its viability and effectiveness. We need to look more closely at the theory and tactics that support it, its interaction with the principles of economic peacekeeping, and its usefulness as a complementary security strategy.

Security Through Civilian-Based Defense

Sharp defines civilian-based defense as "defense by civilians . . . accomplished by reliance on social, economic, political, and psychological weapons . . . nonviolent weapons . . . used to wage widespread noncooperation and to offer massive public defiance."[11] According to Sharp, "Civilian-based defense rests on the theory that political power, whether of domestic or foreign origin, is derived from sources *within* each society. By [nonviolently] denying or severing these sources of power, populations can control rulers and defeat foreign aggressors."[12] The idea is to make it impossible for a government to enforce laws or policies that a significant part of the population considers abhorrent, as well as to prevent foreign aggressors or domestic leaders of an authoritarian coup from consolidating power and governing the country. He argues that it is even possible to use nonviolent action to undermine the loyalty and reliability of the soldiers, police forces, and administrators of those who are trying to seize or maintain control illegitimately.

The underlying insight here is that, however they came to power, rulers are entirely dependent on others to carry out their orders from the very top to the very bottom of the political and social chain of command. They can do little or nothing by themselves. The only real power they have is the power that others give them, by virtue of their active support, cooperation, or at least passive acquiescence.

Through others, rulers have a variety of tools available to elicit support, cooperation, or acquiescence from the people they govern. Some of these tools are ideologies that convey legitimacy, from the "divine right of kings" to a belief in the validity of electoral democracy. Some are the tools of coercion, intended to induce submission through fear—both economic coercion, from deprivation of income (demotion or loss of jobs) to confiscation or destruction of property; and physical coercion, in the form of physical assaults, imprisonment, torture, and death, delivered by means of military forces and police. These tools are often effective. But if large enough numbers of people refuse to comply no matter what the cost, these tools become ineffective and the rulers that have stood behind them become powerless.

This is hardly a new idea. More than 450 years ago, Étienne de la Boétie, one of the founders of modern political philosophy in France, wrote about tyrants, "He who abuses you so has only two eyes, has but two hands, one body, and has naught but what has the least man . . . except for the advantage you give him to destroy you. . . . [If tyrants] are given nothing, if they are not obeyed, without fighting, without striking a blow, they remain naked and undone, and do nothing further, just as the root, having no soil or food, the branch withers and dies."[13]

It is often thought that the effective use of nonviolent action requires achievement of a deeper and more profound moral and philosophical understanding, as well as a higher level of spiritual and religious consciousness. That is simply not true. The capability for effective nonviolent action comes from a much less lofty place. As Sharp puts it, "the capacity to disobey and refuse political cooperation is simply rooted in our human capacity to be stubborn when it suits us. . . . Very young children, as well as many youths and adults, become very skilled in disobedience and noncooperation quite naturally."[14] While that is certainly true, it is also true that nearly all of us are conditioned to obey authority from a very early age, and that conditioning can be hard to overcome.

Obedience to Authority

The power of our conditioning to obey those in authority is nowhere better illustrated than in the groundbreaking experiments carried out by psychologist Stanley Milgram in the early 1960s.[15] Motivated by a desire to understand why so many ordinary people supported and even participated in the brutal and inhuman policies of the Nazi government of Germany (1933–1945), there were two simple but powerful questions underlying Milgram's research: How could such a thing happen? and, Could it happen "here" (meaning "anywhere")?

Milgram ran many versions of his experiment, but the setup was always essentially the same. There were three kinds of participants: a "teacher," a "learner," and an "experimenter." The experimenter (the authority figure) would begin by explaining that the experiment was part of a study of the effects of punishment on learning, and would then go over the procedure to be followed. The teacher was to read pairs of words and the learner had

to respond to a question about each word pair. If the learner answered correctly, the teacher was to move on to the next word pair. If not, the teacher
was to deliver an electric shock to the learner by flipping a switch attached
to a control board to which the learner's hand was connected. There were
thirty switches that marked in increments of 15 volts the strength of the
shock they would deliver, from "15 volts" to "450 volts." Each time the
learner made a mistake, the teacher was to flip the switch that delivered
the next higher shock. To make sure there was no ambiguity about the
strength of the shock being delivered, each successive group of switches
was marked, "Slight Shock," "Moderate Shock," "Strong Shock" . . . all
the way up to "Danger: Severe Shock," and finally "XXX."

But this was an experiment in obedience, not learning, and it was the
teacher who was the subject, not the learner. Both the experimenter and the
learner were part of the experimental team. No shocks were actually being
delivered, but the person playing the part of the learner was trained to react
as though he/she was being given increasingly severe shocks. The question
was, how far would the teacher go in obeying the authority of the experimenter and delivering increasingly severe shocks to the learner? Before
running the experiments, Milgram asked groups of college students,
middle-class adults, and even psychiatrists how far they thought subjects
would go before refusing to obey the experimenter any further. The average
break-off point they predicted was at the eighth or ninth switch (120–135
volts), and no one predicted that the teacher would go beyond the twentieth
switch (300 volts). After all, there was really nothing the experimenter
could do or even threaten to do to any teacher who rebelled and refused to
obey the rules. Then Milgram ran the experiment. The average point of
disobedience was at the twenty-seventh switch (405 volts), and fully 65 percent of the subjects went all the way to the final switch. Through many versions of the experiment, the level of complete obedience (going to the last
switch) was depressingly high; even with the teacher told to physically hold
the protesting learner's hand down on the shock plate, it was 30 percent.
With experimenter absent while the test procedure was going on, it was still
more than 20 percent.

In eighteen different versions of the experiment, there were only five in
which the level of total obedience fell to 10 percent or less. Those five cases

offer some tentative rays of light in an otherwise depressingly gloomy picture of human behavior. Most interesting for our purposes was the version in which the teacher's tasks were divided into three parts and performed by three different individuals, two of whom were confederates who rebelled at a preset point in the experiment. In Milgram's words, "The effects of peer rebellion are very impressive in undercutting the experimenter's authority. Indeed in the score of experimental variations completed in this study, none was so effective in undercutting the experimenter's authority as the manipulation reported here."[16] A version in which two authority figures issued contradictory commands triggered a comparable level of disobedience.

Taken together, the results of these two versions offer insights important in effectively overcoming a strong and widespread tendency to obey even malevolent authority, a tendency that could undercut the effectiveness of civilian-based defense. The first insight is that people have a much easier time rebelling against malevolent authority when peers are doing the same thing. This puts a premium on organizing nonviolent civil disobedience as a form of collective action, rather than an individually heroic act. The second insight is that it is easier for people to disobey malevolent authority when there is a more benevolent alternative to which they can switch their allegiance. That highlights the importance of finding or creating alternative authorities that carry the banner of the cause at hand. Both these insights are entirely consistent with the character of civilian-based defense as a security strategy.

Because nonviolent action works much better when large groups of people participate, the condition and vitality of nongovernmental organizations and institutions make a considerable difference in applying nonviolence effectively. It is much easier to organize collective action through religious groups, ethnic and cultural groups, trade unions, business organizations, cause-oriented organizations (such as environmental groups and peace and justice groups), fellowship and service organizations (such as Rotary Clubs and Lions Clubs), political parties, and the like. They are, in effect, places in which the interests, attention, and loyalties of groups of people converge. Furthermore, they also represent potential benevolent alternative sources of authority. These organizations and institutions can form the nuclei around which much larger groups of people can coalesce, driven by a shared determination to protect that which is most dear to them.

Key Nonviolent Tactics

Sharp argues that there are three broad classes of tactics key to civilian-based defense: nonviolent protest and persuasion, nonviolent noncooperation, and nonviolent intervention. Among the methods of nonviolent protest and persuasion are public speeches, candlelight vigils, petitions, symbolic public acts (such as burning ID cards), leafleting and informational picketing, and mass public demonstrations. The idea is to make it clear that there is meaningful opposition regarding what the participants are protesting, to raise awareness of the issues to increase support among the wider public and grow the movement, and to influence opponents. Noncooperation, on the other hand, has social, economic, and political dimensions. Social noncooperation involves refusal to carry out normal social relationships with individuals or groups that are regarded as being complicit in perpetrating some grievous wrong, such as refusing to talk to or even acknowledge the presence of soldiers of an occupying force. Economic noncooperation includes boycotts (such as refusal to buy certain products or the products of particular nations), disinvestment or refusal to invest, and work stoppages or slowdowns. Political noncooperation includes ignoring the edicts of particular agencies of government or government as a whole; deliberate delay or inaction of those in the government employ who oppose the government's actions; and, perhaps best known, the intentional, open, and peaceful violation of laws thought to be unjust or illegitimate.

The third class of tactics, nonviolent intervention, differs in that it involves directly interfering with and disrupting activities so that they cannot continue unless the interveners are removed or otherwise overcome. Included in this category are nonviolent sit-ins, building occupations, disruptive picketing, and blocking of movement or access. It can go so far as to include the setting up of parallel governance structures, or even an entire parallel government that is regarded as legitimate and worthy of the public's respect and willing compliance. During the primarily nonviolent phase of the American movement for independence (1765–1775), for example, the colonists organized provisional legislatures and committees of correspondence, governance, and resistance that took on various governmental functions.[17] In total, across these three classes of tactics, Sharp lists 198 methods of nonviolent action.[18]

In addition to its efficacy as a reactive strategy for overturning objectionable policies, unseating abusive governments, defeating coups, and denying aggressors the gains of occupation, civilian-based defense may also have value as a deterrent. In most cases, military attacks are launched against a nation: 1) to respond to an attack or other offensive action taken by that nation; 2) to preempt a feared attack by that nation; or 3) as an act of aggression against that nation aimed at getting control of its territory, people, and resources. Since by its very nature civilian-based defense cannot be used as a means of attacking another nation, it poses no offensive threat, and therefore could not provoke an attack for either of the first two reasons. But the third reason is key to the effectiveness of civilian-based defense as a deterrent. If it is well known that a nation has put in place a vigorous system of civilian-based defense (in addition to whatever other security systems it has prepared), potential attackers would be forewarned that even a successful military attack and invasion of that country would be followed by a nightmarishly frustrating and costly attempt at occupation and control. It is not unreasonable to expect that this knowledge might lead them to believe that an attack would have little or no chance of bringing them benefits worth anything near the attack's ultimate cost. If so—and if the potential attackers were rational (always a key assumption of any theory of deterrence)—they would be deterred from attacking in the first place.

The tactics of civilian-based defense, especially the tactics of nonviolent noncooperation and intervention, are an active though entirely nonviolent means of fighting. Civilian-based defense works best when those who participate are deeply enough committed to the method and its goals to keep up the fight despite the threat, and often the reality, of violent and even brutal attempts to dissuade or defeat them. Especially in the face of violent repression, it is a strategy that requires a great deal of personal and organizational discipline. Effective nonviolent action often does draw violent reactions from those who oppose its goals. Though this violence is intended to create fear that will elicit obedience, "In case after case, contrary to what might be expected, there has been independent testimony that people have not submitted to such fear. They have either . . . learned to control . . . or, more dramatically . . . apparently lost their fear."[19] Furthermore, "While resisters and bystanders do get wounded and killed during nonviolent struggle, the numbers are consistently much smaller than in comparable violent resistance movements."[20]

Nonviolent action often creates greater problems for its opponents than does violent resistance. Authoritarian opponents, particularly governments, are better equipped to deal with violence; wielding the means of violence is their "comparative advantage." It is harder to justify the use of violence and brutality to their own publics as well as to the wider world when those who are being treated so brutally are entirely nonviolent themselves. Needing to justify their use of violent repression is not necessarily the result of any awakening of conscience, but simply a pragmatic concern with avoiding further alienation of their own public or the people of other countries with whom they have important economic, political, or military relationships. Alienating their own people could multiply the resistance, increasing the domestic threat to their power. Alienating the people of other countries could generate or magnify external threats to their power by subjecting them to various forms of sanctions and pressure. Indeed, one of the standard tactics used by authoritarian forces dealing with nonviolent resistance is to try to provoke the resisters into acts of violence or, failing that, to use their own agents to foment or carry out violent acts they can attribute to the resisters. If they can credibly label the resistance as violent, they are more likely to be able to convince their own people and those elsewhere that the violent repression of those "vicious rebels" or "terrorists" was necessary and appropriate.

Many of the historical cases of nonviolent action were improvised: the resisters had little or no advance training and did little or no advance planning or strategizing; they simply made it up as they went along. Military campaigns, on the other hand, are usually meticulously planned (although the plans almost always have to be revised) and carried out by forces that are both trained in advance and relatively well equipped. Sharp contends that if the same kind of attention were paid to preparing and sustaining a system of civilian-based defense, "it should not be too difficult to produce an effective power . . . at least ten times greater than that demonstrated in the most powerful of the past cases of improvised nonviolent struggle."[21]

None of this is to say that it would necessarily be wise for a nation to completely abandon its military capabilities in favor of sole reliance on civilian-based defense or, for that matter, on the efficacy of a peacekeeping economy. But it does make sense to think seriously about becoming much less dependent on military force by adopting both economic peacekeeping and civilian-based defense as components of a diversified security strategy.

The Relationship Between Civilian-Based Defense and Economic Peacekeeping

Sharp argues, "The likelihood of foreign attack may . . . be reduced by the development of a more 'positive' foreign policy, which can strengthen a civilian-based defense by reducing international hostilities and increasing goodwill toward the country with the nonmilitary policy."[22] The principles of economic peacekeeping are intended to make economic relations an important part of just such a "positive" foreign policy, "reducing international hostilities and increasing goodwill" by creating strong positive incentives for nations to manage or resolve their conflicts short of violence and war. Thus there seems to be a prima facie case for the compatibility of these two approaches.

Economic peacekeeping and civilian-based defense are similar security strategies in that neither relies on the threat or use of physical violence, yet both include elements of coercive force. Two of the three key tactics of civilian-based defense, noncooperation and nonviolent intervention, are designed to apply coercive pressure by disrupting the normal flow of economic and political life, forcing the opponent to bear substantial costs. Although they do not lie at the core of economic peacekeeping, the main function of economic sanctions is also to apply nonviolent coercive force by imposing substantial economic (and perhaps political) pain on the sanctions target.

The principles of economic peacekeeping are intended to reduce conflicts among *and* within states, and to prevent the escalation of those conflicts that do occur to the point at which violence erupts. But when economic peacekeeping does fail and conflict escalates beyond the point where economic self-interest, negotiation, and goodwill can keep it under control, the tactics of civilian-based defense offer a way of fighting it out while still avoiding the magnitude of damage to and destruction of property and people associated with the outbreak of war.[23] The web of balanced mutual economic dependency that characterizes a peacekeeping economy means that the economic disruption associated with civilian-based defense within or between countries will be quickly transmitted to their economic partners. That will automatically create external pressure to resolve the conflict. Economic partners external to the conflict have a self-interested incentive to pay attention and do what they can to help resolve it. They might offer their good offices as interested but objective mediators; they might suggest potential solutions; they might even offer to be directly involved in arrangements created to resolve the conflict. But if it is serious, they will not ignore it.

Of course, economic partner countries external to the conflict could also try to intervene violently, for example, to help the governments involved forcibly repress those practicing nonviolent action. But violent repression of nonviolent action does not typically fail because of the lack of a sufficient capacity for violence on the part on the government that is its target. When it fails (as it often does), it is because it is inherently difficult to use violent repression successfully against determined practitioners of nonviolent civilian-based defense. In practice violence, especially excessive violence, used against determined nonviolent actors can increase sympathy and support for their cause, and quite possibly swell their ranks. It can also bring international condemnation and serious diplomatic and economic pressure against the government trying to violently repress their peaceful opponents. It can even provoke defections of at least some high government officials or military officers, thereby possibly undermining the strength and standing of the nation's rulers. The point is not that violent repression of nonviolent action always fails, but rather that it frequently does fail, and when it does it is rarely if ever because the government reaction was not violent enough.

Furthermore, following economic peacekeeping Principle I creates a state of mutual interdependence characterized by relationships that are balanced in benefits, flows, and decision power. These relationships cannot work well without the cooperation of many people in the network of countries involved. Therefore, if country A were to help violently repress a popular nonviolent movement in country B, A may subsequently have problems making its economic relationships with B work efficiently, precisely because these relationships depend on the cooperation of many people in B whose hopes and dreams it has just helped to crush. It cannot be guaranteed that no country will ever intervene to violently crush an internal nonviolent movement in another country once a properly functioning peacekeeping economy has been set up. But such violent intervention is certainly much less likely to occur in this situation than in an international economy characterized by unbalanced exploitative economic relationships.

As the period of time grows in which peacekeeping economic principles are seriously and successfully applied among and within countries, an ethos of cooperation reinforced by norms of nonviolent conflict resolution will eventually be established. In such an environment countries are far more likely to offer their good offices in resolving the conflicts that affect their economic partners than to think or act in terms of violent military intervention. Not so incidentally, that environment may also help to deepen and widen support for the adoption of civilian-based defense as part of a comprehensive security strategy.

Finally, in the state of balanced high interdependence essential to a peacekeeping economy, the economic disruption some of the tactics of civilian-based defense are aimed at causing will be felt more strongly by more people. That will strengthen civilian-based defense by increasing the leverage of those who use its tactics to protect their political and economic rights against assault by outsiders and insiders alike, and to rid their countries of policies and practices they consider abhorrent.

Is it possible that increasing the power of such nonviolent action is not an unreservedly good thing? Might it promote chaos and instability, rather than greater freedom and democracy? Might it even be used to support vicious policies and authoritarian practices? In order to be effective, civilian-based defense must be carried out by great masses of people, not by just a few disgruntled souls. A nonviolent demonstration of one hundred people in one place is unlikely to accomplish much if it stays at that level. It may not even be noticed. A demonstration of one hundred thousand people or thousands of simultaneous demonstrations of one hundred people all over the country is an entirely different thing. Similarly, groups of protestors practicing nonviolent disruption are not likely to have much effect if they stay small and scattered. But many thousands routinely practicing one or another form of nonviolent noncooperation can bring down governments and change the course of history. Nonviolent movements may begin small (they often do), but they cannot remain small if they are to have real power.

We need not be overly concerned that training populations in civilian-based defense will give the power to destabilize societies to every small group that has any objection to the way things are. Nonviolent movements trying to depose popular leaders or impose policies on a country that the vast majority of the population utterly rejects will not succeed because they will never be able to enlist the support of a large enough part of the population. The tactics of nonviolent resistance empower every individual by providing a way to take meaningful personal action in support of a cause in which they deeply believe. That is very important. But the action they take will "change the world" only if there is widespread support for and participation in the cause among large numbers of people.

Like economic peacekeeping, civilian-based defense is a security strategy that thrives on broad participation and is thoroughly consistent with and supportive of the principles of democracy. But even in a democracy, broad support for a leader or a set of policies does not guarantee that that leader will be benign or those policies laudable. After all, Adolf Hitler and his Nazi Party were elected to power in Germany, and by all accounts many of their most reprehensible policies had the broad support (or at least widespread acquiescence) of the German people. Although in theory civilian-based defense could be used to depose a legitimate and benevolent democratic leader and bring to power a malevolent authoritarian who espouses brutal policies, it is hard even to imagine how or why such a thing would ever happen. In practice, benevolent leaders rarely if ever give rise to mass nonviolent movements in opposition to their governance, and malevolent authoritarians with violent intentions rarely if ever find nonviolent tactics attractive.

As security strategies, both civilian-based defense and economic peacekeeping are more consistent with democratic principles and supportive of individual freedom than are security strategies that rely primarily on the threat of use of military force. Military organizations must be inherently authoritarian in order to be effective. Soldiers must be trained to obey orders. There can be little room for questioning authority, for free and open debate, in the midst of military action. Military forces can and do play a significant role in providing security for free and democratic states, but they themselves are internally undemocratic institutions operating under a value system that is ultimately incompatible with freedom and democracy (see Chapter 10). If an entire society becomes militarized, freedom and democracy will both be under threat. That is certainly not true of the values or practices that underlie either economic peacekeeping or civilian-based defense.

The Costs and Benefits of Civilian-Based Defense

More or less improvised cases of nonviolent action are much more common than carefully planned campaigns. Yet it would be a mistake to conclude that nonviolent tactics do not require preparation to be successful, or that their effectiveness could not be greatly improved by proper training and organization. Planning, training, and organization are never costless. But the kind of preparation most useful for making civilian-based defense more effective is likely to be much, much cheaper than that required for military approaches to security. For one thing, the equipment costs are vanishingly small as compared to the astonishingly high cost of modern military weapons systems. Communications equipment is important to coordinate the campaign, but low-tech systems (from word-of-mouth and telephone calling lists to radio) may suffice. And to the extent that high tech systems would be useful, they can be as simple as cell phones, computers for accessing the Internet, and GPS devices—already widely distributed among the population in many countries and relatively inexpensive compared to billion-dollar bombers.

As for training, most would be best handled by already existing institutions, from churches and secular service organizations to public and private school systems and universities. While one might legitimately object to the idea of such organizations training populations in violent military tactics (such as the use of automatic weapons and the techniques of commando assault) on grounds that it might increase the level of criminal or even terrorist activity in the society, there is no comparable concern about the tactics of nonviolent action. Some specialized state-of-the-art centers might be useful, especially for preparation of nonviolent defense plans and research aimed at improving the tactics of organized nonviolence. But nothing like the size or scope of the present networks of military academies and defense think tanks, let alone weapons research facilities, would be required. The costs of preparation, while not insignificant, would be minimal as compared to the costs of preparation required by military approaches to security.

From time to time, it would be a good idea to do the citywide, regional, or national nonviolent equivalent of war games—practice exercises involving substantial numbers of people taking part in preplanned nonviolent actions. The reliability of any strategy is likely to grow with practice. Without practice, it cannot easily be debugged; and people are more likely to forget some important part of what they are supposed to do or how they are supposed to do it. These exercises would also have the considerable advantage of periodically demonstrating to the population at large that they do indeed have the ability to deny the power to control their society to anyone who tries to seize power illegitimately or attempts to force them to follow policies they find reprehensible. Certainly, these exercises would be costly because they would involve significant disruptions of economic activity. Yet doing them only occasionally and making them short (say half a day to a day) would help hold down costs.

In general, then, the cost of incorporating civilian-based defense into a nation's security strategy is relatively low. As is also true of economic peace-keeping, to the extent that the adoption of civilian-based defense permits the nation to reduce its much more expensive military forces while remaining strong and secure, it will actually save the country a great deal of money while maintaining or improving security. The resources freed up from the security budget will then become available to help address society's other pressing needs, whether through government programs or private sector activities.

One of the obstacles that must be overcome to get nonviolent civilian-based defense adopted as part of national security strategy is the simple lack of awareness of the historical record that demonstrates its power, practicality, and effectiveness in the modern world. But the most daunting challenge may be to get the existing power centers of society, especially the government, to support the adoption of a strategy that has the potential to undercut their own authority and control. Incorporating systematic nonviolent action by the public at large into security strategy requires the willingness to give masses of people tools they can subsequently use to challenge the authority of the very people and institutions who gave them that preparation. It takes a very self-confident leadership and government committed to democratic principles to be willing to do such a thing. Switzerland has included a component of nonviolent resistance in its "general defense" policy for a long time.[24] In the 1980s and 1990s, Sweden, Norway, and Lithuania also incorporated nonviolent resistance into their national security strategies.[25] But for all the rhetoric about freedom and government "of the people" that flows so freely in democratic societies, it may be a challenge for many democratic governments to muster enough confidence in their own institutions, processes, and people to wholeheartedly embrace the adoption of civilian-based defense.

Of course, government is not the only power center in society. Religious institutions and "big business" are also important. On the one hand, they may be less than enthusiastic about civilian-based defense for the same basic reasons as government, that the tools of mass nonviolent action it encompasses can also be used to work against policies they favor, or even undermine their own authority and power. On the other hand, they may embrace the power of mass nonviolent action as a counterweight to abusive government. One important example is the key role the Catholic Church played in supporting the long and ultimately successful nonviolent struggle of the Polish people (led by the trade union Solidarity) against the country's authoritarian communist government. Still, lack of support by any of the power centers of society does not make it impossible for embryonic grassroots nonviolent action to begin what ultimately becomes a formidable mass movement.

It is likely that promoting nonviolent conflict resolution and knowledge of specific nonviolent approaches to expressing strongly held opinions will lead to increased political participation, reduced political violence, and possibly even lower rates of violent crime. Any government adopting this strategy will know that the people at large can use these tactics to oppose government edicts and policies they find objectionable. That alone might make the government more responsive.

The principles of economic peacekeeping and the theory and practice of nonviolent civilian-based defense are more than merely compatible. Though neither strategy requires the other, they complement and reinforce each other. Both provide security without the threat or use of physical violence yet include a component of coercive force. Neither depends upon a fundamental change in human nature or greater philosophical enlightenment, just on the ability of people to look beyond the often-repeated conventional wisdom and see what is actually in their own self-interest. No articles of faith are required, only a willingness to be open-minded in evaluating what works and what doesn't.

Economic peacekeeping depends primarily on creating security by strengthening positive incentives to manage or resolve conflict without violence. Civilian-based defense depends primarily on recognizing that the ultimate power in any society lies with its ordinary people—no leader can continue to lead when, despite the consequences, others simply refuse to follow. Applied within and among nations, economic peacekeeping should be able to do much of the heavy lifting, providing security by making eruptions of mass organized violence much less likely. Civilian-based defense offers effective nonviolent weapons for fighting out conflicts that the parties involved will not or cannot resolve or manage, despite the strong incentives created by economic peacekeeping. Neither is likely to entirely replace military force as a means of attempting to provide security, but both can help ensure that military forces can be sharply reduced in size and used only sparingly and infrequently. Given the importance of security, the high cost of maintaining military systems, and the even higher costs in terms of death and destruction when they are put into action, that is very good news indeed.

10

Demilitarized Security, Development, and Terrorism

WITH THE UNRAVELING OF COLONIALISM in the nineteenth century in Latin America and in the second half of the twentieth century in Asia and Africa came the promise of more rapid development. Freed of their colonial masters, the people of the newly independent countries were told by national political leaders that they could expect a rising tide of material well-being, as well as greater political freedom. In the 1950s, those relatively few academic economists who paid attention to economic development were optimistic about the possibilities for reducing disparities between the more developed countries (MDCs) and the less developed countries (LDCs). The nations that had already developed, they reasoned, had had to invent for themselves the whole new set of industrial age technologies that propelled their development forward, from steam engines to railroads and telephones to all of the machinery and equipment that filled the modern factory. But by the twentieth century the LDCs could simply choose among the vast array of production and infrastructure technologies already invented, accelerating their own development and helping close the gap. Furthermore, because the MDCs already had so much industrial capital, the return to further investment in those countries would be much lower than the return to investing in new equipment in the capital-short LDCs. After all, additional machinery and equipment make a much bigger difference in raising productive capacity in a country with little machinery and equipment than in a country that is already well equipped. The higher return would naturally attract more investment in the LDCs, and that would also help close the gap. With great enthusiasm and hope, the United Nations, itself a young organization at the time, declared the 1960s the first "Development Decade."

But by 2000—fully four officially declared UN Development Decades later—despite the politicians' promises, the economists' optimism, and the UN's enthusiasm, the gulf between LDC and MDC living standards had not dramatically diminished. In September 2000, more than one hundred nations agreed to an ambitious UN-declared set of eight specific "Millennium Development Goals" to be met by 2015. These lofty and worthwhile goals included drastic reductions in the number of people living in extreme poverty (less than a dollar a day), in the rate of child and maternal mortality, and in the number of people without access to safe drinking water (a major source of disease in LDCs). There has been some progress to date in achieving these goals, but there is still a long way to go.[1] By the halfway point (2008), nearly a billion people still lived in extreme poverty; ten million children were dying each year from starvation and disease; half a million women were dying from complications in pregnancy or childbirth; and more than a billion people had no regular access to clean drinking water.[2]

In short, despite lots of rhetoric, academic theorizing, good intentions, considerable effort, and even a few striking success stories, there is still too much poverty and oppression in too many places. What has gone wrong? Development is a complex business of economic, social, political, and even cultural transformation, much more complex than early students of development had appreciated. There are many reasons why progress in both economic and political development has been slower and more difficult than expected, many factors that explain why the promises have not been kept. Nevertheless, some impediments to development are more fundamental than others. In their presence, development is exceedingly difficult, even if everything else is done right. One such impediment is deeply entrenched, extensive systemic corruption. Another is militarization. This chapter focuses on the latter.

To understand the full impact of militarization on economic and political development, it is necessary to consider its direct effects on availability of economic resources and norms of political behavior, as well as its indirect effects through its impact on the mutually reinforcing concentration of economic and political power.

Militarization as an Impediment to Economic Development

The Diversion of Productive Economic Resources

As I argued in Chapter 3, economic development is much more than simple expansion of the money economy, because economic activity is much more than carrying out money-valued transactions. The economy is not simply a money machine; it is a social system that evolved to satisfy the material needs of the population, to provide for its material well-being. As I argued in Chapter 7, it is the quantity, quality, and accessibility of the diverse products of "economically contributive" activity that measure the true size and state of development of the economy.[3]

Whatever else can be said for it, military-oriented activity does not grow food, it does not produce clothing, it does not build housing, and it does not keep people amused. Nor does it create the kind of machinery, equipment, and facilities that can be used to grow food, produce clothing, build housing, and the like. To the extent that it contributes to satisfying other important human needs, such as the need for security, it has value, perhaps considerable value. But it has no *economic* value because it does not directly contribute to providing material well-being, the central purpose of the economy.

Military expenditures cause labor, machinery, equipment, and other important resources to be drawn into the service of the military sector. All these resources could have been used instead to produce and distribute goods and services that do raise the standard of living. The true cost of military-related activity is therefore its "opportunity cost," the material well-being that has been sacrificed as a result of this economically noncontributive diversion of resources. To this must be added the cost of the loss of human life, destruction of property, and economic activity forgone because of the turmoil and upheaval caused when military goods and services are put into action in war. In the MDCs, this cost has been a difficult burden to bear. For the weaker economies of much of the developing world, it has been nearly unbearable.

Economic development cannot succeed without a great deal of investment in the skill and education of a country's workforce and in its systems of transportation, communication, and water and power supply. Without such investment, there will be no real prospect of freeing the nation's economy from pure dependence on the export of primary products. These investments will not make development happen by themselves, but they are a key part of the groundwork that must be laid before real development can be generated and sustained.

There is no force for development more powerful than improvement in the skills and capabilities of the labor force. People are at once the reason for being concerned about development and the most important means for achieving it. We have seen again and again that a skilled and educated labor force can overcome all sorts of obstacles in moving an economy forward. The skilled and educated workforces of the countries of Western Europe were critically important to their success in rapidly rebuilding those devastated nations after World War II, with the help of the Marshall Plan. The same can be said of the development successes of Japan, Taiwan, and South Korea. The flood of skilled immigrants into Israel in the aftermath of the Holocaust was in no small measure responsible for its ability to make effective use of the development aid it received to achieve relative economic success.

But as important as it is, education is not magic and it is not enough. Because education inherently raises people's expectations, if the better life they have come to expect does not materialize, increasing education levels can even be a source of serious social stress. Without critical investment in infrastructure and other necessary capital, education alone will not generate enough good jobs to allow those who have acquired more knowledge to put that knowledge to work in ways that are both economically productive and individually lucrative. Educated unemployment leads not to sustained development, but to growing frustration, frustration that is personally cruel and socially dangerous.

Large-scale investments in education and infrastructure are very expensive. It is not possible for countries of limited means to make these investments on anything like the scale required as long as they insist on using large amounts of their limited resources to support military forces. Understanding this basic fact of economic life, the Costa Rican government eliminated its national military forces entirely in 1948 and directed the nation's available resources to more economically contributive activities. For more than sixty years now, in the absence of any national military, Costa Rica has maintained its independence and remained the most stable, democratic, and economically well-off nation in a part of the world that has been plagued by deep-seated economic problems and wracked by terrible spasms of violence. It is an interesting and important example.

Nearly all of the democratic nations in the world today have military forces. Some, such as Britain, France, and the United States, have very large, well-funded militaries. In all these nations, though, military forces are subordinated to and can only be activated by democratically elected civilian officials. Furthermore, strict and effective rules limit the use of military force inside the borders of the nations themselves. There are also laws, or at least well-established social norms, in these countries that inhibit the formation, and sharply limit the impact, of armed paramilitary forces. They do not always work perfectly, witness the long history of the Irish Republican Army and the Ulster Defense Forces in Northern Ireland, and the alarming growth of the militia movement in the U.S. more recently. But even in the U.K. and the U.S., the level of violence committed by these paramilitary groups, and their general influence on life in the wider societies, have been quite limited.

But when a society becomes truly militarized, a militaristic mind-set replaces the economic urge to develop new resources and create needed goods and services with the military urge to take them from others by force. Apart from the obvious moral distinction, there is a profound difference between acquiring goods and services by confiscation and acquiring them by economic activity. Acquisition by force is at best a zero-sum game, a game of redistribution where the amount winners gain depends on the amount losers have lost. More likely, it will be a negative-sum game, a game of net loss, because some goods and services will be destroyed in the battle. By contrast, economic activity is a positive-sum game, a game in which new wealth is created, and therefore a game in which the potential exists for everyone to win.

Militarization and the Concentration of Economic Power

Militarization aids and abets the concentration of economic power. In societies with vastly unequal distributions of wealth and income, if the rich do not actually run the government, they exert disproportionate influence on its policies and actions. They are ordinarily in a position to see to it that the instruments of control and repression at the disposal of the government, including military force, are used to protect and reinforce their own positions of economic privilege. This may be accomplished through the unapologetic use of brute force, or through the simple enforcement of "rights" or laws structured to their advantage.

In militarized societies, it is not difficult for those who wield concentrated supply-side economic power to covertly encourage or directly arrange for the use of force to intimidate their workers or their smaller, less influential suppliers or rivals. Special tax breaks and government subsidies, all too easy to come by in less militarized societies, are that much easier to arrange in militarized societies, whose endemic inequalities make the granting of further privilege to the powerful almost a matter of course.

To the extent that they can be separated, concentrated supply-side economic power is more likely than concentrated demand-side economic power to mobilize national military forces for foreign adventurism on its behalf. While I do not believe that all or even most wars are fought primarily for economic reasons, it is indisputable that the narrow economic interests of those who wield concentrated supply-side economic power have sometimes been represented as identical to the national interest in order to encourage the use of military force to ensure access to resources or markets. In the seventeenth, eighteenth, and nineteenth centuries, for example, those who advocated classical imperialism—the most extreme example of foreign military adventure in support of economic advantage—did so on the grounds that it was good for the nation. No less an economist than Adam Smith clearly and forcefully argued that far from being a source of "the wealth of nations," the colonial system was a serious net economic drain on the mother country. At the same time, it is difficult to deny that it did further the narrow interests of the economically privileged who urged on the imperial armies.[4]

In more modern times, large oil reserves in Iraq and Kuwait created a "strategic national interest" that made events in Iraq seem more compelling, and played some role in provoking the use of massive military force against Iraq in 1991 and again in 2003, despite other rationalizations for this action.[5] There was no oil (or any other comparably vital resource) in the killing fields of either the Khmer Rouge in Cambodia or the Hutu in Rwanda, and there was almost complete inaction in the face of the genocides that took place in those countries in the 1970s and 1990s, respectively.[6]

The inherently undemocratic and hierarchical structure and values of militarized societies make them unlikely to support any policy that works to counter the concentration of wealth and economic power. Although it is critical to development, those few who sit on top of the economic or political pyramid have little or no incentive to encourage a wider distribution of economic or political largesse, beyond the minimal point that might prove necessary to forestall riots in the streets.

The Effects of Concentrated Economic Power on Equity and Efficiency

Having come to the unfortunate conclusion that people were fundamentally motivated by greed and self-interest, Adam Smith argued that these narrow and unenlightened motives could be harnessed through the mechanisms of free market capitalism for the general benefit of society. As subsequently elaborated by neoclassical economists, intense competition among self-interested producers would keep them efficient and see to it that the benefits of this efficiency were transmitted to consumers. At the same time, however, Smith warned that whenever competing businesspeople got together, their conversation would turn into a conspiracy against the public. When all was said and done, they would much rather collude than compete.

In unrestricted free market capitalism, let alone in crony capitalism or other equally unenlightened economic systems, there is some tendency toward collusion and monopolization. When industries become monopolized, the result is a socially inefficient allocation of the nation's productive resources, even under free market capitalism. Consumers are also penalized twice: once by inefficient production and again by excessively high prices. Thus, when self-interested producers manage to concentrate economic power in their own hands, some of the most crucial benefits of free market capitalism are lost.

The same can be said of concentrations of economic power on the demand side. Markets do not respond to needs or wants as such, but only to "effective demand," needs and wants backed up by ability to pay. It is often said that one of the great advantages of a free market system is that consumers determine the allocation of productive resources by, in effect, "voting" in the marketplace through the choices they make in spending their money. But the analogy between free market capitalism and political democracy becomes increasingly untenable as the distribution of income and wealth becomes less and less equal, concentrating demand-side economic power in fewer hands. It strains credulity to argue that "elections" in which the participants have radically different numbers of votes to cast in any sense meet the hallmark criterion of democratic elections: that they be "free and fair." When the allocation of a nation's resources is decided by such a lopsided voting process, it is virtually guaranteed to be socially inefficient.

Even within free market capitalism then, concentrations of economic power on both the supply and demand sides interfere with and may destroy both equity and efficiency. For the market system to successfully harness individual greed and self-interest for social benefit, undue concentrations of power must be prevented. That is unlikely to be done in a serious and sustained way in any society that is unduly influenced by a military security system grown too large and powerful.

Militarization as an Impediment to Political Development

Military Authoritarianism and Democratization

People do not ordinarily relish the idea of killing other people, nor do they look forward to putting themselves in the position of being killed or seriously injured. Yet stripped of the pomp and ceremony, of the uniforms and rituals, that is what militaries are all about. Soldiers must be ready to offer themselves up to kill or be killed, or militaries cannot do what they have been created to do. Military training must therefore be designed not merely to teach people to use weapons, but to take away their individuality and train them to unthinkingly do what they are told to do, when they are told to do it. There can be little room for questioning authority, no place for free and open debate. In the midst of military action, votes cannot be taken on which tactics to use. Military organizations are not effective without authoritarian command structures. They cannot be built around democratic principles. It is therefore very difficult for truly democratic political systems to develop and prosper in militarized societies.

While the mere existence of national military forces is not incompatible with democracy, it is difficult if not impossible for democracy to reach its full potential in societies that are dominated by large, powerful, and influential national and subnational armed forces. Even where democratic institutions are firmly established, there is no question that a large, well-funded military establishment together with its economic allies exert a corrupting influence on the political life of the nation. On leaving the U.S. presidency fifty years ago, one of the most successful military commanders of the twentieth century, General Dwight Eisenhower, chose to focus his farewell address to the nation on a warning: "In the councils of government, we must guard against the acquisition of unwarranted influence . . . by the military-industrial complex. The potential for the disastrous rise of misplaced power exists and will persist. . . . We must never let the weight of this combination endanger our liberties or democratic processes."[7]

The full flowering of democracy requires that governments be elected by popular vote and structured to reflect the hopes and desires of all of a nation's people. Elections must be free and fair, with essentially all of the adult population able to vote and assured that their votes will be properly counted. The range of political contestants should be broad enough to express the opinions and interests of all the nation's people. There must be a sufficiently free flow of information in the society that those who want to go to the polls can be well enough informed about the issues to cast a considered vote. People of widely differing political viewpoints not only must be free to speak out, but should also have access to whatever it takes to seek political office and make themselves heard by the electorate.

It is not easy to establish these conditions. They are not completely established even in the advanced democracies of Western Europe, Japan, and North America. In the U.S., for example, questions still persist as to whether the votes of all the qualified voters who went to the polls in the 2000 presidential election were actually counted. Likewise, the corrupting influence of money on politics is a perennial problem.

Furthermore, the establishment of a full functioning democracy is not restricted to the establishment of the formal institutions of democratic government. It is also important to build the underlying infrastructure of civil society from which democracy draws its strength and durability. The nongovernmental, nonbusiness formal organizations and informal relationships and traditions that constitute civil society are key because they promote trust, a sense of wider community, and a shared obligation for building a better common future.[8] The formal institutions of civil society are established for a wide variety of reasons: to help those who need help; to raise public awareness of social inequities and political injustices; to further a social or political cause in which their members believe by providing information and encouraging peaceful civil action. A truly democratic society encourages and facilitates the formation of such organizations, operating independent of control by business or government.

The informal relationships and traditions of civil society are also of great importance. Democracy requires open civil discourse with tolerance of, if not respect for, the expression of opinions that may not only be critical of the government, but with which many of the people of the nation disagree. Shutting out those who express very contrary opinions narrows political discourse and has no place in a vibrant and democratic civil society. This shutting out is not so much precluded by government or formal civil institutions as it is inhibited by the culture and traditions of open civil discourse.

The formal institutions and informal traditions of civil society have little room to operate within the authoritarian structure of military organizations. Freestanding, independent organizations of soldiers that might serve as alternative centers of power and influence cannot be permitted. Debate about policies, strategies, and tactics is severely circumscribed. While militaries do encourage cooperation and joint effort in the service of

an objective, their culture of obedience and discipline, their formal hierarchical command structure, and their tradition of rank and privilege are
not conducive to either open discourse or the freedom of action essential to
civil democracy.

Militarization and the Concentration of Political Power

In authentically representative democracy, those who govern are chosen
by free and fair elections that express the will of those who are governed.
Yet without an elaborate constitutional system of checks and balances and
a respect for the rule of law, representative democracy can easily deteriorate into a "tyranny of the majority."[9] It is the combination of representative democracy, constitutional checks and balances, and commitment to
the rule of law—the combination known as "liberal democracy"—that is the
best guarantor of government driven by the will of the majority but protective of the rights of the minority. With the benefit of hindsight and more
than two hundred years of U.S. experience, it is clearer today than in the
eighteenth century that this approach was basically sound. Both elements,
democracy and constitutional liberalism, are necessary to protect individual liberty and secure government "of the people, by the people and for the
people," and both can be severely compromised by the overconcentration
of political power.

Militarization aids and abets the concentration of political power. It is a
sad fact that many of the world's national militaries are used more as internal
police forces to control and repress their own populations than to protect
them against external threats. As political power becomes more concentrated within a nation, the number of channels available for the expression
of alternative political viewpoints tends to shrink. With fewer and fewer
acceptable outlets, the pressure from those who dissent builds, and those
in control find it increasingly necessary to repress them in order to remain
in power. Military force is often the most ready means of repression available. The more militarized that societies become, the more commonplace
and routine is this reflexive reaction to political opposition.

Concentrations of power can undermine even well-crafted liberal democracy. Individuals and vested interests, grown rich and powerful, can

distort government policy and the government's use of military and police force to their benefit and to the detriment of the public. Even apart from outright bribery, they can "buy" elections and the loyalty of politicians through lavish financial support of flashy, high priced political advertising campaigns. More than fifty years ago, in his classic and prescient book, *The Hidden Persuaders,* Vance Packard warned of the dangers we would face as the ever more sophisticated techniques of psychological manipulation, being refined by the booming advertising industry to sell ordinary goods and services, are increasingly applied to sell political ideas and candidates.[10] In retrospect, it is a warning to which we should have paid more attention.

Concentrations of money and power inside government can also give rise to corrupting influences that distort the processes of governance, even in a liberal democracy. Despite all the checks and balances, power can be transferred to and concentrated in one part of the government when the other parts show it undue and inappropriate deference. The growth of an "imperial presidency" spurred by an ineffectual, invertebrate Congress is one American example. In the opening years of the twenty-first century, this concentration of power has been augmented in the U.S. by the Bush administration's adoption of the "theory of the unitary executive," which claims constitutional support for a presidency with broad powers to run the executive branch of government essentially unfettered by congressional (or judicial) oversight. Another example is the excessive influence on both budget and policy of the chronically overfunded American military that, together with its allies in industry, constitutes the "military-industrial complex" about which Republican President Eisenhower warned us in his 1960 farewell address.[11] Two decades after the end of the Cold War, the U.S. military still lays claim to the lion's share of the federal discretionary budget, representing an important pool of financial capital.

Concentrations of political power can also occur in liberal democracies when fewer and fewer people vote or otherwise participate in the political life of the nation. Such "dysfunctional democracy," as Nelson has called it, retains all the institutions and trappings of liberal democracy but comes to be increasingly controlled by a small political elite and their limited constituency of highly motivated voters and activists.[12] Dysfunctional democracy can arise because of a combination of disaffection with the political process and feelings of powerlessness. The electorate may become convinced that government officials listen only to the rich and powerful (whether or not that is true), a conviction that can easily become a self-fulfilling prophecy.

Concentrations of political power are certainly enhanced and enforced by the process of militarization. Forms of government in which power is concentrated may not be as equitable as liberal democracies, but some argue that they are much more efficient. Both classic authoritarian governments and what Fareed Zakaria has called "illiberal" democracies (those whose freely elected leaders exert authoritarian power after taking office)[13] are less likely to get involved in time-consuming debates and deal-making negotiations common in liberal democracies. They can therefore get things done, including things that need to be done to bring about economic development. The authoritarian government of China, a nation whose economy has been growing at an extraordinary rate over the past several decades, serves as an important modern day example.

Authoritarian governments can certainly take action more quickly than liberal democracies. But for most, their apparent efficiency is an illusion, because the actions they take so decisively are often counterproductive in the long run. Concentrations of power give too much weight to the opinions, judgments, ideas, and goals of one or a few leaders. They are not subjected to independent scrutiny and the acid test of challenge from opposing points of view. There is thus a much greater probability that any flaws in the chosen strategies and the tactics used to implement them will not be uncovered until a great deal of effort has been wasted and serious damage has been done. It is not liberal democracies but rather forms of government in which power is overly concentrated that tend to be inherently inefficient, especially in the long run.

However they may come to be, concentrations of power are anathema to democracy, on grounds of both equity and efficiency. The ultimate danger they pose was elegantly expressed by Kenneth Boulding: "A world of unseen dictatorship is conceivable, still using the forms of democratic government."[14]

The Connection Between Economic and Political Power

Economic inequality fosters the concentration of political power. Even if aggregate income and wealth are growing, as they become more unequally distributed, those few in whose hands economic means are being concentrated gain greater relative potential political influence. They can realize this potential in a number of ways. With greater economic means at their disposal, they are in a better position than those of lesser means to seek out corrupt (or corruptible) officials and buy political favors. Economic power can also be translated into political power in less crude ways that offer the benefit of nominal legitimacy. Lavish funding of political campaigns for or against specific political candidates, policies, or programs, can help "buy" elections or sway public opinion. This approach does not always work. But these funds can often buy enough advertising expertise and outreach to tip the balance in closely fought elections or issues campaigns. Even when they fail to "win" in the short run, generously funded campaigns can help build a political base from which more successful campaigns can be launched in the future.

There are likely to be more businesses than individuals wealthy enough to exert decisive influence on the political process. In the U.S., they can do it under the cover of the legal fiction that corporations are individuals and thus have the same guaranteed rights. This, for example, has led to the ludicrous conclusion that the kind of psychologically exploitative advertising against which Vance Packard railed is "commercial speech" and thus protected by the First Amendment. Another approach available almost exclusively to big business is to directly manipulate governments by offering them the carrot of locating their facilities and therefore creating jobs and increasing the tax base in a particular area, provided the right political concessions are made, from tax rebates to environmental waivers to antiunion commitments. The stick may be wielded by threatening to close down economically important facilities and trigger loss of jobs and tax base if the government does not offer the right concessions. This is such common practice in corporate location strategy with respect to state and local government in the U.S. that examples are too numerous to mention.

Among the most absurd in recent times has been the spate of wealthy, highly profitable, cartelized sports teams that, under the threat to relocate, have demanded and received commitments to build lavish new sports arenas at taxpayer expense.

The propensity for corporate manipulation of the political process is hardly news to those who live in developing countries. Since the end of the colonial era, large multinational corporations (MNCs) based in the MDCs have managed to exert substantial influence on political and economic life in LDCs, often enough to the detriment of any liberal democratic impulses. The concentrated decision power of authoritarian governments and illiberal democracies usually makes them easier to work with and more reliable partners than liberal democracies in delivering agreed concessions.

By their very nature, large MNCs are concerned primarily with what is good for business. They are business organizations, not social welfare institutions. Unfortunately, what most often seems to be good for their business in Third World host countries in the short run is political stability, a cheap and pliant labor force, and easy access to abundant natural resources—all of which are more readily delivered by authoritarian regimes. It is not at all surprising, then, that more often multinationals have supported authoritarian regimes than encouraged movement toward democracy and freedom.

Even within liberal democracies, the interests of big business and wealthy individuals have always been well represented by lobbyists and well-endowed special interest organizations.

Yet however unequal their access to resources has been, grassroots nongovernmental organizations (NGOs) have stood as one important democratic counterforce in the political process. By combining the opinions and expressed interests of dispersed people of little individual political or economic power, they have galvanized meaningful political action. Around the world, grassroots NGOs are a critical component of the infrastructure of civil society on which participatory democracy depends.

It is therefore especially disturbing to note the emergence of a class of NGOs having the appearance of grassroots organizations while in actuality they are established and largely funded by small numbers of wealthy individuals, large businesses, or trade associations to forward their own interests. These "astroturf" NGOs look like grassroots organizations from a distance but really have nothing in common with them.[15] Astroturf activism was defined by *Campaigns and Elections* as "a grassroots program that involves the instant manufacturing of public support for a point of view in which either uninformed activists are recruited or means of deception are used to recruit them."[16] In the U.S., their campaigns "typically involve calling a lot of people and persuading some of them to let their signatures be used on telegrams they never see about issues they don't understand."[17] American examples have included: the tobacco industry's National Smokers Alliance; the auto industry's Coalition for Vehicle Choice; and the pharmaceutical industry's Coalition for Equal Access to Medicines.[18] Astroturf NGOs are just one more means of translating economic power into political influence, another corruption of the institutions of liberal democracy.

Just as those who have concentrated economic power can use it to acquire political influence, those who have concentrated political power can use it to acquire wealth, another phenomenon all too familiar to those living in the less developed world. Probably the three most spectacular twentieth century examples are the acquisition of fabulous riches by Ferdinand Marcos in the Philippines; the plundering of Zaire (now the Democratic Republic of Congo) by Mobutu Sese Seko; and the accumulation of great wealth by Suharto under the system of crony capitalism over which he presided in Indonesia.

Those who use concentrated economic power to acquire political power can then use their enhanced political power to further concentrate their economic power. Those who use political power to acquire wealth can then use that wealth to solidify and extend their political influence. It is thus clear that economic and political power are not only fungible, they are also mutually reinforcing. The concentration of both undermines development, and the concentration of both is encouraged and reinforced when the power, influence, and claim of military forces on the nation's resources grows too large.

Demilitarized Security and Development

Movement toward providing security primarily by establishing peacekeeping economic relationships rather than by maintaining large, lavishly funded military forces has much to offer in terms of both economic and political development. Not only does it allow critical resources to be directed to activities that raise material well-being, it also eliminates one key source of support for unduly concentrated economic and political power. This concentration of power undermines economic and political equity and efficiency in the long run, and is therefore a serious obstacle to development.

In the short run, it may be true that authoritarian governments can better stimulate economic development because they can impose the discipline and organization necessary to make it happen. But in the long run authoritarian governments, which necessarily depend on repressive military (and police) force to keep themselves in power, are more likely to behave in ways that are economically and politically destructive. In the words of Olusegun Obasanjo, former president of Nigeria and the first African military ruler to hand over power peacefully to civilian rule,

> [O]ne-man, one-party, non-pluralistic, or military regimes . . . imposed with the excuse of having the potential to provide greater unity, or correcting the ills and abuses to which the operators of the different democratic experiments in Africa subjected their countries, have proven perhaps more divisive and prone to corruption than the regimes they ousted. In most cases, in fact, such dictatorial regimes have tended to exacerbate the ills against which they ostensibly forced their way into the seat of power.[19]

Social order and a degree of discipline are important to economic progress, but when authoritarian governments impose order by force and fear, an atmosphere is created that virtually guarantees that any economic advantages will be transitory.

For an economy to succeed in the long run, an ongoing flow of people who possess a variety of managerial talents must be available. Organizational skill, innovativeness, entrepreneurial flair, and leadership ability are widely distributed among the human population. When criteria such as kinship, social class, political loyalty, or ideology are used to determine who rises to positions of economic authority, some of the most capable people never get the chance to show what they can do. As time goes by, economic institutions come to be run by second- or third-rate managers. This is less likely to happen in countries that are more democratic, especially if careful attention is paid to breaking up concentrations of monopoly power, which are also fertile ground for managerial inbreeding and sloppiness.

Wisdom is even less highly concentrated in a specific ethnic or kinship group, social class, or adherents to a particular ideology than is managerial talent. Without the give and take of free and open debate, bad decisions made by the very small cadre of leaders at the top of the political pyramid won't be criticized before they have led to economic disaster. Democratic societies are more likely to force the abandonment of wrongheaded policies before they have done intolerable damage. That is also true of decisions made in private economic organizations. Unfortunately, hierarchical authoritarian decision-making is often the rule in private business organizations even within free market democracies.

The concentration of wealth and power is a breeding ground for corruption and other behaviors that do not serve the long-term interests of the wider population. In the long run, then, economically free and politically democratic systems have great advantages in stimulating and sustaining real, broad-based development. Yet, for reasons already discussed, economically free and politically democratic systems are hard if not impossible to sustain in militarized societies. Demilitarization therefore opens the door to political and economic development.

Removing the primacy given to military force only makes economic resources available for alternative use and creates the political space for greater democracy; it does not make development happen. Making it happen requires more than removing obstacles; it requires doing a lot of things right. Government can make its most effective contribution to economic development by focusing its attention on ensuring that the economic infrastructure necessary to support consumption and production is created and maintained, and on establishing and enforcing rules of the game that give the private sector the flexibility it needs while ensuring that the broader interests of society as a whole are taken into account.

The economic infrastructure required to move development forward includes systems that provide widespread opportunities for education and access to health care, as well as systems that provide transportation, communication, electric power, clean water, and waste treatment. It may be best for government to provide some of these services directly, while a regulated private sector may be most effective at providing others. But making sure there is widespread access to quality infrastructure is a legitimate responsibility of government. The efficient production and distribution of ordinary goods and services, on the other hand, are best accomplished by a highly competitive private sector, subject only to the kind of broad rules of the game referred to earlier, and to active antitrust policy implemented when necessary to break up concentrations of economic power and to keep markets competitive.

It would be good if it were possible to provide a universal blueprint for a surefire development program, but we do not yet understand enough about development to do that, and there is at least a fair chance that it will never be possible. The particular economic, social, political, and cultural context within which development takes place in a given country is so important to the effectiveness of the process that it is likely that development plans will always have to be tailor-made in order to have a solid chance of succeeding. But two things we do know: 1) the diversion of critical resources to economically unproductive use is a universal drag on development; and 2) excessive emphasis on military security systems and extensive systemic corruption are the two most important forms of economically unproductive activity in the modern world. Shifting to a security system based primarily on economic peacekeeping will allow a substantial reduction in the political and economic primacy of military systems, removing a critical obstacle to achieving real progress in development.

Development and Counterterrorism

Writing in the *New York Times*, both journalist Thomas Friedman and economist Alan B. Krueger have argued that development is not an effective tool for fighting terrorism.[20] Many terrorists are not poor, certainly not desperately poor, and many people living in poverty do not become involved in terrorism. Others, such as Richard Sokolsky and Joseph Mc-Millan of the National Defense University, have argued that development is crucial to countering terrorism, that poverty and the frustration it breeds are key elements in creating the conditions that foster and support terrorism worldwide.[21]

Not every form of violent, destructive, antisocial activity is terrorism. Violent acts or threats intended to instill fear in the public in order to influence the opinion or behavior of government, business, or the public define terrorism and set it apart from many other forms of violence. Furthermore, terrorist acts are ordinarily committed against more or less randomly chosen victims who themselves are unable to meet the attackers' demands. An armed gang that shoots bank guards in order to steal money is committing a violent crime, not an act of terrorism. The violence is perpetrated to stop the guards from interfering with the theft, not to frighten the wider population. Bombing the barracks of an occupying military force is an act of war, violent and murderous, but it is not an act of terrorism. The act targets those who are directly involved in the activity the attackers are trying to oppose, not randomly chosen innocent victims. A habitual sex offender who kidnaps, rapes, and murders a more or less randomly chosen victim is committing a vicious and brutal crime but not an act of terrorism. Though such a crime may well instill fear in the public, it is not done for that purpose, and it is not done to influence public opinion or behavior. But a suicide bombing in a city marketplace to precipitate a change in government policy is an act of terrorism. The more or less randomly chosen victims cannot directly change government behavior, but the indiscriminate slaughter is intended to shock and frighten people into demanding that the government switch direction by convincing them that they will be in danger until those policies change. It is terrorism because its perpetrators are trying to terrorize.

The definition of terrorism has nothing to do with ultimate goals. Whether a group is trying to overthrow a democratic government and establish a dictatorship, create a homeland for a disenfranchised people, trigger a race war, or get more food distributed to the malnourished, if it uses terrorist tactics, it is a terrorist group. Many different types of people motivated in different ways and seeking different goals may decide to use terrorist tactics, as is true of any form of violence. At one end of the spectrum are people who are deeply disturbed, mentally and emotionally. The economic and political condition of such deranged individuals is wholly irrelevant to their desire to commit mayhem. At the other extreme are those who are motivated by a desire to achieve specific and relatively limited political objectives, such as freeing Northern Ireland from British control or ending the Israeli occupation of the Palestinian territories. They have chosen terrorism on the basis of a kind of rational, though horrific, calculation (which may or may not be correct) that it will get their cause enough attention and build enough pressure to help them accomplish that goal.

What, then, are the connections between development and terrorism? All but the craziest, most isolated terrorists (such as Theodore J. Kaczynski, the so-called Unabomber) are to some degree dependent on, and trying to build support among, a broader public for their cause if not for their tactics. Most subnational terrorists do not have the benefit of a wealthy patron or the active support of a state, but even those who do must be able to recruit operatives. They also have to be able to move around, coordinate activities, take care of logistics, and find secure places to store materiel and to do whatever training or preparation is necessary without being prematurely detected by those who are trying to stop them. This is much easier to do if they have a base of support among a wider public.

If a terrorist group wants to recruit relatively reliable operatives and build networks necessary to support them, they must have a cause that can convince more or less "normal" people to engage in and actively or tacitly support acts of terrible violence they would not otherwise condone. There must be a rallying cry powerful enough to enable the group to recruit people who themselves may not necessarily be in the most desperate straights and who have whatever skills are needed, and to motivate them sufficiently to get them to take extreme, perhaps fatal, risks.

A number of causes and circumstances seem in practice to be sufficiently motivating for these purposes. Most, if not all of them, involve calls to the service of some group or force greater than the individuals themselves who are being recruited or solicited for support. If the individuals involved can be made to feel that by engaging in terrorism they become the avengers of some great wrong, the voice of the voiceless, soldiers for the weak and oppressed, they can be made not only ready but eager to perpetrate horrific acts of violence against innocent people who have never directly done them any harm.

It is certainly true that individuals who, correctly or incorrectly, consider themselves personally (or their close friends and families) to be victims of economic and political oppression and marginalization are the easiest to recruit to "fight back" against those whom they can be convinced are their victimizers—either by directly engaging in terrorism or by supporting it in one way or another. But even those who are not particularly oppressed or disadvantaged economically or politically can feel part of a group that is somehow under siege and so behave in a similar way. For example, it does seem to be true that the actual terrorists of the Irish Republican Army were not necessarily the most disadvantaged of the Catholics in Northern Ireland, and their financial supporters in the U.S. were also far from destitute. But they all felt themselves to be fighters against the forces responsible for the economic and political marginalization of "their people."

Similarly, the perpetrators of the September 11 attacks against the U.S. were certainly not the most disadvantaged of our species. Most of them were apparently more or less middle class, and reasonably well educated. At the same time, they undoubtedly saw themselves as striking a blow for "their oppressed people," whom they most likely thought of as their "Muslim brothers" forced to bear the insult of having the soldiers of "foreign infidels" (American military forces) in their holiest of lands (Saudi Arabia) by a powerful Saudi government they believe to be supported by and operating in the service of those same "infidels." They may have also believed they were striking a blow against America because of its strong support of Israel, on behalf of their "Muslim brothers" in Palestine, who are clearly in dire straits.

I want to emphasize that I am not in any way trying to justify terrorist actions that they or anyone else has taken. I don't believe that terrorism, which is by definition always directed against innocent uninvolved civilians, is ever or can ever be justified. But to understand why terrorists and their supporters do what they do, it is important to understand what *their* perceptions and motivations might be.

Inclusive economic and political development can raise the economic well-being and political status of the larger group, of which the terrorists and their supporters feel they are part. That should make it increasingly difficult for the terrorists to recruit operatives, and should also seriously attenuate support among others who feel connected to that same larger group. It is in that sense, then, that economic and political development can help dry up the pool of potential terrorists and the wider support for terrorist groups in the long run.

The feeling that "their people" are not respected and that their views and needs are not taken seriously by the rest of the world can be a source of motivation toward revolutionary as well as terrorist violence. This violent urge too can often be short-circuited by opening up much more peaceful political avenues to the disaffected for getting their agenda heard. Giving them some sort of seat at the political table does not imply that their views necessarily prevail. A 1988 television documentary called *Costa Rica: Child in the Wind* included a look at that nation's decision to unilaterally disarm in 1948 as well as a review of its political attitudes. At one point the interviewer, shocked on learning that communists held about 4 percent of the seats in the legislative branch, said something like, "You've got COMMUNISTS in the legislature!" To which the Costa Rican official he was interviewing said something like, "Yes. We do. We decided we'd rather have them in the legislature shouting at us than in the hills shooting at us."

Providing better means for a wide variety of groups with real political agendas (not terrorist doomsday religious cults and psychopaths) to get themselves heard would go a long way toward diffusing the feelings of frustration and marginalization that can lead some people to turn to violence or to support it. That is why political development is a key part of the counterterrorist package.

The best way to deal with terrorism in the short run, and the only way to deal with the terrorism that arises from individual mental illness or group psychosis, is through first rate intelligence and police work. But crucial elements of the support system for other terrorist groups can be undermined in the long run by economic and political development. It is not the whole answer, but it is an important part.

Some approaches to development are more likely than others to be effective in fighting terrorism. Regardless of the socioeconomic status of either the terrorists or their financial supporters, the crux of the problem lies in the economic and political marginalization, frustration, and humiliation of those the terrorists see as "their people." It follows that the approach to development that should be most effective against terrorism is one that not only reaches out directly to the most marginalized, disaffected, and disadvantaged of those people, but does so in a way that gives them a sense of empowerment, self-worth, dignity, and respect. It also implies that the most effective program will be one that simultaneously addresses the challenges of both economic and political development.

On the economic side, one of the most interesting and apparently effective approaches to reaching out to raise up those mired in poverty is microlending, as perhaps best illustrated by the activities of the Grameen Bank of Bangladesh, created by economics professor and Nobel Peace laureate Muhammad Yunus. Putting a little capital, and the responsibility to repay it, in many different impoverished hands can go a long way toward overcoming the barriers created by lack of access to the means of self-investment, lack of self-confidence, and lack of hope. It is also possible, even necessary, to seamlessly incorporate an element of education into microlending programs. More importantly, as in the Grameen Bank approach, it is crucial to harmonize the rules of the game to the particular cultural environment in which microlending is carried out. This is especially true of the procedures chosen to ensure responsible use of the funds and ultimate repayment, which are likely to be very culture-sensitive. Consequently, those with a deep and personal knowledge of the cultural environment in any particular application of microlending should play a key role in designing the system.

On the political side, the creation of institutions that encourage, support, and facilitate the development of NGOs can be extremely useful in achieving the kind of deep and wide outreach needed. If counterterrorism is the objective, the point is to give voice to the voiceless by providing nonviolent paths for them to make themselves heard and to get their concerns on the political agenda. Real grassroots NGOs will help invigorate their sense of being active participants in political life.

Because terrorism is such a violent tactic, because it inflicts so much pain on the innocent, it fills us with anger and the urge to strike back even more violently against those whom we think might have encouraged, let alone committed, such despicable acts. Although easy to understand, such urges lead to nothing but more pain, more destruction, more taking of innocent lives. Such a response is more than profoundly immoral; it is profoundly ineffective.

If anyone needs proof of the futility of this kind of response as a counterterrorist strategy, consider the Israeli-Palestinian conflict. For decades, Israel has doggedly followed a policy of responding to any act of terrorism with violent military retaliation. A lot of people have died as a result, but there is still no resolution to the problem of terrorism that afflicts Israeli-Palestinian relations. What has been accomplished? The Israelis have had to live with continuing fear; the Palestinians have had to live with continuing misery. That is no way for anyone to live.

There are much more effective ways to respond to terrorism and, even more important, to prevent it. In the short run, high quality intelligence gathering and police work are the most critical elements of a successful strategy. But in the long run, encouraging economic and political development is the single most effective counterterrorist approach, because it is the only one that directly addresses the marginalization, frustration, and humiliation that breed terrorism, as well as many other forms of violence and inhumanity.

PART THREE

THE PEACEKEEPING ECONOMY

11

Bringing It All Together
Toward a More Prosperous and Secure World

> The international system that relies on the national use of
> military force as the ultimate guarantor of security, and the
> threat of its use as the basis for order, is not the only possible
> one. To seek a different system with a more secure and a more
> humane basis for order is no longer the pursuit of an illusion,
> but a necessary effort toward a necessary goal.
>
> —Carl Kaysen, Professor of Political Economy, MIT

THE IDEA THAT MILITARY STRENGTH IS VIRTUALLY SYNONYMOUS with security is deeply entrenched and widely held. For many, it is close to an unquestioned article of faith. But it is simply not true. Security is and always has been primarily a matter of relationships. The threat or use of violent force may sometimes be needed to protect us against those who would do us harm, but it is never capable of keeping us as safe as building relationships that replace hostility with a sense of mutual purpose and mutual gain. Peace is always more secure and robust when we have found ways to turn our former enemies into partners, if not into friends.

If there is one thing we can learn about ourselves from the checkered history of our species, it is that we are adaptable. We most certainly do not always get things right, but we are capable of making progress because neither our attitudes and beliefs nor our behaviors are set in stone. We are capable of change. In fact, change may be the only constant in our tenure on this planet.

What we are after is progressive change, change that makes the world a better place in which to live out our lives. That kind of change requires more than a glistening vision of what could be. It also requires a practical plan for getting from here to there. Without a vision to guide it, it is just an accident if incremental change ever gets us anywhere we really want to go; without a practical plan, even the most workable and appealing vision of a better world is likely to remain a distant dream.

It does not make sense, in terms of either security or expense, to continue to rely primarily on the threat or use of military force as the basis for our national or international security. An alternative security system based primarily on the principles of economic peacekeeping has the potential to provide us with a much higher level of security at a much lower cost, in blood and treasure. Even when we have established a fully formed well-functioning peacekeeping economy, it is unlikely that it will be possible to eliminate military forces completely. We still have too much to learn about getting along with each other. It may be necessary to confront bad actors with force from time to time. But building a peacekeeping economy will allow us to reduce the size and expense of such forces drastically, and make the need and even the impulse to call them into action much more rare.

At its base, a security system that depends primarily on the threat or use of military force relies on the power of fear to influence human behavior. Fear can be a powerful motivator. The problem is that fear also promotes anger and resentment, which can be potent sources of violent confrontation, even when violent confrontation is completely irrational. It is no accident that we refer to violent conflicts as "hostilities." The anger and resentment that the threat or use of force so often triggers can give rise to a compelling desire to inflict pain on and if possible destroy those who are assaulting or threatening to assault us. We have become quite good at working out ways to act on this desire, even when the odds are against us or our actions simply perpetuate instead of resolving a cycle of fear and violence. At the very least, our desire to forcefully threaten those who are threatening us has led to countless arms races, nearly all of which have ultimately ended in wars—wars made that much worse by the buildup of arms that preceded them.

Fear is not the only motivator, and is often not the most effective motivator, of human behavior. We know that it is possible to use positive incentives rather than threats to motivate self-interested human beings to behave in ways that can work to achieve social goals. We have built an economic system based primarily on influencing behavior through positive incentives that for all its many and varied problems has provided the world with unprecedented improvements in material standards of living over more than two centuries. Since a system based on positive incentives does not create the anger and hostility that can be so problematic and ultimately self-defeating for fear-based systems, it seems the essence of practicality to try to create a system based on positive incentives to provide the security we need more effectively.

Because security is so important, it is easy to understand why the proposal to move in a very different direction may provoke anxiety and thus resistance. After all, we are more familiar with the idea of fear-based security systems. They seem logical enough and have even sometimes been effective, especially in the short run. But there has also been some experience with the idea of economic peacekeeping. The European Union (EU) is probably the most prominent and accessible example of the effectiveness of properly structured economic relationships in keeping the peace today. Born in the aftermath of history's most devastating war, the EU's predecessor organization was originally created for the explicit purpose of using economic ties to overcome deep and long-standing enmities that had led to repeated war. For more than half a century, with all its flaws and imperfections, what is today the EU has been remarkably successful in promoting both prosperity and security.

The EU may be the most remarkable demonstration that economic peacekeeping works, but it is not the only one. Canada and the United States have had such a close and long-standing relationship that it is often forgotten that Canadians and Americans were once quite hostile to each other. From the U.S. perspective, Canada was on the wrong side of the American Revolution, remaining loyal to the British. In the nineteenth century there was even a naval arms race between the U.S. and Canada on the Great Lakes. But for many years now, the thousands of miles of border between the U.S. and Canada has been the longest disarmed border in the world. It might be hard to make the case that this was solely because of the extensive mutually beneficial economic connections between the two nations, but even harder to argue that these economic connections are not an important part of the reason.

Revisiting the Peacekeeping Principles

Taken as a group, the four principles on which a peacekeeping economy is based create a context designed to reduce stresses that can lead to the outbreak of violence, while at the same time strengthening positive incentives to resolve whatever conflicts arise without resorting to war. Each of these principles is based on an underlying behavioral premise that is key to its contribution to keeping the peace. The underlying behavioral premise of the first and most important principle, "Establish balanced, mutually beneficial economic relationships," is that fairness matters to the binding power of relationships. It is easy to see the validity of this premise by simply considering the difference in the way people feel and react when treated like valued and respected partners, as opposed to when they are cheated, treated like irrelevant underlings, and not given credit for what they have contributed. In order of descending importance, there are three aspects to the critical issue of balance that are at the core of this principle: balance of benefit, balance of decision power, and balance in the salience of the relationship. Fairness is key in all of them—in sharing the gains that accrue, in sharing power over the terms of the relationship, and in the sense of equal interdependence. All of these contribute to the power of relationships to strengthen positive incentives to keep the peace.

The underlying behavioral premise of the second peacekeeping principle, "Seek independence in critical goods," is that concrete forms of reassurance are very useful in overcoming real or imagined insecurities that can lead to belligerent behavior. By taking specific measures to ensure that the country is independent (or at least not overly dependent on a small cadre of suppliers) for critical goods, it is possible to short-circuit the tendency to think about every possible scenario in which the nation's supplies of critical goods could be compromised as a result of deliberate action taken by another country. Such scenarios lead to insecurities that increase the pressure to build up the nation's military capacity to coerce supplier nations forcefully. Once that capacity is in place, the same insecurities make it more likely that it will be used, not merely to counter hostile actions taken by critical goods suppliers, but even to take preemptive action against suppliers that are correctly or incorrectly believed to be thinking about disrupting supplies. A little self-reliant reassurance can go a long way toward raising a nation's threshold for taking aggressive action that shatters the peace.

The underlying premise of the third principle, "Emphasize development," is the straightforward idea that giving people a greater stake in the outcome of a process makes them more active in ensuring its success. Here this translates into the idea that people who have more to lose by the outbreak of civil or international violence have more to gain in acting to preserving the peace. When this premise is looked at from the opposite direction, people who feel economically marginalized and politically impotent are less likely to see violent disruption of the status quo as threatening. Put simply, people who have little and who feel powerless to do anything about it are less likely to see violence as risky. Raising the level of economic development gives people a greater material well-being, putting more of what they value at risk should violent conflict erupt.

Raising the level of political development (more freedom and democracy), on the other hand, means that people have more to lose if domestic conflicts escalate to the point of violence, potentially threatening their civil liberties and compromising the viability of the democratic process. Political development gives people more of a voice in decisions that affect their lives, obviating the need to engage in violent behavior within the country to get their voices heard, to get their concerns on the political agenda. Advocates of "democratic peace" also argue that a higher level of political development strengthens social norms of peaceful conflict resolution and the tendency to think of violent action as a last resort, which makes violent international intervention and war less likely, at least among democracies.

Underlying the fourth and final peacekeeping principle, "Minimize ecological disruption," is the premise that stewardship of the ultimate common property resource, the physical and biological environment, is critical to everyone's quality of life. As a result, those who waste the earth's vital resources and cavalierly abuse the environment are threatening the future of this generation and generations to come everywhere in the world. It is not necessary to be a back-to-nature purist to appreciate the fact that any natural resource being used up more quickly than it is being replenished will ultimately disappear. Or to understand that while we do not need a pristine environment, we all do need clean air to breathe, clean water to drink, and a workable climate to have a good life. It is therefore easy to see why heavy reliance on virgin depletable resources and the destructive over-use that depletes otherwise renewable resources cannot help but raise the global level of conflict-generating stress. Or how the pollution-related dam-age and environmental disruption done by some can be seen by others as a stress-increasing assault on their forests, beaches, streams, and other valuable natural assets—even on the planet's vital life-support systems. Becoming better stewards of the global ecological system is not simply some sort of mystical "earth-child" imperative; it has become a practical necessity, not least for lowering the level of potentially conflict-generating stress, as well as for simply getting on with the business of living a good material life.

Building a Peacekeeping Economy in a
Very Imperfect World

In a kinder, gentler, more perfect world, it would be much easier to build an economic system based on the four peacekeeping principles. But then, in a kinder, gentler, more perfect world, a peacekeeping economy might be superfluous. We need a peacekeeping economy precisely because the world in which we live is populated with so many contentious, conflictual people organized into nations and subnational groups that still have much to learn about getting along with each other. It is in this world with all its imperfections and conflicting interests that we must be prepared to build a peacekeeping economy. The global economic system has already created some of the conditions necessary for economic peacekeeping, but there is still much that needs to be done. Government, the private business sector, and ordinary individuals and households all have important roles to play, roles that are distinct yet interactive and interdependent.

The most effective way for government to interact with private business is to establish "rules of the game" that help to ensure that the cumulative effect of actions taken by private firms is beneficial to society as a whole, and to establish institutions that keep the game honest. The levers govern-ment has available to affect the behavior of firms and consumers work best when they are operated from a distance to guide behavior. When they are used as crowbars to directly interfere with the market mechanism, more often than not they damage the machinery and fail to produce outcomes that achieve the social goals that set them in motion. This is not a matter of ideology; it is a matter of information, knowledge, and incentive. It is neither efficient nor appropriate for government to try to micromanage private sector decision making.

Private sector firms are not inherently opposed to acting in the public interest, but it is important to keep in mind that their fundamental mission is to produce private benefit, not social welfare. If the context in which firms are operating makes the pursuit of their private interest consistent with the public good, they will happily take actions that help achieve social goals. That most assuredly includes actions that operationalize any or all of the four peacekeeping economic principles. However, private firms themselves are unlikely to take deliberate action to align private and public interests. That is not their business. It is the business of government, on the one hand, and private individuals and households on the other. For the most part, government stands outside the market serving more or less as a rule maker and referee. Among the instruments it has available for making the public and private interest compatible are laws, tax and subsidy policy, and regulation. By contrast, individuals and households are an integral part of the market. The actions they take as consumers and investors directly reward or penalize firms for their behavior in ways that firms cannot afford to ignore. They can base their decision to reward or penalize on any criterion they choose to apply, including compatibility with peacekeeping economic principles. If enough households and individuals apply such criteria in making their purchasing and investment decisions, they will certainly affect the incentive structure facing firms and thus firm behavior.

Strategies for Implementing the Principles

The basic problem in establishing balanced, mutually beneficial relationships (Principle I) is that private firms want to pay the least they can for whatever they buy and exert maximum control over decisions that affect the relationships in which they engage. If the firms have sufficient market power, that desire leads to behavior that is exploitative in terms of

benefit and unbalanced in terms of decision power. Strategies for countering firms' ability or incentives to engage in this kind of behavior include:

1) Organize and coordinate the actions of those in the weaker market position to countervail the power of those who dominate the market, reducing
   imbalances of power. For example, organizing effective marketing cartels
   (like OPEC) would help to balance the market where LDC producers have
   much less market power than the MDC firms that buy from them.
2) Use the authority of national governments to pressure firms not to engage in exploitative economic relationships on grounds that such relationships endanger the nation's security that government is charged with
   protecting. Clear legal precedent for this exists in national security laws
   that forbid private sector sale of militarily relevant technology to rival nations, and laws that prohibit trade in any goods and services with nations
   under economic sanction. Furthermore, fair trade and fair labor practice
   laws serve as precedents for government action in support of more balanced practices by private business.
3) Promote more balanced economic relationships through structural and
   procedural changes in international intergovernmental organizations
   such as the WTO, which is certainly in a position to establish and enforce
   rules for global trade.
4) Encourage LDCs to trade more with each other through regional trade
   organizations and trade agreements. Trade (and investment activity)
   among countries whose producers have more equal market power is naturally more balanced.
5) Through campaigns organized by NGOs, individuals and households can
   participate in shareholder resolutions, disinvestment programs, consumer boycotts, and other forms of pressure through the market in large
   enough numbers to push companies to stop engaging in economically
   exploitative behavior.

In the nature of achieving greater independence in critical goods (Principle II) most strategies depend more on government action. Those strategies include:

1) Establish tariffs on imports of critical goods.
2) Provide production subsidies to domestic producers of critical goods.
3) Have government directly perform, or fund and indirectly subsidize,
   university or private sector research and development aimed at improving the performance and increasing the cost-effectiveness of critical
   goods technologies.

4) Establish national security stockpiles of critical goods.

5) Encourage or require the diversification of government and private sector supplier networks. This can be done by government action, but it might also be undertaken as a risk reduction strategy by the private sector on its own, or in response to pressure from investors.

Strategies for encouraging development (Principle III) include:

1) Expand export markets for producers in developing countries by reducing or eliminating remaining MDC trade barriers against LDC agricultural products. If most of the gains from this increased trade are captured by local LDC elites, the governments of LDCs can use taxes and traditional welfare programs—or, better still, tax-financed programs of targeted public investment in social capital—to distribute the gains of trade more broadly, converting simple economic growth into real economic development.

2) Increase collaboration between donor and recipient country personnel in designing and implementing aid projects. This will promote joint "ownership" of development projects that will make them more likely to succeed. It will also help in tailoring development projects to the economic, social, cultural, and political environments in recipient countries, making aid more relevant and effective.

3) Require implementation of more effective anticorruption programs and reductions in excessive military budgets as conditions of receiving aid. This will reduce the drag on development that results when resources are diverted to economically unproductive uses.

4) Encourage increased investment in the health and education of developing country populations. A more productive workforce is the single most important asset for development.

5) Increase foreign direct investment (FDI) to stimulate development. FDI can stimulate development by bringing outside capital and more productive technologies into capital-short and less technologically sophisticated LDC economies. Care must be taken to ensure that FDI is not confined to enclaves disconnected from the economic mainstream; excessive long run dependence on FDI is also to be avoided.

Minimizing ecological stress (Principle IV) requires strategies that address both environmental pollution and competition for depletable resources:

1) Reduce reliance on depletable resources in favor of greater use of available renewable energy and materials technologies by applying regulatory pressure

to private business through mechanisms such as renewable portfolio standards and clean air laws.

2) Increase taxes on energy and virgin depletable materials, institute pollution and solid waste generation taxes, and subsidize renewables and recycling to create strong incentives for private business and consumers to conserve energy, recycle materials, and otherwise reduce wasteful use.

3) Create positive incentives by providing funding from ordinary tax revenues or public benefit funds, or create negative incentives through regulatory pressures, to encourage research and development to increase the efficiency and lower the cost of renewable energy and pollution-reducing technologies.

4) Use national and local government as seed markets to stimulate the deployment and use of newly proven energy efficiency and pollution-reduction technologies. This mitigates private sector risk, allows production to be scaled up to reduce unit costs, and reassures risk-averse consumers and businesses that the technologies work, increasing the likelihood that they to will buy them.

5) Shift emphasis from quantitative to qualitative economic growth, especially in the MDCs, relieving pressure on the planet's finite depletable resource endowment and reducing environmental pollution.

It is best to think of these strategies as twenty mutually compatible alternatives, each partially effective, each with its own advantages and drawbacks. In any particular country, which combination will work best in furtherance of any particular principle, which approach should be emphasized and which deemphasized or even ignored will depend on a complex of political, economic, and perhaps social and cultural factors. But taken together, these strategies constitute a package in which the government, the private sector, and the public at large can all take practical steps to make a peacekeeping economy a working reality.

The three existing international organizations with both the most relevance to the project at hand and the greatest global reach are the United Nations, the World Bank, and the World Trade Organization. For the UN, it would be useful to establish a specialized Council on Economic Sanctions and Peacekeeping at virtually the same level as the Security Council, but with much broader membership and no veto. For the World Bank, a number of operational changes might be useful, including: 1) modifying the way debt financing is used; 2) emphasizing alternative forms of finance; 3) ensuring greater donor recipient collaboration in designing and implementing development projects; 4) reducing the scale of projects; 5) facilitating microlending; and 6) incorporating social and environmental impact statements into the project decision process. Some modifications of the Global Environmental Facility, whose projects are managed by two UN agencies and the World Bank, could also help provide stronger support for economic peacekeeping.

Much of what the WTO already claims to be on paper is supportive of the principles of economic peacekeeping. The problem is that its practice often falls short of its rhetoric. Changes in WTO's mode of operation that would bring its behavior more in line with economic peacekeeping include: 1) strengthening mechanisms for more active and consequential participation of the organizations of international civil society in WTO decision making, including global environmental groups, development advocacy groups, and, for issues of immigration and working conditions, human rights groups; 2) substantially relaxing the WTO rule that no nation can impose trade restrictions on another because of the way a product has been produced, since the way a product is produced has great importance to its impact on economic development, environmental sustainability, and human rights—and therefore on economic peacekeeping; 3) adopting a broader organizational perspective than that in which free trade virtually always trumps all other considerations, so that alternative human concerns such as environmental protection or workers rights are also given their due; and finally 4) making the WTO's primary mission setting and enforcing rules to encourage greater balance and mutual benefit while expanding international trade, rather than simply removing barriers and expanding trade at all costs.

The experience of the European Union—as a highly successful regional trade organization and example of the power and practicality of economic peacekeeping—holds especially important lessons for other regional trade organizations. Similarly, organizations aimed at promoting LDC-LDC trade and "fair trade" NGOs also have a potentially important contribution to make in building a peacekeeping economy.

Useful changes in international practices include more effective regulation of multinational corporations and greater regulation of the international trade in hazardous materials and products. Regulation of multinational corporations should be directed at strengthening incentives that encourage them to operate in ways that are compatible with and supportive of the tenets of a peacekeeping economy. This could be accomplished by some combination of action through the WTO, treaties among national governments, and the application of pressure by investors and consumers discussed earlier.

Regulation of the trade in hazardous materials should be aimed at restricting and controlling this trade to reduce societal risk. Apart from the possibility of deliberate terrorist attack on shipments of highly toxic chemicals or radioactive materials, accidents that lead to massive releases of these substances also have the potential to raise the level of conflict-generating stress. The legal and illicit trade in small arms and large conventional weapons should be more tightly constrained, and the strongest possible action should be taken to entirely interdict trade in weapons of mass destruction and their components and key precursor materials. Furthermore, exporting countries (usually MDCs) must stop the practice of selling to other countries (usually LDCs) goods or substances considered too hazardous or dangerous to be sold in the exporting countries themselves. This kind of trade sends a message that the health and well-being of the people of some countries is less important, a message that is both immoral and bound to raise the level of international antagonism.

Building a security system based primarily on economic peacekeeping will involve a substantial shift of people, equipment, and facilities, along with considerable change in the structure and focus of the private sector and governmental organizations currently oriented to serving the needs of the military-based system. Handling this transition well requires considerable planning efforts by both corporations and federal, state, and city governments to ensure that the necessary programs for retraining and reorienting the labor force are not only available, but also well designed and well coordinated with the requirements of the abundant new jobs that can be created by shifting resources to more economically productive activities. Years of preparation by the private and public sector during World War II enabled the postwar return to a peacetime economy to be remarkably smooth and effective. Roughly one-third of the U.S. economy was shifted from military to civilian-serving activities within one year at the end of that war, with the unemployment rate never rising above 3 percent. There are important differences between the shape of the problem of military-civilian transition faced then and the nature of the problem today. In some ways it was harder then, in some ways it is harder now. But there is no doubt that with reasonable preparations attentive to the character of the problem as it exists today, we can convert any fraction of the military sector (in government and industry) we choose to economically productive civilian-oriented activity. There is every reason to celebrate rather than fear the prospect of reducing the military burden on the economy that a shift toward greater reliance on economic peacekeeping would permit.

We also explored the power of coordinated mass nonviolent action as an organized way of fighting both internal repression and external threats to security. The effectiveness of coordinated nonviolence, even against the most brutal regimes, has been demonstrated again and again in the unforgiving laboratory of the real world, perhaps especially during the last hundred years. In short, it works, not just in some idealized world of perfect people, but also in the very imperfect world in which we imperfect people live. As is true of all security strategies, including those relying on military force, it does not work all the time. But it has shown itself more powerful than violent strategies often enough that it is worth considering making training in nonviolent mass action a compatible adjunct to an overall security strategy based on economic peacekeeping.

Neither any of this analysis nor any of these suggestions requires a fundamental change in human nature, a revolutionary shift in the goals of society, or a radical alteration in the network of international organizations, but they do require a change of perspective. While the difficulty of bringing about this kind of change should not be minimized, neither should it be exaggerated. It will not happen overnight, but then it need not happen overnight. It is perfectly possible, and likely much more practical, for the shift from a military- and force-dominated security system to one based primarily on economic peacekeeping to come about at a measured though deliberate pace. It is a substantial transition, and transitions that work well and that have staying power take time. Yet recognizing that people and institutions need time to adjust to the change and comprehend its full meaning should not be used as an excuse for inaction. Because this kind of shift will take years to accomplish—perhaps even a decade or two—the sooner we begin to move in this direction, the better. There is too much to be gained to delay.

The Benefits of Demilitarized Security

There are tremendous economic benefits to moving toward a peacekeeping economy, because there are tremendous economic opportunity costs to military-based security systems. Economic activity is not an end in itself; it is a means to the end of enhancing the quality of people's lives. Because we are multidimensional beings, the quality of our lives depends on many different things. If we accept that the economy's contribution to our quality of life lies in providing the material goods and services we need to have a good standard of living, it becomes clear that military-related activities are a net economic drain. The use of military forces for military purposes does not create material goods and services; it destroys them. Even the preparation of forces for future battle is economically unproductive. Building weapons or buying weapons others have built uses labor and capital that could instead be used for making goods or providing services that do contribute to the material standard of living. In the short run and in the long run, attempting to provide security through military means is a form of economic waste, a burden on the economy.

Lifting this burden would by itself convey great potential benefits, freeing up resources for transfer from military-serving to economically productive civilian activities. This shift is especially important to reinvigorating the productive capabilities and competitiveness of producers in economies long burdened by high levels of military spending, like that of the United States. Furthermore, the enormous pool of resources released can be put to use addressing other pressing public needs, economic and otherwise, that have been too long neglected. Even in countries as rich as the U.S., and even in times of economic downturn, it will become easier to find the resources needed to overcome such problems as the neglect of key transportation infrastructure, the disgraceful state of inner city and rural school systems, and the inadequate access of those with lower income to health care. Relieved of much of their military burden, most LDCs could, from domestic sources, more easily find much of the capital they need to make investments that move development forward. They will no longer have to mortgage their futures by excessive borrowing from foreigners.

But as important as these things are, the economic benefits of demilitarized security are only part of the picture. Every war (or even "militarized dispute" short of war) avoided is that much wrenching dislocation and disruption of lives forestalled, that much suffering and death prevented. Though economists have tried, there is no sensible way to put a price on that. Demilitarized societies are also more fertile ground for the growth of democracy and expansion of civil liberties. Because they encourage both economic and political development, they help overturn the economic marginalization and political impotence (if not humiliation) that make it so much easier for terrorist and other violence-oriented groups to find the recruits and support they need.

On Keeping the Peace and Eliminating War

War ordinarily comes not as a sudden bolt out of the blue, but as the culmination of a buildup of tensions that result from a complex of political, social, economic, psychological, and even religious factors. Like plate tectonics, where the buildup of pressure on colliding plates may take a long time to reach the point at which an earthquake suddenly fractures the planet's crust, the events or decisions that immediately precede the outbreak of war or civil violence are only the proximal causes, not the underlying longer-acting forces responsible for the dramatic and sudden change. In plate tectonics, major earthquakes occur when there is no mechanism operating that allows the pressure that the colliding plates exert on each other to be relieved a little bit at a time. Similarly, civil violence or international war becomes much more likely if the practices and institutions needed to forestall or defuse the buildup of tensions are either inadequate or unavailable. War is a probabilistic phenomenon made more or less likely not just by the immediate precipitating events, but also by the social, political, and economic context within which these events occur. The key to keeping the peace is to establish a context that keeps the strain on the system lower than its strength, so that the buildup of pressure rarely if ever exceeds the threshold at which peace is shattered. Since, as a practical matter, we often do not even know precisely where that threshold is most of the time, it makes sense to work toward creating a context that routinely helps to keep stresses as low as possible and the resistance to these stresses as high as possible. That is exactly what a peacekeeping economy is designed to do.

Because the process leading to the outbreak of civil violence and war is typically neither entirely rational nor wholly irrational, the fact that a peacekeeping economy creates a situation in which the cost of violence and war greatly exceeds the likely benefits cannot by itself guarantee the complete absence of war. It can, however, make the outbreak of war much less likely, and thus play a very powerful and important role in keeping the peace.

There has been an ongoing debate as to whether humans are innately aggressive and violent, and thus condemned to war periodically with each other. From Hobbesian ideas that the brutishness of the human state of nature naturally leads to a "war of all against all" to the contentions of Carl Jung and Konrad Lorenz that at least under some circumstances humans are innately aggressive, many have argued that violence is an inherent part of being human.[1] Psychologist Erich Fromm, for example, wrote, "If man cannot create anything or move anybody, . . . he can escape the unbearable sense of vital impotence and nothingness only by affirming himself in the act of destruction of the life that he is unable to create."[2] But psychologists such as B. F. Skinner have taken the view that human behavior, including violent behavior, is almost entirely the result of social conditioning, and an important school of anthropological thought, represented, for example, by Richard Leakey, has argued that human violence is not innate but rather learned and situational.[3] Of course, Mohandis Gandhi's entire philosophy and practice of nonviolence action as an effective strategy for bringing about political and social change was built on the conviction that, whether it is inherent or socially conditioned, people can effectively suppress whatever urge to violence they might have.

Even if the capacity for violence—and perhaps the urge to commit violence as well—are nearly universal among humans, this does not mean that people cannot learn to control them. Furthermore, having a tendency toward violence in certain kinds of interpersonal situations does not mean we are periodically condemned to engage in the spasms of mass organized violence we call civil or international war. We may never be able to completely eliminate criminal violence or the violence that arises from temporary loss of control in situations of overwhelming interpersonal anger and frustration. But war is not merely the eruption of interpersonal violence on a larger scale. It is an entirely different phenomenon. War, as opposed to criminal or interpersonal violence, is a social institution. Most of those who go off to fight in modern wars are not reacting violently to anger that came from what someone else has done to them personally. Most of those who die in modern wars are killed by others who have never actually seen them, let alone interacted with them as a person in any meaningful sense of the word. Where once soldiers could kill only by piercing the living flesh of other people at close range, they can now kill more efficiently at greater distances. Today, operating in computerized control centers in Nevada, pilots of U.S.-built Predator drone aircraft routinely kill people in countries thousands of miles away.

The fact is, all social institutions, including war, are created by people to achieve goals that are important to them. Therefore, even very long-standing social institutions are subject to change when those goals change, when people's understanding of the most effective means of achieving those goals change, or when people's view of the legitimacy of those goals change.

Put simply, as a means of providing the peace and security we all so deeply desire, primary reliance on military force is an idea whose time has gone. War is too destructive and the preparation for war too expensive for human society to continue to rely mainly on the brute force of large militaries to keep us safe. Since war and war-threatening military force are social institutions that are no longer effective at serving their purpose, rather than being an exercise in utopianism, it is the essence of realism to look for more effective social arrangements. There is nothing more hard-nosed and pragmatic than shifting from that which does not work to that which does. It is easy to be cynical, to believe that we cannot change our way of looking at the world, our way of behaving. Nothing seems so immutable as the status quo. But the fact is we do change our attitudes and can change—or completely abolish—even well established deeply embedded social institutions. We have done it before.

One hundred years ago, women were not allowed to vote in the U.S. because it was widely accepted that they were not biologically capable of making sensible political decisions. Sixty years ago, in the southern U.S. city in which this book was written, it was a criminal offense for black Americans to use the same public drinking fountains or the same public restrooms, or to sit in the same classrooms, as white Americans. Yet today, any American political leader who publicly suggests rescinding women's right to vote or reestablishing legalized racial segregation would be considered in serious need of psychological counseling. Attitudes certainly do change.

Slavery was once a generally accepted social institution with its own set of vested interests embedded in the status quo. There were those who even said it was part of human nature, that only dreamers and fools believed it could be changed. Yet today, although sadly slavery is still practiced in some places, there is not a single nation on earth in which it is legal for one human being to own another. Where it once was a widespread, mainstream, and protected institution, it is now a practice widely reviled, under assault, and condemned to operate on the fringes of society deep within the seedy underworld.

Legalized slavery did not disappear on its own. It ended because of changing attitudes, changing technology, and changing political and economic conditions. But it also ended because there were those who believed that human beings could do better and were willing to combine their vision of a world without slavery with the hard work of building a practical path to their dream.

If we ever do succeed in eliminating civil and international war as a human institution, it will be the result of a long and complex process of changes in our practices, behavior, and ways of thinking. Achieving this larger goal is an imposing and formidable task. But whether or not we decide to undertake this ultimate challenge, we can certainly move boldly and decisively toward making the outbreak of civil violence and international war much less likely, and enhancing our ability to put a rapid end to, and limit the damage done by, the violence that does break out.

This book is not about how things could be in some sort of visionary world of more perfect human beings. It is about the practical prospects for creating a world in which we will all be safer, as well as materially better off, despite all the flaws and inconsistencies that are an inherent part of being human. It is not about a perfect world; it is about a better world that is wholly within the power of imperfect human beings to create. There is no doubt that we can do it. The only question is whether we will find the courage to think and act more boldly, and build the political will to make it happen.

In the early years of the twenty-first century we find ourselves living in a time of profound change in the attitudes, technology, and political and economic conditions that surround the institutions of militarism and war. It is possible for us to do better. But well-establish social institutions and practices do not disappear into a vacuum. There must be an alternative that combines a compelling vision with a practical path to that dream. The peacekeeping economy offers such an alternative. It can help us build a world that is both more prosperous and more secure. It is part of what we need to find our way toward making militarism and war a curiosity of our past, rather than a threat to our future.

NOTES

Chapter 1. The Hopeful Science

Epigraph: Kaysen, Carl, "Is War Obsolete?" *International Security* (Spring 1990): p.63. Kaysen is professor of political economy at MIT.

1. See, for example, Stiglitz, Joseph E., *Globalization and Its Discontents* (New York: Norton, 2002), pp.89–98.
2. Osama bin Laden, the "Emir-General" of Al Qaeda, was born in Riyadh in 1957, the seventeenth of fifty-two children of Muhammad bin Laden, who was from Yemen. His father rose from poverty as a dockworker to wealth in the course of building up Saudi Arabia's foremost construction company, the Bin Laden Group. Gunaratna, Rohan, *Inside Al Qaeda: Global Network of Terror* (New York: Columbia University Press, 2002).
3. Based on the definition of war as "any conflict including one or more governments, involving the use of arms, and causing deaths of 1,000 or more people per year," there were at least 234 wars between 1900 and the early 1990s— World Wars I and II, 83 other wars before 1945, and 149 after. See Sivard, R. L., *World Military and Social Expenditures, 1985* (Washington, DC: World Priorities, 1985), pp.9–11. Some of these figures are updated in Sivard, R. L., *World Military and Social Expenditures, 1993* (Washington, DC: World Priorities, 1993), pp.20–21 (estimates of wars and death tolls prepared by William Eckhardt).
4. History is a peculiar teacher. It tells us what was done and what happened, but it cannot tell us what would have happened. We know from history how many wars have occurred; we cannot know from history whether there would have been more or fewer wars had nations taken a different path.
5. This argument does not just apply to relations with the major powers. The United States has never been all that concerned about the nuclear arsenal of Israel, a nation with which we have close ties, but we went to war in Iraq in 2003

citing what turned out to be mistaken fears that the hostile Iraqi government was trying to develop weapons of mass destruction. Today we remain very concerned about North Korea's efforts to build up its stock of nuclear weapons and the possibility that Iran is trying to develop nuclear weapons—mainly because our relationships with those nations are so problematic, so filled with distrust and hostility.

6. Douglass North took Marx to task for exactly this reason: "Marxist theory is deficient because it entails a fundamental change in human behavior to achieve its results, and we have no evidence of such a change (even after seventy years of socialist society)." North, Douglass, *Institutions, Institutional Change and Economic Performance* (Cambridge: Cambridge University Press, 1990), 132.

7. There are, however, important traps, too often treated too cavalierly in the use of both formal mathematical models and empirical tools for such purposes. In the case of mathematical models, care must be taken in the necessary process of making the models mathematically tractable, to ensure that the assumptions made do not cause the models to lose the essence of the real world situation or process being analyzed. If the assumptions do not capture that essential reality, it is very likely that the conclusions drawn from those models will be at least misleading, if not completely wrong. Similarly, empirical tools must be applied using data that capture the essence of the theoretical concepts that they are trying to measure. Using empirical measures that do not properly represent the theoretical concepts being analyzed is also a common flaw in economic analysis, one that has a high probability of yielding misleading or false conclusions.

8. While more recent concepts of the legitimacy of a state (such as that of Max Weber) tend to focus on the processes it involves and the means it employs, this view is broadly consistent with Aristotle's focus on the purposes of the state, and thus the idea that it is reasonable for citizen support for the state to be contingent on how well a state achieves those purposes. (For an elaboration of this Aristotelian framework—and its application to security-related issues—see *New Approaches to Comparative Politics: Insights from Political Theory*, edited by Jennifer S. Holmes [Lanham, MD: Lexington, 2003], Chapter 4, written by Holmes).

9. John F. Kennedy's famous statement "Ask not what your country can do for you, ask what you can do for your country" was a compelling and poetic call to think beyond narrow self-interest to the broader good. But in a literal sense, it was exactly backwards. It is what your country can do for you—in terms of creating the conditions that provide the opportunity to live a good and meaningful life—that matters and that makes the country worthy of support.

10. Ordinarily, we think of this as a problem of poverty, but many whose incomes are very far above the poverty line find themselves in continuing economic distress because they have managed to raise their level of spending and/or debt to the outer limits of their financial capacity. Neither a society whose norms encourage this kind of behavior, nor a society structured to perpetuate poverty, can be considered conducive to personal security.

11. In the most extreme case, a rising level of violence and disruption, along with an increasing unwillingness to bear further economic sacrifice, may lead to so much social unrest that the government feels compelled to use force to repress its own people, causing personal security to deteriorate even further.

Chapter 2. Laying the Foundations

1. Between 1804 (when Napoleon declared himself emperor) and 1813, some 2.4 million men were drafted into the French military. From 1793 to 1813 the French lost 1.7 million dead, out of a population of 29 million. Dyer, Gwynne, *War* (Homewood, IL: Dorsey, 1985), pp.68–69.
2. Ibid., p.87.
3. All the German air raids on Britain during WWI combined killed a total of only about four thousand British civilians. Ibid., pp.84–85.
4. By the end of the twentieth century, with "smart bombs" and precision-guided munitions, the American public began to see aerial bombardment as a more desirable, relatively "clean" way to wage war, with minimal danger to those doing the bombing, and minimal civilian casualties in the areas targeted. The reality is quite different. Since such bombing was typically intended to destroy the war-making capacity of the nation being attacked, the infrastructure on which the civilian economy depended would be high on the target list. Even if bombs could be targeted with such accuracy that they killed no civilians (which is virtually impossible), the damage to the economy would claim victims long after the bombing stopped. The Persian Gulf War of 1991 is a good example. It is estimated that the damage done to the Iraqi infrastructure by U.S.-led coalition forces in that short war, exacerbated by economic sanctions imposed for more than a decade after the war, resulted in the deaths of well more than 100,000 Iraqis.
5. Given that people are inherently fallible (in the sense of being prone to both error and malevolence), as long as large numbers of nuclear weapons and the capability to deliver them exist, the threat of nuclear war, by intention or accident, will also continue to exist. For a thorough treatment of the nature of human fallibility and its implications for interactions with nuclear weapons (and other dangerous technologies), see Dumas, Lloyd J., *The Technology Trap: Where Human Error and Malevolence Meet Powerful Technologies* (Santa Barbara, CA: Praeger/ABC-CLIO, 2010).
6. A detailed analysis integrating military resource diversion into a coherent macroeconomic theory is available in Dumas, Lloyd. J., *The Overburdened Economy: Uncovering the Causes of Chronic Unemployment, Inflation and National Decline* (Berkeley, CA: University of California Press, 1986).
7. Some version of this quote has been attributed to people as diverse as nineteenth century French economist Frederic Bastiat and mid-twentieth century U.S. secretary of state Cordell Hull.

8. The discussion in this section and the next is intended to lay out the basic thinking behind this disagreement, as well as the results of some of the more interesting empirical studies that have been brought to bear on it. It is not intended to be a comprehensive formal survey of the literature. In any case, it is not critical to understanding the core analysis presented in this book. The reader less interested in this background material may wish to skip to the last section of this chapter.

9. Keohane, Robert O., "International Liberalism Reconsidered," in *The Economic Limits to Modern Politics*, ed. J. Dunn (Cambridge: Cambridge University Press, 1990), p.185.

10. Morgenthau, Hans J., *Politics Among Nations* (New York: Alfred Knopf, 1973).

11. Waltz, Kenneth N., "The Origins of War in Neorealist Theory," *Journal of Interdisciplinary History* (Spring 1988).

12. Herz, John H., "Idealist Internationalism and the Security Dilemma," *World Politics* (II, 1950), pp.157–180.

13. Dietrich Fischer suggests a way around the "security dilemma," arguing that the key to security is not so much the amount of power that a nation possesses, but the type. Nations that build up offensive military capability are likely to be seen as threatening by other nations, eliciting a hostile, security-reducing reaction. But nations can increase their security without provoking a hostile response if they build up defensive capabilities, while maintaining little or no offensive military force. Defensive strength serves as a powerful deterrent to attack by others, while offensive weakness prevents others from feeling threatened, short-circuiting fear-induced hostility and the balance of power reaction. Fischer, Dietrich, *Preventing War in the Nuclear Age* (Totowa, NJ: Rowman and Allanheld, 1984).

14. Waltz, "The Origins of War in Neorealist Theory," p.619.

15. Ibid., p.616.

16. Kreisler, Harry, "Theory and International Politics: Conversation with Kenneth N. Waltz," in *Conversations with History* (Berkeley: Institute of International Studies, February 10, 2003).

17. Waltz, Kenneth N., "Nuclear Myths and Political Realities," *American Political Science Review* (September 1990): p.743.

18. As cited in Hoffman, Stanley, "Rousseau on War and Peace," *American Political Science Review* (57: 1963): p.319.

19. Waltz, Kenneth N., "The Myth of National Interdependence," in *The Multinational Corporation*, ed. Charles P. Kindleberger (Cambridge, MA: MIT Press, 1970), p.205.

20. Gilpin, Robert, "Economic Interdependence and National Security in Historical Perspective," in *Economic Issues and National Security*, ed. Klaus Knorr and Frank Trager (Lawrence, KS: Regents Press of Kansas, 1977).

21. Gowa, Joanne S., *Allies, Adversaries and International Trade* (Princeton, NJ: Princeton University Press, 1994).

22. Papayoanu, Paul, *Power Ties: Economic Interdependence, Balancing and War* (Ann Arbor, MI: University of Michigan Press, 1999), p.12.

23. Buzan, Barry, "Economic Structure and International Security: The Limits of the Liberal Case," *International Organization* (38: 1984).

24. Holsti, Kal J., "Politics in Command: Foreign Trade as National Security Policy," *International Organization* (40: 1986).

25. Ibid., pp.3–4.

26. Keohane, Robert O., and Martin, Lisa L., "The Promise of Institutionalist Theory," *International Security* (Summer 1995).

27. Gourevitch, Peter A., "Robert O. Keohane: The Study of International Relations," The American Political Science Association Online, apsanet.org (September 1999).

28. Keohane and Martin, "The Promise of Institutionalist Theory," pp.45–46.

29. How easy or difficult this is to do depends on the specific terms of the contract, as well as on a number of jurisdictional issues.

30. The market system implies a continuing game with many iterations; cooperative strategies can evolve more easily than in a single play game, where violation of the norms may create a one-time gain.

31. Nye, Joseph S., "Neorealism and Neoliberalism," *World Politics* (January 1988): p.238.

32. Keohane, Robert O., and Nye, Joseph S., *Power and Interdependence: World Politics in Transition* (Boston: Little, Brown, 1977; 2d ed., 1989).

33. Gourevitch, "Robert O. Keohane," p.2.

34. McMillan, Susan M., "Interdependence and Conflict," *Mershon International Studies Review* (May 1997): pp.35–38.

35. For example, see Russett, Bruce, "Politics and Alternative Security: Toward a More Democratic, Therefore More Peaceful, World," in *Alternative Security: Living Without Nuclear Deterrence*, ed. Burns H. Weston (Boulder, CO: Westview, 1990). An interesting attack on the idea of democratic peace can be found in Henderson, Errol A., *Democracy and War: The End of an Illusion?* (Boulder, CO: Lynne Rienner, 2002).

36. As quoted in Keohane, Robert O., "International Liberalism Reconsidered," in *The Economic Limits to Modern Politics*, ed. John Dunn (Cambridge: Cambridge University Press, 1990), p.177.

37. Rosecrance, Richard, *The Rise of the Trading State: Commerce and Conquest in the Modern World* (New York: Basic, 1986), pp.24–25.

38. Kaysen, Carl, "Is War Obsolete?," *International Security* (Spring 1990): pp.53–54.

39. Deutsch, Karl W., *The Analysis of International Relations* (Englewood Cliffs, NJ: Prentice Hall, 1968).

40. Mansfield, Edward D., *Power, Trade, and War* (Princeton, NJ: Princeton University Press, 1994).

41. Ibid., p.23.

42. Ibid., p.20. In other words, the concentration/trade relationship is U-shaped, while the concentration/war relationship is shaped like an inverted U (assuming concentration is measured on the horizontal axis and trade or war is measured vertically).

43. Copeland, Dale C., "Economic Interdependence and War: A Theory of Trade Expectations," *International Security* (Spring 1996): p.17.

44. The high trade case doesn't cause a problem: no conflict is evidence for the liberals; conflict is evidence for the realists. Realists appear to believe that high levels of trade will give rise to expectations (or at least fears) of low future trade; liberals appear to believe that high current levels of trade will give rise to expectations of continued high levels of trade in the future.

45. McMillan, "Interdependence and Conflict," 43.

46. Russett, Bruce, *International Regions and the International System* (Chicago: Rand McNally, 1967).

47. Uchitel, Anne, "Interdependence and Instability," in *Coping with Complexity in the International System,* ed. Jack Snyder and Robert Jervis (Boulder, CO: Westview, 1993).

48. Ibid., p.243. Uchitel's point is well taken, although given the nature and ideology of the particular governments in control of both Germany and Japan in the period studied, it is hard to believe that either of them needed any additional incentives to engage in "expansionist policies and offensive military strategies."

49. Barbieri, Katherine, "Economic Interdependence: A Path to Peace or a Source of Interstate Conflict," *Journal of Peace Research* (33: 1996).

50. Azar, Edward E., "The Conflict and Peace Data Bank (COPDAB) Project," *Journal of Conflict Resolution* (24:1980).

51. Polachek, Solomon W., "Conflict and Trade," *Journal of Conflict Resolution* (24: 1980): p.60.

52. Gasiorowski, Mark, and Polachek, Solomon W., "Conflict and Interdependence: East-West Trade and Linkages in the Era of Détente," *Journal of Conflict Resolution* (26: 1982).

53. Polachek used the Granger causality test. This time series regression-based test attempts to predict each key variable using its own past values and the past values of other key variables. Gujarati, Damodar N., *Basic Econometrics* (New York: McGraw Hill, 1995), pp.620–623.

54. Among other things, he included multiple measures of economic interdependence, and weighted the events data he used for conflict by a measure of conflict intensity. See Gasiorowski, Mark J., "Economic Interdependence and International Conflict: Some Cross-National Evidence," *International Studies Quarterly* (30: 1986).

55. Oneal, John R., Oneal, Frances H., Maoz, Zeev, and Russett, Bruce, "The Liberal Peace: Interdependence, Democracy, and International Conflict, 1950–85," *Journal of Peace Research* (33: 1996). Conflict-related variables in this analysis included geographic contiguity, the ratio of the dyad's military capabilities, whether or not the countries were allies, and relative economic growth.

56. Mansfield, *Power, Trade, and War,* 149.

57. Ibid., p.144. Mansfield was careful to point out, though, that his findings do not suggest that the extent of trade is necessarily a more important direct

determinant of war than the distribution of power, just that the distribution of power does not work through its impact on the relationship between trade and war.

58. For example, Kenneth Waltz, "European great powers prior to World War I were tightly tied together economically. They nevertheless fought a long and bloody war." Waltz, Kenneth N., "Globalization and Governance" (1999 James Madison Lecture), The American Political Science Association Online, apsanet.org (2005), third paragraph of the section subtitled, "The State in International Politics."

59. Rosecrance, Richard, "Review of [Samuel Huntington's] *The Clash of Civilizations and the Remaking of World Order*," *The American Political Science Review* (December 1998): p.980.

60. Copeland, "Economic Interdependence and War," 33.

61. Ibid., p.26, fn.42.

62. Collier, Paul, "Doing Well Out of War: An Economic Perspective," in *Greed and Grievance: Economic Agendas in Civil Wars,* ed. Mats Berdal and David M. Malone (Boulder, CO: Lynne Rienner, 2000), p.91.

63. For an interesting discussion of this phenomenon, see Keen, David, "Incentives and Disincentives for Violence," in *Greed and Grievance: Economic Agendas in Civil Wars,* ed. Mats Berdal and David M. Malone (Boulder, CO: Lynne Rienner, 2000), especially pp.26–31.

64. Reno, William, "Shadow States and the Political Economy of Civil Wars," in *Greed and Grievance: Economic Agendas in Civil Wars,* ed. Mats Berdal and David M. Malone (Boulder, CO: Lynne Rienner, 2000), p.64.

65. De Soysa, Indra, "The Resource Curse: Are Civil Wars Driven by Rapacity or Paucity?," in *Greed and Grievance: Economic Agendas in Civil Wars,* ed. Mats Berdal and David M. Malone (Boulder, CO: Lynne Rienner, 2000). De Soysa used multivariate probit models in this analysis, and controlled for rate of economic growth, per capita income level, ethnic pluralism, and democracy (among other things). The number of conflicts involved in the four probit analyses for which results were reported ranged from 63 to 116 (p.129).

66. Collier, "Doing Well Out of War." Collier did a multivariate probit analysis using the share of primary commodity exports in gross domestic product (GDP) as a proxy for what he called "the availability of 'lootable' resources," and a number of variables, including the extent of ethnic/religious fractionalization, asset inequality, and lack of political rights as proxies for grievances.

67. Ibid., pp.96–97.

68. Ibid., p.97.

Chapter 3. The Core Principles of Economic Peacekeeping

1. On the whole, enforcement of accepted international rules of behavior on businesses and individuals depends on national governments taking action to ensure

compliance in accordance with the obligations imposed on them by agreements they have made.

2. There is an important distinction to be drawn between the function of a peace-keeping economy and the function of peacekeeping military forces, such as those the UN has frequently deployed with at best mixed success. Peacekeeping military forces are intended to keep actively hostile armed combatants apart, to see to the evenhanded coercive enforcement of cease-fire agreements, or to prevent the resumption of armed hostilities in situations of fragile and unstable peace. A peacekeeping economy is intended to discourage even the initial outbreak of armed conflict and to make the tendency to resolve or manage conflicts stronger and more robust by creating the proper context and incentive structure.

3. "Prospect theory" argues that positive and negative incentives do not have symmetrical effects on choice. See, for example, Jervis, Robert, "The Implications of Prospect Theory for Human Nature and Values," *Political Psychology* (25, no. 2: 2004); Oliver, Pamela, "Rewards and Punishments as Selective Incentives for Collective Action: Theoretical Investigations" *American Journal of Sociology* (May 1980); Levy, Moshe, and Levy, Haim, "Prospect Theory: Much Ado About Nothing?" *Management Science* (October 2002).

4. Hufbauer, Gary C., Schott, Jeffrey J., and Elliott, Kimberly A., *Economic Sanctions Reconsidered: History and Current Policy* and *Economic Sanctions Reconsidered: Supplemental Case Histories,* 2d ed. (Washington, DC: Institute for International Economics, 1990). See also Cortright, David, and Lopez, George A., *The Sanctions Decade: Assessing UN Strategies in the 1990s* (Boulder, Colorado: Lynne Rienner, 2000), and Cortright, David, and Lopez, George A., *The Sanctions and the Search for Security: Challenges to UN Action* (Boulder, Colorado: Lynne Rienner, 2002).

5. Boulding, Kenneth E., *Stable Peace* (Austin: University of Texas Press, 1978).

6. Modern telecommunications technology makes it possible for firms to hire workers in other countries to work for them without the workers ever having to leave their home country. Such "virtual" immigration has become relatively commonplace, for example, in software design and maintenance.

7. This concept of balance and benefit is consistent with Aristotle's dictum that "the well-being of every polis depends on each of its elements rendering to others an amount equivalent to what it received from them," though in a very different context. Aristotle, *Politics,* trans. Earnest Barker (London: Oxford University Press, 1958), p.41.

8. The economist's models of pure competition produce results that are in general more socially beneficial than those of monopoly mainly because power differentials unrelated to productivity are eliminated by the extreme assumptions of the model. The intensity of competition in product and resources markets strips away any differential bargaining power that could lead to a lack of balance, in the sense we have defined it.

9. This concept of balance is a combination of fundamental ideas of equity and the economist's notion that allocative efficiency requires resources to be compensated in accordance with their productivity.

10. Blumenthal, Monica D., et al., *More About Justifying Violence: Methodological Studies of Attitudes and Behavior* (Ann Arbor, MI: Institute for Social Research, University of Michigan, 1975), p.108.

11. Kapstein, Ethan, *Economic Justice in an Unfair World: Toward a Level Playing Field* (Princeton, NJ: Princeton University Press, 2006), pp.35–36.

12. The strength of that incentive depends on the salience of that relationship to the parties involved. If a relationship is of little significance to either party, the incentive it creates to avoid conflict arising from other causes will be weak.

13. Smith, Adam, *The Wealth of Nations* (New York: Modern Library, Random House, 1937), pp.581–582.

14. Marx, Karl, *Selected Writings in Sociology and Social Philosophy*, trans. T. B. Bottomore and M. Rubel (London: Watts, 1961).

15. In 2007, Adam Okulicz-Kozaryn summarized the main conclusions of the "happiness" studies literature, which began with research by psychologists on self-reported assessments of subjective well-being or life satisfaction. Those things that satisfy the need to belong—such as religion, family, and friendship—seem to have the most powerful impacts on happiness. Political rights and personal characteristics are also important, although age and gender are not strongly related to life satisfaction. "Personal or household income matters in less affluent countries only (with GNP less than $8000 per person). . . . As long as people can afford the necessities, income does not contribute to happiness" (Okulicz-Kozaryn, Adam, "Does Freedom Matter in Transition?," [draft June 2007, unpublished], p.3, citing Myers, D. G., "The Funds, Friends, and Faith of Happy People," *American Psychologist* [55: 2000]: pp.56–67).

16. In a world filled with weapons of mass destruction built and deployed by error-prone human beings, we can be sure that disasters involving these weapons will eventually occur, by accident or intention. For a detailed analysis of this problem and its solution, see Dumas, Lloyd J., *The Technology Trap: Where Human Error and Malevolence Meet Powerful Technologies* (Santa Barbara, CA: Praeger/ABC-CLIO, 2010).

17. Nye, Joseph, "Limits of American Power," *Political Science Quarterly* (117, no. 4: 2002–2003): p.552.

18. Ibid.

19. Ibid., p.554.

20. Ibid., p.551.

21. The sole exception, of course, is that any party to a purely voluntary relationship, unconstrained by contractual requirements to the contrary, is free to end its participation without anyone else's consent.

22. The formation of the ECSC was the result of a proposal by Robert Schuman, the minister for foreign affairs of France, based on provisions in the Marshall Plan.

Rittberger, B., "Which Institutions for Post-War Europe? Explaining the Institutional Design of Europe's First Community," *Journal of European Public Policy* (8, no. 5: 2001): pp.673–708.

23. All nineteen NATO member nations had to agree on the NATO decision to bomb Kosovo. Thirty-six nations contributed troops to the so-called KFOR military force, including Belgium, France, Germany, Italy, Portugal, Spain, and the U.K.

24. Simons, Marlise, "Dutch Voters Solidly Reject New European Constitution," *New York Times* (June 2, 2005).

25. Bernstein, Richard, "2 'No' Votes in Europe: The Anger Spreads," *New York Times* (June 2, 2005).

26. In early January 2006, shock waves rolled across Europe as Russia suddenly shut off its natural gas pipelines to Ukraine when that nation balked at paying the huge increase in price Russia had unilaterally announced. Even though Russia's actions were aimed at coercing Ukraine, the forty-eight-hour shutoff affected the flow of gas to all of Europe and raised serious questions about the vulnerability caused by excessive dependence there. Russia is virtually the only supplier of natural gas to much of central and eastern Europe. Germany is Russia's largest customer, and even France and Italy buy between 25 and 35 percent of their imported gas from Russia. See Landler, Mark, "Gas Halt May Produce Big Ripples in European Policy," *New York Times* (January 4, 2006).

27. World Health Organization (WHO), "Burden of Disease and Cost-Effectiveness Estimates," www.who.int/water_sanitation_health/diseases/burden/en/print.html (July 29, 2005). DALY is the acronym for "disability-adjusted life-year." It is a summary population health measure that includes the effect of illness, disability, and mortality.

28. Nafziger, E. Wayne, *The Economics of Developing Countries* (Upper Saddle River, NJ: Prentice-Hall, 1997), p.345.

29. Fischer, Dietrich, *Preventing War in the Nuclear Age* (Totowa, NJ: Rowman and Allenheld, 1984), p.147.

30. Ibid., p.148, citing Roberts, Adam, *Nations in Arms* (New York: Praeger, 1976), p.103.

31. As of January 2005, the U.S. had proven oil reserves of almost twenty-two billion barrels, and had produced an average of 7.7 million barrels per day for most of 2004. U.S. Department of Energy, Energy Information Administration, "Energy Overview," www.eia.doe.gov/emeu/cabs/usa/html (July 26, 2005).

32. Bureau of the Census, U.S. Department of Commerce, *Statistical Abstract of the United States: 2004–2005* (Washington, DC: U.S. Government Printing Office, 2005), p.581, Table 898.

33. As of July 26, 2005, the Strategic Petroleum Reserve held 698 million barrels (96 percent of capacity). U.S. Department of Energy, "Strategic Petroleum Reserve—Profile," www.fe.doe.gov/programs/reserves/spr (July 26, 2005).

34. Ibid., pp.580–581, Tables 897 and 898.

35. U.S. Energy Information Administration, Independent Statistics and Analysis, tonto.eia.doe.gov/dnav/pet/pet_move_wkly_dc_NUS-Z00_mbblpd_4.htm and tonto.eia.doe.gov/dnav/pet/pet_pri_wco_k_w.htm (accessed February 26, 2010).

36. For more on the relative cost-effectiveness of renewable energy, see Dumas, Lloyd J., "Seeds of Opportunity: Climate Change Challenges and Solutions," Civil Society Institute, www.civilsocietyinstitute.org/media/pdfs/041906%20Seeds%20of%20Oppty%20Dumas%20report%20FINAL.pdf (accessed July 5, 2008), esp. pp.37–38. See also Pratt, Robert L., "The Promise of Renewable Energy" in *Growing the Economy Through Global Warming Solutions,* ed. Lloyd J. Dumas, Civil Society Institute paper series, www.civilsocietyinstitute.org/reports/GEGWS-PrattChapter.pdf (accessed July 5, 2008).

37. Dumas, Lloyd J., *The Conservation Response: Strategies for the Design and Operation of Energy-Using Systems* (Lexington, MA: Lexington, D.C. Heath, 1976).

38. U.S. Department of Defense, "Strategic and Critical Materials Report to the Congress: Operations Under the Strategic and Critical Materials Stockpiling Act During the Period October 2001 Through September 2002," Washington, DC: Department of Defense, FY 2002, pp.1 and 6–8.

39. Ibid., p.17, Appendix A: "Strategic and Critical Materials Stockpiling Act" (50 U.S.C. 98 *et seq.*), Section 2, paragraphs (a), (b), and (c).

40. Based on defining war as "any conflict including one or more governments, involving the use of arms, and causing deaths of 1,000 or more people per year." See Sivard, R. L., *World Military and Social Expenditures, 1985* (Washington, DC: World Priorities, 1985), pp.9–11; updated in Sivard, R. L., *World Military and Social Expenditures, 1993* (Washington, DC: World Priorities, 1993), pp.20–21. (Estimates of wars prepared by William Eckhardt.)

41. Keohane, Robert. O., "International Liberalism Reconsidered," in *The Economic Limits to Modern Politics,* ed. John Dunn (Cambridge: Cambridge University Press, 1990), p.192.

42. Nye, Joseph S., "Limits of American Power," *Political Science Quarterly* (117, no. 4: 2002–2003), p.549.

43. Ibid., pp.549–550.

44. Collier, Paul, "Doing Well Out of War: An Economic Perspective," in *Greed and Grievance: Economic Agendas in Civil Wars,* ed. Mats Berdal and David M. Malone (Boulder, CO: Lynne Rienner, 2000), p.91.

45. Ibid., p.97.

46. de Soysa, Indra, "The Resource Curse: Are Civil Wars Driven by Rapacity or Paucity?," in *Greed and Grievance: Economic Agendas in Civil Wars,* ed. Mats Berdal and David M. Malone (Boulder, CO: Lynne Rienner, 2000). The number of conflicts involved in the four probit analyses for which results were reported ranged from 63 to 116. (p.129).

47. Collier, "Doing Well Out of War," p.106.

48. Michael Renner, "Security Redefined," in The Worldwatch Institute, *State of the World, 2005* (New York: Norton, 2005), p.5.

49. Homer-Dixon, Thomas F., "Environmental Scarcities and Violent Conflict: Evidence from Cases," *International Security* (9, no. 1: Summer 1994), p.6.

50. The UN Food and Agricultural Organization (FAO) estimated that during the 1990s, 16.1 million hectares of natural forest were lost every year worldwide. FAO, *State of the World's Forests* (Rome: UN Food and Agricultural Organization, 2001), http://www.fao.org/docrep/003/y0900e/y0900e00.htm (accessed December 25, 2010).

51. Wolf, Aaron T., Annika Kramer, Alexander Carius, and Geoffrey D. Dabelko, "Managing Water Conflict and Cooperation," in The Worldwatch Institute, *State of the World, 2005* (New York: Norton, 2005), p.84.

52. Ibid., pp.83–84.

53. Homer-Dixon, "Environmental Scarcities and Violent Conflict," 14.

54. Ibid., p.19.

55. Ibid., pp.39–40.

56. McGinn, Anne Platt, "Phasing Out Persistent Organic Pollutants," in Brown, Lester, et al., The Worldwatch Institute, *State of the World 2000* (New York, Norton, 2000), p.80.

57. Ibid.

58. Ibid.

59. Kintisch, Eli, "Climate Change: Panel Urges Unified Action, Sets 2° Target," *Science* (28 January 2005), p.496.

60. Environment Canada (The Environmental Ministry of the Canadian Government), "The Science of Climate Change," www.ec.gc.ca/climate/overview_science-e.html (September 10, 2005), p.2.

61. World Health Organization, "Climate Change and Human Health: Risks and Responses," www.who.int/globalchange/climate/summary/en/ (August 11, 2005), p.1, paragraph 13.

62. Epstein, Paul R., "Climate, Ecology and Human Health," *Consequences* (3, no.2: 1997), p.3.

63. Chang, Kenneth, "British Scientists Say Carbon Dioxide Is Turning Oceans Acidic," *New York Times* (July 1, 2005). Ocean water today is somewhat alkaline, with a pH of approximately 8.1. It is expected to become more acidic (although still alkaline), with a pH of approximately 7.7 by 2100.

64. Intergovernmental Panel on Climate Change, *Climate Change 2001: IPCC Third Assessment Report*, www.grida.no/climate/ipcc_tar/wg2TARchap6.pdf (July 7, 2005).

65. National Oceanic and Atmospheric Administration (NOAA), "Population Trends Across the Coastal United States: 1980–2008," Coastal Trends Report Series, www.oceanservice.noaa.gov/programs/mb/supp_cstl_population.html (February 20, 2006).

66. Sample, Ian, "Warming Hits 'Tipping Point,'" *Guardian* (August 11, 2005). Siberia is not alone in this. According to a 2004 report prepared for the Pew Center on Global Climate Change, "The Alaskan tundra has already experienced much

stronger warming trends than the rest of the United States. . . . During 1983–1987 and again in 1990, the tundra across the North Slope of Alaska was acting as a source of CO_2 to the atmosphere, instead of the sink it had been." Parmesan, Camille, and Galbraith, Hector, "Observed Impacts of Global Climate Change in the U.S.," prepared for the Pew Center on Global Climate Change, November 2004, p.33.

67. As quoted by Renner, Michael, in "Security Redefined," The Worldwatch Institute, *State of the World 2005* (New York, Norton, 2005), p.8.

68. Conca, Ken, Alexander Carius, and Geoffrey Dabelko, "Building Peace Through Environmental Cooperation," in The Worldwatch Institute, *State of the World 2005* (New York, Norton, 2005), p.149.

69. Dumas, Lloyd J., *The Conservation Response: Strategies for the Design and Operation of Energy-Using Systems* (Lexington, MA: D.C. Heath, 1976).

70. Innovest Strategic Value Advisors, "Climate Change and the Financial Services Industry: Module 1-Threats and Opportunities," prepared for the UN Environmental Program Finance Initiatives Climate Change Working Group, July 2002, pp.5 and 24.

71. Kammen, Daniel M., Kamal Kapadia, and Matthias Fripp, "Putting Renewables to Work: How Many Jobs Can the Clean Energy Industry Generate?," *Report of the Renewable and Appropriate Energy Laboratory*, University of California, Berkeley, April 13, 2004, pp.2–3.

72. Ibid., pp.12–13.

73. Hopkins, Barry, "Renewable Energy and State Economies," The Council of State Governments, Lexington, KY, May 2003, p.29.

74. Ibid., p.26.

75. Hopkins, "Renewable Energy and State Economies," 22–23. Since a typical American home uses an average about 25kWh per day, a living room–sized solar collector operating at 30 percent efficiency should be able to provide enough power.

76. "Cap and trade" systems are a way for governments to create both positive and negatives incentives for pollution reduction without micromanaging industry. For more details, see Burtraw, Dallas, "Cap and Trade Policy to Achieve Greenhouse Gas Emission Targets," in *Growing the Economy Through Global Warming Solutions,* ed. Lloyd J. Dumas, Civil Society Institute paper series, www.civilsocietyinstitute.org/reports/GEGWS-BurtrawChapter.pdf (accessed July 5, 2008).

77. Many have argued that a large endowment of valuable, easily extractable natural resources can be a curse as much as a blessing. The "resource curse" not only diverts attention from more diversified and sustainable development, but also gives rise to violent struggles for control of these "lootable" resources that are both economically damaging and politically destabilizing.

78. Nuclear plants are a class of "dangerous technologies," technologies that are subject to producing major disaster, by intention or accident, as the result of our unavoidable fallibility as human beings. See Dumas, Lloyd J., *The Technology*

Trap: Where Human Error and Malevolence Meet Powerful Technologies (Santa Barbara, CA: Praeger/ABC-CLIO, 2010).

79. For the most part, nanotechnology today uses atoms as building blocks to create new materials in the laboratory with very interesting and potentially useful characteristics. If and when it progresses to using subatomic particles like neutrons, protons, and electrons as its building blocks, it will technically allow any element to be created from any other element. If that can ultimately be done at a low enough cost, it will fundamentally alter the relationship between humans and the materials they use. Any material will become the raw material for manufacturing any other material.

80. These totals, in constant 2005 U.S. dollars, are calculated from data published online by the Stockholm International Peace Research Institute (SIPRI) in the SIPRI Military Expenditure Database, www.sipri.org/contents/milap/milex/mex_wnr_table.html (July 17, 2007).

81. Bilmes, Linda, and Stiglitz, Joseph, "The Economic Costs of the Iraq War: An Appraisal Three Years After the Beginning of the Conflict" (Working Paper 12054, National Bureau of Economic Research, Cambridge, MA).

82. Calculated from data in the SIPRI Military Expenditure Database, www.sipri.org/contents/milap/milex/mex_wnr_table.html (July 17, 2007), and in the U.S. Census Bureau, U.S. Department of Commerce, *Statistical Abstract of the United States, 2006* (Washington, DC: U.S. Government Printing Office), p.522, Table 757. This is a comparison in roughly equivalent constant dollars. There is nothing particularly unusual about the fifteen years chosen, or about the year 2003.

83. Calculated from data in the SIPRI Military Expenditure Database, www.sipri.org/contents/milap/milex/mex_wnr_table.html (July 17, 2007), and in the U.S. Census Bureau, U.S. Department of Commerce, *Statistical Abstract of the United States, 2006* (Washington, DC: U.S. Government Printing Office), p.527, Table 767. This is a year-by-year current dollar comparison. There is nothing particularly unusual about those five years chosen, which include three years of military budgets before the terrorist attacks of September 11, 2001, and two years after.

84. Oak Ridge, Argonne, Pacific North West, Lawrence Berkeley, National Renewable Energy Labs, "Scenarios for a Clean Energy Future" (Washington, DC: U.S. Department of Energy, 2001).

85. Innovest Strategic Value Advisors, "Climate Change and the Financial Services Industry," 14.

86. General Smedley Butler, former commandant of the U.S. Marine Corps, felt very strongly about using coercive military threats, and military forces paid for by taxpayers, in the service of private business. In 1935 he said, "I spent 33 years in the Marines, most of my time being a high class muscle man for big business. . . . I was a racketeer for capitalism . . . I helped in the rape of half a dozen Central American republics for the benefit of Wall Street. In China in 1927 I helped to see to it that Standard Oil went on its way unmolested. . . . I had a swell racket. I was rewarded with honors, medals and promotions. I might

have given Al Capone a few hints. The best he could do was to operate a racket in three city districts. The Marines operated on three continents."

87. Smith, Adam, *The Wealth of Nations* (New York: Modern Library, Random House, 1937), pp.581–582.

88. Kahneman, Daniel, and Tversky, Amos, "Prospect Theory: An Analysis of Decision Under Risk," *Econometrica* (March 1979).

89. Jervis, Robert, "The Implications of Prospect Theory for Human Nature and Values," *Political Psychology* (25, no. 2, 2004). Although it has considerable empirical support, prospect theory is not universally accepted. For a critique, buttressed by contrary experimental evidence, see Levy, Moshe, and Levy, Haim, "Prospect Theory: Much Ado About Nothing?," *Management Science* (October 2002).

Chapter 4. Making It Happen

1. In "The Problem of Social Cost" (*Journal of Law and Economics* [3: October 1960]: pp.1–44), economist Ronald Coase set forth the proposition that markets will produce a socially efficient allocation of resources, *even in the presence of externalities,* as long as property rights are well defined and no significant transactions costs exist. In practice, the assumption of no significant transactions costs is more restrictive than it seems. Also, it matters a great deal from the point of view of social optimality (equity) who has the relevant property rights, even in theory. For a simple example, see Harris, Jonathan M., *Environmental and Natural Resource Economics* (Boston: Houghton-Mifflin, 2006), pp.51–54.

2. This is an example of the so-called principal-agent problem.

3. These results include socially optimal (efficient) allocation of resources, production of goods and services at the lowest possible unit cost, and sale of products at the lowest price consistent with the viability of producers. This theoretically pure case of competition is based on extremely unrealistic assumptions, including: perfect information; costless entry and exit; identical products, identical cost structures; and the inability of any producer to individually influence the price.

4. Galbraith, John Kenneth, *American Capitalism: The Concept of Countervailing Power* (Boston: Houghton-Mifflin, 1952), p.118.

5. Ibid., p.119.

6. Since more competitive markets are theoretically more efficient, in allocative as well as operational terms, and since fair trade practice laws generally promote competition, it can reasonably be argued that such laws increase efficiency. Since fair labor practice laws result in workers being paid a wage that more closely reflects their productivity than the artificially undervalued wage they might otherwise receive, it could also be argued that these laws also increase allocative efficiency. Further, to the extent that fair labor practices result in better-motivated workers, productivity is likely to be higher, increasing efficiency for this reason as well.

7. One case in point was the 1984 amendment of the U.S. "General System of Preferences." The System exempted some goods produced in less developed countries from U.S. tariffs. The amendment allowed these goods to be denied duty-free status if their country of origin were found to be violating internationally recognized worker rights. Broad, Robin, and Cavanaugh, John, "The Corporate Accountability Movement: Lessons and Opportunities" (prepared for the World Wildlife Fund, 1998), p.27. (see www.umass.edu/peri/sweat.html).

8. This case is admittedly a bit more ambiguous, since blocking the acquisition by CNOOC involved disadvantaging the shareholders of one large American firm (Unocal) while benefiting the shareholders of another large American firm (Chevron).

9. Weisman, Jonathan, "Chinese Firm Gives U.S. Details of Bid to Buy Unocal," *Washington Post* (July 2, 2005); and Kahn, Joseph, "China's Costly Quest for Energy Control," *New York Times* (June 27, 2005).

10. Nafziger, E. Wayne, *Economic Development,* 4th ed. (New York: Cambridge University Press, 2006), p.642.

11. "Colonial mentality" is the ingrained idea that everything that comes from the "mother country" is somehow better than what is produced locally, whether it be goods, services (most especially including education), or ideas, cultural and otherwise.

12. Bureau of African Affairs, U.S. Department of State, "Fact Sheet: Economic Community of West African States (ECOWAS)," Washington, DC, November 22, 2002, paragraph 2 (www.state.gov/p/af/rls/fs/15437.htm [March 21, 2006]).

13. Association of Southeast Asian Nations, "Overview," www.aseansec.org/64.htm (March 21, 2006).

14. European Union, "The EU's Relations with Mercosur," Section 1, "Mercosur," paragraphs 2–3, europa.eu.int/comm/external_relations/mercosur/intro/ (March 21, 2006).

15. Nafziger, *Economic Development,* 642–643.

16. Todaro, Michael P., *Economic Development in the Third World* (New York: Longman, 1985), p.426.

17. Todaro, Michael P., *Economic Development,* 6th ed. (New York: Addison-Wesley, 1997), p.490.

18. Friedman, Monroe, *Consumer Boycotts: Effecting Change Through the Marketplace and the Media* (New York: Routledge, 1999), p.173.

19. Broad and Cavanaugh, "The Corporate Accountability Movement," 14. In addition to its resolutions aimed at educating other stockholders and applying pressure to the companies targeted, ICCR has also developed a wide-ranging set of "Principles for Global Corporate Responsibility" that underlie what it considers to be socially responsible corporate behavior. See Mansley, Mark, "Private Financial Actors and Corporate Responsibility in Conflict Zones," in *Profiting from Peace: Managing the Resource Dimensions of Civil War,* ed. Karen Ballentine and Heiko Nitzschke (Boulder, CO: Lynne Rienner, 2005), pp.214–217.

20. Mansley, "Private Financial Actors and Corporate Responsibility in Conflict Zones," 217–218. At 10.5 percent, the resolution did better than most. For the text of the shareholder resolution, see www.pirc.co.uk/shell4.htm.

21. Ballentine, Karen, "Peace Before Profit: The Challenges of Governance," in *Profiting from Peace: Managing the Resource Dimensions of Civil War*, ed. Karen Ballentine and Heiko Nitzschke (Boulder, CO: Lynne Rienner, 2005), p.473.

22. Strom, Stephanie, "Make Money, Save the World," *New York Times* (May 6, 2007). Goldman Sachs has produced reports of this sort on a wide range of industries, including the media, mining, steel, and food and beverage industries.

23. Sparkes, Russell, *Socially Responsible Investment: A Global Revolution* (London: John Wiley, 2002), p.389.

24. Social Investment Forum (SIF), *Report on Socially Responsible Investing Trends in the United States* (Washington, DC: SIF, December 2003), p.i. See www.socialin vest.org/areas/research/trends/sri_trends_report_2003.pdf, as cited in Mansley, "Private Financial Actors and Corporate Responsibility in Conflict Zones," 211.

25. Mansley, "Private Financial Actors and Corporate Responsibility in Conflict Zones," 211.

26. There have also been attempts to organize campaigns to reward companies whose behavior has been exemplary by encouraging consumers to preferentially buy their products. In markets dominated by a relatively few firms, such successful consumer "buycotts" are more likely to be noticed and to positively influence the behavior of other firms in the industry.

27. Jackson, Janice E., "Crisis Management Lessons: When Push Shoved Nike— Boycott of Nike by People United to Serve Humanity," *Business Horizons* (January– February 1993).

28. Mueller, William, "Who's Afraid of Food?" *American Demographics* (September 1990): p.40, as cited in Jackson, "Crisis Management Lessons."

29. Connor, Tim, "Nike's Labor Practices in the Three Years Since CEO Phil Knight's Speech to the National Press Club," *Global Exchange* (May 2001), published online at www.globalexchange.org/campaigns/sweatshops/nike/stillwaiti.

30. Ibid. Some of Nike's critics remained unconvinced that it had fulfilled the commitments made in Knight's speech. A variety of organizations continued to call for consumer action against the company.

31. Ballentine, "Peace Before Profit," 63. For more details on the Kimberly Process see Smillie, Ian, "What Lessons from the Kimberly Process Certification Scheme?," in ibid., pp.47–68.

32. Martin, Andrew, "Burger King Shifts Policy on Animals," *New York Times* (March 28, 2007).

33. Barbaro, Michael, "Home Depot to Display an Environmental Label," *New York Times* (April 17, 2007).

34. Lev, Baruch, Christine Petrovits, and Suresh Radhakrishnan, "Is Doing Good Good for You? Yes, Charitable Contributions Enhance Revenue Growth," unpublished manuscript, July 2006.

35. Strom, Stephanie, "Make Money, Save the World," *New York Times* (May 6, 2007).

36. Ibid.

37. See, for example, "Broken Promises" (Chapter 2), in Stiglitz, Joseph E., *Globalization and Its Discontents* (New York: Norton, 2002).

38. Indirect purchasers of critical goods are those who buy goods for which the critical goods were inputs, such as cars made of steel that is subject to tariffs.

39. Panel on the Government Role in Civilian Technology, Committee on Science, Engineering and Public Policy, National Academy of Sciences, National Academy of Engineering, and Institute of Medicine, *The Government Role in Civilian Technology: Building a New Alliance* (Washington, DC: National Academy Press, 1992), p.109.

40. Alic, John A., David C. Mowery, and Edward S. Rubin, "U.S. Technology and Innovation Policies: Lessons for Climate Change," Pew Center on Global Climate Change, www.pewclimate.org/docUploads/ (January 17, 2006), p.1.

41. Panel on the Government Role in Civilian Technology, *The Government Role in Civilian Technology*, 54–55. While military procurement provided an important early market for semiconductors and computers, the explosion in semiconductor and computer technologies that has occurred in recent decades has been driven by the demands and requirements of the civilian commercial market, not by military requirements, which have a very different character.

42. According to the U.S. Department of Energy, 54 percent of the nation's oil supplies came from foreign sources in 2003, a much higher level than the 34 percent dependence prior to the OPEC oil embargo that shook the U.S. in 1973. U.S. Department of Energy, "Renewable Energy: An Overview," www.eere.energy.gov/erec/factsheets/renew_energy.html (March 28, 2003).

43. In any case, a military blockade of all critical goods shipments is an extreme action that amounts to laying siege to a whole nation. It is an act of war.

44. From the 1970s to the beginning of the twenty-first century, empirical studies have shown that there is at best a weak relationship between foreign aid and economic development in less developed countries. See, for example, Papankek, Gustav, "The Effect of Aid and Other Resource Transfer on Savings and Growth in LDCs," *Economic Journal* (September 1972); Dacy, Douglas, "Foreign Aid, Government Consumption, Savings and Growth in LDCs," *Economic Journal* (September 1975); Gyimah-Brempong, Kwabena, "Aid and Economic Growth in LDCs: Evidence from Sub-Saharan Africa," *Review of Black Political Economy* (Winter 1992); Boone, P., "Politics and the Effectiveness of Foreign Aid," *European Economic Review* (40: 1996); Graham, Carol, and O'Hanlon, Michael, "Making Foreign Aid Work," *Foreign Affairs* (76, no 4: 1997); Burnside, Craig, and Dollar, David, "Aid, the Incentive Regime and Poverty Reduction" (Working Paper #1937, World Bank Policy Research, April 1998), and "Aid, Policies and Growth," *American Economic Review* (90, no. 4: 2000); Everhart, S., and McNab, R., "Rethinking International Aid," *Business and Economic Review* (April–June,

2003); Burnside, Craig, and Dollar, David, "Aid, Policies and Growth: Revisiting the Evidence" (Working Paper #3251, World Bank Policy Research, March 2004).

45. Khakoo, Farahnaaz H., "Development in Sub-Saharan Africa: Examining the Effects of Disaggregated Official Development Assistance" (Ph.D. diss., School of Social Sciences, University of Texas at Dallas, June 2006), Chapter 1, p.1.

46. Ibid., pp.93 and 120.

47. Shirley, Mary, "Can Aid Reform Institutions?" (working paper, Stanford Center for Institutional Development, 2004).

48. Everhart and McNab, "Rethinking International Aid," 15.

49. Khakoo, *Development in Sub-Saharan Africa*, 42, citing Azam, J., S. Devarajan, and S. O'Connell, "Aid Dependence Reconsidered" (Working Paper 189, Center for the Study of African Economies, July 1999).

50. The problem of creating incentive and accountability mechanisms to address the inappropriate and sometimes unethical behavior of international development consultants is discussed in detail in Dumas, Lloyd J., Janine R. Wedel, and Greg Callman, *Confronting Corruption, Building Accountability: Lessons from the World of International Development Advising* (New York: Palgrave Macmillan, 2010).

51. Dumas, Lloyd J., *The Overburdened Economy: Uncovering the Causes of Chronic Unemployment, Inflation and National Decline* (Berkeley, CA: University of California Press, 1986).

52. Every Country Assistance Strategy at the World Bank must now include a plan for how it will account for issues of corruption and governance.

53. Dumas, Wedel, and Callman, *Confronting Corruption, Building Accountability*.

54. Sivard, Ruth L., et al., "Military and Social Trends" table, *World Military and Social Expenditures*, various years from 1983 to 1996 of this no longer active annual publication (Washington, DC: World Priorities).

55. Stockholm International Peace Research Institute (SIPRI), www.sipri.org/contents/milap/milex/mex_database1.html (July 2006).

56. Leonard, David, and Straus, Scott, *Africa's Stalled Development* (Boulder, CO: Lynne Rienner, 2003).

57. For example, see Chenery, Hollis, and Strout, Alan, "Foreign Assistance and Economic Development," *American Economic Review* (56, no. 4: Part 1, 1966); Chenery, Hollis, and Eckstein, Peter, "Development Alternatives for Latin America: Key Problems of Economic Policy in Latin America," *Journal of Political Economy* (78, no. 4: Part 2, July–August 1970); Harrigan, J., and Mosely, P., "Evaluating the Impact of World Bank Structural Adjustment Lending: 1980–1987," *Journal of Development Studies* (27, no. 3: 1991); Gyimah-Brempong, Kwabena, "Aid and Economic Growth in LDCs: Evidence from Sub-Saharan Africa," *Review of Black Political Economy* (Winter 1992); Firbaugh, Glenn, and Beck, Frank, "Does Economic Growth Benefit the Masses? Growth, Dependence and Welfare in the Third World," *American Sociological Review* (59, no. 5: October

1994); and Khakoo, Farahnaaz H., "Development in Sub-Saharan Africa: Examining the Effects of Disaggregated Official Development Assistance" (Ph.D. diss., School of Social Sciences, University of Texas at Dallas, June 2006).

58. Wei, Wenhui, "China and India: Any Difference in Their FDI Performances?," *Journal of Asian Economics* 16 (2005): p.727.

59. Ibid.

60. All figures are in current dollars. World Bank, *World Development Indicators, 2003*, as cited in Wei, "China and India," 721.

61. Although real Gross Domestic Product (real GDP) is frequently used as *the* measure of development, it is actually only a partial and imperfect indicator. It is, for example, only one of three components of the UN Development Program's Human Development Index (HDI). Nevertheless, it does have some relevance.

62. Wei, "China and India," 720.

63. We will have to await the results of such studies to have a clearer picture of the relationship between FDI and real development, as opposed to simple growth.

64. Smith, Adam, *An Inquiry into the Nature and Causes of the Wealth of Nations*, Modern Library edition (New York: Random House, 1937), p.395 (originally published in 1776).

65. Schneider, S. H. and Goulder, L. H., "Achieving Low-Cost Emissions Targets," *Nature* (389: September 1997), as cited in Goulder, Lawrence H., "Induced Technological Change and Climate Policy," Pew Center on Global Climate Change, October 2004, p.28.

66. The "green revolution" agricultural technologies, for example, were supposed to put an end to world hunger. They did produce a remarkable increase in agricultural yields, but there are more chronically hungry people in the world today than there were when these technologies were first introduced.

67. Dumas, Lloyd J., *The Technology Trap: Where Human Error and Malevolence Meet Powerful Technologies* (Santa Barbara, CA: Praeger/ABC-CLIO, 2010), pp.4–7.

68. This is the essence of the idea of "bounded rationality."

69. Dumas, Lloyd J., *The Conservation Response: Strategies for the Design and Operation of Energy-Using Systems* (Lexington, MA: Lexington, 1976), pp.47 and 103–105.

70. Goulder, Lawrence H., "Induced Technological Change and Climate Policy," p.11. Goulder explicitly cites studies by Laitner et al., "Incorporating Behavioral, Social, and Organizational Phenomena in the Assessment of Climate Change Mitigation Options," in *Society, Behavior and Climate Change Mitigation*, ed. Jochem et al. (Dordrecht: Kluwer, 2000), and by DeCanio, S., "The Efficiency Paradox: Bureaucratic and Organizational Barriers to Profitable Energy-Saving Investments," *Energy Policy* (26: 1998).

71. Dumas, Lloyd J., "Energy Conservation: Some Technical and Economic Possibilities," in *The Conservation of Energy Resources*, vol. 324, ed. Evelyn A. Mauss,

Annals of the New York Academy of Sciences (New York: New York Academy of Sciences, 1979); and in Dumas, *The Conservation Response*.

72. Socolow, R. H., *Saving Energy in the Home: Princeton's Experiments at Twin Rivers* (Philadelphia: Ballinger, 1978).

73. This anecdote was told to me by a highly experienced industrial energy consultant, the engineer who performed an energy audit of the manufacturing plant in question. Dumas, "Energy Conservation: Some Technical and Economic Possibilities," p.19.

Chapter 5. Making It Stronger

1. North, Douglass, *Institutions, Institutional Change and Economic Performance* (Cambridge: Cambridge University Press, 1990), p.83.

2. Ibid., pp.3–4.

3. Ibid., pp.4–5.

4. For example, if a U.S. firm violates a contract with a French firm, the French firm can sue for breach of contract in the U.S. courts (or in the French courts), and enforce the contract or punish the violator without access to a strong international sovereign authority.

5. The threat of withdrawing cooperation works best when no single player is so dominant that it can consistently get away with breaking the rules.

6. Gourevitch, Peter A., "Robert O. Keohane: The Study of International Relations," in American Political Science Association, "Association News," *PS Online* (September 1999): p.4.

7. Ibid.

8. Hufbauer, Gary C., Jeffrey J. Schott, and Kimberly A. Elliott, *Economic Sanctions Reconsidered: History and Current Policy* (Washington, DC: Institute for International Economics, 1990).

9. The reasoning here is essentially the same as that in the discussion of the value of balanced decision-making processes included in the analysis of Principle I in Chapter 3.

10. That such pressure can sometimes be effective against governments is illustrated by the qualified success the nongovernmental organization Amnesty International has had in its "naming and shaming" campaigns calling for an end to torture and the release of specific political prisoners.

11. Some interesting and useful work on specialized and targeted sanctions has been done by Cortright and Lopez. See, for example, Cortright, David, and Lopez, George A., *Sanctions and the Search for Security: Challenges to UN Action* (Boulder, CO: Lynne Rienner, 2002).

12. web.worldbank.org/WBSITE/EXTERNAL/EXTABOUTUS/0 (accessed March 6, 2010).

13. Stiglitz, Joseph E., *Globalization and Its Discontents* (New York: Norton, 2002), p.44.

14. Cernea, Michael M., and McDowell, Christopher, "Introduction," in *Risk and Reconstruction: Experiences of Resettlers and Refugees*, ed. Michael M. Cernea and Christopher McDowell (Washington, DC: The World Bank, March 2000).

15. United Nations Development Programme (UNDP), *Human Development Report 2005: International Cooperation at a Crossroads; Aid Trade and Security in an Unequal World* (New York: Oxford University Press, 2005), p.279, Table 18.

16. The G8 countries are the U.S., Canada, Japan, U.K., Germany, France, Italy, and Russia.

17. This decision did not relieve them of the significant debt they owed to their other creditors.

18. United Nations Development Program (UNDP), *Human Development Report 2005*, p.283, Table 19.

19. Ibid.

20. Anderson, Sarah, "Debt Boomerang 2006: How Americans Would Benefit from Cancellation of Impoverished Country Debts" (unpublished draft, Institute for Policy Studies, Washington, DC, March 2006), citing data from World Bank, World Development Indicators online, 2005.

21. Jubilee Debt Campaign, Action Aid UK, and Christian Aid, "In the Balance" (June 2005), as cited in Anderson, "Debt Boomerang 2006," p.3. There are eight UN Millennium Development Goals, agreed to by more than one hundred nations in September 2000.

22. Anderson, "Debt Boomerang 2006," p.233 (Appendix 1: "Heavily Indebted Country Sample").

23. Corruption occurs whenever individuals use for their own personal gain—the authority, power, or information that was given to them only for the expressed purpose of furthering the interests of others. It is *not* exclusively a creature of the public sector, as has been clearly illustrated in recent years by the behavior of top corporate executives at companies like Enron and Worldcom (among others). They greatly enhanced their personal wealth while destroying the current incomes and future pensions of the employees they were supposed to lead, and the equity of the stockholders whose financial well-being they were duty-bound to protect.

24. For example, there are gift-giving practices common in some cultures that are seen as symbols of politeness, graciousness, and respect that would be seen as forms of bribery and buying favors in other cultures.

25. For example, see Knight, Malcolm, Norman Loayza, and Delano Villanueva, "The Peace Dividend: Military Spending Cuts and Economic Growth" (Working Paper 1577, World Bank, Policy Research Department and International Monetary Fund, February 1996); see also Fickling, David, "World Bank Condemns Defense Spending" *Guardian* (February 14, 2004).

26. Dye, L., "Japanese Hint at Establishment of Ambitious 'Global Marshall Plan,'" *Los Angeles Times* (July 12, 1986).

27. Cernea and McDowell, "Introduction" (see subsection "Reconstructing Reset-tlers and Refugees Livelihoods"), www.worldbank.org/ external/default/WDSContentServer/IW3P/IB/2000/05/25/000094946_0005040531052/Rendered/INDEX/multi_page.txt (September 23, 2006).

28. Ibid.

29. Smith, Steven C., *Case Studies in Economic Development*, 2d ed. (Reading, MA: Addison-Wesley, 1997), p.45.

30. Nafziger, E. Wayne, *Economic Development*, 4th ed. (New York: Cambridge University Press, 2006), p.204.

31. For a brief discussion of Grameen's modus operandi, see Smith, *Case Studies in Economic Development*, pp.45–62. For a more detailed discussion of the history and operation of the Bank, see Yunus, Muhammad (with Alan Jolis), *Banker to the Poor: Micro-Lending and the Battle Against World Poverty* (New York: Public Affairs, 1999).

32. For example, since the 1990s, an organization called the Plan Fund in the relatively affluent city of Dallas, Texas, has had some success with microlending as a means of helping economically disadvantaged people in the city address their own economic development problems.

33. Peet, Richard, *Unholy Trinity: The IMF, the World Bank and the WTO* (New York: Zed, 2003), p.135.

34. The Montreal Protocol to the Vienna Convention on Ozone Layer Depleting Substances (signed in 1987), along with the Convention on Biological Diversity and the UN Framework Convention on Climate Change (both of which ultimately emerged from the UN Conference on Environment and Development—the Rio "Earth Summit"—in 1992), are three of the most important treaties for which GEF provides support. It also supports a variety of regional and international water agreements, as well as the Stockholm Convention on Persistent Organic Pollutants (since 2001) and the UN Convention to Combat Desertification (since 2003).

35. Persistent organic pollutants are very stable chemical compounds that circulate around the world as they go through repeated cycles of evaporation and deposition that can carry them far from their original source. They concentrate in biological organisms that ingest or inhale them, and cause a variety of problems including cancers, immune system dysfunctions, and birth defects. See www.gefweb.org/Projects/focal_areas/focal_areas.html (October 10, 2006).

36. Ibid.

37. Young, Zoe, *A New Green Order? The World Bank and the Politics of the Global Environmental Facility* (London: Pluto, 2002), p.8, citing Banuri, T., and Spanger-Siegfried, E., *Strengthening Demand: A Framework for Sustainable Development*, RING of Sustainable Development Institutions (2000); and Imber, Mark F., "The United Nation's Role in Sustainable Development," in *Rio, Unravelling the Consequences*, ed. Caroline Thomas (London: Frank Cass, 1994).

38. At the Rio "Earth Summit" in 1992, the less developed countries argued for the creation of a more general purpose "Green Fund" that would support a broader range of projects related to improving their environmental conditions. See Soroos, Marvin S., "Global Institutions and the Environment: An Evolutionary Perspective," in *The Global Environment: Institutions, Law and Policy*, ed. Regina S. Axelrod, David L. Downie, and Norman Vig (Washington, DC: CQ Press, 2005), p.37.

39. According to SIPRI (the widely regarded Stockholm International Peace Research Institute), in 2008 worldwide military spending totaled $1.5 trillion, 41.5% ($607 billion) of which was spent by the United States alone; www.sipri.org/research/armaments/milex/resultoutput/trends (accessed March 6, 2010).

40. Mansfield, Edward D., and Milner, Helen V., "The Political Economy of Regionalism: An Overview," in *The Political Economy of Regionalism*, ed. Edward D. Mansfield and Helen V. Milner (New York: Columbia University Press, 1997), pp.1–2.

41. Dinan, Desmond, *Ever Closer Union: An Introduction to European Integration*, 3d ed. (Boulder, CO: Lynne Rienner, 2005), p.11, citing Fontaine, Pascal, *Europe, A Fresh Start: The Schuman Declaration, 1950–1990* (Luxembourg: Office for Official Publications of the European Communities, 1990), p.44.

42. Keohane, Robert, and Hoffman, Stanley, "Institutional Change in Europe in the 1980s," in *The New European Community*, ed. Robert Keohane and Stanley Hoffman (Boulder, CO: Westview, 1991), pp.10–13.

43. "Overviews of the European Union Activities: Regional Policy," europa.eu.int/pol/reg/print_overview_en.htm (accessed February 3, 2005).

44. Ibid.

45. See, for example, Mausel, Justin, "Economic Convergence in the European Union: Evaluating the Impact of EU Structural Funds, Institutional Quality and Governance," Ph.D. diss., University of Texas at Dallas, 2007.

46. Ibid.

47. Bergsten, C. Fred, "The Threat from the Third World," *Foreign Policy* (Summer 1973): pp.107–108.

48. See Maizels, Alfred, "A New International Strategy for Primary Commodities," in *A World Divided: The Less Developed Countries in the International Economy*, ed. G. K. Helleiner (London: Cambridge University Press, 1976).

49. Transfair USA, "Frequently Asked Questions, Basic and Advanced," www.transfairusa.org/content/resources/faq.php (accessed November 28, 2006).

50. Ibid.

51. Transfair USA, "Fair Trade Overview" and "Frequently Asked Questions, Basic," www.transfairusa.org/content/resources/faq.php (accessed November 28, 2006).

52. Transfair USA, "Frequently Asked Questions, Advanced," nos. 5 and 6, www.transfairusa.org/content/resources/faq.php (accessed November 28, 2006).

53. www.worldofgood.com/about/ (accessed January 18, 2007).

54. Ibid., no. 18. It is also worth mentioning that not all the coffee-based sustainability initiatives have met with joy by Third World coffee producers. See Neilson, Jeffrey, and Pritchard, Bill, "Green Coffee? The Contradictions of Global Sustainability Initiatives from an Indian Perspective" *Development Policy Review* (25, 3: 2007): pp.311–331.

55. Ul Haq, Mahbub, "Beyond the Slogan of South-South Cooperation," in *Dialogue for a New Order,* ed. Khadija Haq (New York: Pergamon, 1981), as cited in Meier, Gerald M., *Leading Issues in Economic Development,* 4th ed. (New York: Oxford University Press, 1984), p.561.

56. The main ideas contained in this paragraph were generated by Teresa Nelson, in conversation with the author.

57. See Yarbrough, Beth V., and Robert M., "Dispute Settlement in International Trade: Regionalism and Procedural Coordination," in *The Political Economy of Regionalism,* ed. Edward D. Mansfield and Helen Milner (New York: Columbia University Press, 1997), pp.139–148.

58. Caplan, Richard C., "Tracking Transnationals: United Nations Centre on Transnational Corporations," *Multinational Monitor* (July–August 1989): p.1, multinationalmonitor.org/hyper/issues/1989/07/caplan.html (accessed January 8, 2007).

59. The classic book approaching multinational corporations from this general perspective is Barnet, R. J., and Muller, R. E., *Global Reach: The Power of Multinational Corporations* (New York: Simon and Schuster, 1974).

60. Mansley, Mark, "Private Financial Actors and Corporate Responsibility in Conflict Zones" in *Profiting from Peace: Managing the Resource Dimensions of Civil War,* ed. Karen Ballentine and Heiko Nitzschke (Boulder, CO: Lynne Rienner, 2005), p.220.

61. Ibid., pp.227 and 212.

62. Lobe, Jim, "Church Groups Launch Global Corporate Code of Conduct," Inter Press Service, May 21, 2003, www.commondreams.org/headlines03/0521-01.htm (accessed January 8, 2007).

63. Sparkes, Russell, *Socially Responsible Investment: A Global Revolution* (London: John Wiley, 2002), p.389.

64. Mansley, "Private Financial Actors and Corporate Responsibility in Conflict Zones," 211.

65. Ibid., p.215, citing the text of the ICCR code, and Lobe, "Church Groups Launch Global Corporate Code of Conduct."

66. Ackerman, Frank, "The Unbearable Lightness of Regulatory Costs," *Fordham Urban Law Journal* (May 2006): pp.1076–1079.

67. Stockholm International Peace Research Institute (SIPRI), *SIPRI Yearbook 2006: Armaments, Disarmament and International Security* (summary version), p.15.

68. "The Uranium Trade: All Roads Lead to Khartoum's Black Market," *Africa Report* (January–February 1988): p.6.

69. Ibid.

70. Dumas, Lloyd J., *The Technology Trap: Where Human Error and Malevolence Meet Powerful Technologies* (Santa Barbara, CA: Praeger/ABC-CLIO, 2010). pp.92–96.

71. Broad, William J., and Sanger, David E., "Pakistani's Black Market May Sell Nuclear Secrets," *New York Times* (March 21, 2005).

72. Dumas, *The Technology Trap*, Chapter 2, "Dangerous Technologies and the Terrorist Threat."

73. Rizvi, Haider, "UN Passes Arms Trade Treaty over US Opposition," Inter Press Service (October 27, 2006), citing "independent experts who have worked closely with the United Nations," www.commondreams.org/headlines03/0521 -01.htm (accessed January 9, 2007).

74. Bar codes are in wide commercial use as product identifiers. Chemical taggants are tracers carrying identifying information as to product origins (among other things) that can be manufactured into chemicals such as explosives. RFIDs are radio frequency identification devices, built into or onto products or their packaging, which transmit product-identifying signals that can be read by appropriate electronic receivers.

75. Shah, Anup, "Arms Trade—A Major Cause of Suffering: A Code of Conduct for Arms Sales" (October 29, 2006), www.globalissues.org/Geopolitics/ArmsTrade/ CodeofConduct.asp (accessed January 9, 2007).

76. Ibid.

77. Rizvi, "UN Passes Arms Trade Treaty over US Opposition."

78. For example, Russett, Bruce, "Politics and Alternative Security: Toward a More Democratic, Therefore More Peaceful, World," in *Alternative Security: Living Without Nuclear Deterrence*, ed. Burns H. Weston (Boulder, CO: Westview, 1990). An interesting attack on the idea of democratic peace can be found in Henderson, Errol A., *Democracy and War: The End of an Illusion?* (Boulder, CO: Lynne Rienner, 2002).

79. McMillan, Susan M., "Interdependence and Conflict," *Mershon International Studies Review* (May 1997): pp.35–38.

80. The U.S. was able to help establish vibrant democracies in Japan and West Germany after their utter military defeat in the Second World War and subsequent occupation. Attempts by foreign armed forces to impose functional liberal democracy since then have been far less successful, as recent U.S. experience in Iraq has illustrated. At the same time, local populations imbued with the deep desire to play a larger role in political decision making in their own countries have been remarkably successful in overthrowing authoritarian governments and replacing them with democracies through nonviolent action in the Philippines, Poland, East Germany, Czech Republic, Slovakia, Hungary, and a number of other countries.

81. Huntington, Samuel P., *The Clash of Civilizations and the Remaking of World Order* (New York: Simon and Schuster, 1996).

82. Ullmann, John E., "The Reorganization of Hatred: Missing Out on Peace After the Cold War," (unpublished paper, prepared for the Conference on the Centennial of the Nobel Peace Prize, Hofstra University, Hempstead, NY, 2001), p.6.
83. Ibid., pp.6–7.
84. North, *Institutions, Institutional Change and Economic Performance*, 16.

Chapter 6. Does Globalization Contribute to Economic Peacekeeping?

1. For example, Robert Gilpin, "Considered in relation to the size of national economies and of the international economy, trade, investment and financial flows were greater in the late 1800s than they are at the end of the 1900s." Gilpin, Robert, *The Challenge of Global Capitalism: The World Economy in the 21st Century* (Princeton, NJ: Princeton University Press, 2000), pp.294–295.
2. Inevitable, that is, if we manage to avoid fighting an all-out war with the weapons of mass destruction that our technological prowess also provided—or in some other way doing intolerable damage to the natural environment on which our lives depend—and thus becoming the first species responsible for its own extinction.
3. Friedman, Thomas, *The World Is Flat: A Brief History of the Twenty-First Century* (New York: New York Times Books, 2004).
4. Kapstein, Ethan B., *Economic Justice in an Unfair World: Toward a Level Playing Field* (Princeton, NJ: Princeton University Press, 2006), p.16.
5. There may be economic limits to the economies of scale made possible by globalization, but there are even more important political, social and environmental limits. See Weber, Steven, Naazneen Barma, Matthew Kroenig, and Ely Ratner, "How Globalization Went Bad," *Foreign Policy* (January/February 2007). Woodin and Lucas focus on the environmental and social limits. See Woodin, Michael, and Lucas, Caroline, *Green Alternatives to Globalization: A Manifesto* (London: Pluto, 2004). Globalization without any limits is not necessarily economically efficient, politically viable, or socially and environmentally acceptable.
6. The combined sales of the two hundred largest corporations were $7.1 trillion, while the combined GDPs of the 182 nations remaining after eliminating the nine largest economies (U.S., Japan, Germany, France, Italy, U.K., Brazil, Canada, and China) were $6.9 trillion. Interestingly enough, at the same time, they directly employed less than 1 percent of the world's workforce. Anderson, Sarah, and Cavanagh, John, "Top 200: The Rise of Global Corporate Power," Corporate Watch, 2000, p.2, www.globalpolicy.org/socecon/tncs/top200.htm (February 5, 2007).
7. Being a neurosurgeon, a janitor, a machinist, a manager, or a teacher allows us to specialize and become better at performing a relatively narrow range of tasks, and then to use the money we are paid for doing that work to buy all the other goods and services we need (and can afford) that have been made by other

people who also specialize in a relatively narrow range of tasks. If each one of us had to teach ourselves, provide our own medical services, build our own houses, etc., we clearly would be worse off.

8. Changing the stock of large fixed capital (such as buildings and roads) is generally a slow process. But the stock of capital such as tools and small machines can be rapidly changed and much more easily moved. With the changes in international financial institutions and regulations, financial capital has become extremely fluid.

9. "Approximately 40% of all U.S. international trade is intra-firm trade, or international trade that occurs within the firm"; in Clausing, Kimberly, "Tax-Motivated Transfer Pricing and U.S. International Trade," *Journal of Public Economics* (87: 2003): p.2207. According to Stephen Kobrin, "While estimates are hard to come by, it appears that between 30 and 50 percent of world 'trade' is actually composed of intra-firm transfers between units of multinational firms" ("Technological Determinism, Globalization, and the Multinational Firm," Wharton School, University of Pennsylvania, 2003, p.15). The World Trade Organization's estimate for 1995 falls within that range: "About one third of the $6.1 trillion total for world trade in goods and services in 1995 was trade within companies" (See World Trade Organization, *Understanding the WTO*, 2005 edition, available online at www.wto.org, p.72).

10. Nye, Joseph S., "The Information Revolution and American Soft Power," *Asia-Pacific Review* (9, no. 1: 2002): p.63, citing Quinlan, Joseph, and Chandler, Marc, "The U.S. Trade Deficit: A Dangerous Illusion," *Foreign Affairs* (80, no.3: May/June 2001): pp.92 and 95.

11. One interesting historical critique can be found in Arthur MacEwan, *Neo-Liberalism or Democracy? Economic Strategy, Markets and Alternatives for the 21st Century* (London: Zed, 1999), ch.2; another is at the core of Chang, Ha-Joon, "Kicking Away the Ladder: The 'Real' History of Free Trade," *Foreign Policy in Focus* (Silver City, NM: Interhemispheric Resource Center, December 2003), available online at www.fpif.org). The discussion of the critical historical argument presented here draws heavily on these two sources.

12. Chang, "Kicking Away the Ladder," 2.

13. Ibid., pp.2 and 6.

14. Stiglitz, Joseph E., and Charlton, Andrew, *Fair Trade for All: How Trade Can Promote Development* (New York: Oxford University Press, 2005), p.23.

15. Chua, Amy, *World on Fire: How Exporting Free Market Democracy Breeds Ethnic Hatred and Global Instability* (New York: Anchor, 2004).

16. Ibid., pp.9–10.

17. Ibid., pp.5 and 11.

18. Kapstein, *Economic Justice in an Unfair World*, xii.

19. Carr, Nicholas, as quoted by Fort, Timothy L., and Schipani, Cindy A., *The Role of Business in Fostering Peaceful Societies* (New York: Cambridge University Press, 2004), p.73.

20. World Trade Organization, "Understanding the WTO: The Organization: Members and Observers," www.wto.org/english/thewto_e/whatis_e/tif_e/org6_e.htm (accessed March 12, 2010).

21. World Trade Organization, *Understanding the WTO* (Geneva: 2005 edition), p.10 (www.wto.org).

22. Ibid., pp.10–13.

23. In fact, in 1994 the U.S. enacted a law (the Uruguay Round Agreements Act) that legally binds the country's national, state, and local governments to the decisions made by the WTO dispute settlement panels, with the Congress officially denied the ability to do more than express its opinion on whatever enforcement actions the president chooses to take. Kirschner, Orin, "Triumph of Globalism: American Trade Politics," Political Science Quarterly (120, no. 3: 2005): pp.497–498.

24. World Trade Organization, *Understanding the WTO* (Geneva: 2005 edition), p.101 (www.wto.org).

25. Ibid., p.110.

26. Ibid., p.111.

27. Ibid., p.104.

28. Peet, Richard, et al., *Unholy Trinity: The IMF, World Bank and WTO* (London: Zed, 2003), pp.160 and 162.

29. Hanrahan, Charles E., and Schnepf, Randy, "WTO Doha Round: The Agricultural Negotiations," CRS Report for Congress (Washington, DC: Congressional Research Service, September 12, 2006), p.1.

30. It is important to note that WTO agreements do allow for "special and differential treatment" for developing and for least developed countries, though rather than giving them special benefits or privileges, many of these arrangements simply involve allowing them more time than developed countries are given to meet the conditions laid out in particular WTO agreements.

31. Wallach, Lori, and James, Deborah, "Why the Doha Round Talks Have Collapsed—and a Path Forward," Common Dreams News Center, www.commondreams.org, August 14, 2006, p.1.

32. Ibid., p.2.

33. World Trade Organization, *Understanding the WTO* (Geneva: 2005 edition), p.65 (www.wto.org).

34. Ibid., p.66.

35. Richard Peet, *Unholy Trinity*, 182.

36. Munck, Ronaldo, *Globalization and Social Exclusion: A Transformationalist Perspective* (Bloomfield, CT: Kumarian, 2005).

37. This, for example, is one of the central themes of journalist Thomas Friedman's best-selling if deeply flawed book, *The World Is Flat: A Brief History of the Twenty-First Century* (New York: New York Times Books, 2004).

38. Gartzke, Eric, and Li, Quan, "War, Peace and the Invisible Hand: Positive Political Externalities of Economic Globalization," *International Studies Quarterly* (47: 2003): p.569.

39. So is more than 90 percent of phone calls and Web traffic. See Ghemawat, Pankaj, "Why the World Isn't Flat," *Foreign Policy* (March/April 2007): pp.56–57.

40. Gartzke and Li, "War, Peace and the Invisible Hand," 578–579 (Tables 2 and 3).

41. Polachek, Solomon, Carlos Seigle, and Jun Xiang, "Globalization and International Conflict: Can FDI Increase Peace?" (Working Paper #2005-004, Rutgers University Newark, September 2005), p.1.

42. Ibid., Abstract, p.i. and p.18.

43. Data as of June 15, 2007, 2006 ASR data from UNHCR/Governments compiled by UNHCR and FICSS.

44. Smith, Adam, *An Inquiry into the Nature and Causes of the Wealth of Nations* (New York: Random House, Modern Library edition, 1937), Chapter X, Part II, pp.134–135 (originally published in 1776).

45. Ghemawat, "Why the World Isn't Flat," 59.

46. Cohen, Robin, and Kennedy, Paul, *Global Sociology* (London: Palgrave, 2000), as cited in Munck, *Globalization and Social Exclusion*, 107.

47. Munck, *Globalization and Social Exclusion*, 107.

48. DeParle, Jason, "A Global Trek to Poor Nations, from Poorer Ones," *New York Times* (December 27, 2007).

49. World Bank, *Global Economic Prospects: Economic Implications of Remittances and Migration* (Washington, DC: World Bank, 2006). Only some 8–24 percent of this total is sent home by poor-to-poor country migrants each year (DeParle, "A Global Trek to Poor Nations, from Poorer Ones").

50. Sassen, Saskia, *A Sociology of Globalization* (New York: Norton, 2007), pp.154–155.

51. Ibid., p.155.

52. Ibid., p.156.

53. International Labor Organization, "Conventions and Recommendations," www.ilo.org/public/english/standards/norm/introduction/what.htm (accessed March 12, 2007), pp.1–2. As of 2005, there were "over 1200 ratifications of these conventions, representing 86% of the possible number of ratifications."

54. World Trade Organization, *Understanding the WTO* (Geneva: 2005 edition), p.74 (www.wto.org).

55. See, for example, Diamond, Jared, *Collapse: How Societies Choose to Fail or Succeed* (New York: Penguin, 2004).

56. Over a fourteen-year period, they produced average to good yields of peaches, apricots, apples, cherries, and a variety of other crops in a desert in which annual rainfall was only one to seven inches. See Dumas, Lloyd J., *The Conservation Response: Strategies for the Design and Operations of Energy-Using Systems* (Lexington, MA: D.C. Heath, 1976), pp.247–248.

57. Ibid., pp.25–30.

58. According to noted anthropologist Richard Leakey, the !Kung of the Kalahari were an extremely peaceful people until they encountered and were conscripted

by the apartheid era South African military. See Leakey, Richard, *The Making of Mankind* (New York: E.P. Dutton, 1983).

59. Roosevelt, Franklin Delano, as quoted in Barry, Tom, et al., "A Global Good Neighbor Ethic for International Relations," *Special Report of the International Resource Center and Foreign Policy in Focus* (May 2005): p.26.

Chapter 7. The Economic Promise of Demilitarized Security

1. Stiglitz, Joseph E., and Linda J. Bilmes, *The Three Trillion Dollar War: The True Cost of the Iraq Conflict* (New York: W. W. Norton, 2008).

2. For a much more complete version of the argument elaborated in this chapter, see Dumas, Lloyd J., *The Overburdened Economy: Uncovering the Causes of Inflation, Employment and National Decline* (Berkeley, CA: University of California Press, 1986).

3. Economically noncontributive activities fall into two categories: those that produce outputs that help to satisfy noneconomic needs and wants (called "distractive activities") and those that are purely wasteful, redundant, and unnecessary (called "neutral activities"). Ibid., pp.52–70.

4. Smith, Adam, *An Inquiry into the Nature and Causes of the Wealth of Nations* (New York: Random House, Modern Library Giant edition, 1937), p.325.

5. Ibid.

6. See Weber, Max, *The Protestant Ethic and the Spirit of Capitalism* (New York: Scribner, 1958). This is Talcott Parson's translation of Weber's original essay, "Die protestantische Ethik und der Geist des Kapitalismos," the first version of which was published in 1904–1905.

7. Smith, *The Wealth of Nations*, 325.

8. A more detailed discussion of this issue can be found in Dumas, *The Overburdened Economy*, 213–217.

9. Ibid., pp.208–211.

10. Ramo, Simon, *America's Technology Slip* (New York: Wiley and Sons, 1980), p.251.

11. According to the U.S. Department of Labor, "hourly compensation costs to employers" for production workers in manufacturing (including fringe benefits) exceeded those in the U.S. in Belgium (by 31.8 percent), Sweden (by 25.1 percent), West Germany (by 22.6 percent), Netherlands (by 21.7 percent), Luxembourg (by 18.1 percent), Norway (by 12.9 percent), Switzerland (by 11.5 percent), and Denmark (by 4.4 percent). Office of Productivity and Technology, Bureau of Labor Statistics, U.S. Department of Labor, unpublished data cited in Melman, Seymour, *Profits Without Production* (New York: Alfred Knopf, 1983), p.309.

12. President's Commission on Industrial Competitiveness, *Global Competition: The New Reality* (Washington, D.C.: U.S. Government Printing Office, 1985), p.19.

13. U.S. House of Representatives, Subcommittee on Science, Research and Technology, Hearings on the "Role and Balance of Federal R&D Support" (June 18, 1987).

14. News Office, Massachusetts Institute of Technology, "President Emeritus Jerome Wiesner Is Dead at 79," web.mit.edu/newsoffice/1994/wiesner-obit-1026.html.

15. Eisenhower, Dwight D., "Farewell Radio and Television Address to the American People" (January 17, 1961), www.eisenhower.archives.gov/speeches/farewell_address.html.

16. Comparison of data contained in U.S. Census Bureau, Economics and Statistics Administration, U.S. Department of Commerce, *Statistical Abstract of the United States, 2007* (Washington, D.C.: U.S. Government Printing Office, 2006), Table 491, "National Defense Budget Authority and Outlays for Defense Functions: 1990–2006," p.328; and Table 658, "Gross Savings and Investment: 1990–2005," p.436.

17. Dumas, *The Overburdened Economy*, pp.217–221.

18. The book value of capital owned by the Department of Defense is taken from Department of Defense, *Real and Personal Property* (September 30, 1990). The book value of capital in U.S. manufacturing as a whole is taken from Bureau of Economic Analysis, U.S. Department of Commerce, *Survey of Current Business* (January 1992), p.113.

19. In the late 1970s, my colleague Seymour Melman and I met privately in New York with Boris Rabot, former secretary of the Social Science Division of the Soviet Academy of Sciences. Rabot had just left his post as a key adviser to Soviet Premier Leonid Brezhnev, defecting to the United States. He spent several hours with us, describing in great deal the extraordinary economic (and social and political) priority accorded to the military in the Soviet Union of that day.

20. The only apparent exception might be in cases where there is an ongoing major net inflow of fresh resources from outside the economy, as, for example, in the case of Israel's net in-migration and huge inflow of foreign aid. I say "apparent" because such inflows only cover over the underlying economic opportunity costs of the military burden; they do not eliminate them.

21. The fourteen categories of physical infrastructure that received a grade included: aviation, bridges, dams, drinking water, energy, hazardous waste, navigable waterways, public parks and recreation, rail, roads, schools, solid waste, transit, and wastewater. See American Society of Civil Engineers, *2005 Report Card for America's Infrastructure*, www.asce.org/reportcard/2005/index2005.cfm (accessed May 20, 2008).

22. "Raising the Grades—Small Steps for Big Improvements in America's Failing Infrastructure: Action Plan for the 110th Congress," in ibid., www.asce.org/reportcard/2005/actionplan07.cfm (accessed May 20, 2008). President Barack Obama emphasized infrastructure investment projects as a component of his

administration's stimulus package aimed at pulling the U.S. economy out of the seriously deepening recession from which it was suffering when he assumed office.

23. Stiglitz and Bilmes, *The Three Trillion Dollar War.*
24. For a much more detailed analysis of the climate change problem and effective policies for mitigating the global warming that drives it, see Dumas, Lloyd J., *Seeds of Opportunity: Climate Change Challenges and Solutions,* Civil Society Institute, www.civilsocietyinstitute.org/media/pdfs/041906%20Seeds%20of%20Oppty%20Dumas%20report%20FINAL.pdf (April 2006). See also the ten paper series, *Growing the Economy Through Global Warming Solutions,* Dumas, Lloyd J., ed., Civil Society Institute, www.civilsocietyinstitute.org/csiresearch.cfm (December 2007).
25. Kennedy, Paul, *The Rise and Fall of the Great Powers: Economic Change and Military Conflict from 1500 to 2000* (New York: Random House, 1987).

Chapter 8. Removing Barriers to Demilitarized Security

1. Boulding, Kenneth E., in Foreword to Dumas, L. J., ed., *The Political Economy of Arms Reduction: Reversing Economic Decay* (Boulder, CO: The American Association for the Advancement of Science and Westview Press, 1982), p.xiii.
2. Dumas, Lloyd J., "Payment Functions and the Productive Efficiency of Military Industrial Firms," *Journal of Economic Issues* (10, no. 2: June 1976): 454–473.
3. See Mehring, George, "Restructuring the Organization: The Importance of Strategic Learning in Conversion," in *The Socio-Economics of Conversion: from War to Peace,* ed. L. J. Dumas (Armonk, NY: M.E. Sharpe, 1995).
4. See, for example, Dumas, Lloyd J., *The Overburdened Economy: Uncovering the Causes of Unemployment, Inflation and National Decline* (Berkeley: University of California Press, 1986), pp.64–70.
5. One striking anecdotal example was the B-1 bomber plant in El Segundo, California, which, at the height of its operation, had 14,000 workers: 5,000 production workers; 5,000 engineers; and 4,000 managers. Very few if any civilian manufacturers, low tech or high tech, could survive supporting one engineer and close to one manager per production worker.
6. As a general rule of thumb, the retraining and reorientation to civilian work is unlikely to require less than six months or more than two years.
7. For a more detailed discussion of the nature of and strategies for conversion and conversion planning, see, for example, Dumas, Lloyd J., ed., *The Socio-Economics of Conversion from War to Peace* (Armonk, NY: M.E. Sharpe, 1995), and Dumas, Lloyd J., and Thee, Marek, eds., *Making Peace Possible: The Promise of Economic Conversion* (Oxford, U.K.: Pergamon, 1989).
8. Bay Area Rapid Transit District, "About BART/History and Facts/History," www.bart.gov/about/history/history_5.asp (accessed June 5, 2008).

9. Boeing, "History," www.boeing.com/history/ (accessed June 5, 2008).

10. Melman, Seymour, *Profits Without Production* (New York: Knopf, 1983), pp.253–259.

11. Vought Heritage, "Non-aircraft products, airtrans," www.voughtaircraft.com/heritage/products/html/airtrans.html (accessed June 5, 2008).

12. For analysis of the success/failure of some more recent military contractor efforts to move into civilian markets, see Bertelli, Dominick, "Military Contractor Conversion in the United States," in Dumas, ed., *The Socio-Economics of Conversion*, 67–98.

13. The psychological readjustment of returning soldiers, especially those who as active combatants or prisoners of war have suffered severe psychological and/or physical trauma, is an entirely different and much more difficult problem.

14. Prendergast, John, "Applying Concepts to Cases: Four African Case Studies," in Lederach, John Paul, *Building Peace: Sustainable Reconciliation in Divided Societies* (Washington, DC: U.S. Institute of Peace Press, 1997).

15. Kingma, Kees, "Post-war Demobilization and the Reintegration of Ex-Combatants into Civilian Life" (paper presented at USAID Conference, "Promoting Democracy, Human Rights and Reintegration in Post-conflict Societies," October 30–31, 1997).

16. Ball, Nicole, "Demobilizing and Reintegrating Soldiers: Lessons from Africa," in *Rebuilding Societies After Civil War*, ed. Krishna Kumar (Boulder, CO: Lynne Rienner, 1997), p.86.

17. Ibid.

18. In Uganda, for example, demobilizing soldiers and their dependents were briefed about legal issues, family planning, and AIDS prevention as well as about how to open bank accounts and start income generating activities. Their demobilization package also included payment of one year's school fees for their children. Kingma, "Post-war Demobilization and the Reintegration of Ex-Combatants."

19. The bill was introduced into the Senate as the Defense Economic Adjustment Act as a bipartisan measure by George McGovern (D-South Dakota) and Charles Matthias (R-Maryland) in 1977 and later into the House of Representatives by Congressman Ted Weiss (D-New York). Reintroduced in many subsequent years, the bill at its peak had ten cosponsoring senators and dozens of cosponsoring representatives. See "Model Specifications for a National Economic Adjustment Act," in Dumas, *The Overburdened Economy*, Appendix, 261–271.

Chapter 9. Extending Demilitarized Security

1. See, for example, Sharp, Gene, *Social Power and Political Freedom* (Boston: Porter Sargent, 1980); *Civilian-Based Defense* (Princeton, NJ: Princeton University Press, 1990); and *Waging Nonviolent Struggle: 20th Century Practice and 21st Century Potential* (Boston: Porter Sargent, 2005).

2. Easwaran, Eknath, *Gandhi the Man* (Berkeley, CA: Nilgiri, 1978), or Kripilani, Krishna, ed., *All Men Are Brothers: Life and Thoughts of Mahatma Gandhi as Told in His Own Words* (New York: Columbia University Press, 1972).

3. The sole exception was Romania, where the revolution that overthrew the government of brutal dictator Nicolae Ceausescu was short but bloody. It is interesting that Romania subsequently had a much harder time moving forward, economically and otherwise, than did the other nations of Eastern Europe.

4. See Kandelaki, Giorgi, "Georgia's Rose Revolution: A Participant's Perspective" (United States Institute of Peace, Special Report No. 167, July 2006); and BBC News, "Profile: Eduard Shevardnadze" (November 23, 2003), news.bbc.co.uk/1/hi/world/europe/3257047.stm (accessed August 16, 2008).

5. Karatnycky, Adrian, "Ukraine's Orange Revolution," *Foreign Affairs* (March/April 2005): p.1.

6. Ibid., p.5, and Quinn-Judge, Paul and Zarakhovich, Yuri, "The Orange Revolution," *Time* (November 28, 2004): p.3.

7. Karatnycky, "Ukraine's Orange Revolution," pp.6, 7, and 9.

8. Some twenty additional cases can be found in Sharp, *Waging Nonviolent Struggle*, 69–356.

9. Nathan, Andrew J., "The Tiananmen Papers" *Foreign Affairs* (January/February 2001): pp.1–2.

10. "Tiananmen Square Protest," *Microsoft Encarta Online Encyclopedia 2008*, encarta.msn.com (accessed August 19, 2008); "1989: Massacre in Tiananmen Square," BBC, *On This Day* (4 June 1989), news.bbc.co.uk/onthisday (accessed August 19, 2008). For a much more detailed account of this period and the events leading up to it, see Nathan, "The Tiananmen Papers."

11. Sharp, *Civilian-Based Defense*, p.6.

12. Ibid., p.7.

13. De la Boétie, Étienne, *Discours de la servitude volontaire (Discourse of Voluntary Servitude)*, as quoted in Sharp, *Civilian-Based Defense*, 23–24. For more on de la Boétie, see his *The Politics of Obedience: The Discourse of Voluntary Servitude* (written 1552–1553), trans. Harry Kurz, introduction by Murray N. Rothbard (New York: Free Life Editions, 1975).

14. Sharp, *Civilian-Based Defense*, p.26.

15. Milgram, Stanley, *Obedience to Authority* (New York: Harper and Row, 1974).

16. Ibid., p.118.

17. Sharp, *Civilian-Based Defense*, p.47.

18. Sharp, *Waging Nonviolent Struggle*, pp.49–65.

19. Sharp, *Civilian-Based Defense*, p.55.

20. Ibid., p.57.

21. Ibid., p.84.

22. Ibid., p.147.

23. They are likely to be more effective at dealing with escalating domestic rather than international conflicts, though they may also have some value in the international arena.
24. Sharp, *Civilian-Based Defense*, p.134.
25. Sharp, *Waging Nonviolent Struggle*, pp.4–5.

Chapter 10. Demilitarized Security, Development, and Terrorism

1. For more on these goals and the progress that has been made to date see United Nations Development Program, "Millennium Development Goals," www.undp.org/mdg/basics_ontrack.shtml (accessed September 19, 2008).
2. Cook, Joy, and McGowen, Max, "Millennium Development Goals: Who's Succeeding, Who's Lagging," *The Interdependent* (United Nations Association of the United States of America, Fall 2008): pp.20–21.
3. See Dumas, Lloyd J., *The Overburdened Economy: Uncovering the Causes of Chronic Unemployment, Inflation and National Decline* (Berkeley, CA: University of California Press, 1986); and "Finding the Future: The Role of Economic Conversion in Shaping the Twenty-First Century," in *The Socio-Economics of Conversion: From War to Peace*, ed. L. J. Dumas (London, U.K., and Armonk, NY: M. E. Sharpe, 1995).
4. Smith, Adam, *The Wealth of Nations* (New York: Random House, 1937), pp.581–582.
5. The two compelling public justifications used for the U.S.-led attack and occupation of Iraq in 2003 were that the government of Saddam Hussein: a) was directly aiding and abetting the activities of the international terrorist organization Al Qaeda; and b) possessed and stood ready to use significant arsenals of weapons of mass destruction. By early 2004, it had become clear, and was even admitted by the Bush administration, that neither of these allegations were true.
6. The communist government of war-torn Vietnam, having recently won the war to reunify their own country, did attack the Khmer Rouge in Cambodia and ultimately succeeded in deposing the government responsible for the killing fields in 1979.
7. Eisenhower, Dwight D., "Farewell Radio and Television Address to the American People," delivered from the President's Office, January 17, 1961, Section IV.
8. See, for example, the Civil Society Institute at www.civilsocietyinstitute.org.
9. It was the concern of James Madison and his colleagues Alexander Hamilton and John Jay about such possibilities that led to their belief that representative democracy was superior to direct democracy. Attacked by their critics as elitist, they believed that representative democracy, with checks and balances, would provide "filters" that would refine the will of the people to the general benefit of society. See especially Madison, James, *Federalist Paper #10*, and *Federalist Paper #51*, in Frederick Quinn, ed., *The Federalist Papers Reader* (Washington, DC: Seven Locks, 1993), pp.70–77 and 131–136.

10. Packard, Vance, *The Hidden Persuaders* (David McKay, 1957).

11. Eisenhower, "Farewell Radio and Television Address to the American People," Section IV.

12. Nelson, Teresa D., in conversation with the author. Some argue that if the majority is fully enfranchised but does not participate, it must either be because they are satisfied with the existing political outcomes (an economist's "revealed preference" argument) or they are apathetic and therefore can legitimately be seen as having forfeited their right to be represented. But neither of these explanations is necessarily true.

13. Zakaria, Fareed, "The Rise of Illiberal Democracy," *Foreign Affairs* (November/December 1997).

14. Packard, *The Hidden Persuaders*, 155.

15. Astroturf is the trademarked term for artificial grass often used in indoor sports stadiums. Its name derives from the Houston Astrodome, the world's first domed stadium, where it was first used because it proved so difficult for real grass to survive there. Texas senator Lloyd Bentsen is probably responsible for the term "astroturf NGOs." In commenting in the 1980s on this type of NGO, he said that he knew the difference between astroturf and real grass.

16. As quoted from *Campaigns and Elections* in Holmes, Paul, "Who's Poisoning the Grassroots?," *Reputation Management* (July/August 1998): p.1.

17. Holmes, "Who's Poisoning the Grassroots?," 2.

18. Ibid., pp.3, 9, and 10. See also Sanchez, Samantha, "How the West Is Won: Astroturf Lobbying and the 'Wise Use' Movement," *American Prospect* (no. 25, March/April 1996): pp.37–42 (epn.org/prospect/25/25sanc.html).

19. Obasanjo, Olusegun, "Africa in the Twenty-First Century," *Security Dialogue* (24, no. 2, June 1993): p.199. Obasanjo was president of Nigeria from 1976 to 1979, and then again from 1999 to 2007.

20. Friedman, Thomas, *The Lexus and the Olive Tree* (New York: Farrar, Strauss and Giroux, 1999); Krueger, Alan B., "Economic Scene," *New York Times*, December 13, 2001; Nobel laureate economist Kenneth Arrow also expressed a similar viewpoint in conversation with the author.

21. Sokolsky, Richard, and McMillan, Joseph, "Foreign Aid in Our Own Defense," *New York Times*, February 12, 2002.

Chapter 11. Bringing It All Together

Epigraph: Kaysen, Carl, "Is War Obsolete?, *International Security* (Spring 1990): p.63. Kaysen is professor of political economy at MIT.

1. See Hobbes, Thomas, *Leviathan: With Selected Variants from the Latin Edition of 1668*, ed. by Edwin Curley (Indianapolis, IN: Hackett, 1994); Jung, Carl G., *Psychology and Religion* (New Haven: Yale University Press, 1938); and Lorenz, Konrad, *On Aggression* (New York: Harvest, 1974).

2. Fromm, Erich, *The Anatomy of Human Destructiveness* (New York: Holt, Rinehart and Winston, 1973), p.366.

3. Richard Leakey made a particularly interesting version of this argument in "Survival of the Species," the last program in his public television series *The Making of Mankind* (British Broadcasting Corporation in association with Time-Life Films, 1983). For B. F. Skinner's approach to this issue see Skinner, B. F., *Beyond Freedom and Dignity* (New York: Knopf, 1971), and *Science and Human Behavior* (New York: Free Press, 1953).

INDEX

Ackerman, Frank, 195
active nonviolent resistance, 298–299
AFTA. *See* Asian Free Trade Area
"aid" or "trade," 126
Airtrans, 290
Alic, John A., 122
Altrushare Securities, 117
American Academy of Arts and Sciences, 69
American Society of Civil Engineers (ASCE), 272–273, 399n21
Amnesty International, 230, 387n10
And 1 shoe company, 117
Anderson, David, 74
anticorruption, 129, 137, 168, 355
antidumping. *See* fair trade practices
antitrust policy, 106, 120, 132, 212–214, 247, 338
apartheid system, 111–112, 231, 234, 397n58
ASCE. *See* American Society of Civil Engineers
ASEAN. *See* Association of Southeast Asian Nations
Asian Free Trade Area (AFTA), 110

Association of Southeast Asian Nations (ASEAN), 110
astroturf, 335, 403n15. *See also* grass roots
atomic bomb(ing), 17–18
Azar, Edward E., 29

balanced decision-making, 48–50, 93, 387n9; power, 51, 94, 96, 136–137, 219
Ball, Nicole, 294
Ballentine, Karen, 113
Barbieri, Katherine, 29
Bay Area Rapid Transit (BART), 290
Ben and Jerry's, 117
Bergsten, C. Fred, 184
Berlin Wall, 300
Big Grab, 135
Bilmes, Linda, 85, 252, 273
black box model, 133–134
Body Shop, 117
Boeing, 279, 290
Boulding, Kenneth, 38–39, 64, 332
boycott, 99, 124, 159, 162, 211, 299, 308; consumer, 113–116, 156, 211, 308, 354; financial, 156–157; partial, 162

brain drain, 264–266
Brown, George E., 278
Bumble Bee, 114
Burger King, 115
Bush administration, 9–10, 75, 201, 221, 331, 402n5
Butler, Smedly, 380n86
Buzan, Barry, 22

CACM. *See* Central American Common Market
cap-and-trade, 80
capital: diversion, 268–269; flows, 40, 126, 141, 233–237; fluid (fluidity), 394n8; mobile (mobility), 234, 316; physical (plant, facilities), 31, 87, 120, 126, 127, 157, 236, 247, 260, 261, 268–269, 279, 284–285, 322; stock, 26, 237. *See also* foreign direct investment (FDI)
capitalism, free market. *See* free market: capitalism
Carr, Nicholas, 222
Carroll, Eugene, 267
cartel(s), 104–105, 115, 334; primary product marketing, 182–185, 187, 204, 354
Central American Common Market (CACM), 109
Central Selling Agency, 184
Cernea, Michael M., 171
CESP. *See* United Nations: Council on Economic Sanctions and Peacekeeping
chalk theory, 38–39, 64
Charter of Principles for a Responsible Market Economy, 193
Chicken of the Sea, 114
China National Offshore Oil Corporation (CNOOC), 108, 382n8
Chirac, Jacques, 193
Chua, Amy, 219–220, 222
civil: conflict(s), 19, 32, 65, 70, 90, 91, 110, 115, 189, 198, 312, 351, 402n23;

disobedience, 299–303, 307–308; war, 21, 31–34, 65, 67, 88–91, 198, 201, 293. *See also* civilian-based defense
civilian-based defense, 304–320, 400n1
CNOOC. *See* China National Offshore Oil Corporation
code(s) of conduct, 153, 192, 194, 195, 198–199, 205
coercion. *See* economic: coercion
Cold War: and Gorbachev, 300; and Reagan, 266; and Melman, 296; arms race, 300; Berlin Wall, 300; Britain, 47; Buzan on, 22; China, 47; contingent food independence, 55; East Germans, 300; economic overburdening, 271; Eisenhower on, 331; France, 47; Huntington on, 202; Japan, 265; lay-offs, 268, 296; military-industrial complex, 331; military-to-civilian transition, 296; noncontributive military activity, 271; nonviolent resistance, 300; nuclear war, 18; nuclear weaponry, 5, 47; physical capital, 269; postwar LDC spending, 130; postwar weaponry spending, 85, 130, 196; President's Commission on Industrial Competitiveness, 266; proliferation of nuclear weapons, 18; Russia, 196, 265; the Soviet Union, 5, 47, 271, 296; spin-off, 265; Stockholm International Peace Research Institute (SIPRI), 130; Sweden, 55; Switzerland, 55; United States (U.S.), 196, 265, 269, 271, 331; West Germany, 265
collaboration: country context for, 133; donor-recipient, 128–129; expanding it, 169; and microlending, 173; as strategy for encouraging development, 355–357; value of, 135–137; *See also* global: Marshall Plan; World War II: Marshall Plan

Collier, Paul, 32, 34, 65, 67, 373n66
collusion and monopolization, 326
Common Market for Eastern and Southern African States (COMESA), 110
Community Economic Adjustment, 291–292
comparative advantage. *See* theory of comparative advantage
complex interdependence, 25
conditionalities, 120, 164, 168
conflict(s). *See* civil: conflict(s)
Congressional Research Service, 226
Conservation Response, The, 58
consumer boycott. *See* boycott
contingent independence, 54, 55–57, 59–62, 82–83
contributive activities, 255–259, 274, 322–324; and Costa Rica, 324; diversion from contributive economic activity, 268; technology, 263, 265–266, 269
conversion, 280, 283, 285, 288–297, 399n7, 400n12; after the Cold War, 268; after World War II, 279–280, 289, 292; capital equipment and facilities, 284; converting management, 282–283; economic transition problem, 272; external or internal, 285–287, 288, 289, 290, 291; gains from, 206, 251, 274; precedent for, 278; reconversion, 279, 280, 283, 289; technical and economic obstacles, 278. *See also* military-civilian transition
Copeland, Dale, 27, 31
corruption: anti-corruption, conditionality as part of Principle III, 355; concentration of wealth and power, 337; definition of, 388n23; economic power into political influence, 335; as a form of resource diversion 129, 137–138; Obasanjo on Africa, 336; as obstacle to sustainable (economic)

development 67–68, 321, 338; Shevardnadze, 301; student demonstrators in China, 302; World Bank (or IMF) conditionality, 168
cost-push inflation, 259, 260
costs and benefits, xi, 8–9, 178, 242; from balanced relationships, 102; benefit of private property, 48; CESP and norms of international behavior, 161; of civilian-based defense, 315–319; classic problem of negative externalities, 177–178; divergence from private costs and benefits, 147; economic cost, economic benefit, 257; economic viability, 67; external threat and military buildup, 14; IPCC on energy saving from GHG emissions reduction, 87; Kaysen on calculus of war, 26; of mass production or large scale projects, 169–172; military spending, benefit and economic sacrifice, 251–253; private, as part of private decision making process, 101, 147; Polachek on trading relationships and conflict, 29; "rules of the game" for globalization, 212–214; sensitivity of consumer-oriented firms, 115; social, from maximized benefits in private sector, 49, 100; tariffs vs. security in critical goods, 118–119; trade violations and WTO, 161; Uchitel on interdependence, 29
Council of State Governments, 79
counterterrorism, 338–344
countervailing power, 104–105; John Kenneth Galbraith's theory of, 182–183; strategy for implementing the Principles, 354
Country Assistance Strategy, 385n52
critical goods, 21, 52, 90, 102; compatibility between Principles I and II, 76; compromised independence, 101; cost effectiveness of, 84–88;

critical goods (*continued*)
  development and compatibility
  between Principles I and III, 81–83;
  and ecological stress, 83–84; government action for independence in
  critical goods, 354; independence in,
  94, 118–126, 232, 350, 354; National
  Defense Stockpile, 60; Principle II,
  52–61; stockpiling, 55, 57, 59, 82, 84,
  123–124, 355; strategic, 59, 101–102;
  Sweden, 56; U.S. inventory definition of materials for stockpiling, 124.
  See also stockpile/stockpiling;
  strategic goods

De Beers, 115; subsidiary of De Beers,
  the Central Selling Agency, 184
de la Boétie, Etienne, 305
de Soysa, Indra, 33, 65, 373n65
debt relief: civil society campaign for
  Millenium Development Goals, 166;
  Debt Initiative for Heavily Indebted
  Poor Countries, 166
democracy, representative, 199, 330,
  402n9
democratic peace argument, 25,
  64–65, 200–202. *See also* liberal
  theory
Deng Xiaopeng, 303
Deutsch, Karl, 27
disinvestment, 99, 111, 308, 354;
  campaign, 112–113, 234; against
  apartheid in South Africa, 112, 231
disobedience. *See* civil: disobedience;
  noncooperation: disobedience;
  nonviolent action
distancing, physical, 241–245
distractive activities, 397n3
distribution of power, 11, 21–22;
  demand-side economic power, 327;
  Edward Mansfield on, 27, 30, 373n57
diversification of foreign suppliers, 54,
  55, 56, 82, 124–126; raw materials
  independence, 59, 84; strategy to

reduce economic and ecological
  costs, 86–87
Doha Round, 226. *See* Fourth
  Ministerial Conference
domestic conflict. *See* civil: conflict
domestic subsidies. *See* subsidies:
  domestic
donor-recipient collaboration. *See*
  collaboration: donor-recipient
downsizing, 274, 283–285
Dubai Ports World (DPW), 108
dumping. *See* fair trade practice
dysfunctional democracy, 331–332

EC. *See* European Community
ecological stewardship, 204, 351–352
economic: coercion, 61, 304; critical
  goods, 61; equity, 111, 326–327, 336,
  375; Nye's economic power and
  coercion, 48
Economic Community of West African
  States (ECOWAS), 109–110
economic development, definition of,
  62
economic power, concentration of,
  325–327, 333–335
economic sanctions. *See* incentives
economically contributive. *See*
  contributive activities
economically distractive. *See* distractive activities
economically neutral. *See* neutral
  actives
economically noncontributive. *See*
  noncontributive activities
economies of scale, 125, 169, 189, 210;
  global scale, 211–213; globalization
  and multinational corporations,
  247, 393n5; government as seed
  markets, 356; "green purchasing"
  and the scale of operations, 143;
  and the Soviet era economy, 135
ECOWAS. *See* Economic Community
  of West African States

ECSC. *See* European Coal and Steel Community

EEC. *See* European Economic Community

Eisenhower, Dwight, 268, 328; on "military-industrial complex," 331

Elliott, Kimberly, 156–157

enclave economies, 130; and FDI, 355; and trade, 130

energy efficiency, 26, 57, 70, 81, 83, 119, 142–145, 147–149, 243–244, 356; security, 274; taxes, 147–148. *See also* renewable energy

Enron, 194, 258, 388n23

Equator Principles, 193

equity and efficiency, 326–327, 375n9; concentrations of power and, 332, 336

EU. *See* European Union

European Coal and Steel Community (ECSC), 50; formation of, 180, 375n22

European Community (EC), 180

European Economic Community (EEC), 50, 180

European Recovery Act, 270

European Union (EU), 23, 50–51, 190, 237, 246; and beef ban, 223; chemical safety and environmental regulations, 195; and code of conduct, 199; and Doha Round, 226; experience with economic peacekeeping, 349, 357; lessons from, 180–182

Everhart, S., 128

expected utility, 92

export subsidies. *See* subsidies: export

external conversion. *See* conversion: external

externalities, 80, 99, 381; and the environment, 101, 177; negative, 99, 101, 177; positive, 101; security, 119

fair labor practice, 105, 107, 354, 381n6

Fair Trade Certified, 185; farms, 186; Federation, 186–187; Standards, 185–186, 188; social premium, 186;

fair trade practices, 105, 107, 354, 381; NGO, 185–188, 204, 357

Fairtrade Labeling Organizations International (FLO), 186

false consciousness, 44–45

FDI. *See* foreign direct investment

Federal R&D Support, 267

Fischer, Dietrich, 56, 370n13

FLO. *See* Fairtrade Labeling Organizations International

for-benefit corporations, 116

foreign direct investment (FDI), 40, 139–141, 218, 235–236, 240, 247, 355, 386n63

fourth sector, 116

Fourth Ministerial Conference, at Doha, Qatar, 226. *See also* World Trade Organization: Ministerial Conference

free market: Adam Smith on capitalism, 326; capitalism, 94, 134, 326–327; Chua on democracy, 220; and democracies, 337; economic promise, 187; economics, 48; economy, 7, 107, 219; ideology, 214; keeping the game honest, 106; market failure, 99

free rider problem, 102–103

free trade zones, 109, 182

freezing assets, 156

Friedman, Thomas, 209, 338, 395n37

Fromm, Erich, 362

Fuller, Buckminster, 37

gains, economic, 296; from balanced relationships, 42; of expanding economic activity, 63; of globalization, 219; of a peacekeeping economy, 92; security gains, 102; of trade, 35, 90, 189, 355

Galbraith, John Kenneth, 104, 182

Galtung, Johan, 10

Gandhi, Mohandis Karamchand, 298–303, 362

Gartzke, Erik, 234, 235, 236
Gasiorowski, Mark, 29, 30, 372
GATT, 131, 156, 189, 222; GATT/WTO, 156, 229
GDP. *See* gross domestic product
GEF. *See* Global Environmental Facility
Ghemawat, 235, 237, 396n39
GI Bill of Rights, 292
Gilbert, Coen, 117
glasnost, 300
Global Environmental Facility (GEF), 175–180, 357, 389n34
Global: flow/mobility of capital, 233–237; flow/mobility of people/labor, 237–240; Marshall Plan, 169
GNP. *See* gross national product
Gorbachev, Mikhail, 272, 300
Goulder, Lawrence, 145–146, 386n70
Gourevitch, Peter, 23, 25
government-funded stockpiling, 124
Gowa, Joanne, 21–22
Grameen Bank, 172–173, 335, 343, 389n31
grass roots, 318; non-governmental organizations (NGOs), 174, 334, 335, 343
green purchasing program, 143
Greenpeace, 230
gross domestic product (GDP), 31, 61, 166, 253; in Collier's analysis, 373n66; and debt relief, 166; of economies compared to corporations, 393; gross sales of MNCs, 210; per capita in EU countries, 181; per capita in 1980, 140; as prominently used measure, 149, 386n61; shortcoming of, 63
gross national product (GNP), 63, 253; for assigning votes, 158; in happiness analysis, 375n15; Hufbauer, Schott, and Elliott's analysis, 157; as prominently used measure, 149
growth: qualitative 77, 79, 142, 148–150, 356; quantitative, 77, 79, 81, 142, 149, 150, 247, 356

G-6, 226
Guidelines for Multinational Enterprises, 192
guns: into butter, 252; vs. butter, 86, 252

Haq, Mahbub Ul. *See* Ul Haq, Mahbub
hard power, 47, 52
hazardous materials. *See* international trade in hazardous materials
Heavily Indebted Poor Countries (HIPCs), 166
Hermes Principles, 193
Herz, John, 20
Hewlett Packard, 266
HIPCs. *See* Heavily Indebted Poor Countries
Hiroshima, 17, 18
Holsti, Kal, 22
Home Depot, 115
Homer-Dixon, Thomas, 69, 70
homogeneous, 109
homogenization, 241–244
House of Representatives Subcommittee on Science Research and Technology, 267
Hu, Yaobang, 302
Hufbauer, Gary, 156–157
human capital: buildup of, as substrategy, 67; company exploitation of, 112, 192; investment in, 127, 133, 138–139, 292; pool of, after World War II, 128
human rights, 194, 198–199, 231; as counterweight to WTO influence, 230; and economic migrants, 240; and personal security, 13; political development, 62; strengthen WTO peacekeeping principles, 357
Human Rights Watch, 230
humanitarian aid, 127
Huntington, Samuel, 202, 203, 373n59
Hurricane Katrina, 74, 170
Hussein, Saddam, 201, 402n5

IBRD. *See* International Bank for Reconstruction and Development

ICCR. *See* Interfaith Center for Corporate Responsibility

illiberal democracy, 332, 334

ILO. *See* International Labor Organization

imbalanced decision-making, 158, 226–227, 334. *See also* balanced decision-making; unbalanced decision-making

IMF. *See* International Monetary Fund

import quotas, 225

incentives: economic, 6, 38, 61, 65, 126, 150, 157; establishment of a peace-keeping international economy, 89; international economic relation-ships, 35; negative, 38, 91–94, 143, 148, 356, 374; operational for cost control, 283; peacekeeping, 276, 319; profit-based, 118, 168; technology-based, 126. *See also* positive incentives; sanctions

individual security. *See* personal/individual security

inflation, cost-push, 259

Institute of Medicine, 122

Interfaith Center for Corporate Responsibility (ICCR), 112, 193, 382n19

intergovernmental agreements: cartel-style, 184; code of conduct, 192; coercive, 88. *See also* intergovern-mental bodies

intergovernmental bodies: activity, 151; institution, 101; international, 154; joint marketing agency, 184; organizations, 155, 157, 192, 229, 354; supranational, 154. *See also* United Nations; World Bank; World Trade Organization

intergovernmental institution, 101

intergovernmental organizations, 155, 192, 229, 354

Intergovernmental Panel on Climate Change (IPCC), 72–73, 74, 87

internal conversion. *See* conversion: internal

International Bank for Reconstruction and Development (IBRD), 164

International Coffee Agreement, 184

International Labor Organization (ILO), 240

International Monetary Fund (IMF), 120, 164–166, 168, 224, 233. *See also* conditionalities

international trade: comparative advantage, 217; and development, 132; gains from, 20; intrafirm, 394n9; liberals and, 34; Mansfield on, 30; multinational organizations, 216–217, 394n9; organizations, 156, 180, 184–185, 189; Polachek, Seiglie, and Xiang study, 236; regulation of, 205; and relationships, 43, 107, 184; Ricardo on, 217; rules and WTO, 229, 232, 357; and war, 25, 30. *See also* GATT/WTO; United Nations

international trade in hazardous materials, 195–199, 205, 358, 398n21

interstate war, 64, 68, 70, 88, 90

investment: balanced international, 96; business, 181; capital, 269, 273, 323; contributive, 256–257; domes-tic, 64; financial, 247; fixed, 235–236; government role in, 122–123, 143; in education, 132–133, 139, 323, 355; in health, 133, 355; in human capital, 127, 133, 138–139, 292; in infrastructure, 54, 133, 189, 247, 323, 398; in nutrition, 133; in physical facilities and equipment, 31, 87, 236, 247, 269; in public works, 133; in social capital, 355; of Fair Trade social premiums in development, 186; private sector, 133, 143; relation-ships, 94, 102; socially responsible, 113, 193. *See also* disinvestment;

investment (*continued*)
  foreign direct investment (FDI);
  Social Investment Forum
IPCC. *See* Intergovernmental Panel on
  Climate Change
Irish Republican Army, 324, 341

James, Deborah, 227
Jervis, Robert, 92, 374

Kahneman, Daniel, 92
Kant, Immanuel, 25, 200
Kapstein, Ethan, 209, 220
Kaysen, Carl, 3, 26, 347
Kennedy, John F., 267, 368
Kennedy, Paul, 275
Keohane, Robert, 20, 23–25, 62, 153, 154
Khakoo, Farahnaaz, 127–128
Khan, A. Q., 197
Kimberly Process, 115, 383n31
King, Jr., Martin Luther, 152, 298–299
Knight, Phil, 114, 383n30
Krueger, Alan B., 338
!Kung, 244, 396n58
Kyoto accords, 75

labor mobility. *See* Global: flow/
  mobility of people/labor
League of Nations, 230
Leakey, Richard, 362, 396n58, 404n3
Leonard, David, 130
liberal theory, 20, 23–24; McMillan
  on, 25
liberals, 19, 23–28; compared to
  realists, 23; economic, 25

military non-contributive sectors or
  spending, 264, 269, 271, 272, 322
military security system, 85–86, 206,
  272, 274–275, 277, 295, 327, 338,
  359–360
military-civilian transition, 278,
  279–280, 284–285, 287–292, 297.
  See also conversion

military-industrial complex, 328, 331
military-oriented research and
  development (R&D), 264–270, 271
militia movement, 324
Millennium Development Goals, 166,
  321, 388n21, 402n1
MNCs. *See* multinational corporations
mobility of capital. *See* Global: flow/
  mobility of capital
mobility of labor. *See* Global: flow/
  mobility of people/labor
money value, 253, 255, 322
monopoly power, 55, 104, 183, 211–212,
  337
Montesquieu, Baron de, 25
Montgomery bus boycott, 299
Morgenthau, Hans, 20, 22
Mowery, David C., 122
multinational corporations (MNCs),
  391n59; bargaining power, 103; and
  boycotts, 114; conduct or rules of the
  game, 192, 205; control of trade, 132;
  in developing countries, 232, 236;
  economies of scale and competition,
  247; global competition, 209, 211,
  216; international migrant labor,
  238; manipulation of the political
  process, 334; regulation of, 358;
  security concerns, i.e., Dubai Ports
  World, 108; trade practices, 106,
  394n9

NAFTA. *See* North American Free
  Trade Agreement
Nagasaki, 17–18
Nakajima, Masaki, 169
National Academy of Engineering,
  122–123
National Defense Stockpile, 59–60
Nazi party, 314; regime or government
  of Germany, 8, 29, 305
Nelson, Teresa, 188, 331
neoliberals. *See* liberals
neorealists. *See* realists

Nestlé, 114
neutral activities, 397n3
New York, landmark, 3; World Trade Center, 4, 8
Nike, 114, 383n30
noncontributive activities, 255–263, 269, 271, 272, 322, 397n3; military, 259–264, 269–272, 322, 397n3;
noncooperation: disobedience, 305; economic, 308; nonviolent, 302–304, 308; political, 308; Sharp on, 304, 305; social, 308. *See* civilian-based defense; nonviolent action
non-critical goods, 61
nonrenewable resources: addiction to, 142; appetite for, 79, 96; competition for, 95; depletion/depleted, 69, 80, 149, 213; energy, 58, 82, 144, 147; mineral, 34; more efficient use of, 147–148; primary, 65; recycling of, 77; shift from reliance on, 142; subsoil, 33; taxing, 147–148
nonviolent action, 313, 315–318, 343, 359; availability of pathways, 65; Catholic Church, 318; civilian-based defense, 312, 317, 318; conflict resolution, 200; Czech Republic, 392n80; East Germany, 392n80; Hungary, 392n80; intervention, 308, 311; Lithuania, 317; movements, 314–315; noncooperation, 302–303, 308; Norway, 317; Philippines, 392n80; Poland, 318; protest and persuasion, 314; repression of, 311–312; sanctions as nonviolent coercive force, 312; as a security strategy, 316–317; Slovakia, 392n80; Sweden, 317; Switzerland, 317; tactics, 308–311, 315–316. *See* civil: disobedience
North, Douglass, 152, 153, 204, 368n6
North American Free Trade Agreement (NAFTA), 217–218
Nye, Joseph, 24–25, 47–48, 62

Obama, Barack, 289, 299, 398n22
Obasanjo, Olusegun, 336, 403n19
OECD. *See* Organization for Economic Cooperation and Development
oil embargo, 56, 57, 184, 384n42
Oneal, John, 30
OPEC. *See* Organization of Petroleum Exporting Countries
opportunity cost: CESP agreement, 161; contribution of economics, 9; idea of, 9; of military activity/spending, 86, 275, 322; of military burden, 398n20; of military-based security systems, 350; of noncontributive activity, 259
Orange Revolution, 301–302
Organization for Economic Cooperation and Development (OECD), 171, 192
Organization for Security and Cooperation in Europe (OSCE), 301
Organization of Petroleum Exporting Countries (OPEC), 57, 104–105, 184–185, 354, 384n42
Outreach International, 230
Oxfam, 230

P&O, 108
Packard, Vance, 331, 333
Papayoanu, Paul, 22
Peet, Richard, 225, 229
perestroika, 300
personal/individual security, 11, 12–13, 14, 368n10, 369n11
Polachek, Solomon, 29–30, 236, 372
political development, 62
political equity, 111, 336
political power, concentration of, 330–335
pollution-abating/abatement technologies, 8, 77, 79
positive incentives, 38, 61, 93, 94, 98, 350; conflict avoidance, 35, 94, 251, 298, 311, 318, 350; as core to

positive incentives (*continued*)
peacekeeping from economic
relationships, x, 35, 96, 163, 318, 350;
to generate cooperation, 37; as a
motivator of self-interest, 348–349;
and negative sanctions, 37, 91–94,
148, 163; for pollution control, 76,
148, 356, 379; and Principle I, 76;
prospect theory on, 374; for supplier
diversification, 125; technological
development, 143
positive peace, 10–11, 15; and development, 65
Powell, Colin, 299
Preferential Trade Area for Eastern and
Southern African States (PTA), 110
President's Commission on Industrial
Competitiveness, 266
primary product marketing cartels.
See cartels
Principles for Global Corporate
Responsibility, 193, 382n19
proliferation of nuclear weapons, 18;
See also technologies of mass
destruction
prospect theory, 92, 374n3, 381n89
PTA. *See* Preferential Trade Area for
Eastern and Southern African States
purchaser of first resort, 144

qualitative growth. *See* growth:
qualitative
quantitative growth. *See* growth:
quantitative

Rainforest Alliance, 186
Ramo, Simon, 266
REACH, 195
Reagan, Ronald, 266
realist(s), 19–21, 43; and alliances, 22;
compared to liberals, 23, 28; concept
of strategic goods, 52; critical goods,
52, 60, 118; disagreement with
liberals about causes of war 19–23,

39; distribution of power, 21, 27;
economic sanctions, 38; empirical
evidence, 28–31; extending the
theory, 34–36; from Rousseau, 21;
Gilpin on, 21; Gourevitch on, 23;
Gowa on, 21, 22; Herz, 20; Keohane
on 20, 23; Mansfield on, 27;
McMillan on, 28; Morgenthau on,
20, 22; on economic interdependence, 21, 22, 28, 52; Papayoanu
on, 22; Russett on, 28; security
dilemma, 20; trade balance or
imbalance, 40, 41, 372n44; Waltz
on, 20, 27–31, 34–35, 38–41, 43, 52,
60, 118, 372n44
realist theory, 19–20, 43
reconversion. *See* conversion
recycling, 60, 71, 77, 81, 83–84, 95,
147–148, 356
refugees, 32, 89; from conflict, 237;
development, 165, 170–171
regional trade, 189; agreements, 180,
354; arrangements, 180; organizations, 188–190, 354, 357
religious, fanaticism, 203–204;
fundamentalists, 203
renewable energy, 81–82, 83, 123;
benign, 142–144, 148, 274; cost-
effectiveness of, 377n35; efficiency of
resource use, 144; encouraging, 147;
impracticality of, 58–59; and job
creation, 78–79; Kammen, Kapadia,
and Fripp on, 78; national availability of, 59; reducing ecological stress,
77–79, 355–356; security from,
58–59; UNEP study, 78; U.S.
Department of Energy study
renewable resources, 33, 68–69, 78,
142–144, 213, 352
Renner, Michael, 66, 379n67
Report Card, 273, 398n21
representative democracy. *See* democracy, representative
resource curse, 379n77

Ricardo, David, 215, 217
Rice, Condoleeza, 299
Rockwell International, 266
Role and Balance of Federal R&D Support, 267, 398n13
Rose Revolution, 300
Rosecrance, Richard, 25, 31
Rousseau, Jean Jacques, 21. *See also* realists
Rubin, Edward S., 122
rules of the game. *See* code(s) of conduct
Russett, Bruce, 25, 28, 371n35, 392n78. *See also* democratic peace argument; realist theory

Saakashvili, Mikheil, 301–302
sanctions. *See* CESP; incentives; nonviolent action; positive incentives
SAPTA. *See* South Asia Association for Regional Cooperation Preferential Trading Arrangement
Sassen, Saskia, 239
scale of operations. *See* economies of scale
Schott, Jeffrey, 156–157
Schumacher, E. F., 245
Schuman, Robert, 180, 375n22
security, 11–15; dilemma, 20, 94; energy, 274; externality, 99, 119; negative, 99, 101, 119, 121; strategy, x, 5–11. *See also* personal security
Security Council. *See under* United Nations
seed, capital, 133; market, 122–123, 143–144, 356; money, 169
Seiglie, Carlos, 236, 271
self-interest, x, 7, 9, 48, 100, 312; in balanced relationships, 42–44, 94; concentrated economic power, 327; of economic theory, 99; for the general good, 8, 106, 326–327, 348, 368n9; glue in market system, 24, 155; individual, 5; Keohane on,

154–155; liberals on, 23, 25; realists on, 35; Smith on, 326; The Ultimatum Game, 41–42; toward a peacekeeping economy, 100, 152–154, 182, 318
Senate Armed Services Committee, 278
shareholder activism, 113
Sharp, Gene, 298, 304–305, 308–309, 311, 400n1, 401n8
Shevardnadze, Eduard, 300–301
Shirley, Mary, 128
shock therapy, 134
Singapore Ministerial Conference, 240. *See also* World Trade Organization: Ministerial Conference
SIPRI. *See* Stockholm International Peace Research Institute
Sitch, Stephen, 74
Skinner, B. F., 362, 404n3
Smith, Adam, 141, 389n31; on balanced relationships, 44; on business behavior, 326; on colonial relationships, 88; on colonialism and economic net drain, 325; on free flow of labor, 237; on globalization and economic well-being, 215; on motivations, 326; on unproductive activity, 257, 262
Smoot-Hawley Tariff, 217
social: costs and benefits, 115, 147, 165; equity, 106, 107, 111, 381n1
Social Investment Forum, 113
socially responsible: business practices, 117; corporate behavior, 113, 116, 382n19; investment, 113, 193; rules of the game, 192
soft power, 46–48
Sokolsky, Richard, 338
SONY Corporation, 267
South Asia Association for Regional Cooperation Preferential Trading Arrangement (SAPTA), 110
spin-off, 264–266

standard of living, 45, 149, 150;
definition of, 255; economically
contributive, 255, 264; energy use,
58; from contributive consumption,
257; from economic development,
62, 66–67; from foreign aid, 131;
from military expenditures, 86; in
America, 271; in the Soviet Union,
271–272; and global warming and
climate change, 274; material well-
being, 254; and the military,
270–271, 322, 360; and noncontributive activity, 263, 271; peace and
economic development, 66–67; and
performance of the economy, 63;
and personal security, 13; and quality
of life, 46; and technology, 72; and
tradeoff, 256; and wages and
salaries, 259–260, 264
Starbucks Coffee, 187–188
StarKist, 114
Stiglitz, Joseph, 85, 164, 168, 218, 252,
273, 367n1
Stockholm International Peace
Research Institute (SIPRI), 130,
380n80, 380n82, 380n83, 389n34,
390n39
stockpile/stockpiling: contingent
independence strategy, 57, 59–60,
82, 84; critical goods, 84, 123–124,
355; emergency oil, 57, 124;
government-funded, 124; high value
raw materiels, 124; key foods/critical
foods, 55; in Sweden, 56. See also
critical goods; strategic goods
Strategic and Critical Materials
Stockpiling Act, 59
strategic goods, key, 21. See also critical
goods; stockpile/stockpiling
Strauss, Scott, 130
structural funds, 181–182
structural violence, 10,
subsidies, 134, 285, 353; and comparative advantage, 232; for critical

goods, 354; domestic, 226, 354; to
domestic producers, 121; export, 223,
225–227, 231; for fossil fuels, 58;
government funded, 121–123, 164,
166, 227, 325, 354; in the form of
dumping, 106, 223; military-civilian
transition, 287, 288, 291; and NAFTA,
218; for nuclear power, 58; pollution
tax, 8; and the poor, 120; in primary
products, 232; production of critical
goods, 354; and quantitative growth,
150; recycling and renewables, 148,
356; short-term, 133; as an unfair
trade practice, 106, 223
supplier diversification. See diversification of foreign suppliers

Taliban, 8
technologies of mass destruction, x,
393n2; and Al Qaeda, 402n5; the
black market and terrorists, 198; for
enforcing trade sanctions, 162; and
error-prone humans, 375; and Iraq,
9, 367n5–368n5, 402; as source of
security, 46; trade in, 358
terrorism, 4, 74, 108, 203, 320–346;
development and, 226. See also
terrorist: attack; terrorists
terrorist, 320–346; activity, 316; attack,
3, 57, 84, 226, 358, 380n83; target of,
199; threat, 108; thwarting, 4;
weapons, 195
terrorists, 8, 18, 46, 197, and nuclear
weapons, 198, 310, 320–346, 361,
402n5
Texas Instruments, 266
theory of comparative advantage, 22,
39, 214–218, 288, 310
think simple, 146
Three Gorges Dam, 170
Tiananmen Square, 302–303
Todaro, Michael, 110
Tower, John, 278
Transfair USA, 185–187

transition (transitioning). *See* conversion

Tversky, Amos, 92

Tyco, 258

Uchitel, Anne, 29

Ul Haq, Mahbub, 188

Ullmann, John, 202, 203

Ulster Defense Forces, 324

Ultimatum Game, The, 41

unbalanced decision-making; process, 158. *See also* imbalanced decision-making

unemployment, 134, 216, 260, 278, 323, 359,

United Nations (UN), 9, 23, 155, 156–163, 392n73; Centre on Transnational Corporations, 190; Council on Economic Sanctions and Peacekeeping (CESP), 158–163, 192; Development Program (UNDP), 66, 175, 386n61, 402n1; Environment Program (UNEP), 78, 175; General Assembly, 199; Global Compact, 192; Monitoring Organization (UNMO), 160–161; Norms on the Responsibilities of Transnational Corporations and Other Business Enterprises with Regard to Human Rights, 192; Office of the UN High Commissioner for Refugees (UNHCR), 237, 396n43; Security Council, 157–159, 163, 356

Unocal, 108, 382n8

Uruguay Round, 227, 395n23

U.S. Department of Energy, 87, 376n31, 376n33, 384n42

U.S. National Academy of Sciences, 121–122, 123, 384n39

Vegetius, 4, 10

Vertol. *See* Boeing

Vietnam War, 277

Vought Corporation, 290

Wallach, Lori, 227

WalMart, 115

Waltz, Kenneth, 20–21, 370n16, 373n58

War. *See* civil: war; interstate war

wealth, concentration of. *See* economic power, concentration of

weapons of mass destruction. *See* technologies of mass destruction

Weber, Max, 258, 368n8, 397n6

White House Office of Management and Budget, 252

WHO. *See* World Health Organization

Wiesner, Jerome B., 267, 398n14

Wolf, Aaron, 70

World Bank: anticorruption mission, 129; Country Assistance Strategy, 385n52; debt relief, 165–169; and empirical studies, 384n44; estimate of FDI to China, India, 140; Global Environmental Facility, 175, 179–180, 232; global reach, 155–156; greater donor-recipient collaboration, 169; HIPCs, 166; inception, 156; and microlending, 172–173; and migration, 238; and military spending, 168; minimizing ecological stress, 356–357; scale of projects, 169–172; servicing sustainable development, 164–165, 204; social and environmental impact, 173–175; Stiglitz on, 168; versus the WTO, 224

world government, 24, 153, 192, 245–246

World Health Organization (WHO), 53, 73

World of Good, 187

World Trade Center, 4, 8

World Trade Organization (WTO), 188; and its agreements, 395n30; and CESP, 161; the decision process, 224–225; and development, 226–227; and the environment, 227–229; estimate of international trade, 394n9; General Council, 223; and

World Trade Organization (*continued*)
  globalization, 155, 222–233; Green
  Room meetings, 224; inception,
  155–156; Keohane and Martin on,
  23–24; Ministerial Conference, 223,
  226, 240; reducing trade barriers,
  107; reform of, 229–233; regional
  trade, 188–189; role in minimizing
  ecological stress, 356; rules of the
  game, 101, 107, 192, 247; sanctions,
  192; Secretariat, 224; as a strategy
  for implementing principles, 354,
  357–358; and trade, 189; Trade and
  Environment Committee, 227;
  Uruguay Round, 395n23
World War I (WWI), 4, 8, 17, 30–31,
  122, 156, 369n3, 373n58
World War II (WWII): Buzan on,
  22; civilian deaths, 17–18, 128; and
  development, 61, 323; Dwight
  Eisenhower on, 268; and economic
  overburdening, 217; end to US
  isolationism, 6, 31; and Germany, 8,
  31; the Holocaust, 8; and Japan, 31,
  138; liberal argument, 31; and the
  Marshall Plan, 127, 323; and the
  military, 205, 252, 268, 271, 279;
  military-to-civilian transition, 278,

280, 288–289, 358; noncontributive
  military activity, 271; nuclear, 18,
  279, 292; and post-war aid, 138; and
  post-war human capital, 127–128,
  138, 323; post-war tarriffs, 217; return
  to peacetime economy, 358; and
  Sub-Saharan Africa, 127–128; and
  the Soviet Union, 271; sustaining a
  military force, 271; treaties and
  institutions since, 37; twentieth-
  century war, 4; and Western Europe,
  127–128, 323. *See also* Cold War
World Wildlife Fund, 230, 382n7
Worldcom, 258, 388n23
WTO. *See* World Trade Organization

Xiang, Jun, 236

Yanukovych, Viktor, 301
Yeltsin, Boris, 300
Young, John, 266
Young, Zoe, 176
Young Commission, 266
Yunus, Muhammed, 172, 343, 389n31
Yushchenko, Viktor, 301–302

Zakaria, Fareed, 332
zero sum game, 10, 42, 324